CW00952576

OF LIONS AND DUNG BEETLES

Terence Gavaghan

ARTHUR H. STOCKWELL LTD
Elms Court   Ilfracombe   Devon
Established 1898

British Library Cataloguing-in-Publication Data.
A catalogue record for this book is available
from the British Library.

ISBN 0 7223 3231-9

Printed in Great Britain by
Arthur H. Stockwell Ltd.
Elms Court   Ilfracombe
Devon

CONTENTS

ACKNOWLEDGEMENTS

I am indebted to the whole company of those introduced, for whom I have ventured to make "some room to dance" (Lonsdale), albeit unwittingly, within this personal chronicle. It would be invidious to single out individuals. All are presented as I found them, among many others, to be exemplars of the diverse ways in which the dogmas and whims of colonial policy were transmuted in our relations with the colonial people. Had we been otherwise so might the outcome of the 60 year span of colonial rule in Kenya. On the other face of the coin, I owe thanks to the masses of Kenya for affording me a wonderful life, as they also pursued the vision and reality of Independence, their way.

I am grateful in particular to those 'fellow travellers', friend or foe, who over the years enabled me to assemble the fragments of mosaic, some broken or lost in recollection. I have leant upon their inspiration, critical opinion, writings and information, for the use of none of which are they responsible. They include:

George Adamson; Tom Askwith; Peter Barnes; Dr Bill Barton; Vee Bellers; Elizabeth Usher; Alan Bobbé; Monty Brown; Barbara Brown; Toune Carbonnel; John Carson; Cardovillis Family; Dick Cashmore; Charles Chenevix-Trench; David Christie-Miller; John Cowan; Deirdre Cowan; Pat Crichton; Caroline Elkins; Michael Evans; Leda and John Farrant; Colin Fuller; John Golds; Jock Green; Charles Hayes; Christopher Hill; Richard Hughes; Philip Jones; Peter Johnson; Paul Kelly; June Knowles; Oliver Knowles; Bernard Kunicki; Hilary La Fontaine; 'Tubby' Lewis; John Lonsdale; Mervyn Maciel; Erica Mann; Alastair Matheson; Meg. Maxwell; Jackie Milne; Marguerita and Derrick North-Lewis; Peter Pearce; Diana Pritchard; Philip Ransley; Barbara Rigby (Harper-Nelson); Mirella Rocco (Ricciardi); Johnny Rowlands; Joan Rosinger; Sylvia Storey; Douglas Taylor; Tommy Thompson; Joy Thursby-Pelham; Dr Geoffrey Timms; Erroll Trzebinski; Hugh Walker; Elizabeth de Warenne-Waller; John White; Eric Wilkinson; Charles Wilks; Bobby Winser; John Wreford-Smith; Martine Zacher.

My family bore the brunt of living both within the story and with the writer, for which I thank them for their forbearance and support, and our granddaughter Lauren for her drawings.

The entire labour of typing and endlessly correcting the typescript was carried by infinitely patient and painstaking Gail Erasmus.

T.G.

FOREWORD
by John Lonsdale
Director of Studies in History
Trinity College, Cambridge

It is a pleasure and a challenge to write this Foreword, taking up an invitation which Terence Gavaghan threw down in the guise of a gauntlet. Over the years he has been kind enough to read what I have written on Kenya's history and to comment, often pungently. I have focused on Africans in the colonial period and how they argued their way through the oppressions and frustrations, challenges and opportunities of alien rule. They have occupied the centre of my historical stage. 'That's all very well but why', asked Terence, 'do you have to cast us others into outer darkness?' He has a gift for the dramatic turn of phrase; it makes this book a splendid read; but all the same, and making due allowance for Irish overstatement, it was a good and troubling question. Most readers will enjoy this book for what it is, a fine account of a full life, well charged with risk and good companions along the way. But it is more than that, and this Foreword suggests what his memoir of colonial administration also says to the longer history of Kenya.

The Nigerian writer and exile, Wole Soyinka, once offered wonderfully humane advice to historians. In a play to welcome his country's independence he had one of his characters reiterate the injunction 'Leave the dead some room to dance.' It was advice too often unheard in the recent past; historians of Africa have tended to bury the dead under a sesquipedalian heap of theorization about such processes as modernization, the advance of capitalism, or underdevelopment, and so on; real people were flattened under our academic juggernauts. But if we are nowadays, and we are, paying more heed to Soyinka, why should we leave room only for the black African dead to dance? Are not colonial rulers equally worthy of notice, equally able to play a responsible human role in that different country we call the past?

There were once two reasons for their neglect, good reasons they seemed at the time but — if I may take up the Gavaghan gauntlet — now insufficient as guides to historical explanation. The first reason was, and remains, that historians tend to argue that all political change is underwritten by continuities in thought. Most reform, even revolution, is conservative in intent. We all approach an uncertain future by judging it against what we think we know about the past — not just any past but 'our own', as lived by forebears whom we think we understand and who may even understand and judge us. Inheritance of thought enables people to weigh up what must be done to preserve a future of which the past would be proud. All creative thought, universal though it be, occurs within quite small moral or social or linguistic communities who try to live up to their past and civilize their successors. How then can the African historian fit an alien ruler into local traditions of thought — temporary intruder that he was, not 'racy of the soil' as the Colonial Secretary Leopold Amery once inimitably put it?

The second reason was our manichean view of colonialism's place in African history; we saw it as fleeting episode rather than fiery crucible. We saw African subjects divided from European rulers by the intolerances of race, incomprehensions of culture, the mutual privacies of sex and family, inequalities of law and standards of living. We did not see how the outsiders in this impasse of mutual separation could strike root in local history; they were interlopers to be resisted, removed, and then forgotten when Africans got back to the business of their own painful history. My generation of historians, moreover, took up the challenge of rescuing Africans from the intolerable condescension of the imperial history written by our seniors, in which African history was conceived as the story of how energetic white men had stirred up a stagnant continent. In going back with such a mission into that divided colonial world it is not surprising that we made our British officials out of cardboard, not Aunt Sallies — they were not so interesting — but faceless operatives of an imperial force which followed its own impersonal logic and permitted few agonies of indecision to its servants. We did not imagine the colonial service that Gavaghan knew, questioning its pride with its pain; the men whom we met in their despatches seemed self-confident. We were, in effect, simply reversing the colour bar. White settlers, officials, judges, often sighed that they could not fathom the native mind; too often historians did not trouble to fathom the official mind, the unfeeling anvil on which we hammered out our African history.

African history is no longer so tied to these preoccupations. While not forgetting continuities we are increasingly interested in discontinuities. We also understand better the historical openness and interconnectedness of the small-scale African societies that we used to enclose into self-sufficient tribes. Both changes in our approach to African history should allow us to number district commissioners among the dancing dead — along with our usual cast of chiefs and witchdoctors, warriors and herders, peasant men and women. The great discontinuity in the recent African past is colonialism's imposition of the modern state, once staffed by Gavaghan and his colleagues; and now that we no longer assume that African societies were closed communities we can more easily include outsiders in their world, not least their DCs. Colonial rule is at last entering African history, as an integral element in the continent's story of continuity and change, and as one aspect of the larger world with which all small societies have always had to engage in order to survive.

The imposition of the state has altered the course of African history, not least in Kenya where hierarchies of power were once almost entirely unknown to its chiefless peoples. Conversely, the peoples of Africa have made their own recent history by penetrating or colonizing the opportunities for power and profit which the state has offered them, as politicians, officials, soldiers and professionals. Gavaghan and his generation of colonial officers, and a couple of generations of officers before him, were midwives to this modern African history. He and they are inextricably part of it. Of course colonial officials are also part of recent British history, part of the British self-image and our imagination of our place in the world. Once upon a time they were a proud part; recently a rather defensive one; but in the 1990s their reputation has benefited from respect for an ability to get things done in the Third World with more tangible benefit, more willing co-operation from its peoples and only a fraction of the resources that make possible some of the colossal cockups of today. But the DC, the man in the middle, is also an actor in African history; he helped to make it, not only in deeds but also in words.

Today's historians, for instance, are grateful to colonial servants for pioneering our own research. Before the Second World War, Kenya's administration contained some notable scholars. Gathering the knowledge they needed in order to rule, they did more; they enabled Africans, their informants, to write their own past. No historian of Kenya's peoples can do without 'wobbly' Hobley or 'H. E.' Lambert, self-taught anthropologists, perhaps most sensitive among their many enquiring colleagues. One of Africa's most important collections of oral history is the three volumes of evidence given before the Carter Land Commission of 1932–33 and put together with furious energy by Sid Fazan, whose own demographic and economic surveys are full of data indispensable to the social historian. Postwar officials were too busy pushing official paper to emulate their predecessors' scholarly output; but one must not forget their generosity in reminiscing to young scholars in whose judgment they had no reason to trust; nor the diplomatic ingenuity with which Dick Cashmore rescued so many files, especially the irreplaceable political record books, from the burning before independence.

If historians of the pre-colonial past cannot do without DCs, much of the political history of colonial Kenya is the record of dispute between DCs and their seniors or the technical departments of government. In this they were driven by a sense of what their African chiefs and other allies, or clients, could and could not get away with among their people. Without the vote at national level until 1956, Africans can nonetheless be heard influencing policy long before that, less in their own petitions than ventriloquially, through their DCs. Officials' anger on behalf of their people — who had suffered much in the Great War — stiffened the Colonial Office's stand against the settlers in the crisis of the early 1920s. From 1925 onwards the minutes of Local Native Councils also echo vigorous debates between Africans and between Africans and their DC-president. At the end of the colonial period, the hardwon experience of the administration in pushing forward land consolidation and registration, the expansion of smallholder cash crops, and local industry, was in large measure responsible for the later success of Kenyatta's Kenya, at the time one of tropical Africa's few success stories. The DC has his place in Kenya's post-colonial history too. One of Gavaghan's most significant jobs was to plan the Africanisation of the senior civil service.

The most traumatic event in Kenya's past century was the Mau Mau emergency, ostensibly a revolt against white settlement and British rule but also a Kikuyu civil war. It was the Kenya administration's third war, scarcely global but as harsh as the two world wars in its making and breaking of reputations; 'it was the time the school prefects came to the fore' as one retired official, not among them himself, once remembered to me. Terence Gavaghan looked on the duty that was laid on him to help bring the emergency to an end as the test which — by reason of his early release to the colonial service — he had not been called on to face with his regiment in Normandy. British and Kenyan history could be interlinked in personal honour.

Gavaghan's task in 1957 was to unblock the massive but now stalled process of 'rehabilitating' Mau Mau detainees, so as to accelerate their release back into civil — and civic — life. Rehabilitation was, in retrospect, the precondition for his later role in Africanisation. Approved by the Colonial Office, it was a programme of political re-education unparalleled in the history of British counter-insurgency. The continued incarceration of the 20,000 remaining detainees was clearly incompatible with the political emancipation of Kenya then in train. Some readers may nonetheless be shocked by the physical violence used to break the detainees' will to resist their warders' robust insistence that they dare to be free. Why should men who in their own lights were freedom fighters, prisoners of war, be forced to conform with what their foreign rulers chose to define as co-operation, even if it was to advance their mutually convergent interest in freedom? It is a hard question, where the pride and pain of service are most knotted. Readers will make up their own minds on this, one of the severest tests of the British reputation in Africa and one which Gavaghan himself does not dodge.

Two points may be added to his own reflections. First, whatever other explanations of Mau Mau later scholars have offered — and it is one of the most disputed topics in recent African history — to the British it was not only a treacherous rebellion but also a darkness of the spirit. It was a measure of the seriousness with which they went about 'nation building' in their own image that they decided to recreate out of Mau Mau's seemingly malign obduracy, by however desperate measures, the socially responsible individuals who alone could ensure that independence would also bring self-government. The second point is that this resolve did not stem from an arrogant and injured British self-esteem alone; Gavaghan could not have succeeded, and with so little force, had it not been for the largely Kikuyu character of his team. Rehabilitation was as much an argument between Kikuyu — even within Mau Mau — as a re-education enforced by the British. One may dare to say that rehabilitation was as much a Kenyan dispute about civic responsibility as a rearguard action in the imperial retreat.

In making up their minds on this and other issues, readers will find themselves in the splendid company of many great characters in Gavaghan's story, African as well as European or Asian. If this was a manichean world, then it was made human by these many brave men and women who crossed its internal divides and who dance their individuality in his pages. Readers could wish for no better model as a critic than Senior Chief Lengerassi, who welcomed his new DC into local history with the terrifying promise to weigh him up against what the Samburu people, past and present, took to be a proper man. 'We see you, but we do not bid you welcome because we do not know you. When we have come to know you, we shall tell you what we think of you.'

J.L.

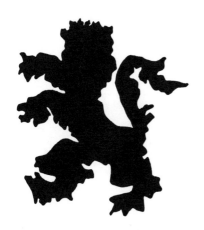

Of
Lions
and
Dung Beetles

OF LIONS

*"The lion, sure, is not so fierce or stout
as foolish men do paint or set him out."*
                              (R. Watkins: 1662)

*Lion — 'Pantheros Leo' of order 'Carnivore' —
is hailed since olden times in myth
and song, pigment, stone and bronze, as
'King of Beasts', feral image of power;
from Rome to Venice, Carthage to Babylon,
Judah to Sheba, Kashmir to far Cathay —
Trafalgar Square, Safari Park, to cartoon Disneyland!*

*Lion were hunted in earliest Mesopotamia, when
the constellations were first descried in Heaven
four thousand years ago. They took fifth
place among the signs of the Zodiac,
the 'Kuklos Zodiakos' — circle of small animals.*

*Lion cull lightly from nervous teeming herbivores.
Females stalk stealthily to feed the pride.
The male roars splendidly at casual glut,
but in decline may take to scavenging.*

*Symbol of Imperial rule, in conquest and peace,
maned head-dress of spear-blooded Maasai Moran,
A lion rampant was chosen and remains
                    the crest of Kenya.*

AND DUNG BEETLES

"... The poor beetle, that we tread upon.
in corporal suffrance finds a pang as great as when a giant dies."
(Shakespeare: *Measure for Measure* 1604)

The dung beetle, 'Scarabeus Laevistratus' is attracted
in blind myriads by the fragrance of droppings.
Intense excitement heats energy for wing-whirring
power for vertical take-off and landing, whereupon
they perform their tidy work of sculpting,
moulding and rolling in faithful breeding pairs,
as ordained for the Garden of Eden.

Ancient Egyptians saw in the ball-rolling beetle
a living symbol of regeneration and renewal,
a microcosm of cyclical processes of nature,
a manifestation of Sun God 'Khepri' propelling
his radiant orb daily across the Heavens.

The scarab — karabos is Greek for beetle —
is not a priceless jewel of romance,
but the engraving of the sacred beetle,
'Scarabeus Sacer', on a gem or signet ring.

Dung beetles preserve the vast plains of Africa
from smothering in deep herbivorous animal dung;
humble servants of God and nature, cleansing
the lion's demesne.

WITHIN THE COLONIAL MAZE

(Author's Note)

This autobiographical account of my service in Kenya as a Colonial Administrative Officer, covers the years between the Second World War and Independence in December 1963. It is neither typical nor exemplary. Situations, events and characters are described as they appeared to me at the time. I have tried to avoid revision by hindsight, but I only became aware of changing external influences and internal pressures as I progressed between the quite different Provinces and Districts.

The Colony and Protectorate of Kenya was a piecemeal British confection, named in a pastiche of local variants of the highest mountain, and given arbitrary land boundaries, within which it chafed against a circle of disparate neighbours:

Tanganyika (Tanzania when joined with *Zanzibar*) to the south bore the imprint of Arab conquest and culture, extending into the Kenya coastal Protectorate and inland along the slave raiding trails. It divided the Maasai ranges with Kenya and may have owed the inclusion of Mount Kilimanjaro to the indulgence of Queen Victoria to her grandson, Kaiser Wilhelm II. German East African colonization of the area in the 'scramble for Africa' was transmuted after wartime defeats into a League of Nations Mandate, then a United Nations Trusteeship under British Colonial Administration, but subject to scrutiny.

Uganda, dubbed the 'Pearl of Africa' for its lush beauty, was colonized early by Britain, evangelized by militant Christian missionaries, pacified by Captain (later Lord) Lugard and rendered accessible by the railway. Under the name of the nearest and largest of four traditional kingdoms, Buganda, a form of quadripartite indirect rule was operated throughout with the Kabaka as ceremonial but resented figurehead. He was exiled by a socialist ideologue Governor and direct rule on the standard 'Whitehall' model was applied until Independence. The large Indian immigrant community, without competing white settlement, grew powerful commercially and through large scale sugar plantations and peasant cotton processing, in addition to the Missionary introduction of coffee.

Sudan. Above the pastoral Nilotic Northern Province of Uganda and the adjoining Kenya Turkana area west of the Rift (once included in Uganda) lay the enormous Moslem, Mahdist and pagano-Christian, Anglo-Egyptian

Sudan, which became the Republic of Sudan on Independence in 1956. An isolated area of southern Sudan, termed the Ilemi Triangle, was amicably serviced from Turkana until effectively annexed to Kenya prior to Boundary Commission changes. (The remoteness of Turkana later provided secure places of detention for the top echelons of Mau Mau, including Jomo Kenyatta.)

Ethiopia. To the north east the ancient pre-Coptic Ethiopian Empire, under British Army restored Haile Selassie, re-established its African pre-eminence as a purportedly enlightened feudal despotism. It was courted by the British Foreign Office, despite the Semitic Amhara disdain for the Negroid peoples of Kenya and for the expansionist Cushitic Somali nomads astride its ill defined borders.

Somalia. The south-westerly urge of the Somali also engaged the Administration of the Northern Frontier District of Kenya. 'Italian' Somalia was loosely administered for a decade by a Civil Affairs organization set up by the British Military Administration after overthrow of the fascist colonial government. Many ex-colonials remained with their language, culture, legal and financial systems and banana production tied to the Italian domestic market. This facilitated the granting to Italy by the United Nations of a ten year trusteeship which expired in 1961 with Independence. An uneasy and complex fusion was then arranged with the former British Somaliland Protectorate to the north in a single Somali Republic, which still represented only two of the five points of the Somali Star on the national flag, symbolizing the notion of a Greater Somalia.

On the wider front American and Soviet Russian nuclear powers competed during the closing decade of British colonial rule to supersede the Empire of 'Pax Britannica' and bring the mass of sub-Saharan Africa, not least Kenya, within their spheres of influence. Kenya was also touched by a series of foreign revolutionary incidents. Israel, in 1948, on the crest of victorious Independence, was actively seeking ties in Africa, the departed British Mandate having just deported Irgun Zwei Leumi (the Stern Gang were likened to Mau Mau) terrorists to Kenya to be detained in the Rift Valley Province, (envisioned 40 years before by Winston Churchill, Colonial Secretary as a Jewish National home!). Cyprus, under British colonial rule in 1956 deported the 'turbulent priest', Archbishop Makarios, who was transhipped with ignominious dignity in Mombasa harbour on route to exile in the, formerly French, Seychelles Islands (once the place of exile of three Southern African Kings). The Anglo-French-Israeli attack on Egypt to secure the Suez Canal, halted by Kruschev's and Eisenhower's threat of intervention, caused the canal route to Europe to be closed and provoked Colonel Nasser to open his doors to Kenya nationalist leaders, notably Kenyatta's respected friend (and future Minister) Joseph Murumbi.

As a British Crown Colony, Kenya was not, by definition, a democratic society. In the virtual absence of Kingly leaders, a system of direct rule was applied, moderated somewhat by the presence of immigrant interest groups which served as disparate checks and balances. White settlement had several strands. Farmers and soldier-settlers were a productive and instructive nucleus to provide freight, income and imports for the otherwise 'lunatic line' (Lord Harcourt's remark) constructed both humanely to quell sectarian strife and suppress slavery in Uganda, and strategically to avert French encirclement through southern Sudan and Ethiopia. Settlers in Kenya had since developed strong elected and farmers' union lobbies, including adventurist extensions of the British landed aristocracy-cum-squirearchy with family pull at 'home'. There was a notorious coterie of scandalous hedonists whose 'white mischief' (sic) served only to sully the reputation of Kenya. Asian immigrants, many of them descendants of railway construction workers and dhow-borne merchants, proliferated in 'bush' trade and commercial enterprise, preserving cultural and religious identities and refreshing their links with India, while asserting political clout in Kenya. Beside, but apart, was a close-knit Goan Catholic community serving in Government and railways with pride and dedication. The Christian missions, both European and American, jostled (peacefully) to deliver with holy inducements their versions of 'Good News' and exerted both sectarian and group influence on modern education and the ending of atavistic mutilation. Anglican professing Governor Mitchell, on his retirement to become a settler farmer, hung up his ceremonial sword in Nairobi Cathedral.

All special interests, as well as the conduct of Colonial Government, were made subject to an over-riding principle set out explicitly in the 1923 Devonshire (Duke of: Colonial Secretary) Declaration, peculiar to Kenya, asserting the 'Paramountcy of African Native Interests' which must prevail in the event of conflict. The principle was put to a test and partially circumscribed by the 1933 Carter Land Commission reporting in 1934, which demarcated in complex detail separate 'scheduled areas', effectively restricted by a Highlands Board to white occupation (hence loosely called White Highlands), and 'native land units', from which whites and lawyers were excluded. Kenyatta had represented the Kikuyu before the Commission, claiming land rights which continued to be a burning issue through the war and up to the Mau Mau Emergency in 1952.

At the apogee of the pyramid of colonial power was the Constitutional Monarch of the democratically elected Government of the British people in

Parliament. The Monarch's titular representative and plenipotentiary in Kenya was the Governor and Commander-in-Chief, executively responsible through the Colonial Secretary to the Prime Minister. Colonial Administrative officers came under the command of the Governor, although, as Her (His) Majesty's Oversea Civil Service appointed at the Colonial Office, they were transferable between Colonies. Everything done in the discharge or conduct of administrative duty was ultimately traceable and accountable through the Governor to the incumbent colonial power. Governors were sometimes turned over quite quickly or retained unaccountably.

The Colonial Administrative Service in Kenya over half a century did not exceed about 200 at any one time, not counting irregular, auxiliary or Emergency appointments. This related to a population ranging between 4,500,000 in 1948 and 8,000,000 in 1960. The administration was both a framework and an instrument for peace, law and order, taxation and co-ordination of development, with a parallel loyalty to the Crown and to the well-being of the colonized people of all sorts. Officers were recruited mainly from a select range of leadership-inculcating schools and universities as well as the armed services. All were assumed to be versed in the commonly held social, ethical and Christian moral values called for in carrying the 'white man's burden' of Empire. Most were also reared in the less conformist qualities of ambition, idealism, adventure, physical courage and self-reliance. A good few (of us) tended to eccentricity with the ego-inflating exercise of authority, from a young age and at close encounter, over large numbers of proud and vigorous people existing in cultures much closer to the bone of life. At all levels and throughout the field services there was a certain 'creative tension' between the amateur Administration and the qualified Specialist Departmental officers, outnumbering them by ten to one, who could be irked by differences of social and official status, even salary, inherent in the stratified colonial system. Another form of tension lay in the restrictive nature of relationships with the indigenous people, largely implicit in the social acceptances of the time, but sometimes adverted to by comically oblique general circular handed down from the Colonial Office. "Arrangements of Concubinage." (sic)

The command structure of the Administration itself was simple, having only four levels, although secondment to the Central Government offered a separate career path of Secretaryships. The titular head was the Chief Native Commissioner (CNC), later styled the Minister for African Affairs (MAA). It was a prestigious but amorphous role, pervasive and influential in policy, rather than executive. He co-ordinated up to ten Provincial Commissioners (PC) and Officers-in-Charge (Oi/c), who had direct authority over geographical or urban units with populations up to a million or more depending on density, terrain or tribal composition. Each PC commanded around seven District Commissioners (DC) in charge of Districts, which might contain more than one distinct ethnic group. A large District could have several District Officers (DO) who might be posted to Divisional Offices, the DO in charge having senior status. DOs in the field increased with Closer Administration for security or development. There were no women in the District Administration and few at the centre.

The human pyramid of the colonized indigenous people of Kenya, was quarried from the greatest diversity of races and tongues locked within the colonial boundaries of any African country, posing a challenge of peace and stable government to colonial or independent ruler alike. There were three distinct populations of circumcised Bantu (people saying 'man' or 'men' in similar tongues also extending down to South Africa), the uncircumcised Nilotes spreading out south from the Nile Basin, the Islamised eastern Hamites or Cushites, ranging past the Ethiopian Semites, and Nilo-Hamitic tribes in varying degrees of fusion between converging flows, who included the tightly knit Kalenjin linguistic group. Around each main mass were formed clusters of related smaller tribes with a multiplicity of dialects.

The Colonial Administrative apparatus was in concept an external scaffolding and an internal frame, designed to fall away when the stone blocks of the people rose up to the apex of the pyramid. In practice it both nurtured and inhibited growth. We, the Administrators, wearing the badge of the rampant lion, often mocked as the 'heaven born', were the 'men in the middle' between the power of an 'Empire upon which the sun had not (yet) set', and the powerful human aspiration to freedom from tutelage. We bore the badge with some pride.

Bertha Matilda's
Gravestone.   *(Married)*
Arconam 1896.

Laurence Patrick
(with) Edward Laurence.
Bangalore 1896.

Laurence Patrick.
Madras Cemetery, 1901.

River Ganges at dawn.
Allahabad.
Author born 1922.

ORIGINS

My paternal forbears lived astride County Mayo and County Sligo in undivided Ireland, as six hospitable Parish Priests and a tumbled clutter of stone Celtic crosses attest. When the Great Famine of 1845 stripped Ireland of half her peasantry, my great-grandfather, Patrick Laurence, found work in London at Hackney Railway Station. He sent his son, Laurence Patrick, to the South India Railway construction at Madras.

There Laurence Patrick met and married Bertha Matilda White, who was visiting church relatives of her father, Edward, a private chaplain to Queen-Empress Victoria. Bertha died of sepsis, aged 21 at Arconam Railway Town, after delivery of my father, Edward Laurence. I found her inscribed tombstone of polished Aberdeen Granite gleaming through the scrub of a century in a long forgotten graveyard.

Promoted to Traffic Manager, Laurence bought a horse, from which he was thrown to his death out hunting, leaving his son an orphan in India at five. Through the kindness of Bertha's family and the Railways, he was sent to Mount St Mary's Jesuit College near Sheffield. Such accidents of social mobility landed Edward Laurence back in India to become a chartered accountant, an Indian Cavalry Officer in war and Comptroller General within the Indian Civil Service — 'The Old Steel Framework', which held imperial sway over the 400,000,000 people of the 'Raj'. His career was cut short after appendectomy in the Great Quetta Earthquake of 1935.

Within the cocoon of pride of service, duty and privilege, Edward Laurence met my mother, Christine Margery Hill, of that other world. Her family came of London merchants romantically linked with the family of Babington, evoking the ill-fated conspiracy to unseat Queen Elizabeth, who first chartered the old Celtic town of Derry (The Oaks) to the burghers of London — hence Londonderry. I never met nor heard of a living relative of my father's surname, save my two elder siblings, hatched during long leaves in England. I was born in Allahabad, Hindu holy city on the Ganges, into the peripatetic life of the 'Raj', soon to join the others in their nest, cherished by a tweedy governess. The maternal White family connection flourishes in Texas.

For me there followed boarding at a Catholic convent for well endowed girls, a rigorous Protestant preparatory school and the disciplined cornucopia of teaching at Jesuit Stonyhurst College, where my small talent for portraiture found outlet in drawing noble lion and 'noble savages' all looking like Paul Robeson, for posters urging penny and prayerful support for the foreign missions. This was capped at seventeen by an unexpected open scholarship, endowed by American philanthropist Harkness, to Presbyterian St Andrews University in Scotland. Robustly serious Scottish and Scotch conviviality, blended with Polish officer-student culture, vodka, Rugby, drama, and the discovery of womankind, jostled with sectarian free thinking and iconoclastic learning for a dizzy year.

This was overtaken by recruitment into the one technical military unit for which I rashly but correctly declared incompetence — signals. Having surmounted this obstacle by becoming a despatch rider instructor, a misdirected posting to instruct officer cadets, not to become one, led me to a commission in the Royal Ulster Rifles, South Coastal Defence and Combined Operations assault course training at Inverary and the Inner Hebrides.

A forgotten record of the University Selection Board which had visited St Andrews, led to an offer of competitive interview in London for the only colonial administrative place urgently to be filled in Kenya, my recorded preference after India. My gallant CO, Colonel 'Trotsky' Davis, advised me to go for the 100 to 1 chance. When selected by the redoubtable Captain Newbolt of the Colonial Office, I accepted fatefully what then seemed to me the wider adventure.

I

VOYAGE TO AFRICA
1944

The *Ville de Majunga* was a Madagascar-bound tramp steamer of the Messageries Maritimes Line, rusted in service of the French Overseas Empire. It carried also eight passengers in four oblong iron boxes with two-tier bunks and a clamped brass porthole. Six were Irish missionary priests, freshly delivered from Maynooth Seminary — poker champions all and adept at conducting mass over a recumbent fellow passenger. My civilian counterpart was a coarsely handsome Police cadet, redolent of the sparring ring, whom I never met again.

The ship's officers were surprisingly sophisticated, even elegant, and played wildly inspirational — and profitable — Gallic, 'Grand-slam', bridge. One grizzled deckhand had served in the Imperial Russian Navy and was a survivor of the Sevastopol Mutiny. He proudly manned a Great War rotary magazined Lewis machine-gun, mounted on the poop deck to fend off any German torpedo planes which might be alerted to attack us by enemy spotters near Gibraltar. As our convoy wallowed past the Pillars of Hercules towards Tangier, torpedoes hit three nearby ships under the protective cover of our own smoke-screen during the daily mock alert.

Having quartered the Atlantic from Glasgow via Casablanca, after some six weeks afloat we hove to briefly off Port Said, to the joyous greetings of bum-boat hucksters and 'Gully-gully' magicians, addressing us blithely as 'Mrs McGregor' in fond memory of prudent memsahibs bound for India. The crew relieved our unrefrigerated 'Franglais' diet with triumphant catches of baby shark, flakily tender when soused in vinegar.

Salt-water dunking with mottled kitchen soap in rusty drums, steam-scalded, left us with an unassuaged thirst for any kind of alcohol until, at last, we berthed at Port Sudan. Quayside lighters were festooned with listless, tattered and emaciated Danakil dock labour, sadly reduced from their prowess as the fearsome 'Fuzzy-wuzzies' confronted by young Churchill at the battle of Omdurman, the culmination of Kitchener's ponderous march from Port Sudan to relieve Gordon at Khartoum.

With shame and greed we watched and slavered while they disgorged crates of Youngers Scottish Ale from the hold and took them on screeching trolleys along the sweltering quay to the dignified Sudan Club. There we were rebuffed by a stern notice newly placed on the steps — 'Members Only' — (a fate to be identically re-enacted 40 years on, when I returned with a United Nations disaster mission). We slunk back to our hulk disconsolate, past the neo-Palladian headquarters of the Anglo-Egyptian

Sudan, surmounted by the wind-ripped flags of the nations of the condominium. I rescued a lonely empty bottle of Beehive Brandy from the unswept, unguarded steps, mounted the deserted inner stairs and presented it to an astonished official in tribute to local hospitality and national pride.

Our only other stop before Mombasa was at Aden, coaling station of Empire, shielded from dastardly French or Italian imperial ambitions by treaty with the warrior Somalis on the opposite Horn of Africa. The ship's officers had watched with surly profanity the French colonial naval base and railhead at Djibouti glide by, depriving them of the unsurpassed delights of the famously entrancing Somali courtesans. Their imprecations turned to whoops of excitement, when it was learned that a branch salon had been set up near Aden Port, to which they quickly repaired, taking me in half-reluctant tow. I did not understand what it was that caused me, in youthful incandescence, to refrain from full enjoyment of the fragrant charms so warmly and laughingly pressed upon me.

And so along the desolate mirage-hazed coast of British Military Administered (former Italian) Somalia to the calm green shores of Kenya. There our voyage ended in the wartime bustle of Kilindini Docks on Mombasa Island, leased still for cash from the Sultans of Zanzibar and an earlier cockpit of Arab strife with the maritime Portuguese, whose blood and bones nourished the ancient baobab trees for centuries.

Such was my training course for colonial service. Ten weeks convoy in a tramp steamer afforded only some mariners' French, Latin mass responses from a horizontal posture, impoverishment at bridge and poker and a dearth of any other stimulus, mental or physical. One real treasure, found on the tiny saloon bookshelf, was a dog-eared copy of *Men of the Trees* by Richard St Barbe Baker, a respected Conservator of Forests and founder of the equivalent Kikuyu movement, 'Watu Wa Miti', with Senior Chief Josiah Njonjo, both of whom I later met.

True, imagination had been fired if misguided by fantastic yarns of a lost Roman legion, the Empire of Prester John, King Solomon's Mines and Sheba's breasts, Sanders (and Paul Robeson) of the River, Livingstone and Stanley, the slave trader Tippu-Tip of Zanzibar, the landings of Vasco da Gama, the 'vision' of Cecil Rhodes, the invasion of Abyssinia, the Uganda Martyrs, the explorer-adventurers, the zealot missionaries and the colonizing settlers. For the heart there was the enchantment of Karen Blixen's *Out of Africa*, culled from the 2,000 year old saw of Pliny: 'Ex Africa semper aliquid novi'. Recent influences were the contrasting works, *Facing Mt Kenya* of Kenyatta, the pith and prescience of Elspeth Huxley's seminal work *White Man's Country*, which in its essence if not the colour of its title has stood the test of 60 years, and her published debate with Margery Perham, *Race and Politics in Kenya*.

With such jumbled personal baggage and cluttered mind did I have the temerity to approach the ideals of service and responsibility for the existence of millions of fellow human beings in a colony, as then perceived. No 'white man's burden' did it seem to me, rather a sense of high adventure which unfolded over two decades in every part of Kenya, during which I tried to meet 'those imposters triumph and disaster just the same'.

II

NAIROBI ARRIVAL
1944

"Entirely a pleasure, old man!" came oddly from the pleasant, cheery, face of one of the two middle ranking secretariat officers, who had been deputed to meet me off the Mombasa overnight train at the original, and still only, Nairobi Railway Station. The oddity of the remark in English was happily lost on the eager porter being rewarded for hefting my cabin trunk through the carriage window and on to his trolley.

The two were my first encounter with the English colonial administrator: Eton and Oxford of the mid thirties, self assured, courteous and tolerant of an unsuitably dressed, palpably green, arrival straight from the 'poor bloody infantry'. Roger Wilkinson was tufty of hair, eyebrow and upper cheek with an engaging glow of friendly optimism; John Webster, more conventional and perhaps constrained by the burden of the looks of Ronald Coleman.

I found myself, so escorted, in the aged taxi of a preposterously racist eccentric, Miss Maclean, who always demanded the front of the rank, to the salubrious bungalow on 'The Hill' of the Deputy Chief Secretary, well named Ernest Rex Surridge, with a wife of discreetly subdued if pleasantly faded charm. He set me to read Lord Hailey's *African Survey* (so heavy a tome that the Lord later told me he rated anyone who claimed to have read it a fool or a liar). She lent me a thriller to read between dutiful pretences. They also provided an old black bicycle to perform ritual calls on selected service dignitaries, placing hastily prepared visiting cards on silver salvers in bungalow hallways, with due care not to be surprised in the act. Invitations duly followed and my 'good suit' was pressed into service — with smartly zipped, high mosquito boots.

Happily I was moved on to the house of P. Wyn-Harris, Everest climber, Labour Commissioner and Governor to be of the Gambia. His comfortable part-Maori wife 'Mo' kept cigarette boxes supplied with admonitions "No! P. Wyn"! He was short of neck, thick of skin with dark greying, bristly hair, double crowned and so restlessly mobile that the Kikuyu called him 'The chicken that runs about with his head cut off'. At crisp, dewy dawn their garden attracted snorting Zebra up from the Athi Plains.

We were within two hundred yards of Nairobi Club, grey dressed-stone bastion of proper civil servants and sporting cricket and tennis players, with a leavening of business. It was the counterpart of the early settlers' pink stucco, Trianon style, Muthaiga Club across the city, which enjoyed a certain raffish superiority, being frequented also by the social and diplomatic set and the expatriate aristocracy, the odd landed Duke or two. Keeping up the quality and esteem of both clubs were impeccable domestics, or 'boys' however aged, in tasselled tarbooshes, red cardinals' cummerbunds encircling ample white cotton robes or *Kanzus*, the head waiters with braided bolero jackets, all silent on shiny, scrubbed, balletic feet, swoopingly alert to every call for service.

Muthaiga Club's remarkable instinct for adaptive survival evolved from post war exclusion of blackballed, 'unsuitable' Jews and Africans to such broad acceptance as to convert the new dispensation into fervent adherence to old standards.

III

KITUI DISTRICT
1944

So to my first field posting as District Officer-Cadet, Kitui Administrative District. Forty years earlier, when administrative maps were being drawn up and Districts apportioned roughly on a tribal basis, the Akamba people were shown as occupying the vast expanse of Ukamba Province, some twenty thousand square miles south east of Nairobi and between South Maasailand District and Tanaland Province, extending southward to Kibwezi on the Mombasa railway line.

When maps were revised, the whole of Ukamba was divided between a separate Machakos District, with headquarters at old Chief Machako's village nearer to Nairobi, and at more distant Kitui District. Machakos took over about 5,000 square miles with 360,000 inhabitants, leaving 14,000 square miles and 210,000 people in Kitui. To me it was a much more attractive proposition to be sent to the wilder, more sparsely populated region.

The Akamba, though of the Bantu language group and practising circumcision, speak a dialect distinct from that of the Kikuyu to their north and in large part have a semi pastoral mode of life attuned to savannah country with low population density. Their skill as bowmen and metal workers is legendary, as is their home-brewed conviviality, both qualities making them popular as soldiery. Their stubborn courage later stood them in good stead against infiltration by Mau Mau influences.

Before leaving Nairobi I was guided first to Ahamed Bros., Jimmy and Taj, tailors by appointment to officials, settlers, the gentry, white hunters and their clients, to dump my 'demob' felt hat and flannels and emerge for about one hundred shillings or five pounds as a khaki-drill clad, brass-buttoned District Officer; then to Kenya Fish and Provision Merchants to collect and order monthly a straw quarter-moon basket, stitched with twine over kippers, thick bacon and semi perishables; and not least to Erskine and Duncan's classier store for whatever canned and glass-jarred delicacies could be afforded for the larder. How I managed on tick, or one month's arrears of my net salary of under £30 (less card losses on board), I know not for I had not a penny, but in those times trust was common currency.

The journey to Kitui of over 100 miles was rough going by robustly rattling, pre-war, 3-ton Bedford truck along a deeply rutted dirt road via Thika, past Bulley's Tannery and Athi River Abattoir, to Ndolo's Corner, the evocatively named turn-off to Kitui. Outsiders often ask, with a tinge of envy, which district I liked most in Kenya and I am evasive. I believe that the answer lies not so much in any place, but chiefly in where one has felt most at ease with oneself as a transient human being, helped by a sense of some achievement and comradeship left behind, or of imagination fired. With an already wonderful sense of anticipation, I loved Kitui on sight and bless it still as the happiest introduction to the rest of my service in Kenya.

My first home in Africa, my first house anywhere was like many another colonial bungalow. It had steps up to a wide verandah against sun and rain; thick walls of whitewashed mud-mortar blocks; a red oxide painted heat-cracking, rain-roaring corrugated iron roof, its ceiling lined with soft-board stained by acrid bat droppings from their cheepy nocturnal clustering. The floors were of cement float, thickly coated with shiny red Cardinal polish daily buffed by sheepskin foot pads, piston driven in a ski-walking motion.

Three main rooms, interconnected, served for sitting, sleeping and dining, which turned out to be a regular feature of social life. An *en suite* bathroom was, like the whole, encased in mosquito gauze shutters, snibbed in place with wooded swivel catches. Inside was a wooden lidded commode for emergency use when confined with dysentery and unable to make it to the outside 'long drop' with 'thunder box'.

There was a standard set of Public Works Department furniture made of hardwood from the ubiquitous 'Mvuli' (umbrella) tree: two wooden frame arm chairs which had rattan seats and adjustable backs, with swivel extensions to hold a drink in a circular slot, or sustain a casually relaxed and mosquito-booted leg. A tall Dietz or Tilley pressure lantern stand was in the corner for close reading and as a target for bombardment by light-crazed, kamikaze, sausage flies which somehow penetrated the gauze to seek immolation by frying crisply on the scorching glass globe or funnel of the lamps.

All this was had for a mere 7½% of salary docked for house rental plus 2½% for furniture, on top of income tax on basic gross monthly salary of £30. These more than cancelled out the new 10% cost of living allowance, the first increase after some 30 years of nil inflation. With what Sam Weller like relief one departed the office on foot or lorry safari, to liberation from office chores and a free share of goat meat, cheap muscular chicken, tiny suspect eggs, mealies and bananas with a princely night allowance of two shillings for the pleasure of it.

Everywhere I went, at home or on foot safari, I was cared for, fed and crisply turned out by my inseparable companion, cook-housekeeper and friend, Ogoma Wakaya, whom I was lucky to find available in Kitui, at above the local going rate of 40 to 50 shillings a month with all, but not much, found. He came from far off Luo country at Kendu Bay on lake Victoria (-Nyanza). His people were Nilotic, uncircumcised, sun dried fish and millet eaters. Their diet was so replete with calcium that they tended to heavy bones and joints with retaining ankle sinews like fence buttresses.

Ogoma had large, upper lip thrusting teeth, through which he would issue a companionable siffilation while engaged in any tasks of concentrated effort, like scrubbing, polishing, charcoal ironing or loading a camel. He stood forward later as my champion at wrestling contests when selecting recruits for the Tribal Police, an evening entertainment much enjoyed, especially if I was finally thrown. He could whip up small meringues baked on a fragment of newspaper laid on a scorching rock.

Ogoma was a gentle, sober man with vanity of white grooved parting in wooden combed hair, toothbrush moustache, smart walking out drill suit and always a tactfully attentive presence. We shared each others lives for 10 years, through eight districts until he retired to open a teashop at Kendu Bay. In a large sense he gave me a basis for my life with Africans in Africa. Not surprisingly such a closeness of experience can fail to survive the changes which occur naturally from bachelor to married life, when the memsahib takes overall control. In such a time Ogoma once intervened in a domestic crisis by taking possession of a brandished kitchen knife.

The Boma, or government campus which, in its Swahili meaning of a thorn enclosure to protect livestock always seemed to be appropriate, was idyllic. The whole peaceful ambience was park like and leafy with towering silver barked, lemon scented, moisture draining eucalyptus trees, lining crisp, red ironstone, gravel roads, called 'Murrum', interspersed with Nandi Flame trees and azure blossomed, fan leaved Jacaranda, with waxy pink and creamy amber frangipani, demanding to be plucked and inhaled. Everywhere stood upright, heavily pregnant, papaya and dark mangos laden with fleshy fruit and the occasional pear green avocado. To stroll at cool dawn through this perfumed paradise to do physical training with the Tribal Police was both a sacrilege and an exhilaration, a sensual delight.

Apart from government offices and bungalow quarters, there was a one street trading centre, clean and well drained, of corrugated iron shops, headed by the general store of Willie Pereira, a Kenya settled Goan trader, with long established Swahili shopkeepers, mainly Moslem, elderly, leisurely and dignified. There was a small Mosque, an open vegetable and livestock market, a cottage hospital, a lock up jail with thick mud walls and high barred window. At a distance was a fine government secondary cum intermediate school and the distinctly superior premises of the local British American Tobacco Company buying station and drying flues. Our colonial community was small, friendly and thrown in on itself for entertainment. Mail was scarce and the telegraph only recently installed, bringing the Olympian voice of the Provincial Commissioner, Charles Tomkinson, down from the misty mountainside at Nyeri in Kikuyu country, unwelcomely closer in the cable room with instant orders and announcements of visits. It was said he had a younger French wife!

The District Commissioner, Paul Osborne, was in his forties, burly

CONTEXTUAL PLACE NAMES

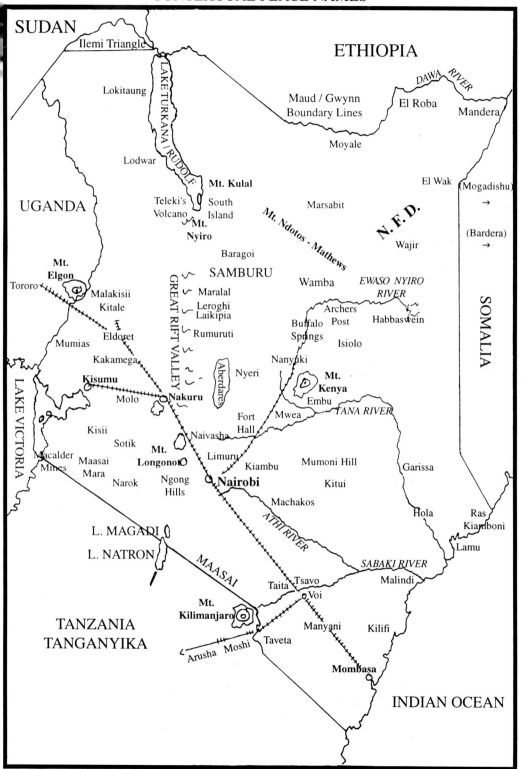

SUDAN

Ilemi Triangle

ETHIOPIA

Lokitaung

LAKE TURKANA / RUDOLF

DAWA RIVER

Maud / Gwynn
Boundary Lines

El Roba

Mandera

Moyale

Lodwar

Mt. Kulal

El Wak

(Mogadishu)
→

UGANDA

Teleki's
Volcano

South
Island

Marsabit

N.F.D.

(Bardera)
→

Mt.
Nyiro

Baragoi

Mt. Ndotos - Mathews

Wajir

SOMALIA

Mt.
Elgon

SAMBURU

Wamba

EWASO NYIRO
RIVER

Tororo

Malakisii

Maralal

GREAT RIFT VALLEY

Kitale

Leroghi
Laikipia

Archers
Post

Habbaswein

Eldoret

Rumuruti

Buffalo
Springs

Isiolo

Mumias

Kakamega

Nanyuki

Kisumu

Aberdares

Nyeri

Mt.
Kenya

Molo

Nakuru

Embu

TANA RIVER

LAKE VICTORIA

Kisii

Fort
Hall

Mwea

Sotik

Naivasha

Mt.
Longonot

Limuru

Kiambu

Mumoni Hill

Garissa

Macalder
Mines

Maasai
Mara

Narok

Ngong
Hills

Nairobi

Kitui

Machakos

Hola

Ras
Kiamboni

L. MAGADI

ATHI RIVER

SABAKI RIVER

Lamu

L. NATRON

MAASAI

Tsavo

Malindi

Taita

Voi

TANZANIA
TANGANYIKA

Mt.
Kilimanjaro

Manyani

Kilifi

Arusha Moshi

Taveta

Mombasa

INDIAN OCEAN

c

Nairobi Railway Station, built 1897, with Tribal Class Garratt.

1958 reenactment of Colonial Secretary Churchill's 1907 visit to Port Florence (Kisumu) Station and Docks, pursuing his vision of a Cape to Cairo link-up. (Cast includes author and NCG arrowed.)

Alan Bobbé, Restaurateur, in his ' Bistro', 1960s.

Gerald 'Uncle' Reece Officer in Charge N.F.D.
(at Moyale District).

Author in front of DC's house, Mandera.

Salute to 'Willie' Keir, 1946.
Old soldiers and new DC's office to rear.

Burial party for 'Willie' Keir, DC,
killed in border raid 1943.

Somali 'Dubas' (Red Turban) Guard.

Kenya Police Guard of Honour.

Kenya Police Inspectors Watson and Eglen (with TG).

Chief Mohamed Jarré — Chief Abdi Nur Gersi — Chief Hussein Salad.

Chief Hussein Salad, Degodia Section, represents Somali needs.

Paramount Chief Mumia.
Died 1952 c.102,
as met by author, 1947.

(Author), Kenneth Hunter PC, Sir Philip Mitchell, Governor, H. A. L. Williams, DC
with Imam of Kakamega Mosque, (1947).

Colonel Ewart S. Grogan DSO.
'From the Cape to Cairo', 1900.

Grogan's Castle 'Girigan'
at Taveta.
(Photos De Villiers.)

Presiding Genius!

topped with a fine head, thin dishevelled hair and amiable spectacles. He and his queenly wife Anna were a well matched pair, intellectuals of the (Manchester-) Guardian-reading persuasion, hospitably 'good' on bridge, tennis and conversation. For some odd, and not strictly apposite reason, they dubbed me 'Oscar', perhaps because I wore an outmoded wing collar with my white 'Bum-freezer', mess jacket, and practised irreverent flippancy. The DC unhappily fell victim to diabetes and had to take leave, but not before he had contracted a mysterious and alarming fever while visiting me in bush camp to the North, with irregular pink spots burning on his white torso. Strangely, the spots were found to match the perforations in his worn cotton golf shirt and it was diagnosed as 'Aertex Itch', from which he made a rapid recovery.

The Senior District Officer was Tom Askwith. He was tall, lean and hesitantly stooped. His lantern jaw was ever clamped on a 'Sherlock Holmes', smooth briar pipe, at which he sucked without false hope on a moistly resistant dottle. It came as a surprise that he was a double Diamond Sculls champion, though this matched a quietly disciplined yet stubborn sense of right and wrong, laconically stated and rarely lit by any revealed humour or sense of fun.

His wife, Pat (neé Noad), was Kenya settler born, pale golden rose and slender stemmed as a girl. Their garden had an exotic profusion of established plants, being that of the original 'Collector's' house in Kitui, still so named above the door since it had been transported by sea, piece by piece, from the Indian Civil Service before the Great War and reassembled by Indian artisans. Tom too later succumbed to a bout of cerebral malaria and departed to convalesce.

With both my senior officers invalided away, I was happily not left stranded in my complete inexperience to hold the fort. There were good companions. Among these were 'Nzuki' Javens, Agricultural Officer, nicknamed after the Kamba word for a bee, since his zooming energy, black tufty hair and bushy brows over bright button eyes, gave him the air of busy pollination. Indeed, he and his wife Nancy infused us all with their joy of life. It was a time when colonial agricultural wisdom was reverting to maize and legume interplanting, having earlier warned peasants of its iniquity.

'Nzuki's' veterinary counterpart was Senior Livestock Officer, Bill Lewis, much older but driven like a bull buffalo by a compulsion to break all records inoculating Kamba range cattle against the decimating disease of rinderpest, so rampantly destructive of Maasai herds. He performed prodigies without proper transport or equipment, inspiring his scouts to exhaustion by his dominant example to catch, to hold, to stab with life saving needles. I was a little afraid of an old bushwhacker's reaction to a rookie.

D

There was no post for a qualified doctor, but an Indian medico ranked as Sub Assistant Surgeon did a noble job of stitching with twine my lower lip, through which my top teeth had lodged in the cannon ball forehead of an opposing centre forward at the Secondary School. It was my only attempt at football. He had also repaired the botched surgery I had to perform with Blue Gillette razor blade, cotton lint and Listerine on the spear ripped belly of a man carried by litter to my camp 100 miles to the north, and then sent on by trader's lorry. All of us survived.

The Public Works Department Foreman and jack-of-all-trades was a rugged Bulgarian refugee known only as Kristoff, an evening with whom, plus slivovitz and pungent goulash made only of the choicest illegally shot venison, aged underground for three days, was a boisterous riot of 'basso profundo' bludgeoning of the English language.

A special person for me was the Headmaster of the Government Secondary School, Bill Glanville, a gentle, lonely, formally courteous man, who came from County Cork. He could talk and teach about many things, as well as being a whimsical partner at bridge. Years later in Nyanza Province he was stigmatized in his Education Department Annual Report as having a reputation for 'tippling' — a difficult enough stain to remove. He sat with friends at bridge one evening, a glass of whisky at hand, went quietly home and shot himself. He left me his small French Mab-Brevête, sleeve-action, pistol, with three silver rounds, and a maroon leather volume of *The Vision of Dante*, which I treasure yet. The pistol was the only personal weapon I ever owned.

The only European merchant living among us was the gangling, cultured manager of the British American Tobacco Company, John Belsham, who later became chief of the whole vast B.A.T. Co. enterprise in West Africa. His bachelor establishment with its canteen of cutlery, linen napery, cut glass table crystal and miraculously generated electric light was the envy of us basic householders. His well served dinners surpassed the general run of soup, Tilapia lake fish, roast meat and soggy cabbage with the inevitable 'creme caramel', followed by cheese and 'second toasties' of grilled sardines on toast or 'devils on horseback'. Such glimpses of luxury were only matched at the DC's table by inherited silver partridges, condiment sets and candelabra, but we were comfortable, companionable and content with our universal Queen's Maroon plates and metal teapots, and we all had flowers.

What of my duties as DO Cadet, so rapidly raised by mischance to command over so wide and strange a reality? They covered quite a span considering also the fourteen thousand square miles and quarter of a million people spread so thinly with minimal dry weather roads, one District 3-ton lorry and no other means of communication, save the bicycle and runner! Such duties fell to the lot of most junior DOs in Kenya Colony and the pattern need not be repeated for other districts where I served.

From my tiny room at the end of the DC's office I was required to carry out in detail a number of unfamiliar tasks. There was the boring grind of checking, ticking and signing endless vouchers against a huge ledger meticulously entered under the avuncular eye of Mr De Souza, the Goan cashier and office potentate, in case I skipped a few to get it done. I was assisted by a sweet, plump, wholesome, messenger lad who awoke thoughts of corresponding, but missing, attributes in for me the proper sex, which were later suggested to me discreetly.

I had daily enjoyable and instructive sessions with people who came to have *shauris* (problems) attended to. The queue outside was presided over, with deceptive affability, by the Head Interpreter, Chumpati, a personage of authority, of whom it was said that small inducements might facilitate a rapid, even favourable, hearing. It was difficult, and probably fruitless, to detect or correct any lurking abuse of this kind, since no one ever complained and anyway it followed the natural order of things from customary usage, 'oiling the wheels', through respectful inducement, to straight bribe, rather as is often alleged in the home press of the former colonial power. It was important that the DO, parading as a sort of Solomon, should not be thought amenable to squinting bias in dividing the infant.

Supervision of the Tribal Police Force of some 50 men was a pleasant task involving things of which I had experience, drill, .303 Lee-Enfield rifles, unarmed combat, gymnastics, basic law and so on. As distinct from the Central Government Kenya Police, of which there was a small detachment, the Tribal Police in every District were an administrative auxiliary force, carefully recruited from the local Kamba and answerable only to the DC. The Sergeant in charge was thus another significant personage. Sergeant Masabi was a bit of a roustabout, tending to choler, whether sober or home brewed drink taken, with much parade ground stamping, quivering salutes, and emphatic bulging of the eyes. His barked commands revealed jagged, sputum-flecked front teeth, the upper four filed to points, the lower removed in the old Kamba fashion, which somehow contrived horrendously engaging smiles. Masabi and Chumpati would not openly cross each other.

Two orderlies were assigned to me, named Mbiti and Chembeni Wa Nzau (sons of a bull). They were half brothers by one father, but the jet skin of Mbiti, the older, so contrasting with the russet of Chembeni, made me curious. It emerged that the latter's first name was a corruption of that of former District Commissioner Champion, after whom he had been named. Later, it was suggested to me that I might call on a mature and comely lady in the village said to be the widow of another DC, affectionately remembered as 'Daddy' Cornell. It was thought that my oral

Kiswahili might benefit, while under more formal instruction by a noted teacher next door.

As a District Officer I was 'ex officio' gazetted a Third Class Magistrate, with limited powers of imposing fines and imprisonment up to six months or of committal to the Supreme Court for specified serious offences. This function required study and examination in the (formerly Indian) Penal and Criminal Procedure Codes, tomes on the Law of Evidence and subsidiary rules and regulations, then spattered confusingly in some twenty beige, hard back volumes. When so qualified one could be gazetted a First Class Magistrate with much wider scope and powers. I never discovered how I did not become Second Class on the way, like a railway carriage, or perhaps I did.

Rape was an example of an offence for which committal to the Supreme Court on prima facie evidence was appropriate. My only such case as presented by the Police was finely balanced, since the molested maiden alleged that, while stooping to fill her vessel at a water hole, the accused, rather ambiguously translated to me by Chumpati "came running in her behind". Though serious this was hardly circumstantial enough to brook the scrutiny of a bewigged and red-robed Circuit Judge. A fitting alternative charge was successfully laid.

In itself the extraction of cash, often at the cost of sale of small stock, from people in bare subsistence, was unedifying and burdensome. It was also a tedious and grubby task. Cash was brought by taxpayers on appointed days in orderly, if reluctant, queues to a folding wooden table where sat the junior DO, me, to count. Each payer was cross checked by a clerk in a register of, sometimes confusing and nearly identical, names for the specified location, whose paid headman stood at hand. An individual would be due to pay 10/- annually, which could come in 10 cent pieces with a hole for tying, blackened silver shilling coins, one shilling notes or even the full amount.

The money saved for tax had been secreted in the payer's hut, and walked with him a long way and had probably been tied in an odour-enriched, knotted kerchief with other valuables like pungent snuff or tobacco. The coins, however rimed, could be slid quickly across the counting table and piled in fives or tens, but the single shilling notes were a trial, being small and crumpled and shaped like an old cigarette card. They needed repugnant licks of the fingers to separate them and defied piling without twine or a band and a stone to weight them. The activity was not enjoyed by either party.

When all was done the shillings were poured in two thousands into deep wooden boxes with grooved, sliding lids drawn by thumb slots which could be sealed with stamped red wax. A box was a single head load on a grass pad for a team of about ten porters, who would march in line ahead linked by a stout metal chain passed through an iron hoop set into each lid, made fast at front and rear. Porters received up to one shilling each a day with rations and they sang rhythmically of their enjoyment of this sociable task, with ribald references to the stipend and their benefactors.

There were sundry other tasks related to the continued waging of war against Japan. One was the firm encouragement, short of legal or physical compulsion, of workers to come forward for plantation labour, sisal cutting and the like. Certainly there was a close connection with non-payment or inability to pay tax, which might in turn be connected with a desire on the part of a Chief or Headman to stand well in the tax collection stakes, as well as fulfilling an assigned quota. But in my experience it was rare or unnecessary for any sanction to be imposed. I hoped so. Another duty was keeping up a meat supply for the war effort. Meat involved an added pain in that the Kamba, as all pastoral people, have an affinity with their steers and heifers which can lead to violent explosions of emotion, if called upon to give up a treasured or ceremonial beast. A fatal example happened later in Maasailand.

More personal and enjoyable work was helping a visiting regular officer of the Army Pay Corps to distribute and record family remittances to demobilized soldiers back from Burma or North Africa. Captain Bobby Caid was a leathery, deeply seamed and grizzled man with long, eroded teeth displayed in a charmingly life-mocking smile. He invariably drove up in his 4 x 4 truck, unannounced, for an expected dawn breakfast of bacon and eggs. He rewarded me by his tales of hunting the huge tuskers still to be tracked in the remote area of Kitui called the 'Yatta'. We would ensure that fees had been paid in advance by hunters and clients for the two annual licences allowed by the Game Department in Nairobi, on a substantial and escalating scale designed to discourage slaughter for undue profit on the ivory.

My first real fall from grace came when, my DC and Senior DO being *hors de combat*, I was expected, as acting Chairman to address a full meeting of the Local Native Council made up of chiefs and notables of the entire district. The Council had powers of supervising markets, roads and drains, fees, primary education etc. It was a forum for debate, long and vibrant but much enjoyed. Meetings were held in an open sided hall with the standard hail-rattling, rain-crashing, heat-cracking corrugated-iron roof.

I thought it only dignified and proper to offer some homily about the last stages of the war in Europe and onward with Japan. I studied parrot-fashion with the elderly village Professor (male) and memorized an opening Swahili sentence of shining grammatical purity. Its delivery is still sharply etched in memory; *Isithaniwe wala kufikiriwa kama tutashinda kwa mara moja!*, meaning hopefully "Let it not be imagined nor believed that we shall win speedily". At that precise moment a well-known village simpleton, perhaps not so simple, who had been standing approvingly outside, burst into a vigorous imitation of a donkey braying in descending chest-rending gusts. My chagrin was not lessened when my orderly, collapsing with laughter, told me that a donkey's refrain, with reference to its own situation rather than mine, lamented; "I can't do it — I can't do it — I can't do it — yees I caan!". I at once set about passing my preliminary oral Swahili exam.

Before this face-losing mishap while my seniors were laid low, came the chance of my first lorry and foot safari. The East African Desert Locust Control gave warning of a vast swarm heading towards Northern Kitui, seeking greenery to strip and an open egg laying ground. This biblical and cyclical plague was by no means unusual and the local chiefs and people were alerted by locust scouts and messengers to prepare for a campaign of destruction after the swarm landed and eggs hatched.

I took off with ill-concealed excitement in the one and only DC's open 3-ton truck of pre-war vintage, carrying its own supply of fuel and water in 44 gallon steel drums behind the cab, a prestige and vantage point for the Tribal Police escort. The only route to the wondrously wild sounding northern locations of Katse, Muvukoni, Tseikuru and Tharaka was a bumpy dirt road sliced across by rain runnels, which passed through the relatively populous cultivated area. Half way, without a sign, it cut across and along the strategic war-time highway from Nairobi to Somalia via the border district of Garissa, after which it was named. It was a strangely evocative encounter of nothing with nowhere.

Our first stop was at the small brick built office of the Mutonguni Location Chief, Charles Ileli, who greeted us with the air of a prosperous businessman, formally attired in brass buttoned khaki suit and pith helmet with lion badge. We took orange soda together, with the rather stilted conversation, partly through interpreter, of a courteous elder secure in his station, and a young tyro of unknown relevance, but representing the authority of the lion.

Our next meeting at Migwani location office was with Senior Chief Kasina wa Ndoo, who was then at the height of his influence throughout Kitui District and beyond. I had no experience of the nature and extent of his power although he reputedly had wealth in land and cattle, as had many another chief, but I was struck by his matter-of-fact manner of quiet, contained authority lacking any ostentation or condescension to myself. I felt, however, something reserved, even sinister in his plump fox-like mask with watchful almond eyes, marked beneath by that slanting shadow found in some feline predators. His determined control of his people much later warding off Mau Mau infiltration may have caused the savage amputation of his hands by fanatics, which he bore and survived with pride and stoicism.

We passed by a towering knob of rock called Gai, which challenged me by its steep rugged beauty to mount on the return journey, and onwards jolting over the transverse rivulets on rigid leaf springs to the fork leading to Muvukoni which was to be our base camp for the locust campaign. The gasping silence after the grinding roar of the lorry was palpable. The heat was flat and complete, unrelieved to the eye by the gnarled and seamed grey, leafless, bulk of ancient baobab trees, looming with embryonic arms above the low thorn scrub. The only sign of life was the occasional soundless glide of a magpie hued parakeet, flitting from bush to bush emitting a single insulting 'quark', commonly given another rendering by exasperated travellers.

To the oblong grass thatched shack which served as a Government Rest House came the Chief of Muvukoni Location. He had been awaiting our arrival in the small mud walled, tin roofed shop of the only Indian shopkeeper, who, from his fixed position, cross legged atop his smooth worn counter, purveyed tiny quantities of cigarettes in paper packets, sweet fizzy drinks, sugar, salt, flour, old onions and oddments like hand mirrors. He could also supply a scrawny chicken from his thorn girt yard.

Chief Mutheki was not impressive, as was evidenced by the dilapidation of the camp hut which leaned precariously on its rough corner post, rendering its balding thatch useless for shade or shelter. Nevertheless, in his sly and evasive manner he had set in train the gathering of many thousand women as locust beaters to cover the area between his Chiefdom and that of the adjoining Location of Katse, under the craggy and more outspoken Chief Kabindu. To my own disappointment, neither the locusts nor I reached the enticingly desolate territory of Tseikuru and Tharaka.

Migrant red locusts can fly immense distances without stopping, even crossing the sea, in dense swarms greater than 1,000 sq. miles. In East African invasions they seek out open savannah upon which they can land after their flight temperature has been reduced in cooling rain. When they have been spotted from trees or hilltops by keen eyed, solitary Locust Scouts, accurate predictions can be made for planning the destruction of the next generation. From landing and egg laying in the moistened soil a biblical span of 40 days elapses before hatching, which can at once be detected as countless millions of small black 'hoppers' emerge to bob rhythmically up and down, heading inexorably in the same direction. The march continues for a further 40 days of mobile growth and change of colour to a greenish hue before take off in mass; a new swarm voraciously seeking fodder and another seasonal breeding ground.

The vital interception and destruction of the hoppers on the ground depended upon sufficient numbers of local people, mainly women and girls, being assembled under direction of local headmen and elders. Without the more scientific broadcasting of huge quantities of arsenic and molasses impregnated cotton seed as poison bait, or of lethal, orange 'Di Nitro Ortho Cresol', DNOC, powder, it was necessary to carry out crudely effective practical measures by hand.

In advance of the legions of hoppers, from flank to distant flank, shallow trenches were dug by hoes or sticks in a fall-back of barriers, the spoil being thrown forward of the line of march. The trenches were filled with tinder-dry and trampled brushwood sprinkled, if available, with flammable fuel like a Christmas pudding. The hoppers, at whatever stage of growth, would thrust blindly forward into the trench, ignited or not, piling and tumbling relentlessly over each other. The women beaters, facing the hordes from beyond the spoil, would then crush the writhing, tangled, rustling bodies, pile upon pile, until a filled trench ceased to be an effective barrier, when they withdrew to the next and the next.

While this wanton, visually disgusting and malodorous task proceeded to exhaustion and extinction, the elders guided the attack from place to place with tactical skill and absence of confusion. I was much struck throughout, not so much by the lissom beauty and tireless vigour of the scantily clad young women beaters, many with babies slung asleep on their heaving backs, as by the demeanour of the male supervisors, which was every bit the equal of competent NCOs anywhere. One mature, finely built, copper skinned man in toga-like attire with a high-domed forehead, intellectual even if illiterate, closely resembled a wartime American Deputy Secretary of State, Sumner Wells. He would have cut a splendid figure in the Senate.

When the gruelling days were done, we joined in a vast celebration dance in the spacious sandy bed of a dried up tributary of the great Tana River, where there was water for the digging by man and elephant, enough to refresh the multitude. The scene pulsated with astonishingly acrobatic male performances, spurred on by thunderously rhythmical, taut cowhide drums, stuttering police whistles, in a frenzy of sinuous pelvic gyrations and seemingly self propelled oscillations of full nippled, abundant breasts. It was a wondrously stirring spectacle of a whole community in uninhibited rejoicing.

Back in the ramshackle guest house of the flaccid Chief of Muvukoni, the simmering oppressive silence, broken by the contemptuous swoop of the same macaw, was relieved by the DC's fever scare and my bush surgery. With the DC's lorry had come a basket of tired inedibles forwarded from Kenya Fish, which relieved my regular diet of deprived chicken and mushy onions or chargrilled baby goat with burnt chestnut smelling mealies.

By then we had run out of drum water and relied on the scourings of a deep dug water hole, pounded and urine soaked by urgent, scrabbling livestock. Treatment was complex and drastic. First a piece of alum was dropped in to precipitate solids. The still murky fluid was then filtered through my grey woollen army socks to clarify, followed by lengthy boiling over smoky fire. Finally it was poured through a clean handkerchief laid over a thick lipped tooth glass or enamel mug. The potable product, two gin bottles of delicate amber colour and indefinable bouquet was crisply flavoured with a cocktail of the new disinfectant 'TCP' and old fashioned Roses lime juice from the elegantly decorated bottle. It was an elixir to be savoured in the absence of *usquebaugh*.

While up north beating locusts, I had a message from the DC by trader's lorry to take on another job. It involved a gruelling foot safari over the mass of Mumoni mountain in Katse Location to check on an abandoned German Lutheran mission station and school in the valley beyond. It had been established in the heyday of German colonial rule in East Africa, before the Great War swept them out of Africa, leaving such small outposts of education untenanted and gone to waste.

Being still 'wet behind the ears' and wearing a borrowed felt trilby hat, for lack of my size in a pith 'Bombay Bowler' at Ahameds', I found the pounding heat of the arid country almost unbearable. I pretended to move as if by chance from one naked bulging baobab to another, embracing vertical slivers of shade where I could. As we laboured to the tree girt top of Mumoni exposing literally breathtaking views of limitless bush, I can remember the vertical sun beating on my ill-protected neck; then no more.

Many hours later I came to under a dry grass thatch and thorn shelter built over me where I lay. Good Ogoma, whistling nervously, was placing wet cloths on my forehead. After a bowl of chicken soup and aspirin washed down with the life giving nectar, followed by cool sunset and ten hours dark sleep, I woke refreshed enough to make the descent towards the deserted Mission. We passed through peaceful villages in which clusters of wide eyed children had without doubt never seen a white man, a 'Mzùngu' (an object of amazement), and few adults ever. The bush dogs, with bristled ruffs, rigidly curled back tails and high pitched yammering, made their territorial rights plain in less friendly fashion.

The Mission buildings were in remarkably sound condition, affording secure shelter for goats and fat tailed sheep, with no human usage for defecation which was discretely done in the sanitizing bush. The German Mission type of construction was quite different from the dried brick or mud and wattle Kenya style. Upon raised foundations the walls were built up with smooth balls of black volcanic rock set in lime plaster blended with the finely digested spoil of iron hard termite towers. What use was ever made of this 'Rip Van Winkle' school, ready for awakening by living pupils, I do not know. Apart from the violent pain as if of a molten cannon ball shifting inside my head when leaning forward, I felt no ill effects from the 'heat stroke', save a lifelong reaction anywhere to rays striking the nape of the neck or the tendons of the knees at slanting sunrise.

On the way back from Muvukoni by waiting lorry we stopped, as planned, at the looming phallus of Gai Rock, rooted in a pubic fringe of dark euphorbia candelabra. Mbiti wa Nzau and I scaled the crinkled flank triumphantly with gasping delight and at the summit I knew the meaning of Wordsworth's "The tall rock, the mountain and the deep and gloomy wood, their colours and their forms were then to me an appetite a feeling and a love". The "... still sad music of humanity ...", came later! The descent, in a thigh quivering gallop down the shifting scree of the upper slopes, brought me to earth with a bump. We found ourselves at the unavoidable mouth of a 40 foot vertical funnel with a few stunted roots protruding as the only handhold to clutch. I confidently eased my way downward, as trained, with back to one wall tensed against feet on the other, suddenly to lose grip and balance and crash wildly and painfully to the bottom of the chute — there to be greeted by an inscrutably smiling Mbiti, who had done it his way. We set up camp beside the Kamba cattle and goat enclosures beneath the falling shadow of the Rock.

The chill before sunrise woke me, inside the body snug canvas of my bedroll, in time to enjoy peacefully the sensual awareness of an African dawning. Colours were dusky and muted, softened by the misty half light. Human figures moving slowly about in silent isolation from each other emitted throat scouring mucus, spat into the bush. The strangulated yell of a male goat called plaintively as if for help, or perhaps a mate, the sound hurled back by the echo of the overhanging rock.

Before leaving Kitui for my next learning post as a cadet DO in Nyanza Province, I was sent on a swift, in our terms, lorry trip to the southern locations of Kanziku, Mutha, Ikutha and as far as the Tana river Mombasa road bridge at Kibwezi, where there was a sisal estate factory and three tin frame shops selling lukewarm cola and such, under the thin shade of yellow bark fever trees. The dryness of the countryside was so pervasive that DC Osborne had reported despairingly that only a network of 1,000 small dams and pans could provide some basis for subsistence, albeit with spindly cassava bushes providing edible ground paste from their bulbous roots. The very names of the locations conjured up the scorched, thorny undergrowth and spiky sanseveira, called elephant sisal, with curved black poisonous tip which once penetrated behind my shin bone causing weeks of exudation of rotting black pus. Yet this wild cousin of sisal, when stripped by tusk, masticated and rumblingly digested makes the fibrous structure of the steaming medicine balls of dung which plop fragrantly to carpet elephant walks and excite the waiting flights of myriad dung beetles to scoop out and roll their orbs of procreation.

Chief Mutuku, whom I was sent to meet at Ikutha, was delicately boned and sprightly, as stylishly turned out as a country squire. He wore brass buttoned regulation khaki jacket, well skirted, with brown leather, softankled cavalry boots over knee breeches, which he slapped nonchalantly with a hunting crop, or was it a switch, and his felt Tyrolean hat was embellished with an iridescent feather from a helmeted guinea fowl. It came to me as a happy revelation that the administration of even the most remote pockets of people could be in the charge of alert and stimulating leaders, who seemed to be informed about affairs abroad, no doubt partly through soldiers returning from the distant warfare in Egypt or Burma.

IV

IMPRESSIONS
1944

After my first posting to Kitui it was difficult to sum up the impressions I had formed of the 'colonial condition', or even to be aware that I had such perceptions.

In mid 1944 I did not have an inkling of how Kamba society, as found by first intruders before the Great Wars, was changing and responding to the socially more open, technically skilled, literate young soldiers returning from active service among men and women of other races in North Africa, India and Burma. The social impact was much sharper and more disturbing than that of their bucolic medal-proud, fathers, who had foot-slogged through German East Africa (Tanganyika) 30 years earlier and who still served as what was termed in law the 'Native Authority'.

Over the same time-span there was also a change from the motley of soldier-adventurer-administrators of the kind celebrated by Dutton, a senior secretariat official and repressed romantic chronicler, in his nostalgic, hero-worshipful saga *Lillibullero or the Golden Road* ... (to Samarkand). There were Archer and Kittermaster, the giant striding *Dioscuri* of the North; Zapphiro, the Levantine Greek guardian of the Ethiopian boundary; Glenday, the ambiguously named, 'Faras Ad' or 'White Stallion' of the Somali nomads; Ainsworth, stern builder of *bomas* and bridges, and those other chosen many, after whom were named peaks and camps and waterfalls.

The next wave brought notable eccentrics and individualists; H. Blackwood-Murphy, absurdly grand in 'Irish Court Dress' at dinner in the bush; 'Frog-Face' Jennings, alleged founder of the often re-invented desert 'Wajir Yacht Club'; pistol-toting Major Grant, who fell uncomprehending to a vengeful Maasai spear, Everest challenger, P. Wyn-Harris; and 'Uncle' Reece, sonorous beadle of the vast Northern Frontier District. They in turn were crossed with a gentler and more liberal breed of peacetime graduates, plucked fresh from the older universities. Their steady careers were properly recorded in Official Gazettes, which concealed career comets', like Turnbull, later to be dubbed 'Tiger of Tanganyika'.

During suspension of normal recruitment between 1939 and 1945 it happened that, other than releases within Africa, two administrative cadets were appointed direct from the Home Forces. First was Bobby Winser, javelin champion and 'parfit knight', whose six month odyssey via the Cape to Kenya was punctuated by a torpedo off the former German port, Walvis Bay, on the Skeleton Coast of the Namib Desert. Much later my own slow boat limped in convoy through the reopened Mediterranean with no such baptismal greeting.

Falling into the line of march of such 'forerunners', I have tried to convey the sense of being a green cadet, charged briefly with responsibility for hundreds of thousands of people of another race and mode of life, placed under the tutelage of an avowedly benevolent oligarchy of white 'strangers' or *wazungu*. I know I felt surprised and pleasurable relief and wonder that the still recent phenomenon of colonial rule seemed to be accepted readily, even with warmth and a sort of inculcated loyalty, without equality. It seemed as if the natural order of things, conducted in the tradition of the mother power, according to ordained 'stations in life'.

Lest I entertained any doubts on this score, a visiting Senior Veterinary Officer, John Hart, with the rank and style of Major, assured me; "There are only two classes of men; officers and other ranks". In a strange way this robust, and not quite joking concept, seemed loosely to dovetail with the local traditional society, which remained firmly patriarchal and regulated by semi-warlike age grades, with gradations of respect upwards. A curious, if provocative, reaction to the mingling of European social groups was a question sometimes put to me as to whether the Colonial Administration and Police were of different tribes. The latter were certainly paid even less!

Neither at Kitui nor later did I begin to penetrate the paradox of unequal relationships and mutual incomprehension between the races. Few Administrative Officers then expressed doubts of the nature and moral base of colonial rule and the famed recruiting sergeants of the Colonial Office, Sir Ralph Furse and Captain Newbolt, went on forecasting a full career until nigh on Independence 18 years later.

The 'Devonshire Declaration' of 1923, asserting that in case of conflict with the "immigrant races ... the interests of the African natives should prevail", was vaguely known to me, but it hardly impinged on relations between expatriates of either gender and the 'natives'. This was particularly so in Kitui where land disputes with settlers had no cause to arise without common boundaries. We had all heard of the two great 'milk barons', Frank Joyce and F. O'B. Wilson of Ulu, whose ranches marched with the Kamba of Machakos District near the Mombasa road, but when, famously, dispute did arise it was put down to unexplained 'grudgery' between two robust Irishmen, who each enjoyed excellent relations with the 'natives'.

Starting at the bottom of the Administrative ladder, I had no occasion to feel doubt or fear, unease, cultural deprival or loneliness and was lucky in health without preventive medicines or domestic refinements and without money. There were practical lacks which also conditioned our behaviour. Transport was minimal, battered and ancient, roads awful, inspection visits happily rare, even after the telegraph intruded. We heard a little of the outside world by battery radio, though villagers thronged to the flickering mobile cinema, presented everywhere by the indefatigable young administrator/impresario, Paul Kelly, with Charlie Chaplin competing with propaganda for the war effort. (His evangelistic fervour and innate goodness ultimately exchanged the lion for the dog-collar).

Under the symbolic power of the lion badge, I developed a certain presumption, even easy arrogance, of command, tempered perhaps by a burgeoning affectionate familiarity with the people around me, which persisted and grew through seniority and change.

There were sceptics at several levels of the Administration who wondered whether we were involved in a huge confidence trick of human manipulation. If it was so it remained unexposed for many years during which we may have led the peoples into a never-never land of expectation following a will-o'-the-wisp of our own ideals and yearnings.

V

NAIROBI STOPOVER
1944

Exhilaration at my next posting to distant Kisumu on Lake Victoria-Nyanza was scarcely broken by a necessary stopover in Nairobi ('Engare Nairobi' meant 'cold water' in Maasai), for official reporting and dental repairs. I had to present myself at the fine, but not over grand, sandstone Government building, designed by Baker of New Delhi fame, together with Jan Hoogterp, in harmony with the adjoining Kenya Uganda Railway HQ. It served both as Law Courts and Colonial Secretariat, the right hand quarter of the top floor housing the office of The Chief Native Commissioner, head of the Provincial Administration. I was not detained for long and at Assistant-Secretary level, as befitted a cadet with little of significance to impart.

The dental appointment, on service recommendation, was with the long established practice of Jack Melhuish and handsome Jimmy Guest in the old Corner House, looking to the rear of the seated Delamere statue commanding his own main avenue. 'Jack' himself was ageless, with straggly hair of faded orange, sinewy-agile cunning at squash and quicksilver charm. He enjoyed a reputation for rare skill, a fashionable clientele and blithe disregard of convention in his unchurched devotion to his redoubtable companion, Joan Waddington, respected custodian of ciphers and secrets at Government House.

I was in need of capping a front tooth, split upon colliding with the forehead of the opposing centre forward in my clumsy attempt at football at the Kitui secondary school. Mrs Watson, bustling motherly receptionist with the spirited wit of a Londoner born, was about to usher me into the surgery, when in swept an unmistakable lady, scented, permed, bestockinged, with a sharp-eyed fox fur thrown across her shoulder and a tiny felt hat.

"Oh Lady Saltau, would you mind waiting a moment while Mr Melhuish has a look at this young man?"

"Not Lady Saltau!" snapped the glamorous but impatient personage: "Lady ..." and she mentioned the current spouse.

"Never mind, dearie," retorted Mrs Watson comfortably, "the teeth are the same, aren't they?"

It was my only brush with one of the small, overrated circle of upper crust vagabonds known as the 'Happy Valley set', whose nest had recently been fouled by the roadside murder near Karen of Lord Errol, Premier Earl of

Scotland, a crime of passion still wrapped in a web of concealment, which few could then penetrate and none yet chose to do so. The murder car was a Buick leased from a future uncle-in-law of mine.

Having as yet no personal friends in Nairobi, I stayed at the (not so New) Stanley Hotel, where the Assistant Manager, fresh from the Army, was Alan Bobbé, gracefully golden with a wry, barbed wit protecting a gentle heart. He introduced me over time to an engaging coterie of friends. Among them were Stephen Death, Government Fisheries Inspector, in from Kisumu, where I later found his official launch cabin decked out with yellow chintz curtains, and Peter Hield, once Household Cavalryman, of family wealth in woollen mills from which he could draw remittances only on banker's certificate of gainful employment. This was elegantly undertaken in bush hotels where his culinary skills and five star reception confounded the far from elegant passing trade. I once found him up a ladder, in dinky blue shorts, overpainting the 'Voi Hotel', a whitewashed block house, as 'Hotel de Voi'.

There were others, such as aristocratic Fabian Wallis, friend of 'Sharpie', gardener extraordinary of the Administration, who congregated on small estates along 'Buggers Ridge' near Thompson's Falls. They were cultivated, amusing, lovers of music, food and wine and happily tolerant of my 'non-involvement', as of Mickey Migdoll, standard setting proprietor of Esquire Tailoring House, and Peter Colmore with Harry Winfield, popular bandleaders at Torr's Hotel, deliberately built to rival London's best by Colonel Grogan (of whom more later). Alan Bobbé, friend from then on, peerless restaurateur (for forty years) at Alan Bobbé's Bistro and musical broadcaster to the changing generations, gave me a long, rope handled, mortar bomb box full of wonderful '78' records of Caruso, Gigli, Swan Lake and Nutcracker ballets and classical ballads, which later made magical sand-silent, lone evenings on the Ethiopian border.

I do not recall meeting any Africans or Asians at that time, except in shops, offices or public places. When I cast a hopeful eye on a young white woman, I was warned mockingly "Don't waste your time dreaming, old boy, strictly Majors and above". By lucky chance I met 'the Bowring girls', three graces who carried the respected name of the Colonial Administrator who had fought incessantly for the realization of former Colonial Secretary Churchill's dream of a railway network through Africa, using the Great Rift Valley and lakes as a conduit. Gladys Hughes, a widow, gave me an inscribed leather quarto size Shakespeare, whence the 'Poor Beetle' of this book. Her sister was married to Granville Roberts, journalist and broadcaster, prophet of 'nouvelle cuisine' culled from his Karen garden and future Kenya Agent in Grand Buildings, Trafalgar Square. The third, a tantalizingly beauteous nymphet was victim of alleged rape by her garden 'boy' at Eldoret, whose successful defending counsel, an ebullient retired magistrate from Palestine, Mervyn Morgan, became her husband and opened the door to legal representation of African clients.

Having thus innocently tasted a fragment of Nairobi's Bohemian society, in contrast with earlier Secretariat propriety, and formed some lasting friendships, I gladly made tracks for Kisumu, with the resurgent confidence of a 'Mr Toad' emerging unscathed from confinement in the wild woods. I was no longer the 21-year-old tyro without household goods. Ogoma, too, was a cock-a-hoop at our posting to his Kisumu homeland.

VI

RAIL ACROSS THE RIFT
July 1944

Nairobi railway station was already 50 years old and looked good for a century. The substantial single storey span of dressed stone under red Bangalore tiles was dignified by a central rectangular clock tower, sloping upwards to a decorative iron filigree rim like a coronet, in the manner of a Loire château. Its great extent amply housed all services to the daily east and westward bound passenger trains, including a friendly farewell saloon and a quite fashionable restaurant.

The broad platform was long enough for some 30 carriages, propelled up the steep gradients of the westerly journey over the Great Rift Valley by two widely spaced Garratt steam locomotives, their massive bulbous tanks extruding power to thrust or reverse the huge pistons. There were three classes of carriage, in like clusters, mainly but not exclusively for European Asian and African travellers, there being little in material comfort to mark the difference in cost between the first and second class sleepers, save perhaps the squatting arrangements in the European or Asian labelled WCs. A coupé for two was the ultimate in privacy, opportunity and status. Third class was given over to slatted wooden seating, without facilities to sleep or eat, the latter provided for at halts by eager jostling wayside vendors offering aromatic roast mealies, bananas and local fruits.

Access to the train was simple and efficient via a small booking alcove with a clerk and a cashier in a glass cubicle, through an unfussed but crowded ticket gate to a facing line of notice boards displaying name, carriage, and cabin, even seat number, with location of classified restaurant cars. Each notice was scrutinized for the names of fellow passengers and the chances of good company, or otherwise, on the long trek.

Mounting excitement, blasts of steam and whistle, slamming of doors, warning shouts, parting valedictions and a scampering of late beer drinkers, heralded departure. Exactly on time the enormous vertebrate beast lumbered jerkily into motion until the comforting rhythm of bogey on track took over on the level curve towards Dagoretti corner, in Kiambu district.

Almost at once a khaki uniformed cabin steward appeared to ascertain needs of canvas bedroll and bedding, with or without mattress separately charged, and early morning tea. He was followed by a more important official issuing different coloured cards, well thumbed, for first or second gong announced dinner sessions, each having advantages of quantity, cuisine and service. In this and other railway journeys of the time the friendly and skilful service, almost entirely Goan and African, was remarkable. The food cooked and presented from cramped, steaming galleys on acrobatically balanced trays was quite out of proportion to the minuscule prices charged, a few shillings for full breakfast or five course dinner, with wine and 'collectible' cutlery and napery to match.

We shrieked, snorted and thundered our smoke plumed way for nearly 300 miles through many strata of geology and history, while glimpsing also layers of my own experiences to come. The slow climb up the eastern ramp of the Rift cut through the confused pattern of the southern Kikuyu land unit, or 'reserve', which fitted like pieces of a jigsaw puzzle into the hedged or fenced 'scheduled areas', similarly reserved in practice for European settlers and often loosely called the 'white highlands'.

The Kikuyu lands, beneath a certain fecund visual splendour, were a pullulating rural slum of poorly thatched, smoke blackened, toadstool huts set in clusters among straggly plantations of maize and tattered banana fronds. Some open spaces showed the half filled scars of contoured soil conservation trenches, but more often revealed the wounds of deeply eroded gullies spewing down slimy red mud scoured from overgrazed or steeply tilled hillsides. The settled farms seemed to roll more leisurely past in idyllic parklands, dotted with fine grade cattle, sometimes the hardy-delicate Jersey cross, or in orderly lines of ripening coffee bushes, their long triple stems stooping gracefully or single pruned and smartly upright, protected from sun and hailstorm by golden flowering Gravillea trees. The occasional homestead could be glimpsed festooned with blazing Bougainvillaea beneath feathery fronded purple Jacaranda.

Although the urchin children of farm labour, herding worm ridden and scrawny Kikuyu cattle and goats along the embankments, screamed and waved delightedly at us, their patiently awaited daily entertainment, the contiguous and contrasting land holdings had been the subject of bitter friction for over twenty years since pioneer nationalist Harry Thuku's abortive revolt of 1922 had resulted in 25 riot deaths in Nairobi outside the Kingsway Police Station and opposite the famed Norfolk Hotel, complete with hitching posts for settlers' horses. He became a pioneer 'gentleman farmer' and friend, but retained his untouchably detached prestige.

Harry's protégé and follower, born Muigai wa Ngengi, dubbed Johnstone,* whence 'Jomo' at the Church of Scotland Mission, and nick-named 'Kinyatta', after his bead decorated belt, had since emerged as Jomo Kenyatta, persistent if Delphic advocate of Kikuyu claims to settled land for which he gave evidence in front of the Kenya (Carter) Land Commission in London. His absences from Kenya due to study at the London School of Economics, publication with Malinowski of *Facing Mount Kenya*, visits to Russia, his English second marriage, surprisingly, his lectures to the Army Bureau of Current Affairs and the practical constraints of war, delayed

---

*Being denied both John and Peter as Christian names he combined John with Peter meaning Stone!

return to his people and homeland until 1946. It was at that point of his rise to power that my own encounters began with a personality so powerfully absent while we rolled through Kikuyuland.

As we steamed higher we passed through neat rows of crisp green tea in the impeccable plantations of the Brooke Bond international company, altitude, temperature, heavy mists and acid soil being found as well suited to tea planting as Assam. The expatriate management of the tea companies always seemed to enjoy a rather superior social status and better conditions of work, which extended, in some measure, to their nimble fingered pluckers and their well kept labour compounds. On the open windswept plateau, farmed by Kikuyu Co-operatives with their own whitewashed oblong offices and depots, were expanses of pretty white Pyrethrum flowers, like the miniature Chrysanthemums they are, yielding the profitable insecticide powder processed and marketed by factory and statutory boards in Nairobi and Nakuru. The locally made and ubiquitous mosquito spray guns used for the produce, 'Flit', were indispensable bedside companions in camp, hotel or railway sleeper, determining rest or sleepless misery.

In the cool pastures near Limuru we saw champion Friesian cows swinging their splendid udders with heavy gait to the model dairies of their bucolic owners. Tom Brown was one, a ruddy, side-whiskered 'Farmer Giles', a model of skill and reputation in development of the national herd. With such neighbours no dispute arose at that time.

Limuru township and railway sidings were a cockpit of converging and conflicting economic and social activities. There was clamorously competitive loading and unloading of supplies and exports; of the well conducted tea companies; of the powerful, non-Communist Czech Bata shoe factory of exiled 'Tommy' Bata; of Pyrethrum Co-operatives and saw millers, while lurching, lop-sided lorries carried crabwise their bulging nets of vegetables for pre-dawn delivery to the waiting Nairobi market. All was set within a sordid crush of mud huts and flimsy hovels, huddling together unknown numbers of unemployed landless or evicted Kikuyu, distilling and consuming lethal Nubian gin, or brewing traditional beer in vessels. From them I later gained the Kikuyu nickname of 'Karuga Ndua'.

We toiled on, past the turn off to Uplands Bacon Factory, shrewdly managed by another John Bull figure, 'farmer' John Bicknell, whose stout cudgel conjured up the picture of him prodding a gruntled pen of fine pigs greedily, if unwittingly, awaiting their turn. His incoming successor was a handsome young middle-European 'thinking man's farming expert', renamed Southall. He was experimenting with the application of music to production. A voluntary payment of 10 cents monthly entitled workers to gramophone music of their choice, but Southall decided the records put on in relation to the rhythm and speed needed for matching the revolutions of the manually operated slicing machines to the current appetite of the market. No other volume control was necessary.

At last we emerged into the thin, clean, pine scented air of the Crown Forest plantations, extending up to the lip of the Rift. The winding track clung to the escarpment side beneath the bamboo forest road. It passed near a miniature gem of a Catholic church built by the remaining Italian prisoners of war, exhibiting their national genius for creative enjoyment of misfortune. Happily for all concerned they were put to construction of the new tarmac highway directly assaulting the eastern wall of the Rift down which we came. The enormous vista opened during the descent was a marvel of nature, even when half tamed by man, whether Maasai or settler. The shapely, near extinct, volcano Longonot reared its crinkly sided crater from the bed of the Rift to a height of 3,000 feet. It was an instant challenge to me to run round the narrow lip. It was later pointed over dramatically towards the Ruwenzori Mountains by Clark Gable to Ava Gardner as "gorilla country".*

The immense, seemingly empty, expanse of grazing land conjured up the foreboding in Maasai folklore of a great snake appearing to divide and consume their pastures. Their tribal domination was exercised seasonally and at will for their vast herds of cattle before their catastrophic depletion by rinderpest, and the grass had been too sour for sheep until Lord Delamere found the key to its use by introducing a trace mineral cobalt lick. On both counts the central Rift was to see the fulfilment of the prophesy because the powerful Purko, Kekonyukie and other clans had been induced by the Colonial Government in an explicitly "enduring" treaty to withdraw in confused stages to two separate "reserves". The one was over the Mau Escarpment to the Loita Plateau in the south west, the other to Laikipia Plateau in the north. More trouble arose when the northern migrating clans and their herds had grazed down and sweetened the coarse Laikipia grasses, and settler ranchers claimed them back as their 'promised land'. I was to become closely involved in this situation from the Samburu direction since the same 'promise' was cited by all parties in respect of differing claims.

Whatever the interpretation put upon pre-colonial settlement Maasai land rights, the evidence of their nomadic dominion and passing is still generally recognized in place names on survey maps showing towns — Nairobi — Narok; grazing plateaux — Merti — Uasin Nkishu; mountains; the twin peaks of Mount Kenya, Nelion and Batian — Ol Donyo Sabuk — Sattima — Lolokwe — Menengai, and rivers such as Guaso Ngiro, which is duplicated north and south reflecting the to and fro movements after the divisive intrusion of the great snake. The word 'Ngai', alone or attached,

*In the 1950s cult film *Mogambo*, described later.

conveyed both god and rain, being of common significance as epitomized by the power of the rainmakers — 'Oloiboni' or 'Laibons', of whom more later. Even a one hut railway halt we passed was named 'Il Kek', after the ostrich which abounded.

The elongated giant's trough of the Rift, gouged by nature down from the Red Sea, where the water miraculously divided for the Israelites, to the sunken game-sheltering 'lost world' of Ngorongoro Crater, was seen by the Colonial Office as a convenient natural boundary for demarcating two of the territories secured by Britain in the European powers' 'Scramble for Africa' of the 1890s. Up to 1902 the boundary line between the initial East African Protectorate and the Uganda Protectorate extended from Lake Rudolph, astride the 'Abyssinian' border, directly south past Lakes Baringo and Naivasha to a point on the border of German East Africa between Lake Natron and Mount Kilimanjaro, ceded by Queen Victoria to her grandson, Kaiser Wilhelm II. Only after 1902 did confused argumentation between Foreign and Colonial Office interests result in the shifting from Uganda of responsibility for the area between the Rift and Lake Victoria, leaving the future Kenya to take its subsequent shape from Lake Victoria to the Indian Ocean.

We stopped briefly to take on water at Nakuru Station, before entering the thriving lakeside town, Provincial Headquarters and hub of Kenya Farmers' Association activities. The principal Hotel beside the Kenya-Uganda highway, The Stag's Head, was later the scene of my first involvement in a direct racial clash implicating prominent personalities yet to appear. Somewhere there I met George Carlos Meredith Dowson, naturally called John, and his Romany-Rosetti wife. He was then District Commissioner Kajiado, stronghold of the south eastern Maasai. He and 'gentle parfit' John Carson, DC at Kapsabet in Nandi District, came to epitomize for me the humorously unassuming core of normal decency in our service, brave, stubbornly principled and noticeably unrewarded in the perplexing role of colonial ruler and careful trustee, in which career ambition could guide conduct willy-nilly in response to fluctuations of policy.

From Nakuru we made good speed to the opposite wall of the Rift and spiralled upwards out of range of Maasai incursions and into the looming fertile uplands of the Lumbwa whom they derided as 'diggers', the Nandi, the Kipsigis and cognate groups. All are of mixed Nilo-Hamitic stock and follow the tradition of circumcision into warrior age-grades, but practice more stable and intensive livestock and mixed farming suited to their terrain. They were sometimes known collectively as 'Kalenjin', both as a convenient label of political and social cohesion and in its meaning that they can converse with each other, that is when they choose since men tend to the taciturn, 'the silent culture', and greetings are restrained with long pauses. They were renowned for physical beauty, athletic prowess and sturdy independence. In the British parlance of the day they were counted with approval as among 'the fighting tribes'.

I was once present at Kericho when a newly appointed Kipsigis Assistant Minister in the Colonial Government, Taita arap Towett, rated more as a poet than a politician, came home to address a 'baraza' of his elders. They were seated on the ground with their lower faces respectfully covered by their blankets. He indulged himself at length in fancy and didactic discourse. When he ran dry a severe and upright elder, at least two grades his senior, stepped forward deliberately. With fine disdain and pointed fly switch he told the Minister, "Young man, we have listened patiently to what you wished to say and now we shall tell you what you are to do." Democracy in action.

We had taken the westerly fork to Kisumu, where the other line switched via Eldoret and north of Lake Victoria to Uganda. Ours climbed to Mau-Summit, said to be the highest railway station in the Empire, where we saw fortresses of stacked logs from Tinderet Forest waiting to be loaded. On top of the world, we rolled by Turi village, famed both for its butchery, which despatched succulent Molo lamb throughout Kenya, and for the academic success and cultural regimen of Turi School, chosen by many Europeans, settlers and others, in preference to sending their children away to boarding schools 'at home'.

The air was heady and bracing, the sun crisply burning and Mr and Mrs Wenmans' family hotel at nearby Molo so simply welcoming that many came to find health and peace there, even though it was hinted that the altitude eventually touched the minds of the ruddy cheeked denizens. Indeed, when I was sent there for a week's recuperation after amoebic and bacillary dysentery, stuffed with Emetine by mouth and depleted by Iatrine washouts, I had to collapse with my case on the steps half way up the steep hotel lawn from the bus stop, heart and head pounding with nausea.

At Wenmans' bar I first met Punch Bearcroft, rumbustious young pilot of a single engined Piper aircraft, who challenged all comers at table tennis, despite the loss of a hand in an explosion. His defiantly fearless service with the Kenya Police Airwing brought us together in harsher days to come. Along the same ridge was the Highlands Hotel, enjoying a more classy clientele and the proximity of Captain Tryon's livery stables, with suitably thoroughbred horses. The hotel keeper of nearby Kaptagat Arms was 'Sweetie' Cooper, a gentle but zany man, who in 1955 attempted with three friends to drive the hazardous overland route to Europe across the Sahara in a Morris Minor Traveller. Tragically having lost the desert trail south of Tamanrasset in Algeria he and Freda Taylor died of thirst. Seventeen-year-old Peter Barnes of the Prince of Wales School in Nairobi was rescued near death together with Barbara Duthie of the East African Women's League by a French Foreign Legion patrol.*

Freewheeling down the sinuous incline to Muhoroni, we could discern in the glow of the false dawn a sheltered arena, the focal point of deep folds in the shadowy hills, which offered settler farmers a sense of calm seclusion and independence. Up the Mteitei Valley, a veritable Shangri-La to me, lived 'O.C.' Harries and his wife Allie, while high on the far side were Colonel and Mrs Southon, retired to an austerely hospitable, if somewhat religious, sunset retreat. Their tipple at meals was delicious skimmed milk separated in their creamery.

'O.C.' was of the powerful frame of Wordsworth's Grasmere shepherd. His Welsh forebears, emigrants to South Africa, had come north with the late wave of Boer Voortrekkers attracted in 1904 from British dominion by publicity about settlement land along the new Uganda railway. The Harries clan reputedly came more or less barefoot beside their ox wagons, some barely literate, although Allie was a teacher and her two daughters flourished at Turi School.

The four Harries brothers, 'O.C.' plus Ivan, 'Bobs' and 'Black', made a daredevil team who once for a wager arranged, as if in a bullfight without sword or lance, that one as matador should leap upon an outraged charging rhino and be photographed so mounted. 'Bobs', whom I knew later, became an influential pineapple grower and canning industry magnate at Thika. Such affluent farmers were often marked by their curvaceous, trimly fitting safari suits of loden material called 'solaro', shot through with green and red thread in the weave, both colours said to be resistant to the sun's rays.

At the convergence of the valleys was a sprawling and unpretentious club with tennis, riding and less innocent mingling, as a change from isolation. The riding was to be my undoing. Hoping to impress O.C.'s daughter Jean Harries. I rashly took up a challenge to ride her 17 hands, unconvincingly gelded, black horse *Shaitani* — Satan indeed! — in a pony club scurry. My steed fared well with me on top, until the gaping sole of one of my ex-army boots parted to grip the stirrup. Losing balance and reins I slid from the saddle, while kicking vainly to free my boot, only to be dragged helter-skelter by the other foot, side face down, around the tufty field to a bloody finish, inglorious but much enjoyed by other backers.

This fall from grace gained me a kindly invitation to restore my lost face at the Mteitei farm under the sternly trusting eye of O.C. There I fell further for the wit and warmth of my full bodied, bud lipped, musky skinned challenger, who was favoured also by the, to me quite ancient, paleontologist Louis Leakey. Sadly, resisting such addresses, she remained determined to pursue her promising career as an artist and I my posting to

*The full story told me by Peter Barnes in Nairobi in February 1998 was published in *Trek*; Paul Stewart; Jonathan Cape; 1991.

the Somali border 600 miles north. Years later she married a Police Inspector friend, Doug Espie, with whom I struggled 14,000 ft up Mount Elgon, astride the Uganda border in pursuit of a turbulent Kitosh tribal prophet, Elijah Masinde.

Before we left Kalenjin territory on the high plateau of the western shoulder of the Rift, I was shown by regular travellers, with some approbation, a single natural spire of weathered rock towering above the dark skyline. It was known in settler lore as 'Nandi Rock', from which Nandi warriors would throw despised Kavirondo tribal prisoners down to their unhealthy plains. As the sun rose from the Rift behind us, there was a palpable change of pressure, temperature and humidity nearing Lake Victoria, or rather the land girt antechamber of the Kavirondo Gulf, upon which three years of my life were at intervals to be centred.

The hubbub and bustle of wake-up tea set on the floor, cramped shaving in the folding topped steel bowl, dragging out of cases, stacking of bedrolls and bunks, speedy but Full Kenya Breakfast all generated growing excitement. Warning whistle blasts cleared the cane cutters walking the track to their set tasks. The lush sugar plantations from Miwani to Kibos gave out from the refineries the thick burnt aroma of refining sugar and coarse jaggery, the main ingredient of Nubian gin. The glint of irrigated rice paddies spread far into the Kano Plain.

Most strikingly there was a change of human vibration into a kind of undulating bellow of uninhibited voices, deep chested and at full volume, quite different from the staccato metallic din of Nairobi city and the thin high pitched calls across the solitary spaces of Kitui. Through a fringe of workers' maize girt shanties and within sight of the gulf waters the proudly hooting train with blasts of discharging steam drew slowly into the noisy welcome of Kisumu Station.

58

VII

NYANZA PROVINCE — PROVINCIAL HEADQUARTERS
KISUMU, JULY 1944

Jack Flynn, a clearly senior officer from Provincial HQ, met me at the
Kisumu railway terminus. He was a spare, dark haired man in the late
thirties, lean visaged, taciturn and choleric in hue. I was told that his
present position begged the question why he had not yet held a District
command, hurtful enough if unspoken. Without marked enthusiasm he
conducted me to my lodgings. An easy walk with porter and trolley up the
road from the station passed through the grid-plan, storm-drained Kisumu
township streets of mainly Indian, porticoed shops adjacent to the marine
installations and twin berths of the fine Lake Victoria steamers.

Further uphill a grassy belt, clear of clutter, served as a sort of cordon
sanitaire separating the bustling commercial centre, with its surrounding
shanty sprawl, from the more salubrious Government and residential area
above. This consisted in the main of rows of well spaced garden lots with
Frangipani shrubs concealing old colonial bungalows, some raised on stilts.
They ran along either side of a single public road, which followed the upper
curve of the hillside from the hotel to the Kisumu Club, affording a
splendid panorama of the gulf. The humid morning air was heavy with a
blend of exotic odours, rudely pierced by sudden gagging wafts of gutted
lake fish, stretched and sun-dried on tall frames, or stacked flat like huge
poppadoms on delivery lorries. It was a delicacy as prized and pungent as
Bombay Duck.

The long, whitewashed, two storey Kisumu Hotel, indeed the only
superior hotel, may not have won many AA stars, nor an asterisk for
cuisine, but it was the hub of much of the public, business and social
activity from Tanganyika to Mount Elgon, being at the end of the line by
road, rail, lake steamer and air. It boasted a banqueting room as well as a
restaurant, a hairdressing annex and a cocktail bar presided over by
Maurice the dapper barman, hailing from the famously advanced, mission
educated, tea growing, Colony of Nyasaland.

The hotel served both transients and local residents, the latter much
given to membership activities, each with jealously guarded loyalties and
cliques, social, tennis, yachting, and senior white duck clad bowls. There
was a richly endowed and powerful Masonic Lodge, wherein the rank of
the Brothers could turn topsy turvy their service seniority outside; a
prestigious Rotary Club and a robustly tribal Caledonian Society.

The Caledonians, more noticeably Scottish in their exile, had the
capacity in several senses to upset apple carts, while preserving a devout
seriousness of purpose. As a new District Officer and hotel guest I was

invited to 'Burns Night' dinner and was seated behind my personal bottle of Scotch, when John L. Riddoch, American Ford dealer, cotton ginnery owner and wealthiest merchant in the Province, was remorselessly debagged down the hotel steps to adjust his pretensions. Among the boisterous assailants was Ted Robertson, anarchical young prospector, who with distinctly hierarchical Lord Erroll had struck it rich in the gold rush to Rosterman's Mine near Kakamega. Ted was held on a gossamer rein by his enchanting wife Moira, one of the 'three graces' of Bill and Eileen Danks at Maseno Veterinary and Breeding Centre. Bill, with his attractively flattened pugilist's nose once showed me his pride and joy, an imported Sahiwal bull destined to spread its progeny through the native Zebu herds. In a confined demonstration room like a squash court the bull dared to pin Bill against the wall only to stagger back dazed by a vigorous right cross.

Ted had obtained the unobtainable, a black 1940s Chevrolet limousine, probably from the divinely blessed and profitable turnover of imported vehicles permitted to American Missions such as the Elim Missionary Society of Massachusetts, the Seventh Day Adventists and the Church of God Limited! By happy mischance its identical twin was the official car of the Provincial Commissioner, whose known routes were innocently followed by Ted, patriotically flying a larger Union Jack from a taller mast and graciously acknowledging the respectful salutations of the country folk; a *lèse-majesté* not much appreciated.

When I registered at the small grille over the hotel reception counter, a baize functions board to my right, I became aware of a phenomenon advancing from the left towards the board, or me. It assumed the shape of a lady in full bloom, known irreverently as 'Diamond Lil'. She was encased in a silver sheath, like a water-slicked mermaid, with an abundance of bosom which pressed me back to the wall. Once secured on her embonpoint she looked me over with an expert eye, as if a promising colt, and said, with regret rather than offence, "Pity; too young!" Her real name turned out to be Noreen Antrobus and I always remembered the warmth of her welcome.

The table in the dining room nearest to the reception telephone served as all purpose desk for the British Overseas Airways Corporation whose pilots, cabin and local ground staff met, ate and arranged schedules in the most informal way. The air hostess, Hazel McMahon, taut bloused and shadow eyed, unwittingly tantalized my solitary meals, but my courage failed me. The B.O.A.C. operation took over from the Imperial Airways Sunderland Flying Boat service which had earlier fuelled at a wooden jetty off the tiny Crescent Island in the middle of Lake Naivasha in the Rift. A number of local settler children also boarded there to fly to school in England or South Africa. Among them was Barbara Joffé who, like Gigi, grew into the loveliest young woman I met on a Hollywood film set in Samburu District.

When the island mooring was abandoned in favour of the Kavirondo Gulf of Lake Victoria it was acquired by Rift Valley Provincial Information Officer, incurably romantic Charles Hayes and his wife, Jean Parnell, leading lady of Donovan Maule Theatre, as a country retreat and haven within the flamingo fringed papyrus. For several hectic days, unknown to the world media they later gave sanctuary to George, brother of Kabaka 'Freddie' of Buganda, fleeing from the Nilotic usurper President, Apollo Milton Obote, himself to be driven out by General Amin.

Meanwhile, tragedy had befallen Imperial Airways. Successive Sunderland Flying Boats, of the same type as that in which the glamorous Duke of Kent had crashed to his death in 1942, now laden with South African troops returning from the Italian campaign, plunged into the Kavirondo Gulf on landing. The disasters were put down to the peculiarity of temperature changes affecting the buoyancy of the heavy planes on final approach to the confined area of relatively shallow water.

In the midst of this vigorous, largely expatriate community, interwoven with the colonial top hamper of a Province of over one and a half million African 'natives', without yet having exchanged a word with one of them save Ogoma lodged helpfully behind the hotel, I reported to the Provincial Commissioner's office to meet the Departments and study the files under the eye of Jack Flynn.

Kenneth Leggat Hunter, powerful as a Duke of Normandy, presented a complex amalgam of qualities. He was reputed to be tough and a disciplinarian, partly because he had a South African military background from the Great War. In his early fifties he was strongly built, heavy thighed, energetic and self-assured. Thin, greying, tidy hair topped an oblong lively face, often tilted in a quizzical, charmingly attentive way with a curiously feminine crinkle of the eyes matching a subtly disarming voice which did not denote softness, only softening up. His skin was full and smoothly tended and he was the first man I met who carried the aroma of 'Williams Aftershave', to be made popular in Kenya by the visit of Governor 'Soapy' Williams of Michigan.

The PC was impressive and pragmatic rather than sophisticated or intellectual. At a formal dinner, to which I was honoured to be invited, he greeted the magnificent French Begum Aga Khan, towering over the dutifully rotund 'Highness' on his way to be weighed at Dar es Salaam in diamonds for the Ismaili Khoja community chest, with the toast, "Je suis tres jolie de vous voir". Perhaps she thought it accurate. Gertrude Hunter, unkindly nicknamed 'Dirty Gertie', both for alliteration and because she was 'swart' in Afrikaans parlance, was a commanding spouse, if not quite at ease in her unavoidably exalted social position. She and tall, gentle Ann, their comely daughter, tentatively smiling to offset short sightedness, were kind to me in my bachelor state.

The PC personally took pains to see me introduced to his Provincial hierarchy, preparatory to serving with their local staff in the outlying districts. In the medical world there was compactly immobile Dr Ross, comfortably ensconced as Provincial Medical Officer in the only two storey brick house along the 'boulevard'; his matronly wife known for her home-made avocado face cream. The Senior District Medical Officer was well named 'handsome Harden'-Smith, whose wife's warm dinner invitation once conflicted awkwardly with an amorous attachment of mine not mentionable at the time. At the excellent European hospital was calm, thoughtful, meticulous Dr Howett Wiseman, providing with his wife an academic and cultured presence, which inspired both respect and diffidence. He later lifted me from the pit of dysentery.

Rather pompously enjoying the precedence of the judiciary, was Sir Howard Elphinstone Bart, Resident Magistrate and celebrated author of his eponymous Swahili Grammar. His dignity suffered a not unpopular setback when on the Remembrance Day parade in full white Colonial dress finery and sword, after bending cautiously to place his wreath at the Cenotaph he rashly essayed a smart about turn. This so strained his overtaxed trousers that the elastic retaining loop beneath one shining black chukka boot burst, causing the leg to fly upwards revealing a plump white calf in retreat. *Schadenfreude* is too gloomy a word.

The Provincial Superintendent of Police was 'D.D.' McGoun, as tough and craggy an Ulsterman as one might wish to meet, who on my return to Kisumu District was to figure in a passionate affair with the popular wife of a brother officer which split the tight community. The Superintendent of Marine, in Kenya and Uganda Railways and Harbours, was a Scot, Sandy Lochhead, whom I did not then meet, but whose daughter, Molly, had the perfectly chiselled profile and flowing tresses of a schooner's figurehead. I was inspired to make a sketch and offered it to her before she was piloted confidently into church by Tom Watts, fellow District Officer.

I was happy to meet Jock Stirton, Senior Health Inspector, another dryish Scot, and his prematurely silver haired, violet scented, Irish wife Sheila, whose house I took over on return to Kisumu. I then turned Sheila upside down in the Government wartime Ford panel van on her transfer to their next posting. Carrying a Kenya driving licence, newly issued by archetypal Police Assistant Superintendent Johnny Walker, I rashly boasted to Sheila of my Certificate of Competency. She said, "touch wood", tapping my head. Instantly a bee entered my shorts and stung my left buttock just as I should have swung right at Mitford Barberton's corner near Kitale. Disaster! Up the road drain — jammed accelerator — wild swerves — slew into road-repair earth mound — turn turtle — slide 50 yards to halt on roof — silence save for a drip-drip — road gang rights vehicle with pious ejaculations. The cost of repair of fan sliced radiator and leaky battery at Italian ex-POW Peter Conti's garage was £25 in Kenya shillings (two weeks' salary). The Accountant General, no less, approved reimbursement of half, observing that he half believed my accident report.

I do not recall having met any Agricultural or Education Officers at Provincial level, which may have been because their work was carried out on the ground by locally authoritative professional staff or through the active and influential missionary bodies. So it was that, drawn loosely into the warp and weft of the colonial fabric, I was sent out to Kisii District across the plains to the south to complete my apprenticeship among people totally different from the Kamba of Kitui.

VIII

KISII DISTRICT
SOUTH KAVIRONDO/NYANZA
AUGUST 1944–MAY 1945

Kisii Township and District Administrative Headquarters lay nearly 75 miles to the south of Kisumu across the deep alluvial expanse of Kano plains, some eighteen hundred square miles crying out for any form of better land use based on irrigation, whether from the bisecting river or from the lake out of which the plains had once emerged. Two things in particular struck the passing eye. The rain sucking 'black cotton' soil was pimpled with circular homesteads of varying size, enclosing both living huts and livestock. They were small family or village units called *Gweng*. Their perimeters were thickly protected by rooted, dark green, viscous euphorbia shrubs, up to 15 feet in height, leaving one substantial but moveable stile of branches for entry and exit, blocked at night like the biblical 'Eye of the Needle'. Otherwise there was little sign of planned agricultural activity except for the huge thriving market at Ahero in mid plain on a main road junction, with signposts to Kericho District and other centres.

Before climbing to the Kisii highlands I had been urged to deviate to the lake shore at Nyabondo, below the eroded escarpment of Nyakach location inside Kisii district. Whichever came first, the exposed clay or Father Bartels, white-robed Dutch Mill Hill Mission Head, the place was famed for the remarkable school of modelling he founded. The busts of local people, fired an ochre tint, were spread around the world and bore the unmistakable imprint of the Nyabondo School.

The Administrative District of Kisii was as variegated in population as in its terrain and both were of remarkable fertility and productivity. Over half a million people, twice as many as the Kamba of Kitui, occupied one third of the land surface at a density nine times as great, although 150 to the square mile was not yet burdensome. There were two roughly equal but distinct ethnic groups, the Nilotic Luo and the Bantu Kisii, with very different language, customs and food. The former, like all Nilotes, were uncircumcised and followed a hierarchical form of leadership with titles of respect like *Jadwong*, clan leader, and *Ruoth* or King. The latter practised circumcision and observed a clan land based democratic structure. Both systems were overlaid by the scaffolding of government directly appointed Chiefs.

There were two other groups, both of the Bantu (generically meaning 'people') language group. The semi-pastoral Abakuria, commonly called the Tende, lived astride the Tanganyika border and were readily recognizable by their earlobes, stretched on ivory rims or looped up in a tidy knot. The lacustrine Abasuba, grouped on the islands or lake shores, were fishermen who seemed to be an evolving mixture of Nilotic and Bantu intermarriage, with other infusions. They were said to have sailed down from the Northern Uganda shore of the lake. One island in particular, Rusinga, achieved some notoriety in the world of anthropology through the classification of a skull unearthed there by the brilliantly contentious Leakeys as 'Rusinga Man'. The adjoining island of Mfangano also held a government exiled group of Nandi and Kipsigis Laibons (rainmakers), whom I visited later.

On route to Kisii District Headquarters lived two of a formidable array of Location Chiefs, who epitomized some of their powerful differences. The first I met was Gideon Okoth, his name already conjuring up his rugged physique, tombstone teeth from a diet of calcium-rich fish and millet, deep resonant voice and direct address, a veritable Og, Gog and Magog rolled into one rollicking martinet in full command of his location, as indeed was his neighbour the redoubtable Zephaniah Malit. Further along was Karachuonyo Location, benevolently presided over by Senior Chief Paulo Mboya, who was rounded in all his characteristics, head, lips, body, speech and amblingly purposeful gait. He was already famed beyond his chiefly duties as the ideal thinker, proponent of his people and persuasive intermediary in all aspects of advancement. He was the first African 'native' I met who transcended the local scene.

The approach to Kisii township was increasingly undulating with the Kitutu escarpment looming starkly beyond. The small bazaar area lay at the base of a long continuous rise. The road then led upwards past the 'native' hospital on the left, with a turning to the old, massive walled prison, and to the right the modest European Kisii Hotel overlooking the countryside. There followed the Departmental Offices and European staff quarters in roughly ascending order of function, seniority and plot size: Health, Education, Agriculture, Medicine, Administration and so forth.

The Senior Education Officer was to me 'Mr' Cameron, in his youthful fifties with tiny shorts and a round, grey fluffed head like an ostrich chick. He and his dark comely wife, exuding a seemly attraction, were very kind and civilized. Of the Education and Health Officers I gravitated towards Paddy Doran and Jimmy Coombs. Paddy was compact, steady, easy-going, in complete contrast to his social firecracker wife. Jimmy and Eileen Coombs were an intriguing pair. Diffident but stubborn, his sense of romance was revealed in the lively Eileen, who moved with a rather seductive limp resulting from severe polio, which had not deterred her from the birth of their child. She had that glistening olive skin which some American women seem to inherit, as if from an infusion of 'Red Indian' blood.

Up a side track was billeted Captain Jack Sim, Army Pay Corps Family Remittances Officer. He was debonair and leggy, dark hair neatly parted and gleaming smooth like an Edwardian masher's picture in a barber's shop. His pencil moustache curled in line with a sardonic lip raised over an ivory cigarette holder. He was a jaunty roué who walked great distances to his assignations in a smart blazer with Oxford slacks and had just been cited for "impropriety in a tent in Naivasha", two days' march away. He had a Luo housekeeper, whom he also praised for her sultana cake. In the same area I was called out on a Sunday to shoot a rabid dog spotted running, slavering and undeviating, and not to be accosted save by a rifle bullet. The skull confirmed the disease.

Back in the main ascending line of bungalows, raised on stilts to avoid the wash from cloudbursts, lived 'Mat' Matson, Health Inspector and historian. Mat was rubicund, rumbustious and Rabelaisian. His ample frame moved with one shoulder raised in a rolling nautical gait, consistent with simian leaps behind the wicket in his passionately loved cricket. He was devoted to pungent cheroots and twin Dachshunds who assisted him while bathing like animated loofahs. Mat was a happy warrior who gave his life to understanding the territories and people he served. He wrote a significant history of Nandi resistance to British rule and bequeathed his numerous articles and unique collection of books to the Kenyan nation.

Above Matson's were 'Tommy' Thompson, Senior Assistant Agricultural Officer and his wife Mary. Agricultural extension work was of basic importance throughout the District and Tommy's advice was delivered tirelessly, if sometimes tactlessly. Dark haired, sharp featured, florid and impatient he was balanced by the calming influence of Mary with bobbed, grey blond hair, trim figure and very firm chin.

Briefly attached to the Agricultural Office to gain field experience, was a young graduate of the School of Tropical Agriculture in Jamaica. He was 'Sandy' Storrar, a willowy and irrepressible Scot, with dark hair flopping from a widow's peak above mobile eyebrows and an overlapping of the upper lip. I envied his unabashed self assurance. With his green porkpie hat, dangling cigarette, and quirkish charm he rose to be the brilliant silver haired Head of his Department. When we then met again in the house of mutual friends, the Manns, he kindly explained to me the qualities leading to his own success in comparison with my presumed plight.

Between the Thompson's and myself were parallel Macrocarpa hedges lining a 'sanitary lane', up which a long open cart was drawn by a team of oxen to collect and deliver the galvanized iron lavatory buckets. The lugubrious clanking and lowing and cracking of whips disturbed the small hours before dawn. There was access to my bucket latrine 10 paces behind the house where one night I was picked up unconscious by the night soil team after about thirty dehydrating scourings from dysentery.

The next row of houses swung to the right to overlook the whole valley. My front garden was a long steep expanse of flower bordered lawn which stopped short of the steps to a solid stone bungalow. I was proud and happy with my three roomed home. From the bedroom to the rear was a bathroom *en suite* complete with a bees' nest in the angled ceiling, whose daily aerobatics made shaving hazardous from both sting and leather stropped blade. The kitchen at the back of the central dining room was Ogoma's, where he wielded charcoal iron and charcoal stove with impeccable skill and repetitive menu. I learned how to silence his many Luo visitors in Dholuo. The living room furnished with my transported Kitui sofa and chair of maroon hessian and paraffin reflector wall lamps was always scented with garden flowers, Canna Lilies, Agapanthōs and freshly plucked Bougainvillaea.

I bought some Kisii stools decorated with coloured beads hammered into the surface while still freshly carved from the virgin root, and pink grained soapstone figurines of birds and animals. On the walls I hung brilliantly coloured Nubian mats of straw woven over coils wound from the centre in increasing circles, the more tautly to achieve a bowl shape. Mine were brought to my house by a decorously dressed and half veiled young Nubian woman I have called Fatuma.* She carried around a selection from the Nubian village of which there were many settled around Kenya by porters and Askari escorting the early caravans of explorers, traders and missionaries. She was warm, aromatic and graceful and we became intimate. She taught me the intricacies of sex inculcated from childhood involving backward movement across the floor on heels and shoulders keeping a stone suspended by a thong across the *mons veneris* and hanging free between the buttocks.

On the next adjoining plots lived the two Medical Officers and their wives. John Walker, the junior, was handsome, able and vain. He was already exhibiting signs of deserved promotion to Director of Medical Services, at which time I spotted him from the Speaker's Gallery in Legislative Council seated on the government benches and carefully teasing with a pencil strands of dark hair across his fine cranium. The Medical Officer of Health, Hugh Turner, was a delightfully whimsical Ulsterman, with no pretensions at all and a self-deprecating chuckle. When treating me with Stovarsol after dysentery he pronounced across the tennis net upon the analysis of my final exhibit as "pure gold". His chunkily attractive wife, Hilda, was and long continued to be a 'pure dote'. Beyond the doctors, in a discreet hollow on the edge of a deep fold in the hills, lay the house of the District Commissioner where amid chintz and crystal and silver his, to me, motherly wife Elsie fussed over me throughout my posting.

The other side of the fold, higher up on the sideways facing slope, stood a well established complex of two storey clapboard buildings; the

*I referred to her in the BBC TV series *Ruling Passions* in 1995.

headquarters of the Seventh Day Adventist Mission, presenting an image of Spartan simplicity with efficiency. There was a sense not only of spiritual but cultural separateness between the Colonial and the Mission communities. A genteel, but quite tense dispute arose when the Mission milk herd grazed untended on their Sabbath day across the fairways of the golf course, depositing inconvenient hazards to the fury of Saturday golfers, who escorted the ambivalent beasts to the pound. The DC, in the role of both Caesar and God, was found at home by protesting pastors absorbed in his Sunday bible reading and unable to accept full pound fees for release until the Monday.

I recall meeting only three 'Adventists', two men and one woman, who served as both teachers and Evangelists. They had a sort of homogenized, mid-Atlantic style of accent and pin striped seersucker clothing, which did not cover an unseen gap of mutual understanding. They appeared neither young nor old, nor stirred by human frailty or robust humour. An apparent fleshlessness accorded with an abstemious but tasty diet of nutloaf and vegetables, taken without stimulants such as coffee. They had a Plymouth limousine. My tenuously friendly relationship with them was rewarded with the gift of a packet of tracts for camp reading on a projected foot safari. At a glance they were so horrendously illustrated with devilish creatures in ambush of the soul that I left them behind, with some misgivings and wonderment that such passions burned in quiescent breasts, capable also of kindly and creative works.

Such was the chess board of Kisii, on which the pawns and knights and bishops were set out, not to overlook the decisive mobility of the queens. All the pieces were white on black. I reported to the District Office, a sprawling array of low buildings in a large oblong compound, separating the lower and upper levels of the government houses. At the open end was an historic fig tree, 'ficus giganticus', the trampled fruit in season smelling like a brewery, which probably preceded the colonial presence.

Bill Perreau the DC's own office was quite unpretentious in keeping with his relaxed style. He sat behind a file stacked desk, hands clasped in a habitual posture behind a large head with tawny worried hair, displaying the sweat soaked armpits of a beige striped city shirt. He appeared in the later forties and overweight for his stature. He looked to be preoccupied and overworked even as he rose courteously to greet me with a warm smile and a sigh. He was thoughtful, fair and decent and dismissive of the niceties which eased the path to service advancement.

The Senior District Officer, Pat Lowe, was a son of the formidable Archdeacon Lowe, one of a pair of Anglican Archdeacons of the time with trenchant reputations and great influence in 'native' education and welfare. Pat had a well chiselled Roman head with close curled greying hair and finely flared nostrils which suggested a certain fastidiousness. Sloping shoulders threw the balance of his solid body weight downward, like a top, which gave power to his forehand at tennis but which he did not throw about. His tall wife, Rowan, had a disarmingly gentle manner and a new baby son whom I dandled. (40 years later with the UN, I met this son as Director of Oxfam in Port Sudan. Recognizing a family resemblance, I astonished him by asking was he 'Jammy' or 'Mucky', the nicknames of his father or his uncle).

As for myself, I was to be District Officer 'dogsbody', Third Class Magistrate, tax collector, chivvier of labour recruitment and livestock sales around the whole district; a motley but congenial enough bundle of experience which proved a source of lasting friendships. Proudly somewhat apart, but utterly reliable and loyal, was the indispensable cadre of Goan clerks and cashiers who had then a virtual monopoly of the clerical services and were the prop and stay of many a DC, myself included. Catholicism, their club, curry and cricket made them a tightly knit society but their non-abstemious hospitality was legendary.

The senior African staff in the DC's office were the two completely dissimilar Interpreters, each more equal than the other. Ladislaus Agagé was delineated by his name. Square in build he had a huge head and a cavernous mouth, somewhat like a hippopotamus in battle, from which a basso profundo voice was delivered with ponderous authority. His rival at court was Silvanus Olóó, supple and delicate as the sound, with softly refined features and manipulative charm. They separately guided me towards wisdom in local lore with avuncular precept and subtle suggestion. The Sergeant of Tribal police was not to be within my area but the orderly assigned to me near and far, was Musété Maéba, as pleasing and biddable, in the Irish sense, a young guard and companion as could be wished. He was a Mtende of the Abakuria people and a great help in their territory and happily 'mucked in' well with Ogoma on arduous safaris.

While in the *boma* my work was mainly done within a single shuttered, mud and wattle, grass roofed '*rondavel*', the light filtering through the eaves and open door. This served as my Court House where I sat at a small deal table, as did the Police Prosecutor, while Interpreter, accused, escort and witnesses in turn were crammed together. Two cases brought before this mini-court stood out. One was of a woman accused of scalping her husband with a *panga* (machete). The charge of 'assault causing actual bodily harm' was straightforward enough since the husband himself indignantly held out the missing portion which was then presented in evidence by the Police. The Doctor confirmed that it was indeed once attached to the plaintiff's head while the wife claimed extreme provocation and seemed ready to complete the job. Reconciliation and medical attention sent the pair off with a 'guilty' plea and a suspended sentence. The doctor told me later that surgical shock was more readily borne by Africans than by cosseted Europeans, both physiologically and psychologically, while medical conditions were less easily sustained or resisted.

The case was not unconnected with another brought by the Police against a fascinating Kipsigis Laibon visiting Kisii, Kibinot arap Rongoi. He contrived to combine several cultures and customs in one uniquely elegant and harmonious personality. Physically he was tall, lithe and smoothly middle-ageless, with a fine boned cranium and elongated ears, hung with metal and amber earrings. He sported a quality green-check motoring blanket, clasped at the left shoulder by what could only have been a silver Scottish Highlander's kilt pin. His Robin Hood cutaway and furled felt hat was set off by a rakish plume. He carried a slender spear, the leaf shaped blade burnished and glistening with Vaseline, the haft bound with fashionable hospital bandages.

Kibinot was famed abroad as a witch doctor and had been retained in defence of an alleged local practitioner held on remand in Kisii Prison. The formulation of the charge was delicate since it did not seem to come clearly under any provision of the Penal Code of Kenya, consolidated in 1941 and itself based upon the old Indian Penal Code. The trouble was that there was no specific offence of 'witchcraft' and neither section 198 about 'malicious attempt to cause death' nor 207 about 'hastening death' nor 215 'intent to cause death' quite fitted the bill, although undeniably the prospective victim was grievously ill and firmly believed he had been bewitched. I went to see him in hospital to establish the medical facts and question him. He was a young educated Christian Chief called Gideon Okore. He had pneumonia. I saw quantities of fluid drawn from his lungs and his bible clutched fearfully in his hands as he prayed for divine help against the spell. His condition deteriorated and he died of 'natural causes'. Clearly no case could be made out against the remand prisoner and I ordered his release only to meet Kibinot Arap Rongoi outside the prison with what might be called an enigmatic smile. An old Kisii hand called Dick Gethin who attended the Court told me that Kibinot had finessed an unbeatable hand; the 'victim' had succumbed, the 'perpetrator' had been released and Kibinot had been seen both at Court and outside the District Prison. His reputation and his fee had been enhanced.

Dick Gethin himself was a stalwart of the Gethin clan which was famed for the transport business of Gethin and Dawson since the first World War. A towering figure with grizzled hair and powerful forearms, he was surprisingly mild and philosophical, humorously tolerant of the ups and downs of his life. He told me of his hasty midnight departure in his pyjamas on a donkey clutching a whiskey bottle upon sudden warning of an invasion of German led forces of the celebrated and undefeated General von Lettow Vorbeck in 1916. The southern border tribes in contact with Tanganyika (German East Africa) had apparently been sympathetic to the

Germans and some elders I met still spoke German. When the tables were turned and the returning DC decided to make an example of known 'traitors' by shooting them under the old fig tree, the impact was somewhat spoiled when the first shots evoked appreciative applause and calls for more. Like Tyburn of old perhaps.

Dick had a companion, Winifred, always referred to as 'Miss Hall' to indicate the decorousness of their relationship. Their house was beside the Kisii Hotel, a travellers' rest, presided over by a burly innkeeper called 'honest James' Barclay after his skill in filling 3 glasses from a pint drawn. His companion, gentler bred, was dark and mysterious Val Vane of whom romantic stories were told gaining credence from the name of her nearly nubile daughter named Trilby, after Du Maurier. Trilby once told me when we met by chance away from her mother's cosseting at the Pentecostal Mission on the Kitutu escarpment that she suffered exciting nightmares after cheese. Later as a free young woman in Nairobi she won a lottery of £25,000.

A foot safari was planned for me to circle the District for tax collection, livestock sales and labour recruitment and generally show the flag, make contact with Chiefs and field officers, hear complaints and report back to the DC. The first leg was by lorry to our take off point on foot, bowling along the good murrum road to the Asumbi Catholic Mission of the Mill Hill Fathers. On the way we met with a notably eccentric woman labour recruiter. Miss Maclean was unrelated to the Nairobi taxi driver of the same name, who had first delivered me from Nairobi Station to the New Stanley Hotel, although she also was in the habit of upbraiding passers by who had failed to doff their hats, before offering them a job. She was a sort of subcontractor to the upmarket 'Mac' MacInnes and his American wife, who supplied labour from around their Sotik Home to the Kericho tea companies and wonderful Jamaican 'Rum Shrub' to lubricate relationships.

Asumbi lay in the heart of fertile Luo country and the Mission was headed by an indestructible Dutch priest, later to be Bishop at Kakamega, Father Philip Scheffer, known to all as 'Pilipo'. He had entered for a 'life sentence' of service and had already thrown off dysentery, blackwater fever and plague. In his late fifties he was ruddy and robust with the gusty exhaling laugh of a Dutch farmer, his white cassock being equally his serviceable smock or football gear. A streak of innocent cunning in no way connected a list of young men recommended as suitable for conscript labour with sins of the flesh muttered secretly in the confessional, but not otherwise disclosed. His Procurator was Father Macintyre, a caustic but kindly Lancashireman and worldly wise philosopher. The male side of the substantial mission house was served domestically by bustling, cheerful Sisters, all white, occupying adjoining quarters who supplied a solid table at which there was neither excessive fasting nor any abstinence. Dürer's etching of monks fishing and fasting with unblessed *fiascos* of wine on Fridays conveys the companionable scene.

My special and lifetime friend was Father Jaap Molenaar, who managed to be a lovably fallible saint. When we met at Asumbi he was just thirty but kept his joyous optimism till he died at eighty. He was about six foot including a thick shock of silver blond hair which grew *en brosse* from a narrow forehead above small, almond shaped, attentive eyes of vivid blue. High cheek bones, pointed chin, small mouth, with cheroot as comforter, surmounted a frame and limbs of astonishing strength. He loved to exhibit this in little competitions like lifting a wooden backed chair in one hand by a front leg, or raising a 200 pound sack of maize meal under each arm. His lively, gregarious spirit and interest rejoiced in all and everything, about which he would sing in a consciously melodious voice. He also had a BSA 500 motorbike on which we sallied forth among the fields to the admiration of shapely young women secure in flirtation with a celibate if not a pair of them. When I showed off my skill and fell I lost a portion of ankle bone to the footrest. When I first married he was 'best priest'.

From Asumbi the footslog began. We headed via Homa, well named 'fever', Bay where another labour recruiter and commercial agent, 'Mac' Macpherson had a stone house with verandah overhanging the lake. He plied me with aromatic passion fruit juice topped up to the rim unnoticed from a labelled water bottle, actually containing Plymouth gin. He took me crocodile shooting by torch light for their much prized skins. I missed. The next day we marched with tents and porters along the coast of Kasigunga Location to the narrow strip of water through which we waded to Rusinga Island, the site of Professor Leakey's 'find' of Rusinga Man. As I crossed the mainland beach of rock strewn sand a crocodile, cut off from his habitat, broke from the bush behind me and nearly scythed me into the water with a flick of his encrusted tail. Recovering my balance from a desperate leap I shot him once with my .303 so flukily that he died horrendously crunching a rock in the shallows. Fear and nausea gave me momentary pleasure.

From Rusinga across five miles of smooth water to Mfangano Island we had a marvellous canoe race. The canoes were finely dugout logs with uplifted prows tapering to a point. There were eight narrow cross benches for the sixteen crew wielding long handled, leaf bladed paddles. They used the benches to kneel upon leaning outward while cross bracing themselves with the rigid inward leg. Timing of stokes was regulated by a hand cast metal cattle bell hanging from a wooden rod across the bows. The forward paddler, both stroke and cox, altered the time as speed required by pushing a rock towards the bell, thus shortening its swing so that the bell then sounded the rhythm for all. The dipping thrust of the paddles was accompanied by a deep belly grunt which counteracted tearing of the twisted muscles of the abdomen. From the outset of the race between our two canoes it was clear that I must be one of my team of sixteen or else be blamed as dead weight. I did not object until the pain of the aftermath.

Our frantic approach with flashing blades to Mfangano with not half a length between us, resembled the desperate hurling of the 'Red hand of Ulster', severed despairingly to be thrown ashore to gain the first touch and win the land. My crew had no such expedient although they might have considered throwing their amateur paddler overboard. It happened there was a well accepted convention that no live bovine could be introduced to the island which was free of East Coast Fever, Foot and Mouth and most tick borne diseases, to which long isolated cattle would rapidly have succumbed. Though small they were remarkably well formed, sleek, and healthy.

An unusual duty on visiting Mfangano was to check on a small group of Nandi and Kipsigis Laibon who had been exiled from their home districts as fomenters of disturbance and subversion. Originally the Laibon or *Oloiboni* had been the rainmakers of the Maasai with enormous spiritual and temporal influence, but they had infiltrated and become identified with the comparable *Orkoiyot* of their neighbours and been much involved in two Nandi 'uprisings' on such a scale as to have been termed wars or rebellions. I was required to verify the presence and nominal roll of the exiles and deal with any problems, including a 'matchmaker' arrangement for the annual exchange in marriage of maidens and young bachelors between the separated clans, partly to avoid inbreeding but also intended to dilute the strength of the Laibons.

From the islands we landed on the coast of Gwasi Location and trekked through the Lambwe valley, a veritable elephant refectory and dung carpet. The black cotton soil sodden with rain was so glutinous that the porters' loads, singing as they did, must have felt double in weight and I went barefoot to avoid the suction and the uneven build up of mud as it caked on my boots. The whole valley of the elephants was dominated by a prominent Luo traditional elder, a patriarch nicknamed Kasuku, or parrot, from the cast of his features which appeared to be reproduced literally in everyone we met.

Our march led south some 30 miles via Karungu to Muhoro near the Tanganyika border. On the way I was heartrendingly begged by allegedly starving villagers to shoot a hippopotamus from a school seen watching us goggle eyed some 200 yards offshore. To my shame I succumbed to the suspect blandishments which redoubled in sincerity and glee after a single .303 bullet did its regrettable work. The hippo disappeared in double quick time especially into 4 gallon tins of prized fat and certainly no one was left starving. I never shot another animal, apart from legally, and came to love the ponderous, usually placid, beasts long before they became Walt Disney cartoons. Only when interfered with or cut off from the water while grazing ashore do they display their vast destructive jaws, moving at astonishing speed.

At Muhoru we turned eastward inland to visit officially at Macalder's Mines (after Canadian miners MacMartin and 'W.P.' Alderson, a wealthy steelmaker), where a small expatriate community extracted from a rich seam of copper with some gold. I had no business in the mine itself and was farmed out by the happiest chance to the hospitality of Doctor Zoltan Rosinger and his wife Joanna, called Joan. Both were Jewish, he from Hungary and she from Vienna. They were young middle aged and Zoltan was qualified not only as a physician but also in psychiatry which he practised on me at every opportunity for decades thereafter. His smooth domed forehead appeared never to have been encumbered with hair and his dolefully comprehending eyes shone with gentle humour and sceptical compassion through enormous spectacles, an essential 'prop'. Because his 'foreign' qualifications were not recognized by the Medical Department he was only allowed to practice on contract first in Tanganyika then at Macalder's Mines.

When things became more relaxed and open Zoltan served for forty years as much loved doctor in Malindi where his zany methods and passion for Strauss usually won him loving plaudits and with Joan the annual ballroom dancing prize at the Sindbad Hotel. Joan was and stubbornly remained, sometimes with coquettish hauteur, the quintessential cultured Viennese lady of the afterglow of the Austro-Hungarian empire. Music, opera, literature, conversation, café society and a circle of devoted friends were her delight. They sustained her through exile in a mine and the heat and humidity of lone years as the Doctor's wife in far off Malindi by the Indian Ocean.

Fortified by the encounter I walked on some miles to the smaller Masara mine where the manager, tall, elegant Colonel and Mrs Garret treated me to a Wimbledon style interlude at their bungalow set in a lovely 'English country garden'. Both were in their late fifties or more but a strawberry and cream tea on arrival was followed by two sets of tennis, a breather, and three of squash in a private court, all of which I lost. Sherry in a schooner and 'a wee Doch and Doris' nearly finished me off and I had no time or consciousness to learn more about them before early morning departure. He used to leave her love notes under the pillow when he was away for a meeting.

We resumed the daily routine of meeting the Watende elders on route, with my orderly Muséte Maéba as interpreter, registering tax-payers and encouraging stock sales. Our path led directly across open savannah to the Chief's offices at Subakuria and Isibania through small pastoral kraals and herds of fine cattle in the deep red oat and star grasses. The people were a pleasure to meet and handsome to behold with no hint of strain or resentment in their welcome to this young intruder in their life. Before leaving Tende country we met a stout American Missionary of the 'Holy Rollers' who declared quite credibly that he had been a prize-fighter in the States. Although running a small dispensary as well as a prayer house, his sect did not believe in medical treatment and when I asked what he dispensed he declared with the robust humour of a US Marine sergeant, "I give them whitewash as a scourer for their huts and they never come back". Cleanliness next to Godliness?

When we reached the northerly turn of Kisii district boundary as it met the Tanganyika national border we headed directly north towards Kisii via Nyangusi, although this meant short-cutting across a corner of Maasai land, which was probably quite contrary to regulations and etiquette, by trespassing in another's District. Within the nearly empty triangle of Maasailand we stopped outside a ramshackle habitation in the open bush and called *Hodi* to request admission. After several shouts elicited no response we pushed the open door and tried again. A faint disembodied voice rose from behind the remains of a sofa, which we discovered to be emanating from a horizontal Mica prospector in happy inebriation. Having set him to rights and ensured he had food and water we left him to seek his lonely fortune.

With the increasing excitement of the homing traveller we re-entered our district, up the eastern incline to the Kitutu plateau and escarpment which looked westward over the heartland of the Bantu speaking Kisii, half the population of south Nyanza. My main objective was to pay my respects to Senior Chief Musa Nyandusi, the outstanding leader of his people, whose office and home were on the plateau. He invited me to his house for lunch which was much the same as Ogoma would give me at home but with more vegetables and much tea.

Chief Musa was equally comfortable in the very different milieu of a Kisii traditional Elder and able Administrator under colonial rule. (His power and authority later carried through to his son, Simeon Nyachae, who after Independence was to become Secretary of the Cabinet, Chief Secretary, Member of Parliament and Minister.) Before then I had met Musa again as Senior Chief outside the Nakuru Hotel at the pull-in where he and his entourage in an American limousine had been denied entry to the dining room for lunch. I arranged with the Manager, Norman Jarman, to take a snack with them in the closed saloon bar.

One last stop on our long march covering over 200 miles was at a diminutive Mission Station poised on the very lip of the Kitutu escarpment. This was an outpost of the Pentecostal Assemblies of Canada and was conducted by the Reverend John and Sophie Kitts. If ever anyone exemplified simple faith, they did in a touchingly innocent way. John revealed that his father had once struck him in anger at his drinking, whereupon he "saw the light" while Sophie was said to have been a "bareback rider" in an American circus "or even worse". He was short in the leg, long in the body and head as a Lancashire mill-worker; she attractive enough to evoke comment in unseemly variants of her two names. They seemed to see good as they looked at you and gave happy holiday refuge to young Trilby Vane from the hotel below. Fifteen years later John wrote me a letter of congratulation about Africanisation of the Civil Service.

Down the escarpment we went almost in a canter to come at our houses in triumph. In my case also in disaster since by then I was so much wasted by what turned out to be both amoebic and bacillary dysentery which reduced me to only ten stone from thirteen that I had to be treated in Kisumu and convalesce on local leave at Molo. A move to the Kisumu District of Central Nyanza followed.

Kisii had been unalloyed contentment and the separation from friends cast a passing cloud. A happy link between the two Districts was my time in Kisumu Hospital under the care of Dr Howett Wiseman where I shared a ward behind a cotton central screen with Dr Zoltan Rosinger, who vainly repudiated the Doctor's diagnosis that he had a carbuncle, asserting it was a symptom of anthrax to which he had been exposed at Macalder's Mine, surely a more heroic complaint. Stimulated by psychoanalysing me owl-eyed across the screen, in particular with regard to my perceived weakness to overtake women, he recovered from both complaints.

IX

KISUMU DISTRICT
CENTRAL KAVIRONDO/NYANZA
MAY 1945–MARCH 1946

Kisumu District presented few of the anxieties facing a newcomer since my brief spell at Provincial HQ, fieldwork at Kisii, and friendly introductions in Kisumu Township made it seem like a homecoming, especially as I had the house vacated by the Stirtons waiting for me. 'Condemned' unofficially by the Public Works Department for 12 years it may have been, and without remission of rent, but it suited Ogoma's and my needs and had been left impeccable. The only blemish was the immediate appearance from under the rainwater culvert on the lake side fence of my little garden patch of a spitting cobra reared up in serious challenge. Sheila Stirton awaiting departure for Eldoret braved me into action with the encouraging warning that cobra spit aimed at the eyes required instant washing out with milk. My dear friend Bill Glanville's Mab Brévète sleeve action pistol left to me was all I had. Three little silver bullets out of my six nicked the cobra which was finished off with some enthusiasm by the staff of nearby bungalows.

I reported at once to the District Commissioner, Charles Farquhar Atkins at the low, rambling but functional and whitewashed District Office. It was quite airy in spite of the humidity which the DC evidently found oppressive as his ample frame was habitually unbuttoned to the vest. He often used to hum in snatches, suggesting preoccupation or impatience. Although diffident to the point of shyness and rarely looking directly at one, he was clearly able and not unkind. We met again in difficult circumstances years later.

The DC introduced me to his Senior District Officer, Michael Evans, a large, calm, red headed, black belt at Judo with an academic turn of mind and an amiable personality. Two other DOs were in process of transfer; Teddy Eggins was universally regarded, rather to his misfortune, as unbelievably handsome which with his languid style cast him for matinée idol and amateur dramatics on and off the stage. In contrast Tom Watts, he who had won the hand of Molly Lochhead, was a braw, intelligently domineering man, whose post I was to take over. His friendly visits to his neighbouring DC later became known as 'doing a Watts'.

My duties followed much the same pattern as before but involved more travel by lorry or the huge Ford panel van, with accommodation at Chiefs' Offices and Missions; altogether more planned and less arduous. There being a Resident Magistrate and two First Class Magistrates I had no court duties, only reluctant study for the law exam, and checking 'Native Court' registers. I had no regular orderly but was guided a little superciliously by an Interpreter called Opiyo who regulated the constant daily queue of people with *shauris*, minor complaints or queries, in an offhand tenor voice and world weary manner, concealing great acuity.

The continuing task of recruitment of conscript labour, chiefly for the sisal plantations and Mombasa docks, heavy work for powerful Luo, brought me useful experience for much later, and my first nickname *Tich Marach*, Dholuo for 'bad work', referring I hoped to the task rather than my performance or character; 'nasty bit of work'? I had, together with Chiefs or Headmen, to carry out rough and ready inspections of recruits, including giving instructions in Dholuo for squatting, standing, bending and arm exercises. Happily they did not include the lifting of the penis, the 'short arm inspection' for VD required in the Army. A hospital dresser also took a 'skin snip' from the upper arm to examine for trace of the prevalent worm and fly-borne disease, 'onchocerciasis' called 'river blindness' because crocodile and buffalo in riverine thickets were hosts for the flies. Being very debilitating it was a disqualification from labour requiring treatment, a fortuitous health benefit.

A labour transit camp on the outskirts of Kisumu was run by a delightfully cultured, older man called Reilly Cowan, who could well have been a testy Professor of history, or languages in which he was widely versed not least in pure coastal Swahili. He was perturbed by an unexplained outbreak of virulent meningitis in the absence at the time of effective drugs. It was traced, I know not how, to dirty 'gunny' sacks for sugar from the neighbouring refinery and abated as rapidly as it began.

'Professor' Cowan took me to tea at his raised bungalow near the hotel where, on the wide plank verandah enclosed by mosquito gauze, Mrs Cowan dispensed aromatic tea from a superb silver Queen Anne service. There was a delicious Madeira cake, made she assured me with pure oil of rare oyster nuts from the coffee plantation at Kaimosi of retired Mission Doctor Pentreath, frail and delicate, and tended devotedly by his spinster daughter. (The occasion linked a number of much later experiences; Kaimosi as the location of a celebrated lawsuit; Reilly Cowan's son John as acting Prisons Commissioner and my close colleague; the tea service, since languishing in a cupboard in North London.)

To the north of Kisumu in an isolated location was a Leper Colony in which unfortunates, actively ravaged by the abhorred sweet smelling disease for which treatment was embryonic, were accommodated in a fenced encampment supervised by Warders who were themselves infected. My task was to report in general terms and on specific needs as well as to check on stores, food, etc. The visit, during which I tried to behave normally in human contact, caused me some anxiety especially when a suspect white area on my skin was subjected to random scratching with a pin, my eyes closed to test comparative sensitivity. I was cleared. Outside the camps were many cases of parasite borne elephantiasis, shambling painfully abroad on grossly inflated, splitting legs, not as painful to behold as the awful blight on their lives.

Further afield in a sub-Location called Gem Ahono was one of the most heartening examples I ever met of individual imagination, rural self help, and improvement of the environment. The Government and Local Native Council lorries, such as they were, had both a driver, often long-serving, and a mate, a young lad called a 'turney-boy'. The Bedford 3-ton LNC lorry had been serviced and driven, boy and man, by a Luo called Zakayo Opondo. He grew up with his lorry, saving enough to buy it when it was officially 'boarded' and sold as past its useful life. With a burgeoning transport business for cash flow, Zakayo, still young himself set about making a paradise of his father's small-holding. With bananas, maize, millet and vegetables planted, a small copse of wattle established for firewood and bark for tanning, he bought a small foundation herd of improved Zebu-Sahiwal cattle from the Veterinary Centre at Maseno for milk, manure and progeny.

The main family house was oblong of mud and wattle, the mud admixed with straw, liquid dung and salt for smooth binding. The roof was uniquely thatched with dried, then soaked, banana fronds, turned pliant and streaky brown. Each frond was stretched, twisted, bent and knotted over a lateral withy, then beaten with a *Rungu* (long club), to fit tightly against the one before. When the external banana tresses had been combed with a wooden thatching rake and trimmed neat and deep at the overhang, the interior knots and spaces were treated with a sort of home made neatsfoot oil and hoof glue making them both glistening and impermeable as well as warm, sound proof and pleasing. The floor was made of compressed soil and dung mixed with blood, rammed hard and coated with red cardinal polish, buffed to gleam like a mirror.

Outside, Zakayo constructed his own simple methane gas plant. This consisted of a cylindrical 1,000 gallon galvanized corrugated iron water tank, seated on a cement plinth with open top. Into this was placed a 500 gallon tank upside down and closed at the top except for the tap hole into which was fitted a long half inch rubber pipe. The open sleeve created between the tanks was reached by an outside wooden ladder and platform at top level from which buckets of fresh liquidized cow manure could be poured until the sleeve was full. The maturing dung gave off methane gas which seeped into the centre tank from which it exited via the rubber pipe to pass without odour, flies or risk of fire to a home-made gas refrigerator, a stove and three lighting points. The power generator was the backside of five cows which sufficed to renew the supply as necessary when the residue of gas depleted manure could still be used for tilth. The Opondos were a prosperous and happy family.

Further afield I had frequent occasion to call at the impressive Intermediate and Secondary schools. Mainly run by the various Mission denominations, the Protestant ones were well funded and seemed to specialize in splendid young women who could by no means be accurately described as Amazons but performed callisthenics with intimidating vigour in smart gym tunics and sometimes hairnets to contain their beehive coiffures. They were clearly a social if not political force for the future.

The Yala Catholic Secondary School for Boys above the Yala swamp was equally impressive educationally. Unbeknown to all of us at the time, it was to be the launching pad of the future political star, Tom Mboya, who blazed so brightly before he fell to an assassin and whom I was to encounter at close quarters. One of the teachers, Father Hoffman, was a fellow enthusiast for motorbikes and had an old BSA 500 with coil springs, upon which I had trained in the Corps of Signals, which he kindly hired to me for my local leave for ten pounds, a week's salary.

I headed first for Nairobi in quite ridiculous garb of khaki jacket and shorts, pith solar topee strapped under the chin against the slipstream, khaki knee stockings and golf shoes. My wardrobe was a canvas Army knapsack. Despite intermittent chill in the thin air of the highlands, all was well until I reached the then only stretch of tarmac between Nakuru and Naivasha which should have been a doddle. A sudden savage squall of driving hail then tore my face and legs so painfully that I cried out and pulled into the wonderful old Bell Inn at Naivasha for fuel for myself and my tank. There followed such shattering potholes, concealed under choking grey volcanic dust on the neglected road, due to be replaced by a tarmac re-alignment under construction by Italian POWs, that I wobbled into Nairobi with what felt like a red hot bullet up the anus keeping me well above the saddle.

Alderman Doctor Gregory, later Mayor of Nairobi, greeted me with Irish affability, told me to bend over, nicked the offending pile, which he called a grape, with a scalpel, prescribed hot baths, Vaseline and no motorbikes. I had a comforting hot bath in the Stanley Hotel and set forth again the following day. The three hundred mile journey down the Mombasa road, with stops for food and fuel at Sultan Hamud, Mac's Inn named after Game Warden MacArthur, Voi and Mariakani was surprisingly uneventful, although many elephant and giraffe kept my spirits high. Before sunset I chugged triumphantly over the Mombasa Island causeway, past the abattoir, to catch a glimpse of the town before circling back to Port Reitz Hotel.

The hotel was very simple with a path down to the old Port Reitz deep water anchorage where there was a wooden jetty. I shared an outside series of lean-to bedrooms with only one other guest, who was disconcertingly eccentric. He was lean, red faced and angry looking and timed like a metronome. Each morning at seven he emerged in a white towelling robe, another large bathing towel round his neck, strode down to the jetty, disrobed to pre-war belted trunks, plunged tidily into the saline creek and executed some twenty strokes outward, overarm. He then returned backstroke, mounted the wooden steps, towelled briskly and returned to his quarters without a word or passing sign of recognition. By this time I had lamely proffered several respectful greetings. Breakfast done he and I sat in silence across the lounge. Exactly at 10 a.m. he strode to the opening door of the bar and emerged with a tankard of beer. With scarcely altered pace he delivered himself of "Good morning — good morning — good morning, and that will suffice for the day." We were to meet again years later at his celebrated private hotel beside Tororo Rock in Uganda. He was H. H. Aitken.

There were about a dozen other guests including a family from the Belgian Congo, whose luxurious home was on the enchanted Lake Kivu. They had the aristocratic name of Van den Berg van Heémstédé. Mother and father were congenial company for me, as was their suave thirty-year-old son Paul. Their younger son Edouard, who played the piano pleasingly, was something of a problem, since female guests complained of his climbing to peer into their bedroom windows. Madame sighed that it was often thus away from "home" where he had "such a nice Congolese girl" to cool his ardour.

Back in Kisumu again, this time by train to Nairobi taking my bike in the Guard's van, I took up my social life with shaming attempts at tennis against a 'Bounding Basque' of a court hero called Charles Harvey, a zig-zagging yacht with a bent keel which I bought for £12 and my rejected racket, and plenty of dinner invitations as a spare bachelor.

The even tenor of existence had been disturbed before my coast adventure when one night I was awakened instantly by the unmistakable sound of my hob nailed shoes scraping the red cement floor. Knowing which side of the bed they were, I moved both my hands up to grip the sheet under my chin, while the nervous juices trickled noisily in my stomach. I then struck out wildly against whomever was close enough to move the shoes and leaped out naked on the other side towards the bedroom door which was locked. In the blind man's buff that followed, except that I knew the layout blind, I slipped into the adjoining bathroom where one gauze covered window was opened. I stood in the corner exit to the back verandah beside the wooden commode until a shadow appeared in the bedroom doorway. Recognition was mutual and we struggled wildly, he being oiled and naked to the waist, until I struck him senseless against the commode in fear and anger. Ogoma appeared in answer to my shouts for help and with skill and satisfaction tied the intruder by one thumb backwards across his shoulder to the opposite big toe dragged upwards.

The Police took him off in a van and recorded charges against him on several counts. Not only did he break and enter my own house with a grass slasher but he was wearing the Police Superintendent's shorts with the Superintendent of Marine's wallet in the pocket. I was only allowed with some hesitation to proceed on leave since he remained in a prison ward apparently unconscious and, had he died, I might have been charged with manslaughter. As it was he had recovered by my return, was found guilty and sentenced to a total of six years by Resident Magistrate Elphinstone. He escaped on the way to prison and for some time I ostentatiously loaded my Mab Brévète with the last three bullets in front of my bedroom window to discourage a return match.

The gentler side of life was a long and memorable relationship with a young, half Nandi, half Arab woman called Khadija binti Chemuti. She had appeared at the back quarters of a brother officer's house which I had visited on my posting to Kisumu and I was so struck by her that I went out to meet her. It was a classic *coup de foudre*, hopefully on both sides. She was slight, olive skinned, with a delicately formed face set in a fragrant cloud of gossamer hair. Her open smile was made mischievous by one overlapping front tooth on which her upper lip was slightly raised in repose. Our close but free relationship persisted over time and distance.

After nine months in Kisumu, with the learning experience of two widely differing Districts and a Provincial HQ, I was delighted to be posted as District Commissioner to Mandera the most distant District in the Colony. It was early 1946 and I was twenty three.

G

X

MANDERA DISTRICT
NORTHERN FRONTIER DISTRICT (N.F.D)
MARCH 1946–OCTOBER 1947

Mandera was about as far away as possible from Kisumu, nearly a thousand kilometres as the crow flies. It lay at the very corner of north eastern Kenya between Abyssinia (Ethiopia) and Somalia and was one of six Administrative Districts then comprising the 100,000 square mile territory called the 'N.F.D.' or Northern Frontier District, with its Headquarters at Isiolo, so called 'Gateway to the North'. The journey from Kisumu was by rail to Nairobi, where I was looked over and nodded on by Colonel Marchant, the Chief Native Commissioner, a distinguished soldier administrator, and went by the slow train to Nanyuki railhead, where the Mandera DC's lorry awaited me.

Towering over the scene, tantalizing and elusive, was the often shrouded basalt and glacier summit of Ki'inyaa or Kirinyaga, the mountain hallowed variously in the mythology of the Kamba, the Kikuyu and the Maasai. Nanyuki Township, named after the red oat grass on the northern expanse of the high plateau once roamed by the Maasai, was a true one steer frontier town, put together piecemeal by settler ranchers and sheep graziers, suppliers, traders and transitory government functionaries. It lay on the measured but invisible line of the Equator and was an instantly appealing place, with a single main street flanked by tree lined islands and slip-roads for loading at the shopfronts. I called at one, 'The Settlers Stores', owned by generations of Patels, to top up my provisions.

There was a fair complement of characters in the neighbourhood, notably the brilliantly eccentric Hooks, of whom one, ex-Naval Commander Logan Hook, was proprietor of the Silverbeck Hotel, where I spent the night in a comfortable log cabin. He was a 'fundamentalist' British Israelite and accosted me on my morning call at his central crow's nest of a pit latrine to assure me that my movement was unnecessary since the end of the world was nigh. Meanwhile he ran up signals at the masthead beside his entrance, warning visitors of any sickness by a yellow flag and so on. He was a pale, bulky, grand old man, quite different from his nearby mule coping rogue of a brother Raymond; a scholarly, slovenly, splendid Viking wreck who later taught me much and gave me books from his rush-strewn library infested by worm ridden dogs. A solid community could safely spawn, sustain and gain from such eccentrics.

From Nanyuki onwards the plateau broke off in a succession of ridges which the heavily corrugated, dirt road negotiated in great loops and swooping inclines. Long stretches were tautly fenced with sheep wire and cedar posts, behind which it was said that every white fleeced sheep belonged to the Welsh-South African pioneer flock of Powyses and every curly white haired Powys could be mistaken for a sheep. The vast expanse of the frontier emerged from the haze of heat and distance and took a sharper focus as we rattled briskly down the long slope into Isiolo.

The first and abiding impression was reporting to the Officer-in-Charge N.F.D., who enjoyed the status of a Provincial Commissioner, which he became when the adjoining 'Extra-Provincial District' of Turkana was added to his huge bailiwick. I had entered what I had imagined as a mythical place inhabited by Giants of Empire, the last but not least of whom was Gerald Reece. Before confronting him I had a reassuring and imbibingly informative night's stay with the District Commissioner, Isiolo, John Pinney. He was three years my senior, sturdy, steady, square jawed and smiling, and also held the fort while Reece was out and about.

Gerald Reece, or 'Uncle' as we all called him, not to his face nor because he was at all avuncular, had gained by his fifties a formidable reputation and authority overspilling the bounds of his unique realm. It was compounded of a potent blend of force of character, unswerving dedication, incisive knowledge with a strong relish of eccentricity. At the same time there was for him an underlying, sometimes grudging, affection of the kind accorded by youths to an intimidating Headmaster. The post war DCs were indeed all under 30 and known as the *crèche*, although some still carried officer rank.

The seasonally nomadic population of the vast territory varying between one and two hundred thousand were preponderantly Somali and kindred peoples of the Eastern Hamitic migrations from the north, or Boran/Oromo/Galla descending from the Ethiopian highlands. Reece's relationship with them was conditioned by his dutiful, honourable but relentless restraint of the compulsive south westerly movement of the Somali as a matter both of Imperial policy since the 'scramble for Africa' and on behalf of the Foreign Office's permanent bias toward the Ethiopian Imperial interest. There was also the perceived danger of potential confrontation between the converging Somali and Turkana and their penetration into the Maasai and Kikuyu occupied highlands of Kenya, not to speak of the white settled farms.

In some trepidation I reported myself to the extraordinary personage who pervaded the turbulent scene and my life for nearly two years. To my surprise 'Uncle' Reece's physical presence was not in itself overpowering. He was over 6 foot with a rather narrow forehead and thin nondescript brown hair. His shoulders were not broad nor well muscled and the power structure of his frame lay across the box of hips and thighs which served to launch both his heavy tread and the deep boom of his voice. This was often preceded by a thunderous 'harrumph' or 'hèehém', or in Swahili a

84

probing double *Kama* ... *Kama* (roughly 'look here — if') which gave rise to his other nickname 'Bwana Kamakama'. Emphasis was given to his categorical discourse in idiosyncratic Swahili by ferocious twitches of a formidable nasal organ, apparently jointed at the bridge. Perhaps mischievously he used to demolish his *bête noire* in Government, Attorney General Stafford Foster-Sutton as "the Member for Law and Disorder ... extraordinary fellow ... twitches!"

Somehow Reece's assorted fasces of authority were bound together by his manifest sincerity, deep humanity, love of youth and meticulous attention to detail in a gruelling task. What is more he was as cunning as a cartload of monkeys! He kept himself alert to nefarious activities through a network of District 'informers', surreptitiously known to and advised by his DCs. He had a particular affection for the red turbaned 'Dubas', the élite Tribal Police recruited from each clan, although it was one area in which his rather indulgent discipline fell short of his standing order that underpants were not worn beneath their off the shoulder *shuka* (heavy cotton toga). The opprobrious word *shéégat* (a clan parasite) expelled from his diaphragm like a mortar bomb would make a strong man cringe.

His gentle wife Alys wrote of her side of life with him in a touching book entitled *For my wife 50 camels.** They had a dear son born with an impaired heart. I was readily enslaved to this man and listened to his admonitions and exhortations as to how to conduct myself as DC in Mandera with pride of service and self-discipline. Above all he warned me, using the singular, like a Commanding Officer of 'the soldier'; "never love 'the Somali' or you may end up by hating him". It was a harsh dictum which some discovered for themselves to have a grain of truth.

Forewarned if not forearmed, I sallied forth on the next 500 mile slog to the north, calling at the roadside Kenya Police fort of an Inspector in Charge, known in song as "I'm the Bimbashi, the lord of Muddo Gashi, the *Watu* (people) to me they all bow down ... I'm Bimbashi Bullseye Brown". Indeed he was. We drove into mirages puddled like hallucinatory lakes on the road ahead in the searing dazzling heat and I looked vainly for the non-existent camels, elongated and upside down in their non-existent pools. After monotonous hours on a rigidly corrugated dirt road we passed through the nothingness to the sand blown oasis of *Habbaswein* (big dust). There huge dark green Acacia, 'fever trees', overhung pools of water, rising from within the desert where the *Uaso Nyiro* (the red river), spewing seasonally from Samburu District expired reluctantly near giant Kittermaster's Camp into a meandering swamp for nearly 100 miles. *Habbaswein* marked the half way point between Isiolo and Wajir.

In thankful shade from the monstrous heat were scattered under the best

*Alys Reece. Harvill Press Ltd., London, 1963.

cover some dozen constantly changing lorries of varied provenance in every stage of gallant decrepitude. The drivers, many of them diminutive, wizened, ageless Yemeni Arabs with Lamu turbans, their prayer mats, sandals and kettles laid ready beside open fires for brewing tea and washing feet, were engaged in cannibalizing vehicle parts in the most generous way, regardless of time and technical difficulty. Sagging springs were reinforced or splinted, tyre walls gaitered, coils rewound and miracles of fusing performed with silver paper from cigarette packets. What Ogoma was making of all this away from his lakeside people I did not need to ask. He was making tea.

Onward then over the unchanging expanse to Wajir, the hub of the N.F.D. road network with spokes south, whence I came, north west to Moyale and the Ethiopian highlands, north-eastward to Bardera in Somalia, via Baidoa to Mogadishu on the Indian Ocean, and now northward to El Wak and Mandera my new home. The cross-roads was located near a honeycomb of wells sunk deep into gypsum rock and concentrated within a few acres of flat white surface, trampled smooth by an ordered confusion of roaring, bellowing, gagging, squealing camels, clubbed into tribal drinking positions by frantic herdsmen.

Wajir was known to European sojourners as the Beau Geste fort of the N.F.D., not for the beauty of its ideals but for the Foreign Legion style of its buildings and its atmosphere of desert romance. It was also in the heart of the 'purest' groups of Somali nomads to have surged south west into Kenya, and the entrepôt of so called alien Somali traders from Somaliland, vying with Arab importers and transporters from the ancient port of Lamu. Not least among these was a diminutive, bow legged, elegantly attired tycoon known irreverently as Ahmed Bin Salim Bayusuf by Jesus by Christ. He stood a full five and a half feet with lovely embroidered turban, a brilliant shawl and glowing cross eyes enhanced and focused with kohl.

Since I often came back from Mandera to visit Wajir, with which there were many connections of duty and pleasure, I mention now only one significant local colleague. He was Peter Derrick, ex-Royal Artillery Major, whose path I was happily to cross in friendship many times. He was lean and pleasingly handsome in the manner of Shakespearean Peter O'Toole, with a comparable languid drawl and a remarkable rasping trick of projecting his unabashed discourse across any room or din.

After another hundred miles of flat but unmade-up road we entered Mandera District south of *El Wak* ('Wells of God'). This was a minute version of Wajir with a Kenya Police post, a wretched plastered hovel of a shop, and a single, twisted gypsum well in process of vertical realignment by hand. Apart from vital dry season watering for camels and small stock, the produce of the well had a curious reputation arising from the effect of chemicalized water on the hair which stuck out rigidly when combed, fit to crack, and induced an acute version of what was called 'Wajir Clap' lower down, causing crestfallen and anxious officers to head hot-foot to the M.O. at Wajir. It was not established if the two phenomena were related, being sometimes found together.

From El Wak we penetrated thin savannah ripped apart by a tangle of criss-crossing tracks, spanning a width of up to 100 yards, collectively the Mandera road. They marked the individual skill and luck of drivers as they swerved between mud wallows, ruts, sunken brushwood and surviving tree stumps or ground to a halt deep to the axles. The secret of extraction was a contrivance called a 'Tanganyika Jack'. These indispensable contraptions were usually worked in pairs, each with a separate block of wood to serve as a stable base. The jack post was a 5" x 3" hardwood sleeper nearly 2 feet tall with a heavy toothed, vertical gear topped by an open claw bolted to one broad face, which was activated by an attached winding handle. A pit was dug in the mud to beneath each sunken rear wheel, the block was driven flat into the bottom of the pit and the jack at low elevation was stood upon it, with the claw gripping the cross member of the truck body. The gears on each side were then wound to maximum height and brushwood rammed into the space under the raised rear wheels and forward to the front ones. The assembled passengers were then exhorted by a cheerleader's spasmodic roars of *Harāām-bée* (heave together) to a frenzy of effort, the driver revved in bottom gear and simultaneously the lorry was jerked into motion by released engine and human power to topple forward from the jacks on to the brushwood bed. With luck a mud spattering surge of a few yards was achieved to hard ground; without it a few feet were gained and the exercise repeated to exhaustion. In the rains the journey could take a week, but three tons had been moved.

Our driver triumphantly skirted the worst hazards and we sped on at over ten miles an hour through glades of low thorn and *malmal* (gum Arabic) trees. When we stopped to speak with young camel herds the silence was made musical by the melodious clunk of camel bells and aromatic foliage as they tugged and ripped the sweet feathering of leaves down hanging branches spined with thorns with a delicate and contemptuous detachment. It was as if their contemplative mastication had no connection with the foaming acid saliva, which rendered down the thorns, nor with the output when digested through the labyrinth of rumbling stomachs.

Three bold and lissom Somali youths, their glistening fat anointed busbies of hair stuck with carved wooden teasing combs, had waved us down, eagerly offering gourds of camel milk in exchange for a drink of our precious pure water. They were the first nomads I met who were to be my administrative responsibility and their gift of unfamiliar milk was doubly sweet. They were of the Murille sub-section of the Hawiyeh clan family, who ranged far and wide from the north beyond Mogadishu south westerly into Mandera district.

Nothing marked the approach to Mandera *boma* save the visual image of the place name. This was a corruption of *Melka Mêdera Wein*, meaning 'the wide crossing, or watering place of the Dōm palms'. There was a perceptible moist thickening of the dry atmosphere as we neared the Dawa 'Parma' (Italian usage) river fringed by the nut bearing trees. It flowed turgidly between the higher Ethiopian bank and past a knobbly spur on the Somalia border, called *Finan Guba* (The Black Nose), on its way, via Dolo and Lugh 'Ferrandi' (Italian usage), to the benign Juba river confluence in Somalia. A sure sign of arrival was a flaccid wind-sock on a twisted pole, marking the small airfield between the border and the township. The lorry swung past a few wretched, lime plastered petty stores, between barbed wire and palm post gates and came to a halt in a frenzy of shouts in front of a palm-thatched oblong shack entitled 'DC's Office'. Stooping to emerge from the shady interior stepped the District Commissioner, John Howard.

John was the epitome of the Edwardian gentleman, clean cut and correct, with a neatly proportioned head, no moustache and parted brown hair. His long and rangy physique inclined forward from the hips as if clad in knickerbockers and boots striding forth to a distant place. It could easily be divined that he had heard the siren call of the unconquered faces of Everest and Mount Kenya from the often distant focus of his gaze commonly seen on climbers, but the ascetic commitment to the earth and mountains was softened by his smiling courtesy and raffish enjoyment of a cheroot. From first encounter he seemed to me the beau ideal of the Colonial Administrator. His handing over notes and records were impeccable, with diagrams of wells and water holes and suggestions for dam sites, as well as the whole gamut of human problems, including those of our small company through which all was to be achieved.

A special task he laid on me was the erection of a suitable stone memorial to his own predecessor, gallant 'wee Willie' Keir, who had been killed in an ambush by *shifta* (bandits), on a rocky outcrop called Gadeir along the Ethiopian border. Funds came through and this was later done at a full ceremonial parade of Chiefs, townspeople, Kenya Police and Dubas. I saw John Howard off to greater challenges and higher mountains, my admiration mixed with anxiety as to my ability to follow his example.

Because Mandera District commanded over two hundred miles of international boundaries, east and north, a substantial armed Kenya Police force of over 100 men, drawn from many tribes, was quartered with families in the *boma*. In addition there was an élite force of some 50 Dubas in separate 'lines' smartly uniformed, but without 'Uncle'-offending underwear. There was a turnover of expatriate Police Inspectors in what was termed a 'hardship' station, usually three at a time, and they shared an Inspectors mess in a cavernous gabled and palm thatched mud barn. The most experienced was John Doull, streetwise, thick lipped and bodied as a boxing trainer, right elbow raised high with a tankard and a cigarette held down the left seam of his shorts. Don Whitehead was neatly handsome and properly brought up. (Thirty years later as a Major of Security in Smith's Rhodesia he should have arrested me at the airport when on a secret mission for the African Nationalist cause. Happily the surprise of old friendship took us both to the airport bar).

Ken Eglen was a tufty moustached ex Army NCO, hair bristling like the cockade of a Fusilier and alert for any command. Ian MacDonald was short, black haired, nimble and volatile. His explosive aggression had made him a ferociously brave and commended jungle fighter in Burma, and a barefisted bar brawler, whom I saw catch and despatch a vulturine guinea fowl in a running leap from the back of a moving truck. Pat McGhee was smiling, plump faced and phlegmatic, not prone to dispute. A rather sad and gentle oddity was pallid, wispy moustached Smallwood, inaccurately translated into literal Swahili as *miti midogo*, who was a proud son of "'Ull on t'Umber" (*sic*). He wrote wonderfully romantic safari reports about his daily round until "sun went down in blaze of glory", and touchingly declared "I don't know what I'd do without my f...ing chickens". The Company Sergeant Major, Arraleh, was a vinegary old Isaak Somali from British Somaliland. (His great niece worked with me there much later in Save the Children during the upheavals of civil war).

The DC's Office staff were headed by a Goan District Cashier cum Clerk called Victor Fernandes, a robust, outgoing game hunter who yet found the tensions of social isolation hard to bear and often took solace in total immersion in a cool bath. His junior was a sage and assiduous Arab clerk, Ahamed Abdullah, who offset his deceptive ordinariness by flashes of impish humour and later became an Administrative Officer and a Coast Liwali. The Interpreter cum general 'fixer' was Mohamed Alio, who pliantly detached himself from involvement in explaining any hard issues by ending his translations evasively by adding, "that's what he says" (*yeye nasema*), even when 'he' had not.

As all frontier DCs I was much reliant upon the Dubas for close contact with the people. I introduced them at dawn to newly constructed horizontal and parallel bars, partly because I enjoyed my remembered gymnastics and also their nomadic style of life left them relatively weak in hands and arms. An exception to this was a very dark, heavy shouldered, Corporal, Adullahi Dabasso, nicknamed *Ndofu* (the elephant) upon whom I often depended in difficult situations. Conversely there was a young Murille, Ahmed Ali, very handsome and somehow giving rise to unease, as emerged more clearly in later political developments. The Dubas in their turn put me through my paces in learning to ride the small hardy Somali ponies we had on strength for hot pursuit. The airstrip was our training arena but I failed to overcome the difficulty of stirrups dangling so near the ground that I tried to steady myself as if on a bicycle.

I went to call on the Town Mayor, an unimpressive individual called Sheikh Ibrahim, wearing a simple, off white cloth *kanzu* (gown) still stamped with its former user 'Unga Flour Mills'. His manner resembled the mumbling Emperor Claudius, though he doubled up as Imam of the wretched Mosque, which was all the small traders could then afford. A task ahead. A pivotal character in the conduct of the *boma* was Osman Muslim, Head Station Hand. He was cast in the mould of a Lewis Carroll figure, squat, paunchy, pockmarked, melon-headed and bandy. In a plain linen shirt over shorts, his rolling walk was half waddle, half limp. His manner, not without charm, was one of respectful familiarity, as befits a retainer who has done discreet personal service to a variety of officers. He was also 'uncle' Reece's local informer and I found it sensible to trust his judgement in prior discussion of what might be helpful information to impart.

A delightful and invaluable adjunct to our small foreign society was a 'lost patrol' of former Italian prisoners of war, still awaiting repatriation. 'Engineer' Ramazotti was their officer, ready to draw up building plans and apply their timeless peasant and artisan skills to any task for which cash or material could be found or adapted. We took to musical soirées on the sand outside my house with a small manual gramophone, wound happily by Ogoma's kitchen *'toto'* (boy) supplied with a steel hard whistling thorn needle for each record. My Gigli, Caruso and Marion Anderson records in the mortar box given me by Alan Bobbé encouraged pasta production and cheap 'must' wine from former Italian Somalia. If alone last thing at night I played for myself a '45 record labelled 'Swan Lake-Scene' which was an enchanting extract of a *pas de deux* on violin which gave peaceful sleep against the blood curdling cackles or voracious who-ops of circling hyena.

The DC's house was a crudely substantial, rubble and lime plastered block. There were two rooms, perhaps ten by twelve feet, with an unshuttered window space in each and a palm thatched leanto across the front. The ceiling cum roof was of *Terminalia Spinosa*, thorn branches, serving as rafters, the gaps between filled with loose concrete, sealed on top with a thick layer of boiled bitumen, flexibly tacky in the heat. The bitumen was looted from the light-rail and roadside dumps of the fantastic 1935 *Strada Imperiale*, the Fascist arrow aimed by the Italians from Mogadishu dead straight into the heart of Abyssinia.

There was a low Indonesian type 'sloshing' tank in an alcove at the back of the living room, into which I fitted a looted iron bath without a bottom which, when seated on wet cement, smoothed and enamel painted, afforded recumbent soaking in boiled brown water from the river bed. Ogoma's kitchen and hut were at the back. Uninvited visitors who shared my bedroom, when sand on the wind drove me inside, were furry, restless bats who slept hanging upside down from the thorn branches, releasing squirts of burning urine which left red weals across my exposed forearms. I was told that this erection, before 'modernization;, had cost four hundred shillings or £20 some years before, but bureaucracy required of me rental of 7½% of my salary (roughly £40 a month). For the barest essentials of hard furniture there was the further 2½% to pay, giving an annual return to the Treasury of over 200% on capital cost. I raised a faint peep of protest to 'Uncle' Reece when instructed to vacate the house and contents for a ceremonial visit of the Governor, proposing instead a suitably splendid tented camp for the entire gubernatorial party. I did not move.

Seasonal migratory 'birds' added colour to our small company. Among them the most bizarre were the regular and part time Locust Officers. *Oom* (Uncle) Scheurkogel had his own farm lorry in Eldoret, in which he brought 3 ton loads of cotton seed, arsenic and molasses for bait which were dumped in a huge mound near the Dubas lines, where our milk herd of impounded cattle were held and thrived mightily on this nourishing diet. He looked like an American bald eagle with wrinkled face and neck above powerful shoulders, bowed as if to bear a milk bucket yoke. His limbs were muscled like a Leonardo anatomical drawing, showing every sinew of unbelievable strength. He lived close to the earth, thriving on *biltong* (dried game meat) and carrying a half walnut shell as an eyebath to use with his own urine to fend of blinding, endemic Trachoma and the like. Killian was a compact, Irish South African 'redneck' who would readily eat spoonfuls of the new orange DNOC locust poison dust to convince nervous cattle owners that their herds could safely graze where it was broadcast.

Gerald Selby-Lowndes was clearly of upper class and education. With his great, cadaverous height and hawk nose he was like a Red Indian Chief at the head of a totem pole. He was accompanied always by his faithful familiar, a black dog suggesting a difficult union between Labrador and Dachshund. It made heavy speed to match his pace on short legs and a bounce off the midriff. It once discreetly helped us out in our flood marooned tent by disposing gladly of surplus camel curds to avoid offending over generous donors. It was always addressed formally as 'Charles Grey'.

The semiprecious gem was F. E. Beale, a regular Locust Directorate employee and a real 'gentleman of the bushveld'. He was 54 and in good fettle, always perfectly groomed from coconut oil anointed, thin grey hair and massaged eyebrows to naked brown torso under a white silk neckerchief. He wore immaculate white shorts revealing useful tanned legs and neat feet in pipeclayed tennis shoes. He toured outposts from his HQ camp near Voi in a well kept, pre-war, box body English Ford upon which he had built a cabin with prettily curtained windows and a frilly bunk bed. In this travelled a lovely young Somali girl friend, Habiba Mohamed, whom he left sometimes nearer her home, sending her gifts like smart sandals and remittances, through my willing care. Despite a scurrilously expressed nostalgia for his former service in the British South Africa Police, his party piece was a repertoire of horrendously mawkish sentimental ditties, like "Once I saw two lovers in a garden ..." and "Come little girl for a sail with me, up in my big balloon", a performance of which once silenced the visiting Governor.

Every few months a single engined plane of the Kenya Police Airwing came on a 'milk run' round the N.F.D. bringing welcome company and *kikapus* (baskets), of fruit and vegetables. Occasionally also the Police Armourer, an Inspector Hamid Wali Mohamed, came by road to service our hundreds of .303 Short Magazine Lee-Enfield rifles, some in use since the First World War. He also cut up the unserviceable camel *baramils*, 14 gallon portable water tanks of copper, whose rivets and metal screw necks had 'started' to an extent not repairable in the Nairobi railway workshops. With sledgehammer and steel cutting rings and interlocking blocks of grooved and embossed hardwood he rammed out ashtray shapes from the thick gauge copper. After rubbing down and burnishing by prisoners with ashes and lime, a 1780 Maria Theresia, or even an Emperor Menelik, silver dollar from Abyssinia was soldered into the hole in the base, making unique and appealing gifts, far too good for smokers to use. The accented í in her name on the coin was said to be the Latin 'recumbent dative' cried in despair by the Hungarian nobles she seduced — "*Moriamur pro rege nostro Maria Theresía*".

Before getting down to the serious business of office administration, I set about becoming familiar with the environs of the *boma*. The lifeline for everyone and everything was the water supply, drawn painstakingly from the Dawa river about a mile and a half away. A fast walk down hill, once keeping tactfully a half pace behind a thundering and breathless 'Uncle' Reece, pained still by First World War wounds, led through spindly trees and thickets alive with squalling, raucous baboons, some carelessly carting underslung babies, others vulgarly presenting their unlovely, bulbous purple rumps, towards the turgid river. John Howard and others before had cleared an oblong irrigated allotment in which a few apologetic paw paw trees, egg plant, chillies and gritty spinach grew grudgingly under the green hand and timeless *sharduf* (weighted lever) pump of the ubiquitous and diminutive Arab gardener. Endless patiently moaning, swaying camels, five to a rope and leader, carried the precious water from roughly filtered mudpits in *baramils*; our only community water supply.

The office, in fact two offices in turn, demanded much attention. The first was the primitive, bat infested, thatched store used by all Administrators since the post was first established, snapped in 1935 with a lissom young Dick Turnbull (later PC) emerging from the gloom. John

Howard had secured funds for a fine dressed stone and tiled building, which I was lucky to enjoy when completed and which I encircled with a hedge of pink oleanders impervious to donkeys' casual nibbling. Under the guidance of interpreter Mohamed Alio and the clerical staff I greeted the first trio of clan elders from the Murille, the Degodia and the Gurreh who called to look me over. There was great pride and snobbery attached to Somali clans of which there was a bewildering complexity across the spread of Somali migration south of the Red Sea back to the time of the Prophet. Most males had an extraordinary memory to recite their own genealogies.

Abdi Nur Gersi was the Chief of the Murille occupying a long gusset of land linking the powerful Darod Marehan and the Hawiyeh Degodia. Although counted as of Hawiyeh descent, they were careful to keep on good terms with the Marehan, who trampled across them at will. Perhaps for this reason Abdi Nur Gersi conveyed a slippery and insincere impression of great earnestness, not rendered more convincing by a shifty habit of alleviating manually the constant itch of chronic piles. He was always ready with a detailed and well substantiated claim for compensation of some kind; the more the references to calves with their tails bitten off by hyaena at night, the less likely the whole tale.

Hussein Salad, the Degodia chief, was a more convincing performer. He spoke deep and little and had an air of earthy humour. He exuded empathy with glowing, slightly wall eyes, grizzled spade beard, large metal trimmed teeth and a loosely furled turban. He was a sturdy, well planted man, comfortable in himself, pliant tanned prayer mat over one shoulder, cudgel in hand, striding out with good will.

Mohammed Jarri was a Hawiyeh Gurreh of the Koranyo sub-clan, as distinct from the Tuf, whom I was told by Mohamed Alio, a Koranyo himself, were somehow less pure. I never quite overcame the irreverent image of stout and curvaceous Mohammed Jarri in company with his Tuf counterpart, spiky Hassan 'Gab' (the short) as Eeyore and Piglet. They had a touching simplicity and honest directness in their constant partnership.

On this occasion all the Chiefs' needs were unspecified, but they prepared the ground for future claims for compensation for wounds and thefts in Marehan raids, cattle taken by lion, trespass on clan water holes and other needs concerned with tax, trade, wells and so on. Much time was expended on a satisfying exchange of protestations, the longer the better.

A quite unexpected caller from Isiolo was Abdallah Farah. He eased himself unannounced into my new stone office, the walls already lined with shelves full of the Laws of Kenya and subsidiary legislation, portending my compulsory law exam as First Class Magistrate. He cut an imposingly bulky figure in a voluminous cotton robe, which appeared to sweep along without benefit of legs, somewhat as a Victorian lady negotiating stairs in a bustle, or a Cardinal at the altar.

'Have a fag', he said smoothly, proffering a silver case which appeared from inside his robe. From then on over many years we had an amiable relationship as our paths crossed. His father, Colonel Kirkpatrick of the Kings African Rifles, had married a northern Somali woman in the Moslem rite with whom he had a son. The Colonel inherited a Baronetcy. When he retired to Britain, leaving Abdallah and his mother behind in Africa, he married again according to the Christian rite and had another son Christened James. On Colonel Kirkpatrick's death succession to the Baronetcy lay between the Moslem Somali and the British Christian son. It was determined through a substantial settlement, in favour of the latter as being of the Protestant faith, according to which, it was represented, the Baronetcy had first been granted by a Christian ruler. Sir James Kirkpatrick Bt., the younger son, became a Game Warden in Kenya and sadly committed suicide. Haji Abdallah Farah (so entitled after pilgrimage to Mecca), became a prominent merchant in Isiolo, known with ironical respect as 'the bastard Baronet'.

It was time to take off on safari and earn the lines composed for the annual song at the first DC's meeting I attended in Isiolo;

> "Now up in Mandera the lorries stay put
> 'cause Gavaghan finds that it's quicker on foot."

I planned to skirt the entire district, along the Ethiopian border via Melka Murri, towards the Moyale District boundary, back eastward above the Wajir border to El Wak, and north again to Mandera, a distance of around 350 miles, plus deviations and halts, to be completed within three weeks.

For this purpose we required a string of ten hired baggage camels with several experienced leaders and two good goats in milk as a mobile supply, saleable on return. The baggage train had to be treated seriously. Camels were not just camels. They needed to have certain characteristics. They should be of the *Gelap* breed and conformation, with powerful shoulders and short in the leg. Their box like chest must provide a broad bone platform for steady loading, with good clearance on each side so as not to cause a sore by rubbing the upper leg joint on the march. They must have a well plumped, centrally placed hump for balance of loads and, in a sense, for living off.

They should be gelded for even temper or, if in rut, have a toggle of knotted rope under the jaw to stop the soft palate ballooning up the neck and out like bubble gum in a foaming ectoplasm, generating such rampant passion as disastrously to buck off and smash a kitchen box. A by-product of the frustration of this orgasmic enjoyment is a series of explosions of noxious gases from the rear after passing through four stomachs, enough to asphyxiate an incautious follower. A bull camel in untrammelled rut, exulting on prancing legs, can see off a lion with its powerful thorn ripping jaws and teeth, from the cover of a thicket. Otherwise snarls, groans, whines and grunts from twisted head are largely declarations of independence and reluctance to be loaded.

Camels march slowly and with dignity at their own pace, which is about 2½ miles an hour and can slither in mud on the splayed feet which serve them so well in sand. It is risky to get too far ahead or cross a *lugga* (dry river) which may separate you in sudden spate from everything you need. Camels also browse slowly and must have time off to keep up strength on a long journey. Two other Mandera breeds, on which I made notes, were the *Horr*, a sort of dual purpose animal of medium height, and the *Sifdarr* with thoroughbred style, long in leg, neck and tail, to tug at sweet upper foliage for good milk, and flick irritating flies from their flanks. *Sifdarrs* are often of creamy hue and are much prized. The silky pelts of their young are delightful to the touch, even as they try to lick salt sweat and tasty shorts from too close an admirer. Some 'foreigners' hated camels. I did not and revelled later in their fresh milk.

Our first objective was Ramu, a watering place on the Dawa River, 50 miles or two days march away. There was a small trading centre for hide buying and the supply of sugar, flour, tiny paper packs of cigarettes and warm sweet drinks. I was met there by Hussein Salad, whose only centre it was for the Degodia, whose lands also spread across the river into the Ogaden area of Ethiopia. He offered us large gourds of sour camel milk with the consistency of junket and protected from dirt and flies by fresh, green feathered thorn sprigs. In return he and his retinue took enamel mugs of tea, to which he beamingly added spoons of sugar until the spoon stood up unaided.

Our only problem on this and the next stretch was to be aware of our location in regard to the disputed international boundary with Abyssinia (the then appellation), which had its humorous and its hazardous aspects. When Emperor Menelik's conquests reached a ragged limit at the end of the Nineteenth Century, a Colonel Maud did a survey in 1903 and proposed a line which was finally agreed on the map by Treaty with Menelik in 1907. This became known as the Maud or 'blue' line. In 1908 an attempt at clearer definition on the ground by a Colonel Gwynn, although marked by beacons, was not agreed and became known as the Gwynn or 'red' line. The wavering discrepancies of a few miles resulted for many years in each side observing the more advantageous border, sometimes confronting each other from the 'wrong' direction. Fortunately no-one's weapons were accurate and formal diplomatic protests delivered by hand in Arabic and French could end like Tweedle-Dum and Tweedle-Dee at six in bush 'dinners', at which *Tej* (mead), whisky (Kenya Government issue), unborn camel in saffron rice and worm pills averted any worse incident. Such matters were properly the affair of the DC Moyale, the Governor of Sidamo-Borana and HM's Consul at Mega (when in post).

The next planned stopover two days later was at Melka Murri another shallow watering place for thousands of livestock, this time deep down in a broad ravine scoured by the river. The cattle while drinking were protected from marauding crocodiles by herdsmen with sticks standing in deeper water splashing and shouting. One lad was taken and dragged down but his brother sprang to his aid striking and gouging at the crocodile's eyes to release the boy only to be taken off to his own death. The report of it was published and earned him a posthumous Commendation for Brave Conduct, perhaps of some comfort.

I savoured the perfection of foaming camels' milk *en primeur*, squeezed in thin squirts directly into a gourd. This is not a single or casual process. A freshly made gourd is cut from the bole or root of an aromatic *malmal* tree, from the bark of which the gum is bled in shiny sticky gouts, like astringent resin from a pine. The block is then adzed with a delicate, razor edged blade stuck in the burnt and inturned head of a thorn stick, until the classical shape of a vessel emerges. The inside is then cut out to leave walls so thin they could emit a hollow sound and show light through the skin, thin as porcelain. A wooden lid is then prepared with a snug fitting rim and leather shoulder strap. Any roughnesses inside are then burned off with charcoals of *malmal*, shaken like a cocktail. Finally the gourd is washed out, scarified and disinfected with any available urine and left to dry on the sand in the blazing sun. Result, a flavoursome receptacle redolent of each treatment and fit to blend its casked flavours with the 'foaming hippocrene' struck out from the desert sand by some cameloid Pegasus. I could never resist it and could happily live on it alone for days.

Without paying much attention to the conflicting Maud and Gwynn lines, which considerably diverged as we left the natural boundary of the Dawa river at Melka Murri, we cut across a triangular salient in the unmarked border towards the Kenyan Police frontier post at El Roba, a small sandbagged fort set on a giant rock girt mound. On the Ethiopian side was a large complex of deep wells, called Gaddaduma, of great importance to cross border clans, while El Roba was largely dependent on lorry borne drums. We at once set about redressing the deficiency by sealing off a large rainwater tank across the flank of a smoothly weathered rock catchment area. The problem of leakage through the base of the containing wall of concreted boulders, set in a chiselled trench, was solved by the application of a thick lining of the invaluable looted bitumen from Somalia. El Roba was a magical halt with a chilly night breeze from the Ethiopian Highlands and blazing fires shining through the tracery of thorn branches to the stars set in the blackness beyond. The sunset lowering of the Union Jack and the plaintive bugle call of the 'Last Post', saluted by the Kenya Police Guard, was so affecting as to evoke the emotional mention by Inspector Smallwood in his Safari Report, "... while sun went down in blaze of glory". It was just so.

In the bush near by we visited a temporary encampment of 'Wata', a people variously named 'Boni' among the Marehan and elsewhere in Kenya generally termed 'Dorobo'. They were descendants of the indigenous occupants of the land before the south westerly drive of the Somalis and they had cleaved peaceably to the clans which overbore them. Although of refined and delicate features, well formed cranium and small stature, they were palpably of a lower level of subsistence than the dominant Somali, keeping mainly goats, avoiding attention and thus eluding registration for tax. Among the minor Somali clans such parasitical attachments would have been stigmatized by 'Uncle' Reece as *shéégats*, barked out with disdain for any defilement of true lineage. Stolid, beefy, bead telling Mohamed Jarri had also come from El Wak to introduce us to a gathering of his local Koranyo people.

Onwards then to cross the Mandera to Moyale Road, where the District lorry, laden with drums of clean water, provisions and any urgent mail, had come to meet us, so that we could continue fully supplied for the more demanding circuit ahead, away from water in arid bush and hill country. I was astounded at the huge intake of water by our baggage camels after a week's march, emptying a half drum apiece, which they seemed to absorb into every part, including the stiffening hump.

The rough, winding, dirt road was under constant repair; draining, destumping, and filling of gouged ruts, by labourers from the vast Turkana District beyond the Rift Valley. Although coming from a fierce warrior race and uncircumcised, they were recruited willingly to undertake the heavy manual work which was repugnant to the proud but less robust Somali nomads. Several N.F.D. roads were maintained in this fashion by isolated gangs of 30 or so under their own Turkana foreman. Equipped with picks and hoes, they would be given a task of measured distance monthly. They were rationed with maizemeal, salt and sugar and allowed to purchase and consume a fixed number of goats or sheep whose skins were accountable, dried and stacked, sometimes with the odd dog skin, and handed in on pay-day, 30/- per man monthly. The supply lorry might also bring them chewing tobacco and cloth. Fids of tobacco evoked delighted crooning noises, but one ounce packets of Epsom salts were pronounced insufficiently dynamic to shift their meat diet, sometimes after two weeks. A particular affliction to which their habits rendered them susceptible was called 'hydatidosis', after the hydatid cysts deriving from close contact with defecating animals, above all dogs, which customarily used to lick the anus clean in lieu of paper, water, grass or stones. Eyes, stomach and skin could be affected and cysts proliferated with alarming speed. Prevention and cure came much later.

In Mandera District the Turkana road workers were all Catholics, evangelized by the Italian Consolata Catholic Mission at Meru, below Mount Kenya 500 miles away. In celebration of their faith they assembled each evening at a thorn bower, shaped like a grotto, in which they placed a blue, white and gold attired plaster statuette of the Blessed Virgin Mary, sent by the Mission and sang devoutly if discordantly, "Ave Maria, Gratia Plena", while telling their flimsy rosary beads. It was a touching sublimation of their menial lot and an assertion of self-respect alone among Moslem Somalis.

Reprovisioned for the more desolate part of our journey, we passed by Gadeir, from where former DC 'Willie' Keir's body had been recovered, and made our way by a succession of imposing rock strewn hills, located a varying day's march apart. The first was Dandu, faced with huge slabs, separated by fringes of stunted vegetation and holding surprising pools of water, an ideal habitat for baboon and rock hyrax. We camped at the foot and held a sort of jamboree for recruitment of Dubas. This consisted of three tests; first, overall physical inspection with some enquiry as to clan, family etc.; then a preliminary range practice with a .303 rifle against a flat rock face at which some were instantly proficient; the short list would then wrestle either with Ogoma or with me, which was very popular entertainment. A challenge thrown out to me by Ahamed, the Murille Dubas, led to him resorting to, apparently legitimate, testicle clutching before he tore free to grab a rifle with evident intent only to be seized and thrown by Abdullahi Dabasso, to my sincere relief and gales of laughter.

Without further incident we camped in turn below Kuffole, Balobleh and Takabba, meeting many bell clonking camels and their welcome draughts of fresh milk. Two other staple foods kept up my energy. Both were recipes from my friend in South Nyanza, Father 'Jaap' Molenaar. One was simply a nourishing but easily prepared Dutch soup called *snoet*, made of dried chick peas crushed and soaked overnight so as to form a thick consistency when boiled, embellished with any bone stock and livened with a shot of grain 'Hollandse' gin. The other was for the chill of pre-dawn consumption while camels were loading. A large enamel mug two thirds full of scalding, jet black Kenya coffee was smothered over with a frothy nog of two or three whipped up raw eggs, laced lightly with brandy, onto which was loaded black sugar until it sank in. A beverage with charge enough for a day's march.

So fortified I broke south from Takabba towards a lone pimple of a hill called *Bur Mayo* in the middle of an arid, grey, cracked, salt earth plain called *korticha*. The only pathetic shelter was of low, desiccated thorn bushes beneath which we squatted at hourly intervals awaiting the laggardly camel train. To stand up too quickly was to invite a blackout due to lack of salt. On route I met my first dung-beetles, who alone, rugged and well armoured as JCBs, seemed impervious to the heat and were busy clearing up pellets after such herbivores as could find sustenance, browsing goats, slender gerenuk and the like. We unkindly interrupted the beetles' purposeful activity, smoothing an oblong, dust walled drome within which to test their ball rolling paces, betting matches on our favourites. We, bearing the noble badge of the lion, were sharing their humble place on earth.

Having arranged to meet again with Peter Derrick, my DC neighbour from Wajir, I rashly pressed ahead of our camel train with Abdullahi Dabasso, each carrying a rifle and water bottle. Some nine hours out of Takabba we approached Bur Mayo to find an *Ilalo*, a khaki turbaned Locust Scout, squatting on top like a watchful bird of prey. He knew nothing of any encampment, but assured us it would be at a water hole in a swampy river bed some hours ahead, which could be reached by lorry track from Wajir. We had no better option than to find Peter's camp, or at least water and a track, leaving the scout to tell our baggage train to head direct to El Wak and await us there. After a dour footslog until sunset, Abdullahi sustained a thorn spike between his big toes, which had to be bound tightly with my handkerchief to stem the blood and I took over his rifle to ease the weight on his foot. Towards ten we saw lights and heard the welcome commotion of a proper tented camp and staggered in to a hearty greeting of, "You are late for dinner!" Torn between hunger, thirst and indignation I swallowed a bowl of oversalted Mulligatawny and vomited. We remained friends.

We begged a lift on Peter's lorry back to the Wajir road and north to El Wak, where our camels had arrived and watered. Hassan Gab had gathered a group of Gurreh of his Tuff section and was joined by some elders of the Leisan, the fourth but smallest Mandera clan of the Hawiyeh, whose women were renowned for their calm beauty, captured by the famous Italian painter Bruno di Sopra, his name by chance describing the posterior view he often favoured for his recumbent models.

The same diminutive Arab mason as on my first arrival at El Wak dangled from his rope within the perfectly chiselled gypsum circumference of the now vertical well. He had broken through the crooked access shaft to the dank, gaseous, water trapped at the bottom of old carved standing ledges. Water-smoothed thorn branch props had enabled a relay of a dozen or more camel herds to reach the malodorous pool, tossing soft, giraffe hide bags to plop onto the water then handing them up again dripping full. Meanwhile, an improved diffusion system was prepared on the surface. This consisted of four thick straightish thorn boughs set in a square frame across the circular lip of the well and bound where they met. Each bough had four grooves made to slide the ropes on which the full hide bags were pulled to the surface, four of one clan to each bough and sixteen to the circumference, working in unison of movement and chant. Behind them was a gypsum plastered apron, sloping outwards towards a wider concentric trough at drinking level. As the workers grasped their full bags they emptied them into channels cut in the apron, which flowed continuously into the main drinking trough, its four clan divisions corresponding to the rope pullers on each quarter of the frame.

Apart from the increased supply, more rapidly delivered with less wastage and commotion, except among the brawling camels, lives could be saved by exposing stagnant, gypsum polluted water to light and air. First entrants to the traditional, crookedly angled, well shafts, driven by the onset of the dry season, risked asphyxiation when penetrating the last dark chamber and disturbing the locked in gases. The boughs needed to shorten the original steps were a possible clue to the existence of a mythical race of giants called the 'Madhanle', whose scattered and mysterious barrows of rock also suggested had once preceded the Somalis. The stature of the two early N.F.D. administrators, Archer and Kittermaster, 6'5" and 6'8", may have encouraged this belief.

From El Wak we loaded our District lorry with kitchen boxes, bedding, food and water, together with our 'returnable' milk goats. An easy drive over 60 miles up the Mandera road brought us to the sandy turn off to a potential dam site on the Korijub *lugga*, where Gerald Selby Lowndes and Charles Gray had set up camp to meet his Locust Scouts. The idea was to build the central part of an earth dam on a loop which would slow a sudden torrent of rain and form an 'oxbow' lake, before partly settling behind the dam, whose spillways would then be blocked to retain a temporary pan of water. That was the theory. The practice was an overnight flood that surrounded our chosen hummock for acres around, leaving us cut off from our staff, with nothing but Gerald's Mogadishu brandy and loads of rancid camels' junket, secretly consumed by Charles Gray. Two days later we waded fairly soberly to our lorry, leaving a rather small dam and thousands of triumphant bull frogs.

After nearly three weeks away Mandera seemed like home, and my mud walled blockhouse a palace. It was good to be known and to know something of the work to be conducted from District Headquarters. There was no laid down pattern for this except in the subject files, regular reports and handing over notes. Broadly it ranged over; international boundaries; clan or tribal movements; law; prison; Police and Dubas; livestock, grazing control and water supplies; health, works and services; tax collection; accounts, communications and reporting. Visits, to and from, were dealt with *ad hoc*. Education scarcely figured except for a form of literacy largely inculcated at 'Duksis', or evening bush schools, by a Sheikh using wooden shards branded with *surahs* of the Koran sung out in chorus.

An early drama was a mass border infringement by the Darod Marehan, driving their livestock through the Murille and engaging in a running battle with the Degodia as they sought grazing across the Mandera triangle into Ethiopia. The Marehan had numbers of Italian rifles from the recent campaign and some ponies, but were engaged by the Dubas who returned to the *boma* with thousands of trespassing camels, sheep and goats abandoned in flight, and some thirty prisoners. For many days the whole area resounded with the bellowing of impounded herds and the plaintive ululations of Marehan women seeking release of their menfolk. Hastily convened court hearings, my first as gazetted First Class Magistrate, led to the confiscation of a proportion of the livestock in lieu of fines and the release of the remainder with all but one of the prisoners, who was found guilty of wounding. As was usual with Somalis when confined, he at once fasted and wasted away in his cell, was admitted to the small dispensary to be fed, but slipped his handcuffs attached to the iron bed and was reported over the Ethiopian border at Melka Murri, 100 miles away, within 24 hours.

The proceeds of disposal of the livestock were, of course, credited to General Revenue. Some 'retentions' from unrecorded goatskins, as opposed to goats consumed, found their way into that invaluable N.F.D. receptacle known as the 'goatbag', which enabled DCs to perform minor miracles with non-existent funds, severely disapproved of by visiting Auditors, if unwisely declared or carelessly discovered in a safe. Much benefit accrued therefrom and I used about four hundred shillings to make a suitably designed roofless store, doubling as a squash court, between our houses. Other government buildings erected with dressed stone and corrugated iron were a new 'secure' prison, a small cottage hospital next to the telegraph office hut, and several whitewashed Dubas 'lines' to an improved pattern. John Howard had foreseen some of the funding and the 'goatbag', with the help of Engineer Ramazotti's 'POW'' team, made it possible.

Our medical lifeline beyond the Hospital Dresser in charge of the old dispensary and the new cottage hospital, was by telegraph or lorry to Wajir, from where a single Medical Officer covered the entire 100,000 square miles of the N.F.D. Dark haired, olive skinned Scot, Doctor Adam, supplied me with the new 'M and B 693' tablets which seemed to serve for various ailments, not least for venereal infections and I was sometimes asked by bashful staff to dole out enough pills to get them on the road to Wajir, crudely nicknamed 'the clap track'. He also advised me about a vile emission of black pus from a long cavity behind my right shin bone following deep penetration by a poisonous black spike of 'sanseveira', (wild or elephant sisal). This hazardous but useful plant delighted elephant who stripped it of green nourishment and passed its fibrous material through in structured balls of dung demolished by eager dung-beetles. The Somali used to break off the tips to secrete drops from the cortex for use in eye complaints such as Trachoma. Dr Adam handed over to a handsome, athletic young successor, Bill Barton, who became a firm friend and later formally inaugurated the new Hospital.

In the village we helped Sheikh Ibrahim erect a miniature but pleasing Mosque and a Gurreh trader Mohamed Ali, was provided, for rental, with a proper shade drying *banda* (shed) of tarred Dôm palm corner posts set in sun baked brick dwarf walls with thatched roof, wire skin stretchers and protective chicken wire. This was part of an experimental contract with a Czech leather expert called Emil Taussig, Manager of Bulley's Tannery (an international subsidiary) at Thika. Having already been struck by the quality, russet or silvery colour and silky texture of baby camel skins and by the slaughter of most of the young males, it had occurred to me that attractive jerkins or waistcoats similar to Persian Lamb, might be made from them, if properly skinned, shade-dried, tanned and styled. At least a few shillings might have got back to the owners. I did not see the result and Bulleys moved on.

Further visits to neighbouring areas were now due. I opted for the more unusual which was through British Military Administration occupied former Italian Somalia to the Indian Ocean at Mogadishu. It was a very odd time, being in the aftermath of the successful East African campaign against Italy involving Somali troops under General Platt and coinciding with an abortive spasm of international support for pan-Somalism, surprisingly enjoying the weighty and characteristically personal backing of the ex-coalminer British Foreign Secretary, Ernest Bevin. Thus for a brief period from 1942–7 most Somalis came under British administration, with the exception of those in French controlled Djibouti.

Only twenty-five miles from Mandera along the Dawa river by a road so atrocious as earlier to have broken the back of an impatient Police Inspector, 'Pissy' Wright, we reached Dolo, a much larger and more complex former Italian border outpost and Somali village with riverine cultivation. It was situated at the inland spear point of the *Strada Imperiale*. There was a substantial presence of the Somalia Gendarmerie, the military force commanded by Brigadier Pat Mundy, in support of the Civil Affairs Administration under the Governor, Denis Wickham, at Mogadishu.

There were two Majors at Dolo. One was Ray Russell-Smith with his German wife Dorothée, a delightful couple who became close friends and settled at Kiambu in Kenya. The other was 'Reg.' Cater, a short, bespectacled chemist from Tanga where his wife still ran their pharmacy. He had a tall Degodia woman 'bodyguard' in uniform who proudly displayed notches on her rifle butt, apparently signifying unsuccessful assailants. There was also an engagingly lugubrious Captain, 'Hutch'

Hutchinson, whose flourishing moustaches wilted under the influence of 'Cioffi's Old and Bold Brandy, *Molto Aromatico*, Extra Extra', guaranteed two weeks in bottle and costing up to six shillings, depending on stated vintage.

Under the genial influence of a superior tipple, 'Cioffi's Dry London Gin', the visiting Civil Affairs Officer from Lugh Ferrandi was reputed to sweep in unannounced and launch an attack on the hilltop Officers' Mess, first by threatening to open fire from beneath his 4 x 4 truck, and then brandishing his sword while charging across the car-park at the defenders. I was told that a bullet of unknown source had once ricocheted round the iron interior and struck an innocently raised elbow at the bar.

Escorted by a 4 x 4 truck from the Italian run Gendarmerie garage, we followed the *strada* on its raised embankment direct to Lugh Ferrandi, passing ostentatious Roman stone pillars with carved fasces every ten kilometres and twisted lengths of narrow gauge rail track used for construction gangs and other materials, including the many battered drums of bitumen and a few rusted officers' baths. At Lugh we stopped between the confluence of the Dawa Parma and the broad Juba River, which swept on to the ocean. We were met at the entrance of a fine two storey *palazzo*, formerly occupied by the Italian *Commissario Distrettuale* (District Commissioner) and now by the Civil Affairs' Officer, Major Charles Keyte.

Charles was, or had become, an unbridled eccentric. Before the war he had played the saxophone in Geraldo's dance band. With good education and address he had gained rapid wartime promotion in the East African Campaign and had been left behind in the Civil Administration of conquered Somalia, certainly because of his ability and probably because of his irrepressibly unorthodox style. In his early thirties he retained Italianate good looks, with glossy black waves and olive skin. Though tall and gracefully fashioned a certain, rather seductive, softening of skin and sinew reflected an indulgent hedonism uninhibited by embarrassment. He floated in a miasma of easy charm, lubricated with Cioffi's Dry Gin and twine bound fiascos of Chianti. He would quaff tablespoonfuls of sizzling *pili pili ho ho* in sherry fortified soup to sharpen his appetite and wit. He was a Dorian Gray unmarked and undaunted by the hidden picture of excess.

He took me once with him as invited guest to the inaugural meeting of the nascent Somali Youth League or SYL, dismissed lightly by some officers as the 'sewing circle'. His *Ilalos* (scouts) in pointed khaki turbans set out a good supply of drink at his lamplit camp table outside. After relieving other entrants of a shilling fee, he and his gin moved to the place of guest of honour on the dais of the hall, screened at the back by palm fronds from unseen ululating women. After we had eaten well of camel on saffron rice, with seethed cubes of sheep's tail fat popped hospitably by one's host into the mouth, he addressed the meeting, "Ladies (*sic*) and gentlemen, I shall introduce my speech by singing to you the famous British patriotic song 'Honey have a hunf on me'." I never heard what impact this astonishing paean of Empire had on the 'sewing circle', the nucleus of an independence movement.

The Commissioner's *palazzo* had marble floors and elaborately plumbed bathrooms. It was presided over by Charles' urbane major domo cum universal provider, Mohamed, and was constantly mopped shiny clean with naphtha by a shapely maidservant, her otherwise seemly dress off one shoulder to reveal a perfect breast. One evening a group of officers were invited to dine alfresco on the river terrace. The major domo had arranged for several very young and pretty local girls to be in attendance, each attaching herself to a chosen guest. Before matters had proceeded beyond chattering flirtation the major domo reappeared visibly perturbed on the upper patio to announce the presence in the hall of Padre Cheese. At once the laughing courtesans, too young for that, were shooed into the riverside bushes where they lurked, almost silently, but for the hysterical barking of Charles' dog at their hiding place.

The Reverend Ethelston Cheese had been well described as "a saint of no fixed abode". Of Anglican family, he had been appointed to the Mission Chaplaincy in Beirut in 1912 and had followed the campaigns of Allenby against the Turks and of General Cunningham, 30 years later, through Italian East Africa. His peripatetic career veered throughout the Horn of Africa until he moved from Addis Ababa to Somalia in 1918. The twenty years until our first inopportune meeting were spent as a revered and protected holy man with the Moslem nomads, translating the Gospels and Pilgrims' Progress into Somali, then lacking its own script. There he stood, calm but frail, in his too large (General Sir Garnet) Wolseley helmet, overlong shorts and large boots, his kit bag by his side, looking benevolently at the disordered scene. "I'm sorry to disturb you," he said, "but I wanted to ask if I could hold a small Sunday Service for you here tomorrow. Does your dog want something, do you think?" With suspicious alacrity a service was agreed for the morrow and Padre Cheese, perhaps not so innocent, was escorted to his lodgings. His service was most reverently attended.

After the exotic excitements of Lugh we drove rapidly down the *Strada Imperiale* to the considerable town and Provincial Headquarters of Isha (or Iscia) Baidoa. We were given curry lunch by Lt. Colonel Hurt, the Provincial Civil Affairs Officer, at which we met the District Commissioner, Frank Goodbody. Roger Hurt was erect, soldierly and distinguished, seeming older than his years, his apparently slow and taciturn manner being due to deafness. Frank was cherubic and bespectacled, honest and bonhomous, but said to cut an outrageous caper in his *Kikoi* on the dinner table. Both our paths recrossed in Kenya. At Baidoa there was a large Italian Catholic Mission School of importance in the education of girls and boys born across the races of all kinds, who fell between acceptance in Islamic and Christian society. One such, about whom I was asked, was said to be the son of the *Ugas* (chief) of the Marehan and an Ethiopian Coptic woman. I suggested his best future might be found in normal upbringing in the Marehan tradition. There was also a well frequented *ristorante* cum *bordello*, continuing to serve its companionable purposes.

By the slanting evening sun we saw the clear blue of the Indian Ocean beyond the raised sandy plateau and white portals of the ancient city of Mogadishu (or Mogadiscio), still plainly a symbolic outpost of the 'new' Roman Empire in the frustrated fantasy of Benito Mussolini, who had once addressed his adoring colonists from a balcony above the 'forum'. I spent two nights only at the two storey principal Hotel, the 'Croce del Sud', known to the British Army as 'the sweaty crutch', which was built about an oblong courtyard sensibly used as dining area. Near by was the Governor's Palazzo, known as 'Cockroach Castle', occupied by unassuming Denis Wickham, who later retired to Lamu in Kenya. His Chief Secretary was Jake Cusack, a russet haired Irish colonial Casanova, said to have been seconded from the Kenya Administration both for his easy brilliant mind and his agility in moving ahead of various irate spouses. Mogadishu was in all externals a European rather than a Somali city occupied by conquerors and conquered on amiable and co-operative terms, with a large Italian commercial community and residual civil service, enjoying a free and easy life. The sandy, seaweed and Portuguese Man o'War jelly fish infested beach was on Sundays something of a beauty parade, of which the unchallenged queen was 'Pussy' Cioffi, daughter of the redoubtable purveyor of the local gin and brandy, which oiled the wheels of society.

South-east of Mandera by over 100 miles was Bardera, whose Civil Affairs' Officer was golden haired 'Duggie' Collins. His bush hat was ringed with a leopard's tail, and he led a pair of cheetahs on a chain, giving out a weird jargon of his own, like "screechers with rage" when in pursuit of "wompoh" (beer), which belied his devotion expressed in a romantic memoir *A Tear for Somalia*. In the wild north-east of the Mijertein territory a formidable and dramatic Irishman, Gerry Hanley, held sway. He told of his experiences in *Warrior*, which revealed him as having an unrivalled insight into how Somalis saw themselves and which laid bare the loneliness and suicidal depression of some of the officers serving them. In *A Consul at Sunset* he recorded a matching insight into the role of these last of the few. A strange empathy yet grew between many officers and their utterly different and reluctant charges.

Any impression left of that ephemeral society as merely a Gilbertian charade must be countered, both by the turbulence of the times and by the guts, self-reliance and adaptability of the, mainly young, officers left to float or flounder in the early aftermath of war. Naturally they were sometimes lonely, loving and randy. Somalia was no easy posting and the rifle bearing Somalis were the least predictable and 'biddable' of people. Two foreign tongues were in use, astride an unscripted 'lingua franca'; funds were scarce to nil, society limited, policy and future direction obscure and timing of release uncertain. It was unsurprising that some of the personalities I came across had burgeoned into flamboyance or eccentricity.

So, back we went without further ado to the seeming normality and ordered routines of a District in an established Crown Colony, where I had quickly to meet the pressing deadline of my law examination. The Penal and Criminal Procedure Codes and Laws of Evidence requiring invigilation, I had to take the District lorry to Moyale, 250 miles to the west, where the District Commissioner was Colin Campbell. Colin, some five years my senior, was an Old Harrovian and graduate from Cambridge with the hallmarks of apparent diffidence and actual self-assurance. He was long, sinewy and hirsute of body, with dry dark hair, a pallid and haggard face and an indrawn mouth, giving a breathy, lisping touch to a slightly mocking style of charm. At squash he was a demon, while always seeming on the point of collapse. His evening ride of three miles return to the look-out over Ethiopian Moyale made up his stint of 'horse and foot miles', required to be reported monthly, the total thus varying in proportion to the days in the month.

This ploy had a certain relevance to a *froideur* between us, which taught me a lesson of trust. Colin was no martinet and Dubas turnout was not one of his preoccupations. He had just been alerted to expect a visit by the Governor and asked if I would send my pristine 'No.1s' over to be sent back by return for my own ceremonial parade. I did. His scruffy uniforms came back. Great Joke! Nevertheless I enjoyed his entertaining company, and his relaxed invigilation of my exam papers left me eligible for 'First Class' confirmation and thus for passing an 'efficiency bar' on the Administrative salary scale.

Early one evening we and some of the local staff, were enjoying a fairly noisy session, with Italian brewed Castle beer from Ethiopia, in Colin's whitewashed mud plaster and corrugated iron house, before tucking in to curry dinner. The ceiling had, over the years, suffered some damage from gun happy drinkers firing at imaginary denizens in the roof space and the holes were left in nostalgic celebration of the, nearly, past. There came a timid but insistent knocking at the crude wooden door which opened, up a single step, onto the forecourt of compacted mica-glinting clay. Outside stood a small, nondescript European in rumpled clothes and outfitters' solar topi usually called a 'missionary'. He blinked hesitantly behind steel frame spectacles, not by any means the intrepid explorer. "I am Reverend

Wiffin," he announced simply. "We have driven down from Addis Ababa on the way to our Mission House at Kakamega and thought we should ask for your clearance through Kenya." Behind him stood a box-body Model T Ford containing several members of his family waiting calmly and unexpectantly. Their unescorted journey, in that simple work-horse of a vehicle, through war ravaged Ethiopia was evidence of faith, hope, courage and endurance of an order possible only for innocents of God. After suitable care and arrangements they went on their pilgrims' way until our next most tragic encounter.

My planned return to Mandera by lorry was ruled out by the sudden onset of the long rains and we had hurriedly to improvise a camel train with which we set forth miserably on a ten day slither, with soaked bedrolls, hoping that the lorry might catch us up. I learned often to hear the tantalizing sound of distance, just like a conch shell held to the ear falsely echoing the memory of its ocean. In a final defiant spurt of exasperation I took up an old challenge and flogged the last forty-nine miles on foot from Ramu in under twelve hours, a day ahead of our baggage camels and a week of our, allegedly, stranded lorry.

The next visit to Moyale was for border liaison in connection with observance of grazing boundaries between the western Gurreh of Mandera and the Ajuran and Sakuye who, together with Boran from Ethiopia and Degodia from Wajir, formed the fluctuating population of Moyale District. In those times there was a sort of genealogical class distinction of Somali clans with gradations downwards from the north and east towards the south and west. The Hawiyeh clans in Mandera were not graded in the first rank and the Ajuran of Moyale even less so, the term 'half-Somali' being used by some officers who seemed to take a vicarious pride in the precedence or purity of their 'parishioners'.

I found twenty-nine-year-old David Christie-Miller, released from the Sudan Defence Force, installed as DC in place of Colin Campbell. He was, by contrast, Eton and Oxford, but any misgivings I may have had dating from inter-college vendettas with Eton at early wartime OTC camp with the Guards at Aldershot were instantly dispelled. In appearance David reminded me of a debonair Prince Albert, with all the graces attributed to him. Languid charm and unaffected concern for people and affairs were his style, not without a certain elusiveness and a mischievous enjoyment of human foibles.

All were intrigued when he upped and married 'Silver Jane' Wynne-Eyton, a good deal older and a famous aviator (strictly not-rix) in peace and war. She had a disconcerting habit of using N.F.D. road junctions as a flight compass, not always taking the right degree or spoke and landing once in a remote bush glade to check position, without hope of take-off. David introduced me to 'Haji' Ali Sigara, the most genial of Moyale traders, one of those worthies upon whose support and wisdom in almost every district young DCs came to rely. Although an 'alien' Somali, an Isaak from the north, Ali Sigara's pilgrimage to Mecca, earning him the title of Haji with hennaed hair, green turban and all, was celebrated with enormous enthusiasm, his spiritual merit conveying prestige on the whole district.

There came the expected visit of His Excellency the Governor and Commander-in-Chief of Kenya and Commissioner of Transport, Major-General Sir Philip Mitchell. This was to be by air, preceded by the Officer-in-Charge, N.F.D., by road to prepare the ground. Two, not closely adjoining, camp sites with well appointed 'double fly' tents and bath compartment were set up in a graceful thorn tree glade some 200 yards beyond my 'inadequate' home. The nearer was for 'Uncle' Reece, the further for H.E. and his staff. An inspection by 'Uncle' was a stringent enough affair without the exacting requirements of His Majesty's representative. He would come in his black Chevrolet saloon car, flag flying, which was robust enough for any passable track, but not designed to sustain any roots negligently left to bash sumps or spike tyres. Their discovery would be the cause of any length of delay while the Officer-in-Charge dug out every one, building up a head of steam for instant release on belated arrival.

The night before the Governor came was such a time and 'Uncle's' booming demands for repeated plates of soup (Boy! Leta soupu ingine!) and, unbelievably, for pullovers, left his respectfully listening hosts despairing of long ruined dinner. He mellowed, offered me his Dubas escort in scruff order for the Guard of Honour and asked for Osman Muslim to report to his tent, about which Osman and I had put our heads together! By lunch time we had gained approval for Willie Keir's memorial, Dubas gymnastics, new buildings and had been reminded of the paramount importance in the exercise of authority of *Heshima* or Prestige. 'Concubinage' was not mentioned, but resident wives were held to occasion a thirty per cent drop in efficiency.

The Kenya Police Airwing twin engine, five passenger plane taxied bumpily to a dusty halt on the airstrip, the windsock limply at ease as the entire male population lined the whitewashed stone runway. Two separated Guards of Honour of Kenya Police and Dubas freshly laundered, were brought to the 'General's Salute; Present Arms', as the cabin door opened, followed by punctilious inspection by His Excellency in full fig, closely accompanied by the respective unit Officers and his entourage. The Officer-in-Charge, N.F.D., then formally introduced his officers and the night-gowned Mayor, Sheikh Ibrahim, to the visiting party before they straggled through the compound to their camp sites. It was crushingly hot.

The routine processes of inspection were followed towards sundown by a gathering of all Officers, presided over by 'Uncle', to greet the

Governor's party, and his pilot. It was my first encounter with the Lion, the head of the pride, of Kenya. It is difficult to identify the essence of distinction or presence. Sir Philip Mitchell had all the attributes customarily associated with that quality, save one. Although Dame Margery Perham had found him fascinating and attractive twenty years before, early in his brilliant African career, his physical impact did not now match the grandeur of power which he exuded and articulated in movement, and the precision and weight of spoken and written word. After writing a powerful Hobbesian agrarian homily in the *Kenya Weekly News*, he ended rhetorically with his hand on The Bible, "There is a Book for the business." The Governor came with his Chief Secretary, Gilbert Rennie, who had no outward pretensions but showed himself to be the ideal, diligent, absolutely reliable, Colonial Civil Servant, ready to record and implement the findings of the visit.

The social event of our year was played out at several levels. John Doull held up the Police side with robust good sense; F. E. Beale treated us all to his uninhibited repertoire of Edwardian love songs, 'Uncle' engaged the Governor in current policy matters and I answered the Chief Secretary's queries about practical needs, the new Colonial Development 'Dixey' (the Hydrologist) schemes, etc., but I was overheard and blundered. "Balls, Gavaghan, I've never heard such unmitigated balderdash in my life! How can you speak of a one or a ten man station when you are surrounded by a human population for whom you are responsible?" Almost verbatim, I was thus upbraided for having spoken to Mr Rennie of the personal problems arising in our remote and isolated situation. I swallowed the rebuke and turned back to the Chief Secretary with the lesson digested. The party resumed in good voice and the visitors flew off at dawn in apparent satisfaction.

With safaris every month and occasional Sunday picnics down the Dawa by canoe, shooting livestock marauding crocodiles, and discouraging Dom palm destroyers as they slashed the bark to bleed alcohol fermenting juices, the time was packed with incident, but no great anxiety. There was constant wind of clan warfare in Ethiopia. Reports spread of Somali Youth League unrest in Somalia and I was warned of plans by Ahmed, the Murille Dubas, to decamp, possibly with others, over the Somalia border just across the airstrip. After checking intelligence with police officers, I attended the Dubas evening parade of about thirty in the *boma*. The Sergeant gave the orders, "Attention; open order march; ground arms; close order march; fall out!" They scattered to their houses in which rifles were usually held and the grounded rifles were placed in the Police armoury.

A report was sent to 'Uncle' by letter and lorry. Not unexpectedly he wrote back condemning the loss of *Heshima* visited upon the Dubas by what he termed my "nervous" action. He also accused the Kenya Police of stirring up intrigue. I explained and protested. He courteously responded, endorsing my "ideas on discipline" which he wished me to "introduce to Turkana", now added to his N.F.D. bailiwick to form the Northern Province, of which he became Provincial Commissioner. A few weeks later, after twenty months as DC Mandera, it was for me to hand over to Arthur Loggin, as kindly, sweet natured and tolerant a man as I had known. Whatever blunders I may have committed, I was happy that he would put them to rights and that I had added something to my inheritance from John Howard.

Since I first passed through Wajir there had been two changes of DC following Peter Derrick. The first was Tony Galton-Fenzi, his large, ruddy face glowing with optimism, because, or despite as 'Uncle' might have had it, of the presence and support of his flame haired, red lipped, wife Daphne. Tony's family name was celebrated on the huge granite ball which marked the central point of Nairobi and the end of the first motor car journey from Mombasa. His DO and office assistant had been small, precise, finger-tipping Gordon Hector, who had intercepted a circular advertising the vacant post of Chief Secretary, Seychelles, which he at once applied for and went on to fill with great career success. Next had come dark, toss-haired, Noel Hardy, Gurkha Officer, baritone singer, romantically awaiting the arrival of his own future Dawn.

I had instructions from the, now, Provincial Commissioner's Office in Isiolo to proceed at once to Nairobi to report to the Chief Native Commissioner about my transfer. Col. Marchant looked at me reflectively and said, "We have decided that Turkana would be too harsh a posting on top of nearly two years in Mandera, so off you go to Kakamega, to put your law exam to good use in the court there and experience a change of life among half a million peasant farmers and indigenous forests."

XI

KAKAMEGA DISTRICT IN NORTH KAVIRONDO/NYANZA NOVEMBER 1947–OCTOBER 1948

The District of Kakamega was a patchwork quilt of peasant farms in 'forty shades of green'. It was predominantly peopled by Bantu speaking Abaluhya, practising circumcision, but the generic word embraced a number of distinctively named traditional groupings, including Wanga, Maragoli, Bukusu/Kitosh and Teso, as well as Tiriki and a few Mount Elgon Maasai. Some distinctions were blurred and clarity was not aided by the use both of the frowned-upon generic *Kavirondo* and the locational description *Nyanza*, nor by the use of Abaluhya (Abbreviated as Luyia) as both a linguistic and tribal appellative. There were said to be 37 dialects in a population of nearly 700,000. This was numerically the largest single administrative unit in Kenya with occupation densities averaging 250, and in Maragoli up to 900 to the square mile.

District Administrative Headquarters had been established at Kakamega Township since the staging posts of caravan and rail at Mumia's and Bungoma on the route to Uganda had become redundant. The District spread north from the Nilotic Luo boundary to include Mount Elgon touching the Uganda border, across easterly to the European settled plateau of *Uasin Gishu* (Maasai for 'striped cattle'), and south again through the forested border with the Nilo-Hamitic Nandi. Many factors contributed to make the District one of the most closely developed and sophisticated in Kenya. There was the influence of the four Kingdoms of Uganda; Buganda, Bunyore, Ankole, and Toro, comparable in his own estimation to the Wanga King, *Nabonga Omuruki wa Basatsa* ('greatest of all men'), Mumia, who had led his Wanga people against the British, before accepting their less polemical and powerful title of Paramount Chief. There was the pervasive influence of Christian Missions, which salted competitive evangelism with education. There were the neighbouring settled farms extending labour skills, literacy and employment remittances. A particular stimulus had been the gold rush in the late 1920s focused on Rosterman's Mine, which attracted many outsiders to try their luck, bringing all kinds of technical skills, work opportunities and income, some of which remained. These together with productive land, industrious people and some indigenous structures of authority had eased the task of creative administration.

On the busy road to Kakamega from Kisumu I was put in mind of two great sadnesses. One was the recent suicide in Kakamega of my Irish headmaster friend from Kitui, Bill Glanville, crushed by his annual report. The other was the cruel irony of the death of the Reverend Wiffin, who had so hopefully travelled through Moyale from Addis Ababa. Before he had even arrived at his earthly destination, his light cross-country box-body Ford slid off the rain soaked, graded earth camber, turned over on his side and broke his neck. I was able only to attend his memorial.

The approach to the spacious township, Indian trading, administrative and residential, was beautifully laid out and lined everywhere with tall Eucalyptus, Nandi Flame and Jacaranda trees, with a verdant golf course as a central park. I went at once to the DC's office, a single storey building lining the upper side of the turn-off to the indigenous Forest Station. Below the road, standing alone, was the Court House which was also to be my office.

The District Commissioner, C. H. Williams, a monumental figure, was doubly well nick-named thus avoiding use of the reality Cyril Herbert. At Cambridge, where the one blot on his heroic escutcheon was a decisively unforgotten miskick in the 'varsity Rugby match, he was dubbed 'Bluff Hall' for his commanding mien, mistakenly rendered into Harold by which he became known. As DC he was generally called 'Ngombé', (generic Swahili for a bovine) because of his bulk not his brains. His hunched shoulder muscles usurped his neck and tendrils of russet hair overlaid a worried forehead. Innocent blue eyes were set in florid cheeks and quietly breathy utterances were economical. They hid a shrewd and lively mind, which could outmatch many an unwary sophisticate. His wife was Joy in name and nature, an unconventional Antipodean with two lively heifers, running free.

Two other District Officers came about the same time as I did, which could have caused some difficulty at work. One was a wartime Brigadier, Pat Hughes, married to 'Ronnie' (Veronica), one of the three formidable daughters of a celebrated Kenya pair, Oscar Watkins, a former Chief Native Commissioner, and Olga, a redoubtable European elected Member of Legislative Council. Pat, lean-faced, rangy and relaxed, added to his physical attributes an amazing natural talent for any sort of sport requiring co-ordination and eye, which gained him ready acceptance in company. He was popular, fair-minded and tolerant. Don Stones, ex-Wing Commander with a DFC, was hawkishly dark and handsome, his intense manner accentuated by a black eye patch. He was constantly protective of the comfort and contentment of his fragile, 1930s coiffed blonde beauty of a wife.

Our relative official positions were in a sense awkward. While I had over 3 years as DO and DC and had passed my law exams, they were both older and far superior in active service rank and military distinction. It worked out well enough, as the magisterial work and The Native Appeal Court, with outside law and order duties, made a clear division of functions and the apparatus of general administration and departmental co-ordination of over half a million people imposed a heavy load on us all, with inadequate staff and finance. The DC said not a word.

Life in the *boma* was lively and sociable, many officers being young and married. The long established Golf Club near Rosterman's Gold Mine provided a well equipped centre for tennis, squash, golf, bridge evenings and fun and games, in which the unconventional 'forty-niners', Cecil Trennery and George Flemmer, who still remained, kept the spirits alive and flowing. There was even room enough for class distinctions to be observed. My bungalow was one of several along the track overlooking the golf course and beside me was saturnine Jonah Jones the Health Inspector and bubbling, attractively horsy, Elsie. Ogoma was delighted to hire an underling to help us entertain properly and one day ushered in Khadija from Kisumu days, who had happily sought me out again. Luckily it was not when a giggle of merry wives bent on mischief invaded my open bedroom and upended me.

The Magistrate's Court work was fascinating. Two cases in particular stand out. Kaimosi, from where Mrs Reilly Cowan of Kisumu obtained her oyster nut oil for her Madeira cake, was the scene of a notable battle over a timber concession, involving an enormous 'Valkyrie' of an Afrikaner widow, Mrs van der Westerhuizen, and an Indian sawmiller, whom she claimed was exploiting 'her' forest without a licence. Unlettered but vocal and enraged, she had mounted the intruder's 'donkey engine' and smashed it with a sledgehammer. Police charge, 'malicious damage to property': counter charge, 'felling trees in Crown Forest without a licence': civil claims for compensation both ways: deposition of an unidentified crate of Black Label Whisky outside the court door: settlement proposed to both parties before any hearing; withdrawal of all accusations and claims, as well as the whisky to avoid bribery investigation and vigorous prosecution each way. The whisky disappeared and so did the protagonists.

Another case presented a terrible dilemma. A middle aged man returning on foot from Uganda was charged with murder. The Police case was watertight. There was no defence nor witness called; only a plea of 'not guilty'. The accused had been on the well trodden footpath round 14,000 foot Mount Elgon into Kenya, when he fell in with a village beer party which he was invited to join. A quarrel arose and an elderly drinker was violently assaulted and subsequently died. The traveller was averred by all present to the Police to have been responsible. My magisterial powers extended only to finding that a prima-facie case existed for committal to the Supreme Court. It clearly did, but I felt bound to add a footnote, however irregular, that the unanimity of evidence might itself be suspect in the circumstances. He was found guilty of murder and hanged.

Legal work also included the supervision of the Native Courts. The increasing importance of individual land ownership had made the people extremely litigious. A parallel indigenous judicial system had been encouraged and codified in the densely populated agricultural Districts, which evolved in tandem with the Local Native Councils as one embryonic application of the 1923 Devonshire Declaration of paramountcy of native interests. The Native Courts had gained impetus in the 1930s from the imaginative inspiration of a Provincial Commissioner, Sydney Herbert Fazan, also Secretary of the Carter Land Commission, who endowed many with classical 'temples' and amphitheatres where justice could be seen, if not always done.

A senior Administrative Officer appointed to co-ordinate the Native Courts visited us from Nairobi to inspect progress. His noble Celtic name was Desmond O'Hagan, but I saw him then rather as a black forest leopard pacing lithely across the broad courtroom, pausing one foot raised at each low window sill to hold forth from alternating profiles his compelling thought and vision. He left me with a sense of unawareness of my existence, until one fine day his aloofness gave way to simple courtesy and kindness. As for the courts themselves, I found tours of inspection with the appointed Appeal Court elders thoroughly enjoyable, particularly at the otherwise drab railway township of Bungoma, then emerging as an Administrative Division and later a District HQ. The elders were as engaging a bench of 'Justices of the Peace' as could be found, and were bastions of stability in a changing society. I would have laid money on their pragmatic observance of their traditional laws, regardless of any legalistic gloss put upon them by our parallel system.

Among the acknowledged leaders of the main tribal groups there were some notable personalities. At the vibrant roadside market of Mbale on the Kisumu road I met the local overlord, Lumadede, a squat yeoman businessman, a classic Irish 'Gombeen man', basking in the authority of patronage and public respect. He was of the Maragoli people who had once migrated from Bunyore and were noted for their social and educational advancement. They were smooth chocolate skinned and their cranial structure was indented at the level of their ears with pronounced frontal and occipital bulges. Their rather short legs were springy, with muscular calves giving a built in thrust from the toes, which added to a reputation for bounciness.

Towards the north was the old 'Cattle King', Senior Chief Sudi of the generic Abakusu, reputed to number his herds in tens of thousands. He farmed them out to his extremely extended and countless families, over whom he exercised unchallenged control; a dignified, shrewd, blanket-garbed, rancher patriarch. Among the Kitosh, between Bungoma on the Uganda railway line and Kimilili, I met a politically active Local Native Councillor and Native Court Chairman called Pascal Nabwana. His name and influence cropped up constantly in all kinds of dubious connections, including heavy indebtedness to the Roman Catholic Mission at Kibabii for his maize milling business. Tall, lantern jawed, saturnine and combative, his manner served notice of his involvement in cult disturbances to come.

On another plane stood Anglican Canon Jeremiah Awori, whom I found on his mixed farm towards Busia, the teeming barter centre on the Uganda border, across which the Teso clan of the Abakusu was spread. Canon Awori was a giant yeoman of Christ, wielding a spade in place of a crozier, gum-booted to shovel steaming muck for his tasselled stands of millet, while delivering sound pronouncements in stentorian tones. His very political minded son, known by his initials W.W. (after agrarian reformist Wycliffe), born to one of such stature, could not but be diminished by comparison.

Above all in historical perspective was Paramount Chief Mumia, with his lineage and titles going back for generations, who spanned the incoming tide of Empire and the separation of the East African Protectorate between Kenya and Uganda, leaving the Wanga Kingdom on the Kenya side. When I first met him he was well over ninety and blind, no longer the splendid warrior in Moslem style finery, but a fragile, rather shabby, figure in white cotton *kanzu* and filigreed hat, seated in a folding deck chair as his throne. It was strange and wonderful to meet a legend at his own place, Mumia's, and make a recommended libation of Beehive Brandy. His response showed that he had all his wits about him.

Mumias was still the ceremonial meeting place for all the chiefs and notables of Kakamega district, to which the Governor of Kenya, Sir Philip Mitchell, came to hold a huge *Baraza*. I was deputed to accompany him and sat on the rear seat behind the driver of the capacious Government House Daimler limousine. The Governor sat in the VIP seat behind the protection of the Police escort, a huge Nubian called Dismas, complete with red *tarboosh*. On the jump seat crouched rheumy old Senior Interpreter, Petro Okondo, his silver braided, black velvet *Kanzu* flecked with spittle, his embroidered hat askew on his straggly grey hair. *"Simama hapa"*, he growled beerily, tapping the driver smartly on the shoulder. "Why are we stopping here?" asked His Excellency, unperturbed. Whereupon Petro explained that every Governor holding a 'Baraza' at Mumias took the last opportunity to urinate behind a flourishing fig tree at the roadside. So H.E. did, feathers and all.

As the Baraza assembled I was approached by a small group of noticeably different Africans, smaller and less ebullient in manner. They were Kikuyu representatives of KAU, the Kenya African Union, on a recruiting tour with their newly returned leader, Jomo Kenyatta, and they asked formally to be seated. I said that they were welcome to attend, but I could not displace eminent local representatives gathering from afar for a concourse of their own people. Thus I missed an early opportunity to talk with a man on the brink of changing Kenya for ever. Instead I followed the Governor on his circuit of power, including the inauguration of a Mosque.

One day came a sudden rumour of an attack on the Catholic Mission at Kibabii in Kitosh country. It was said to have been the work of a rapidly growing quasi-religious cult called the *Dini ya Misambwa*. I was at once sent up there by the DC, who waited behind to obtain reinforcements from Kisumu, with a Police Inspector and a section of Askari in their blue jerseys. We also took six Tribal Police in their maroon, leather-shouldered pullovers, pill box hats with lion badge, khaki puttees above sliced lorry tire sandals. Each had a .303 rifle with 10 rounds and 'side arms' of long bayonets. All were crammed into a 3/4 ton green American Ford V8 pick-up, the small workhorse of Police and Administration.

The *Dini ya Misambwa* was in its pagan or spiritual dimension an expression of animistic reverence for beneficent 'departed spirits' who were believed to influence crops and seasons. I noted the names of three as; *Were Makhoba*; *Were Khakhaba*; and *Were Omwami* (also recorded as *Mrembi*). The appellation *Were* was likened by some to the Hebrew *Yahweh*, the unspoken 'he who is'. Aside from any Old Testament derivation, the spirits were seen as a Trinity symbolized on the back of chasuble-like vestments worn by priests of the cult and by staves split three ways at the top carried by devotees. The cult was thus a complex ferment of traditional animism, early perceptions of a creator God, fragmented Christian missionary teachings, nascent political resentments and aspirations, with a dash of cynical opportunism. Fanaticism and hysteria were further inflamed by a promise that bullets aimed at devotees would turn to water. The cult had been given shape and impetus three years earlier by the disputed release from Mathari Asylum near Nairobi, of a local man, Elijah Masinde, who returned to assume the mantle of prophet. Elijah had a limited Christian education, had been a Court Process Server and a celebrated football player, but had suffered some minor humiliations and setbacks which were sharpened by an obsessive belief in his god-given inspiration to lead his people against European power.

Our small emergency force, joined by the DC who had secured a Bren Gun with two magazines, arrived at the Kibabii Mission to find the Austrian Father-in-Charge in a state, since a huge crowd had assembled not far away threatening to burn the mission to the ground that night. We went over to the fringe of the mob and sent in an oral message by one less hysterical that I would like to come and talk to their leaders. The reply was that I would be welcome but should not expect to return with my head. The DC and I decided against this suggestion and, with his agreement, I gave our party, totalling a dozen by now, the command to fix bayonets with maximum ostentation. Extended order gave us a frontage of about thirty yards. A Magistrate's Order to disperse shouted in Swahili was followed by a very slow advance with bayonets extended, which brought us to within pricking range of those nearest. Fortunately they seemed cumulatively disposed to retreat into the mass, encouraged by advice from our Tribal Police Corporal that bayonets did not turn to water. It was 'Ngombe' himself who reported laconically to author Negley Farson that, "We walked them away."

They did not move far afield so I parked an open lorry overnight in the driveway of the Mission facing the gate with headlights on giving the Bren gun, visibly mounted over the cab, an illuminated line of fire. Despite much wild shouting and leaping around blazing fires the night passed without ado and by dawn fanatics had become farmers. Only the Prophet Elijah and his acolytes had made off towards Malakisii trading centre on the foothills of Mount Elgon. A further violent confrontation took place there between Elijah's adherents and a detachment of Kenya Police under an experienced fifty-year-old Assistant Superintendent, 'Johnny' Walker. In danger of being overwhelmed at close quarters, he gave the order to fire while felled to the ground by an assailant as he fired his revolver. Eleven cult members were killed but Elijah and his bodyguard were seen to make their escape up the mountain to the east.

Kenya Police Inspector, 'Doug' Espie, and I thereupon took off from Kimilili with a full platoon in hopes of intercepting the cult leaders as they crossed the mountain. Doug was a quietly determined Scot, of pawky humour and that freckled orange hue, burnt but not cooked, with washed pebble eyes found only among the Celts. After many hours of lung and thigh bursting climb, at around eleven thousand feet we gave up the search as fruitless in such an impenetrable fastness only to learn to our chagrin that Elijah* and a few followers were believed to be in a prepared 'foxhole' in the foothills, where he was later apprehended. The confused and fanatical convulsion near Mount Elgon on the border of Uganda, led me to venture into that pearl of a country. Its proud Kingdoms had seemed to travellers to be an exemplar for Africa of beauty, fertility and organized well-being, enhanced by the dignity and grace of women, with their superb shoulders and swaying gait. There was some anxiety that the heady lees of the *Dini ya Misambwa* might have left some sediment among the Abakusu living astride the border, but the cult seemed to have headed eastward within Kenya, where it burst out under a new leader.**

I regretted not having a dutiful reason to reach Kampala, the city of many hills, with Makerere University the first beacon of tertiary education

*Elijah Masinde was deported first to Lamu then to Marsabit in the Northern Province. Freed by President Kenyatta in 1963, he was readmitted to an asylum in 1980, persisted in his vision until his death aged 77. He 'earned' a *Times* Obituary on 10 June 1987.

**In 1949 a recrudescence of the 'Dini ya Misambwa' occurred in Marakwet District under a new prophet, Lukas Kipkoech, resulting in the killing by spears of the incoming DC, Alan Stevens, two Police Officers, Taylor and Cameron, and a Constable. 29 Suk were killed by rifle fire. It became known as the 'Kolloa Affray'.

in East Africa, but could only decently justify going as far as Tororo, the limit of Teso occupation. There I met again the redoubtable H. H. Aitken last encountered on local leave in Mombasa. He was, as its notice board announced, the sole, self regulating proprietor of the Tororo Hotel, famed far and wide for its idiosyncratic perfections. The hotel was a charming thatched Devonshire cottage with shaped eaves hugging the bedroom windows. It nestled quaintly beneath the solitary rearing phallus of Tororo Rock.

Mr Aitken was everywhere, as like as not at the door to greet the weary traveller. Once the Governor of Uganda, whom he did not like, turned up unannounced with his ADC on route for Kenya only to be referred to the next hotel, wherever that might be. There were empty rooms. The Governor was Sir Philip Mitchell, later to take command in Kenya. On other occasions guests, who enquired the tariff were puzzled to learn that a room with a bath was 20/- a night, against one without at 25/-. A matter of his personal taste for cleanliness. A late arrival would involve the entire kitchen and dining staff being turned out to serve a full menu, regardless of protestation. Mr Aitken would be at hand with a silver tray and ivory handled brush to catch any carelessly dropped cigarette ash and a tasteful 'sampler' at eye level beside lounge chairs would set out the proper behaviour of a hotel guest. He was a martinet who offered and expected perfection. His memory lived on.

Back again in Kakamega, I was deputed by 'Ngombe' to escort the celebrated American writer, Negley Farson, with Mrs Farson around the prosperous 'alien' Somali village during the taking of the National Census, which was not a popular enquiry among the elusive Somali. He had written *Behind God's Back* on a previous visit to Kenya and then showed a perspicacity and critical insight not always appreciated by the authorities. Personally he veered between crude insensitivity and a sympathetic instinct and prescience in his relations with Africans of all conditions. Given to wearing shorts he would display a ghastly ulcer cavity in his knee, drink and eat intemperately and yet transmute his acute observations into elegant and evocative prose, in which he owed much to the calm observation and meticulous recording of his wife. He sketched our Somali 'boudoir' visits with felicity and embarrassing kindness to me in his current book, *Last Chance in Africa*, which was a farseeing political travelogue covering most of Kenya. He painted a picture of Jomo Kenyatta, well before Mau Mau, more humanly open eyed and open minded than any other before or since. Perhaps he felt an affinity.

I returned to the North West of the District, the heavy-soiled maize growing area of the Kitosh with an Agriculture Department Research Centre and Township at Kimilili, whence 'Doug' Espie and I had set off up Mount Elgon. There New Zealand farmer Peter Thoms, laughing optimist, mounted on his cross country mule of a model T Ford, its fuel mix of paraffin and petrol fed direct through a tube from a can on the roof, encouraged co-operative ploughing by tractor. His father, aged 75, I found mending the corrugated iron roof. He had been Colonel Commandant of the Shanghai Defence Force of the International Settlement and above their open fireplace hung a vivid, Caravaggio-style, presentation oil painting of a ceremonial parade marking his retirement. It throbbed with the emotional tension of the participating forces' Commanding Officers seated in the foreground looking skyward in consternation at Japanese Zero fighter planes heading inland to the Sino-Japanese war.

It was a short drive from Kimilili to join the main road from Eldoret to Kitale where I could check on any infiltration of the *Dini ya Misambwa* and where my old friend from Kisii, 'Jaap' Molenaar, was now installed as Father-in-Charge at the Catholic Church. I booked in at the old established Kitale Hotel where I met the two attractive receptionists from the local settler community, Sonia Fletcher and Cecily Tofte. Cecily's stalwart Australian uncle Cedric and his wife Doreen had a lovely coffee and dairy farm towards the Cherangani Hills, which was just emerging from the lean wartime period when farmers ate *posho* (maizemeal) and depended on the 'cream cheque' for all other expenses. There was discreetly in the offing a substantial Afrikaner farmer's son and local Rugby hero, Bert Steyn, but after a friendly skirmish I was fortunate to find favour with Cecily and her uncle and aunt, if not yet of her distant parents, gentle accountant Jack and unquenchable Hilda. With a dispensation for a 'mixed' marriage granted by Bishop 'Pilipo' Scheffer, formerly of Kisii and now reluctantly elevated to Kakamega Diocese, we were married by Fr. Jaap at Kitale Church.

After a spell of shaking down to married life between the sometimes abrasive cultures of settlerdom and officialdom, enlivened by the social activities of Kakamega Club, we were shipped off to Oxford University to attend the Second Devonshire Colonial Service Course. It was to be my first training experience after over four years service already completed. Although I was not again posted west of the Great Rift Valley, I had served in all three of the then Districts of Nyanza, Luo, Kisii and Luyia, making up one quarter of the population of Kenya. The link with Nyanza was kept open by Ogoma agreeing to wait on our return.

XII

OXFORD UNIVERSITY
OCTOBER 1948–MAY 1949

Honeymoon at Malindi followed by home leave brought us in the autumn to Oxford University to attend what was effectively a post-graduate Colonial Service course. It was named after that Duke of Devonshire who, as Colonial Secretary, promulgated the 1923 doctrine of 'Paramountcy' in regard to conflicts of interest between 'natives' and the 'immigrant races' in Kenya. Having enjoyed only nineteen months of the Harkness Scholarship at St Andrews University before call-up, I was treated as matriculated at Oxford and admitted, rather grandly, to Cardinal Wolsey's Foundation, Christ Church College. I scarcely dared to enter it even to dine, (although for long afterwards I was recognized as a suitable source of contributions to the building fund).

We were lodged in a rambling university annexe, No.3 South Parks Road, close to Rhodes House. We rented a bed-sitting room on a step-up landing, opposite Peter Derrick, my Wajir neighbour, and his delightful wife Meg, of the old Kenya Le Blanc-Smith family. She unfailingly made the world seem a brighter place. From South Parks Road our son Kevin was born in the Radcliffe Infirmary. Cecily was held back for treatment to a breast ulcer while I fumbled with hand washing hairy cotton nappies, disinfecting and preparing feeding bottles of cod liver oil drops in milk, baby bathing, queuing for ration stamps and orange juice. I weakly gave in to each clamorous nightly demand from beside my couch, in order to get some sleep for the day's work. Having contracted a facial 'nappy rash' and sprouted a stubble I queued in the Radcliffe Royal Infirmary for the scrutiny of a woman Consultant, briskly trailing learner skin specialists. "Well, Miss X," she barked, eyeing me with distaste. "Is it coccus or fungus?"

The course work covered a wide scope and consisted of subject lectures, visits, debates and required papers. It was mostly of the current orthodoxy, rather than exploratory or innovative. Colonial history was Professor Vincent Harlow, urbane, silver haired and bland. I remembered nothing I did not know. Colonial Economics was Professor Sally Herbert Frankel, a blunt, bluff South African, to whom the concept that a string of economists placed end to end would never reach a conclusion was unknown. He usually did. Local Government came alive through the fascinating cameos of Senior Lecturer Bryan Keith-Lucus, culled from the byways of history and made somehow pithily relevant to our Kenya experience.

Anthropology *was* Professor Evans Pritchard, acknowledged authority on the Nilotic people of South Sudan. His white polo-neck under Master's gown set off a heroic profile, framed by dashingly backswept hair, to the rapt gaze of his mainly female class. In private I rashly questioned his statement that the Samia people of Nangina, where I had stayed with old Luhya-speaking Père Cöenan, were Nilotic, demonstrated with excitingly mouthed titles like 'Jadwóng' (elder) and 'Ruóth' (king). He dismissed my temerity with a downward glance as if I might be a circumcised Bantu. Mistaken or not, I ceased my voluntary attendance and moved over to genial Professor Max Gluckmann of Manchester, who was illuminating, even once lit up, on the birth rate of the migrant wives of exploited mineworkers of Basutoland (Lesotho); twice a year, he said, in an optimistic moment.

It was a time when a Course Staff Member, a Mr Carne, could still introduce discussion on the current debate about the relative sizes of European and African brains and the significance to intelligence. More practically relevant were the sessions with Dr G. B. Masefield who showed us how to measure the pH factor of acid in the soil of an abandoned monastery, which had not been tilled for eight hundred years, of significance in assessing tea growing potential in the Kikuyu uplands. He also gave us to read his own new book on *Tropical Agriculture* and 'the farming ladder' about the beneficial effect of mobile poultry sheds in spreading highly acid droppings over dead, chalky soil. I chose for my required paper for him a twenty page thesis on Tsetse fly and Trypanosomiasis in Africa, which proved directly applicable in my next posting at Taveta.

We all felt pretty good about being addressed by Lord Milverton, formerly Governor of Nigeria, and Sir Grantley Adams, Prime Minister of Barbados; grandees both. Discussion followed on a most important policy direction, also taken up by Margery Perham, as to whether to induct future African leaders into the 'scaffolding' of Provincial Administration, as for instance ex-Sergeant Major Isaak Okwirri appointed a DO in Nyanza Province, or to promote their advancement through the elective institutions of Local Native Councils. It was of historic importance that the former course was pursued, leaving the way open for the third option, the wayward political stirring and all it brought in train. We also had an inspirational address from mustachioed Major 'Tony' Swann, the appropriate District Commissioner for the 'fighting tribe' of the Kipsigis. He was a dashing Prince Rupert, rather than a Roundhead of the administration in turbulent times, and inherited a baronetcy.

In plenary meetings and in social groups there was a noticeable tendency for Colonial Officers from West and East Africa to be divided into sheep and goats respectively, in the attitudes both of liberal academics and themselves. The shorthand basis could be put simplistically as 'black man's country' versus 'white man's country', but this almost completely discounted the 'Devonshire Declaration' and the beneficial developments associated with white settlement. Certainly there was inter-Colony moral rivalry amounting also to service snobbery. The Indian Civil Service held itself to be pre-eminent, followed not closely by the Sudan Political Service, with Kenya well trained 'pedigree gun dog' in the colonial kennels of the east, as against 'man's best friend' in the west.

In one meeting Dr Rita Hinden of the Fabian Bureau berated Kenya vigorously from the platform for its exploitation and repression, connived at by its Administration. I challenged her evidence, which provoked her to question when Kenya independence could be expected. "Between ten and twenty years," I rashly replied in my blind ignorance. (It was then 1948 and *Uhuru* [freedom] came in 1963!). An antidote to this stinging encounter was a meeting with the almost 'sublime' Margery Perham who, in the full flood of a life of unrivalled variety and distinction, was anchored as Director of the Oxford University Institute of Colonial Studies. She still stood on the liberal ground she had occupied in her close print encounter with Kenya settler born Elspeth Huxley, published in 1944 as *Race and Politics in Kenya*, but there had since been some exchanges of attitude. I found her superb in gum boots and have tried at length elsewhere* to do justice to the whole person whom I met. She took me into her back garden where she continued with the task of forking steaming manure, the fertile and the ethereal in unison, which seemed to convey an earthy understanding of our labours in Kenya.

Socially the Course was a cohesive group symbolized by a revival of the dark blue tie with gold *hartebeest* which I arranged with Walters the Tailors. The symbol was well chosen, but the human animal came in many shapes and sizes, as well as hues. John Drysdale from the British Somaliland Protectorate Administration was embarked on a uniquely dedicated career among the northern Somali in which our paths crossed many times. He conjured up the title 'Prinny' in his fruity utterance and his engaging fascination of gaze, as if in rapt attention at one's discourse. His own ideas he could express in unscripted poetry in the Somali language, with perfect glottal stops and gutturals. One late night after curfew I shouldered him over the high wall of Christ Church College into the waiting arms of the 'Progs' who failed to cushion his lubricated fall. At table my companion told me he knew Kitui, my first station, so I asked did he come across "old Slawkins"? "My uncle, Mr Slade-Hawkins, the District Commissioner," he responded coolly, until I revealed his uncle's pleasing Kamba nickname, *Bwana Kôlôtô* or "He who places his finger along his nose', which indeed he did most knowingly.

One day the housekeeper came to me in distress because she could not

---

*In *Corridors of Wire* published privately in 1995. Obtainable from the author.

obtain admission to the room of a Forestry officer from Nigeria, called Akpata. She asked me to accompany her with a master key in his absence, in case some embarrassment arose. We found a rather sad disarray with a litter of photos of a young woman, his wife perhaps. We set matters to rights and I said nothing save to a genial pair of Malay Rajahs, who were invited course members. They took Akpata on one side in the most tactful manner and explained that a course mark of 100% was not to be obtained by full success in studies alone, but by half in course results and half in social relations. He seemed much happier for the friendly interest they had shown in him.

Near the end of our eight months at Oxford I had a clash with authority in the person of the Senior Proctor. This arose from my arranging with Course Supervisor Giles, to go to the Earl's Court Motor Show in London to order a suitable car within my pocket or loan entitlement for delivery on return to Kenya. Meanwhile, on behalf of the *hartebeest*, I had put in a request to the Senior Proctor for a social function at Rhodes House. On receipt of a summons to present myself on the same day as our visit to the Motor Show, I called in advance to excuse myself and ask for an alternative appointment. "Proctorial summons takes precedence over all other functions." The stolidly repeated injunction from a bowler-hatted guardian at the door left no room for discussion and I penned a formal message of my regret that I would be unable to attend. The balloon went up on my return and I dutifully prostrated myself before the gowned eminence, while contriving to represent myself as among the mature, married and temporary students with overseas service, whose needs sometimes differed from those of traditional undergraduates. "Proctorial summons ...!" The carefully chosen car, a utility Standard Vanguard van, proved back in Kenya a worse disaster, even at less than £500. It was clearly designed as a combustible vacuum cleaner for human propulsion on a cotton wool carpet.

XIII

MOMBASA HQ
MAY 1949

On our landing at Mombasa I was temporarily assigned to revise the European electoral roll, although recreate, even resurrect, would have been a better definition. I was allocated the huge corner room upstairs in the original massive walled DC's office, with a wonderful teak and brass ceiling propeller fan. It overlooked both the huge fig trees in 'Government Square' and the low built Coast Agents' offices, which were important to our leave, our travel and our emoluments. On the slope down to the spacious wood-framed Mombasa Club were the impressively elevated Law Courts, complete with coat of arms, and the steep battlements of Fort Jesus, the historic 1592 Portuguese bastion against the ding-dong maritime incursions of the marauding Arabs from Muscat and Oman, and Zanzibar. Time had given the redoubt of bloody warfare a crusted coral hue, which glowed warmly at the rising and setting of the sun, when its walls echoed with the leather thunk and excited cries of young football players.

The European roll presented few problems. An obvious need was to strike off the considerable numbers of registered Mombasa residents, who had died or departed since the last pre-war census and to attack the task of ascertaining and recording newly eligible voters. A separate project was to carry out a house to house census of the growing Swahili village across the southerly ferry to Likoni. This was a thoroughly enjoyable exercise in futility. Most houseowners were at work or untraceable by questioning. The mud and thatch houses were clean, spacious and in orderly array. The women and old folk at home were charmingly conversational and improved my Ki-Swahili. I drew up plans and vague estimates and took 'Tusker' beer at the nearby bungalow of my hospitable mother-in-law, Hilda Tofte, overlooking the creek where the docking ocean liners sailed gracefully past.

This second and longer spell in Mombasa left me with an appreciation of the then slow-paced, orderly Protectorate in which the communities moved smoothly and without apparent friction within accepted roles. The 5,000 odd European residents and visitors were the pie crust, with the Administration, Law Officers and Municipal Executives as topping. They included the professions and entrepreneurs, such as The Old East African Trading Company, shipping and safari agents, produce brokers, oculists, chemists, car dealers, jewellers, hoteliers and the like. The retail trade was otherwise almost entirely Asian, with names like Choitram, Gidoomal and the lampooned Rahimtullah Uppabhoy. The Arabs commanded the seasonal monsoon dhow fleets and their imports, notably Persian carpets, to the Bonded Warehouse. The Municipal Markets for fish, vegetables, fruit and flowers, well built and conducted, were meeting places for all races, with the adjoining streets jammed with delivery barrows, laden with produce and *makuti* (palm thatching). A still thriving part of the town was the Kilindini docks and railway terminus where the BISN Line (British India Steam Navigation) ships, *Modassa*, *Madura* and so on, were familiar and welcome callers, whether bringing expatriate employees back from leave or the more select and expensive tourists. There were also the larger white Union Castle and Lloyd Triestino ships plying as far as the Cape.

The Port Captain of Mombasa, Captain Hamley RN, cut a considerable figure. This was not only due to his command of the unique Indian Ocean anchorages, deep water harbours, warehousing and loading facilities linked to the railway terminus at Kilindini docks, serving a traffic catchment area from Uganda, Tanganyika and Mount Kenya. It was also because his penetration into every facet of commercial life was backed by the firepower of a sea-dog among landlubberly colonials. He also sailed the figurehead of a comely, russet and freckled daughter, Diana, who allowed the many admirers of her limpid green eyes to careen and paint and polish and varnish her yacht to, not quite, their hearts' desire. Captain Hamley's span of command planted the seed of an idea in my mind which years later germinated in a plan for sea-borne training courses for future African bureaucrats.

I only met one Arab on a social footing. He was Seyyid Seif bin Salim, of the powerful Zanzibari Burgash family, who had a four storey house on the left of the narrow lane past the Mombasa Club on the way to the Bonded Warehouse square. He was an Arab 'David' in beauty of face and form and had a Gymnasium with wall bars hung with boxing gloves and, strangely, a grand piano. Sadly I was moved on before friendship could take root.

We had a chance to repeat our honeymoon visit to Malindi, Vasco da Gama's 1498 port of landing. We drove over the wooden ferries, chain-propelled by chanting and stamping Public Works Department old age choristers, fuelled by largesse, past the mysterious, overgrown ruins of the lost city of Gedi and through the country of the Giriama people, which had been ravaged in the nineteenth century by the warlike Mazrui clan of settled coast Arabs. Malindi was both a leisurely Arab township lightly administered and serviced by a District Officer, and a haven of sea level rest for up country farmers and civil servants. Visitors vied with each other to stay in Lawford's palm thatched elegance standing on an eminence outside the village and only a few paces from the tidal surf. The beach of firm sand, bespangled with ripples of silver mica dust, was broad and long, extending in a golden curve to the gaping mouth of the Sabaki River, which daily disgorged its load of red soil eroded from the Kikuyu highlands and spread a menacing stain of silt far into the Indian Ocean.

The Eden Rock Hotel was constructed as his eyrie by a notorious eagle of Kenya society, Lord Carberry, known only as 'J.C.' Carberry. His hotel was well named for his sybaritic life based on the accumulated 'rocks' of bootlegging during American prohibition and other dubious adventures. He was a grizzled but powerful bronze Neptune like figure as he strode, stripped after snorkelling, harpoon in hand, into his semi-circular private bar. His manner compounded of machismo and noblesse was enhanced by a broken nose and a nasal drawl between Eton and Los Angeles. He was sardonic, amusing and cool as he sipped his whisky, soda water and cold skim milk.

In the bar I met a charming retired doctor to whom 'J.C.' was indulgent, and whom I helped overcome the problem of holding up the wall, his trousers and his functioning member as a pink beach crab scuttled into his underpants on the floor. He recovered rapidly from the shock of my intrusion on his privacy with another pink gin and passed out on one of the Roman reclining couches set into the half moon wall. On the tidal beach below I was fortunate to have to step over Venus Aphrodite in the altogether at the foot of a rocky outcrop, evidently asleep or waiting for Neptune. This was the irresistible 'Junie' Carberry who with her step-daughter Juanita,* was later privy, but not party to, the infamous goings on the night that 'Joss' Hay, 22nd Earl of Erroll and Premier Earl of Scotland, was shot in his car near Karen Blixen's house, to set in train one of the great 'unsolved' murder cases of the century, in which the aggrieved husband, Sir 'Jock' Delves Broughton, 10th Baronet, was tried and found not guilty, only to commit suicide in the Adelphi Hotel in Liverpool.

I was also introduced to a droll and engaging pair with the timeless, joyous pathos of Laurel and Hardy. Sam Spencer was a shrewd investor and prosperous Kenya businessman, whose addiction to Rugby had not succumbed to baldness nor to bulges nor to spluttering gums, all of which he would bring to bear in a 'scrum down' when fully charged at the bar. His faithful Laurel, small, hesitant and full of innocent wonderment was Cyril Breskel, to whom fortune had come in a £25,000 sweepstake, which gave him personal pride as they spent it liberally together. They were boon friends of Hilda Tofte.

Halfway back to Mombasa we stopped at Kilifi District Headquarters on the Kilifi creek to pay respects to Jim and Nora Lurman, 'great' in-laws, who had retired to a bungalow with a veranda looking over the Indian ocean toward his distant homeland, Tasmania, though she was rural English. They were the hewn rock of sound decency and their slow, warm, kindly burr found no need for haste in articulating opinions which would brook no other. They were ageless and indestructible and Jim's monumental

---

*Juanita's mother was Maia, whom 'J.C.' had taught to fly and who died in an air accident on the Ngong road, near which he founded the Maia Carberry Nursing Home.

nose sprouted the vigour of seeds that lay within him.

Before approaching the straggling tourist beach-hotel fringe and the select residential area by the Nyali pontoon bridge, we turned off to Mtawapa creek to call on Edward Rodwell, a distant connection of the Toftes, and his wife Olivia. He had established a niche for himself as local chronicler in an unbroken weekly series in the *Mombasa Times*, entitled 'Coast Causerie'. He offered carefully researched nuggets of historical information and graceful commentary in a style reminiscent of Betjeman's lightly serious versifications of society and the commonly held beliefs and institutions that he loved. Exquisitely courteous citizen of the Coast Protectorate and respected Editor, it was appropriate that he should be awarded the Portuguese accolade of Prince Henry The Navigator. (The later Kenya title of 'Moran [warrior] of the Burning Spear', albeit inspired by Kenyatta's sobriquet, less well reflected his personal style.)

After this elegant summation of our lotus-eating interval beside the Indian Ocean, we headed inland, still within Coast Province, to take up my deferred substantive appointment as District Officer, Taveta sub District, within the Administrative District of Taita-Taveta.

XIV

TAITA-TAVETA DISTRICT
COAST PROVINCE
JUNE 1949–MARCH 1950

Voi was a characterless Township and railway junction, one hundred road miles north west of Mombasa beside the main line to Nairobi. In daylight it appeared as if crouched beneath the 7,000 foot massif known as the Taita Hills, which harboured the 60,000 strong Bantu-speaking people called Taita. By night the station rest house was a cacophony of whistles, shouts, reversing pistons and escaping steam, in which the cold invaded the blankets of passengers awakened by the din and the lights. Taveta sub-District lay sixty miles to the west of Voi along the rail link to the inter-territorial boundary with Tanganyika. Just within the Kenya border was a small forested enclave occupied by the Taveta people. On the face of it a posting to Taveta was something of a side track in both location and experience. It turned out quite otherwise.

Successive caravans of the arch slave trader, Tippu Tip, and of the Church Missionary Society had trekked inland from Zanzibar in quest of bodies and souls. They skirted the rich and populous Chagga country beyond the plateau township of Moshi (meaning 'smoke') which lay beneath 19,000 foot Kilimanjaro, looming white-domed in the clouds, apocryphally called the Kaiser's birthday cake from the indulgent Queen Victoria. Over the Kenya border they had traversed the fertile glen of the isolated Taveta tribal group, densely forested and abundantly watered from the glacier fed streams, which filtered beneath the encrusted toes of the ancient lava flow from the once belching cones of the great mountain. Their landmarks were the pinnacled fastnesses of the Taita, poised above the converging caravan routes from the port of Dar-es-Salaam (Haven of Peace) and from the dhow anchorages of Mombasa, which then proceeded upcountry as one.

North West from the intersection Bishop Krapf of the CMS Mission at Rabai, who had first sighted Kilimanjaro, then espied from Mwendwa's *kraal* (village) the distant snow and basalt outline, known to the local Kamba trackers as *ki-i-nyaa* (the wing of the cock ostrich — with black and white plumage). He noted this in phonetic German as *Kegnia*, the source of much righteous disputation about the correct way to pronounce the African nation of Kénya, or Keenya, as the settlers had it.

At the Tanganyika border in 1916 German and 'native' troops under the undefeated gadfly, General Von Lettow Vorbeck, had made an incursion through Taveta towards Maktau siding, to be turned back at a desperate trench battle on Salaita Hill, with British and Kenya forces under the former Boer war General Smuts advancing from Singido. A certain romance attached thereafter to the otherwise unremarkable sub-District of Taveta. The intrepid District Officer was S. H. La Fontaine, later Colonel, DSO and MC. Upon learning of the German advance, he had climbed on the roof of his bungalow and single-handed fired his .303 rifle as they appeared. No doubt dismayed at this temerity they returned fire and moved on to the main battle, but leaving behind evidence of their bullets in the thick mud walls of La Fontaine's house and the prison.

From Kahé junction on the Tanga to Moshi line a vital railway link had been established between Tanganyika and Kenya, designed to take freight between Moshi and Voi consisting of Chagga coffee, Taveta timber and European fibres and minerals. The flat, undrained and vacant land around the Taveta oasis had been scheduled for settlement by Europeans and 150,000 acres, in three adjacent blocks, had been allocated to a Colonel Ewart Grogan. Sisal, an *Agavé* plant indigenous to Yucatan in Mexico, had been imported from Florida by German and Greek settlers in northern Tanganyika as a plantation crop to meet a resurgence of world demand for natural fibres. It flourished in the propitious climate and easily cultivated soil below Kilimanjaro and in the main redeveloped Taveta estate of Col. Grogan. Fortuitously, an unrelated indigenous fibrous plant called variously *Sansiveria*, beloved of elephant for bulk food and digestive roughage, and thus at second hand of cleansing dung-beetles, already grew wild on his lake Jipé estate. He was so provided by nature with a cash crop, ready to be decorticated free on his Ziwani sisal estate machinery, and marketed as fibre to pay for the replanting of sisal on the cleared Lake Jipé acres. Hydraulic engineers and contractors had been hired from Greece, Cyprus and Italy, and others brought in by the Church Missionary Society, to instal the network of irrigation canals, bridges and bunds required for leaching the heavy impervious soils and deposited salts to render them productive. Sawmillers from Tanganyika and Nairobi were vying for exploitation, and destruction, of the unique hardwoods in the Taveta rain forest, still in the hands of the indigenous owners.

The first formal attempt at reconciling the traditional grazing and watering needs of the Maasai and wildlife around Amboseli with the establishment of the Tsavo (West) National Park had been initiated by the new Kenya National Parks Department under Colonel Mervyn Cowie, of an old settler family. His part was celebrated in the film *Where No Vultures Fly*, with screen idol Anthony Steel, whose shorts famously revealed his all, and co-star Dinah Sheridan. (She went one further in giving birth to a then unimagined Chairman of the Conservative Party called Jeremy Hanley.)

Against this unfolding back-drop, of which I was still largely unaware, I turned off at Voi to report to District Commissioner's Offices at Wundanyi, high in the Taita Hills, before making my way in learning stages onward to Taveta. The DC was Peter Walters and his wife was unusually named Ayesha after the priestess of the flame 'She who must be obeyed' in the novel *She* by Rider Haggard, inspired while he was visiting his brother Jack Haggard, Vice-Consul in Lamu. Peter was tall, dark and well favoured, somewhat cool and aloof, with a supercilious wit accentuated by a slant of the upper lip over slightly prominent teeth. He had the enviable gift of keeping on cordial terms with our masters. He clearly knew his job well and kindly left me with a free rein in Taveta, while calling on me to help with Taita land cases in the hills.

While on such a tour, I visited an eccentric 80-year-old Bulgarian called Verbi. He had worked his passage with the first CMS Evangelists, who had successfully established their schools and churches to which he had long acted as a general factotum and lay preacher. He walked daily 10 miles to and from the vegetable market along the precipitous tracks. He had a youngish Australian wife and a blond daughter of about 10, as well as a son in his 50s whom he said was a Colonel in the East African forces. He showed me a quarto bound volume, dated 1897, of copies of the *Taveta Chronicle*, said to be the first Kenya newspaper. One full page advertisement was for Roses Lime Juice, its embossed bottle tilted enticingly with a caption beneath describing it as "A Sure Preventative of Malaria"; with whisky perhaps!

The not so Reverend Verbi had a macabre way of fixing episodes of his life on a time scale. One evening he had heard sounds as of a fluttering bird pecking at the ripening cobs in the maize patch outside his house. Determined to put an end to it he let off both barrels of his shotgun. A wild commotion was followed by deathly silence, a moment to which he often referred like a calendar as: "I can't remember whether it was before or after I shot my mother-in-law." His successful defence at trial for murder was that he had mistaken her for a black crow.

The tortuous descent from the Taita Hills to the level dirt highway, which ran beside the branch railway along the valley between Voi and Taveta, set up acute nausea. The balancing fluid between the ears and the churned up gastric juices swashed like bilge in response to each surge and swoop of the truck, poised dizzily over nothingness at every hairpin bend. I turned off at Mwatate siding to call in briefly at two adjoining Kyanite mines at Merca inside the new National Park. Kyanite had only recently been found in Kenya. It was an ingredient in the production of a rare aluminosilicate, which was called Mullite because it was only found naturally deep buried in the Hebridean Isle of Mull. There was an increasing demand for Mullite in manufacturing refractory porcelains, thus making the extruded hump of almost too pure Kyanite in Merca hill of exceptional value, especially as so accessible to both transport and labour. Production was about fifteen hundred tons of Kyanite a month, at a sale price of four to seven pounds a ton; say £75,000 to £100,000 a year.

K

Figures were not discussed openly in the cut-throat rivalry of the investment companies, which extended to the employees, some 1,000 Africans and 20 Europeans in all. A huge crushing and smelting machine for conversion to finished Mullite had been set up by Sir Charles Markham Bt. in the teeth of American opposition since they wanted to buy cheap and raw, while India was producing a usable quality of unsmelted Kyanite. There was on site an atmosphere of 'Klondyke' excitement, while sample products were tested. There was something of the alien and bizarre, almost burlesque, about social existence at the two mines of Merca, the smaller run by General Phillips and a Brigadier Blood, the larger, Kenya Kyanite, by Sir Charles Markham, Bt., and his financial guru, Dr Parsons.

Sir Charles, whose family fortune derived from coal, giving their name to the famed Markham Colliery, was a rollicking giant of a man, whose shorts could have sailed a yacht. His twin brother was said to have fared badly at the breast, being unkindly known as 'the unweaned calf'. I later rashly joined the 'weaned' one at the bar of the Pink Elephant Hotel in Moshi until conscious of little else but the blistered skin of my elbows, while he quaffed on regardless. His Mine Manager was a Colonel Bruce-Smith, whose villainous sideburns belied the gentle pride in the photo he showed me of his superlatively beautiful daughter, Philippa, aged 17 who died tragically young in a flash flood in Maasai country, after having married a young coffee residue extractor in Kiambu.

There was a (more or less) European club for entertainment of every kind, at which I danced once with forty-fiveish Beryl Markham, celebrated Atlantic flier and racehorse trainer. I knew nothing of any dispute, about her authorship or her husband Schumacher's, of her epic account *West with the Night*. I found her very tall, cool and queenly, gliding rather than dancing, with translucent blue eyes, seemingly more concerned with contemplation of self than she was to create an impression on others; a cat that walked alone and chose her companions. By way of contrast I was scorched, unresistingly, by a writhing Italian harpy, slinky in black satin, with molten scarlet lips and rather bad, carnivorous teeth, due no doubt also to the rime of the tobacco smoke which lingered with her eager murmurings.

Having left Merca at dawn I pulled in at Maktau Station which had an Indian Railways type *Dak* bungalow traditionally located at the post stages of the old mail coaches. The Maktau one, with Goanese staff, was renowned for its delicious bacon and egg breakfasts. So fortified I drove without further deviation past the roadside signs to Colonel Grogan's Jipé and Ziwani plantations and his Sainté Irrigation Scheme. Approaching Taveta we passed a kind of 'secret garden', concealed behind a dust barrier of tall grasses strapped across by slivers of bamboo. A raised board carried the locally incongruous name of 'Goodwillies', a small irrigated enclave which had been ceded by the former settler owner to the Taveta land unit. A few reputed descendants appeared to be of mixed Scottish blood, or to have albino genes, exhibiting very white, reddish mottled skin, set off by coarse, vibrantly orange hair and pale lashed, strikingly blue eyes.

At last, we crossed the Lumi river bridge through a narrow forest belt and into Taveta village, which hardly rated the status of Township. The single street was a 60 yard dash past a dozen raised wooden and corrugated iron Indian shops, and one manual petrol pump, requiring a change of arms to fill a tank. It was also the main road to Tanganyika. The few Government buildings were in a rough semi-circle, across a scruffy football area from the shops and at the foot of a low ridge, on which the few civil servants had their bungalows. There was an old prison and a small Cottage Hospital, both casual labour rather than casualty.

I was due to have taken over from the decisive, roseately beaming, Tony Galton-Fenzi, whom I had known at Wajir, but he had been transferred after a brief spell in Taveta while we were held back in Mombasa. The DO's office, shoddily designed and built of concrete blocks, had five rooms, a hallway and softboard ceilings under corrugated iron, which had not been bat-proofed at the gables. The result was a sludge of dung and urine weighing down and staining the soft boards with oozing, stinking ammonia — 14 wheelbarrow loads of it. The office staff was headed by the indispensable Goan team; thrusting and vigorous Peter de Souza, staid and elderly Cashier, John Barros, and pert young assistant Clerk, Claro Menezes, the last unusually inclined to tears when pulled up. Taveta Office Boy, Seng'ondo Kariiro, was, as I reported, "the only thing to come between the DO and insanity," in controlling the files.

The numbers of non Taveta people in the sub-District had grown rapidly to over 4,000 Africans and 100 Europeans, overloading the indigenous Taveta population, without counting the infiltration of Maasai, Chagga and Paré from Tanganyika and of nearby Kamba and Taita within Voi district. While the District Officer had no direct responsibility in regard to the affairs of the commercial enterprises, there were many matters of law and order, taxation, registration, employment, public health, livestock disease, safety regulations, communications, water and land usage, grazing rights, game control, timber exploitation and so on, in which the Administration had the right and duty to exercise legal powers.

In 1949 I recorded that, "race relations have been remarkably good throughout the year," among all the heterogeneous and polyglot community. I also made a general note of the effects of the juxtaposition of the multiple exotic influences upon the Taveta community. "While the estates, which might be called the limbs of the district, are flourishing the trunk or backbone is weakening and disintegrating ... it seems clear that in the interest of the whole community, greater attention must be paid to the organization and development of the Native area than hitherto." A classic case of the principles of the Devonshire Declaration presented itself.

Small as the 'vanishing' tribe was, it was sad that "Chief Leng'iriama just escapes being a non-entity", especially as the Chairman of the Native Tribunal, was as sinister and menacing a character as his name suggests, Sowéné Lorógwa. There was a simple and effective structure below the Chief based on three Headmen, each controlling five *Mitaas* or 'lands'. The fifteen *Mitaas* were guided by the *Njama*, a standing committee of thirty five elected from the 2,000 or so adult male members of the tribe, meeting in a General Council called the *Isanga*, which also admitted residents of other tribes. It was traditional and democratic, but not up to the preservation and advancement of the little society of the forest and the streams in their chosen habitat, under threat of encroachment by the great estates.

Before bearding the formidable Colonel Grogan in his den, I called to see his manager, Mr H. H. Trafford, on Taveta Sisal Estate. It was fully established with a large Nilotic Luo labour force under several European foremen with a remarkable pair of young Seychellois, Ray and Trixie Rougé, who had defiantly, with wit and seduction, carved out a niche for themselves among their colour conscious peers. Ray could fix anything and Trixie get around anyone, including Col. Grogan and me. Mr Trafford was an ex DC, deploying his remembered authority with an arrogance matched by his formidable wife, though happily I was exempt from attention. His son Tim became a tearabout friend and later ran a Night Security firm.

Back in the office one Sunday I looked out of the window at a remarkable visitation. Three suited, turbaned Sikhs stepped out of a unique vehicle, a brand new, gleaming black, American Ford V8 saloon, sheer sided and without running boards! They advanced politely and purposefully into my room and introduced themselves as, respectively, Chanan Singh, Kishan Singh and Mohan Singh, from Kilimanjaro Saw Millers in Moshi. Chanan Singh, short and businesslike, opened the bidding, "We are not concealing from you, Mr Gavaghan, that you have the very nicest jungle in East Africa." The Ford regarded me seriously.

I had looked at the 'niceness' of the jungle in some detail on behalf of the Taveta owners and found it a nice surprise. The timber mostly in question was from a particular hardwood tree called *Mvuli* or umbrella, both because of its canopy shape over a clean trunk and because of its rain *Mvua*-forest connection. There were about 50 mature trees inside the Local Native Council common forest area: perhaps twice as many were in individual, if disputed, ownership. A fine tree might yield around 500–1,000 cubic feet of usable straight timber, which when dried in the log would fetch over 12/- per cubic foot. A tree was thus worth nearly three times my annual salary, and thirty times that of a Tax Clerk. It was no wonder that saw-millers from far and near sought concessions, nor that permits, royalties and fees had been levied by Tony Galton-Fenzi. I looked regretfully at the enticingly parked sedan, parted very amicably from my Sunday Sikhs and made even handed arrangements with several applicants, including a Tavetan, for exploitation, in agreement with the Taveta Land Board and the Forest Department, to preserve a standing asset of such importance to the economy and ecology of the whole region.

The first encounters with the new Kenya National Parks Warden, charged with establishing the Tsavo (West) Park boundaries with the Maasai near Amboseli were abrasive. He was a Major W. F. M. Taberer, choleric, overbearing and discourteous, still engaged in his own private war. My reactions were not soothed by his derision when his well grown lion cub leaped playfully on my back outlined against the canvas of his tent outer 'fly', which only just reduced the penetration of its claws. He had odd ways of showing contempt for office functionaries, like stamping through the flimsy seat of my desk chair. I was also reported for 'theft' of Parks' piping by allowing a local small-holder called Dickie Peel and his wife Doreen, formerly married to Sandy Wright of Molo, to pick up some lengths, long left in the roadway outside the Prison, to use for gravity watering their drought stricken orange groves nearby. Their daughter June Wright, a 'ward' of Col. Grogan, was already a famous flier. I was compelled to repudiate the charge to Colonel Mervyn Cowie himself. Happily Taberer's Assistant Warden, 18-year-old spiky blond, Kenya born, Peter Jenkins was his antithesis and showed early signs of being a respected Parks Warden, working with David Sheldrick in establishing Tsavo (East) beyond Voi.

On the main road one day in the District pick-up truck the driver stopped to talk to a Paré man from Tanganyika walking with a *Kikapu* (woven basket) full of flour. My Tribal Police orderly felt deep into the ground maize and produced a 'wet' skin of a superb leopard. "No man would have been carrying the basket," said the driver simply. The poacher's mate was prosecuted, the skin dried and stored for the National Parks and later, improperly I think, I asked Col. Cowie's permission to buy it at the regular office sale of game trophies. Beautifully tanned, it graced our sofa for years until I succumbed to an offer of £25 from Jack Block, owner of the famous New Stanley Hotel and Ker and Downey safari business.

The engineering firm of Theodoropoulos and Michaelidis bulked large in Taveta life, being involved in every kind of works, large and small, on a contract basis, as well as seeking timber licenses. Mr Michaelidis was the business linch-pin based in Arusha, where he had a classical blonde daughter, *Efaris* or Joy, and a son called Xenophon, while 'Theo' who became my dear friend lived in a large white 'palace' near the Taveta airstrip. Theo was permanently of a certain age; white hair still streaked with yellow, lugubrious eyes overflowing with sympathy, husky voice responsive to every nuance and situation, using a curiously engaging Esperanto, enriched by meaningful interpolations. "Terry, down there..." he would address me seriously, once offering to buy me a small refrigerator from our local General Merchant, Mohamed Habib Lalji. "Listen, down there, Ritsa says that Cecily has no refrigerator, down there." Ritsa was his irresistible blonde marshmallow treasure, who served endless Greek dishes and, with the sweetest of smiles, would tap her soft dimpled cheek, never exposed to the sun, and happily repeat her favourite English word, "White! White!" His gift, even borne by a Greek, was transmuted into a tarmac strip he agreed to lay along the shop fronts, with co-operation from Mohamed Habib Lalji, his co-applicant for a timber licence. This I tied to a compulsory closing time for all shops to allow for village volley ball, much encouraged 'down there'!

Theo had as his canals engineer and supervisor the kind of Italian not included in the British mythology. He was Vincenzo, 'Enzo', Barsotti, ex prisoner of war, ex Town Clerk from Firenze and now partner in Silver Star Engineering, Mombasa. He was erect, stern but smiling, straight down the line, and delighted in an evening sparring round with his guard dog Bruno. His elegant wife Iris, serene through every misfortune, had graced Roman society. She it was who later called our two babes "Gli due porcellini" (piglets).

Enzo fell victim to an unexplained fever in the forest, so severe as to paralyse one side and leave one eyebrow rather villainously raised. We tended them in our Guest House until he recovered, when he gave me an oil painting on wood of Brava town in Italian Somaliland. It was signed by Benuzzi, who with him and one other, Giao, had defiantly walked out of their prison camp in Nyeri, climbed Mount Kenya without equipment or map, and on return invited the astonished Commandant to observe the Italian flag placed on Lenana after they had been driven back by storms from the ridge up to the peak of Batian. It became the true adventure story, No Picnic on Mount Kenya. (William Holden, the malleable film hero, told me at a Nairobi City Hall reception years later, that he yearned to play the part of Benuzzi but he meanwhile contented himself with having bought the Mount Kenya Safari Club (formerly the Mawingo Hotel), as a partner with Winston Churchill, from where he planned to floodlight the mountain.)

Our guest house was the strange scene of another Italian adventure. A young saw miller from Dodoma, deep in Tanganyika, Angelo Pavéta, came to Taveta to meet his proxy bride from Rome to solemnize their wedding at Father Witté's famous Waa Mission and Technical School near Moshi. She was Maria Ercolé, who eventually arrived by bus, emerging from a cloud of dust like a marble goddess in gleaming white sharkskin and high heels. There was no onward transport and Father Witté had not appeared so we took them in, disconsolate as they must have been. We put them in single rooms in our Guest House, one on each side of the shared bathroom and lighted them there after dinner. Many years went by before a most impressive formal document came to me from the Sacred Rota in the Vatican asking for details of the circumstances of their night stop and if they would sustain a plea of non-consummation to justify an annulment! I did my best to leave all options open, past and future.

My relationship with Colonel Grogan had too many unexpected facets to bring into a single account and they began with a death and an armed affray. A grey, Straight Eight, shark-snouted, Lincoln Zephyr, with flowing wings, drew up across the office square. Without haste or stiffness an immediately arresting figure stepped out alone, the archetypal pioneer, with silver Vandyke beard, wearing a neck protecting flat topped, thick pith, sun helmet and quilted, khaki, bush jacket with spine pad and long sleeves. He first opened the rear passenger door, allowing the body of an African in khaki to slide to the ground. He then raised the deep trunk cover and threw out bundles of spears, machetes, bows and arrows. As he strolled over drawing on a cheroot, I went out to meet him. He knew who I was and courteously welcomed me to Taveta, apologizing for the nature of his call.

"This wretched fellow is my driver. I warned him to be careful circling down my hillside, but I have just found him overturned and dead so you may need a post mortem for the death certificate. This other stuff I confiscated yesterday from a cattle raiding party whom I disarmed and sent packing."

" Did they not resist?" I asked, eyeing the armoury.

"Oh no," he replied off-handedly. "Their leader was impertinent, but nothing that a kick in testicles could not settle. It saved a lot of fuss," said with a quiet wolfish chuckle. After he had driven home I received a cable from the Tanganyika Police at Paré asking me to charge a certain European estate owner with assaulting a Police party in hot pursuit of rustlers!

At that first of our many encounters Colonel Ewart Grogan, DSO, named after 'Home Rule' Gladstone, was seventy five and it was fifty years since his prodigious march through 'darkest' Africa, recorded in his book, *From the Cape to Cairo*, in pursuit of adventure, wealth and the hand of Gertrude, his bride to be. Through all the vicissitudes of our uneven positions I was proud to have his 'recommendation' to place inside my first edition. A curious feature of our relationship was that I never felt conscious of the gap in our years, though I would not have called him 'Grogs' as he was widely known, any more than he would have used my first name.

The nub of any conflicts of interest between the Taveta and Colonel Grogan was their understandable fear that they would be hemmed in, dried out and swallowed up by the demands of the surrounding estates. In his turn he could justifiably claim many direct and indirect economic and social advantages, from which they stood to benefit. His scientific enquiry and practical inventiveness knew no limits. I tried both to co-operate and to keep a balance within the law. It was a learning experience.

Girigan Hill stood up like a bristly hummock in the arid bush of Jipé estate. Grogan must surely have been conscious of the happy similarity of names. I circled carefully round the hill to park my detested Vanguard in front of a dozen concrete steps curving inwards to a small platform, to the right of which hung from a frame an engraved brass ship's bell with a toggle. After an interval the wrought iron entrance gates to the otherwise severe residence swung open affording a practised appearance for 'Titania' to announce, with theatrical flourish;

"Welcome to Girigan!"

She was, quite possibly, Camilla Towers, Grogan's long time companion whom he had certainly met in Wardles the Nairobi chemists, and who had told me she had once been Mother Superior of a convent. At all events she was devoted to the care of her puckish Oberon, was nicknamed for her appearance and style 'The Marmalade Cat' and was reputed to have as an admirer Captain Boskovic, a freelance Yugoslav pilot. I found her a kindly Queen of the Fairies. She led me down an oblong atrium past a concrete tank dense with vegetation and stocked with Guppy fish to feed on Anopheles malarial mosquitoes. To the right of the hallway and dining room was a vast circular room where she announced my arrival and left me with the chief focus of attention and action in Taveta.

The living room was the greater part of a circle some 40 feet across, with a huge central bole, from the head of which extended spokes of the tapered metal spines of salvaged aircraft struts, serving as rafters. Around the bole at desk height was a giant millstone stacked with scientific journals, set out in layered fans by date and subject. The panoramic plate glass windows commanded Lake Jipé, the forest and the mountains, as well as the flat bush which Colonel Grogan called the "vegetable image of democracy". Rising to greet me, he put down some learned paper and, without carping or condescension, set out some of his plans and problems. On the floor beside his rugged boots was a prospector's pickaxe.

He needed water from the Lumi River to feed into a planned series of fish ponds, like bunded rice paddies, to be seeded with plankton for the breeding of Tilapia, lake fish from Nyanza, economical, popular and nutritious rations for his imported Luo labour force. The rotated ponds would progressively eliminate brack in the soil which could then be put to sunflower for oil and seed. The only obstacle was delay in obtaining a wayleave from the Water Board in Nairobi for the 40 cusec abstraction.

In the increasing need of land for population growth of 3.5%, scientific attention was turned to the vast areas of Africa, particularly in Tanganyika and Rhodesia, locked up by Tsetse fly and Trypanosomiasis, 'sleeping sickness'. A new drug Antrycide showed promise of effective inoculation of cattle for up to six months to replace Stibofen or Surfen C from Germany. Grogan had brought in a Zebu herd for experiment on his infested Jipé land. It was hoped that a combination of Antrycide injections with sufficient density of human and livestock occupation would clear areas of fly which needed thickets for shelter. I had a certain enjoyment of the names of the associated, viciously biting but non-infective, flies. Stomoxys; Haemotopata; Hippobosca; one could swat them with ones tongue more readily than the mind boggling names conferred on the Glossina species by entomologists, Tachinoides, Longipennis, Pallidipes and the menacing Morsitans. I shared Grogan's enthusiasm for the subject, which I had studied on the Oxford course, but other inventions overtook his Antrycide trials.

Across the main road on the Ziwani Estate he had established an irrigated plantation of delicious pink pomelos, oranges and lemons under the supervision of a nimble buffalo of an Afrikaner called 'Prins' Prinsloo, with his wife Queenie who contrived to turn every natural product of bush or beast, avocado or antelope, to domestic use. Camilla Towers invited us to dinner to meet an Israeli team of citrus experts. After the usual elegantly presented meal at his unique *Mvuli* table, inset with six inch square veneers of all the finest African hardwood, lit by candelabra and lubricated with fine wines, there was an expectant silence. Compliments and toasts were exchanged and the delegation leader spoke.

"Colonel Grogan, it has been our pleasant task to review many of the citrus plantations of the world and their parasites and diseases, but we have never before been privileged to be shown them all in one place." It would have taken more than that to faze their host but, as his unimpressed and laconic nephew, Michael, had responded when the Israelis had observed that his uncle appeared to be "God Almighty around here", "Yes, bloody dry isn't it!"

When we next returned from a weekend's local leave in Nairobi, I could scarcely believe my eyes as we passed over a freshly constructed culvert bridge, through which poured and gurgled a torrent of river water looking remarkably like the 40 cusecs applied for, especially with Theo wagging his tail at the canal works ... "down there". Up I rushed to Girigan to be greeted with smiling urbanity. "Ah, my dear Gavaghan, I thought it best to bow to the inevitable while you were away and save any embarrassment." The wayleave came and saved my bureaucratic bacon.

It might have been natural for me to expect that the Ewart Grogan, who had stalked the length of 'darkest' Africa, who had inhabited the halls of fame with the devious Milner, the falsetto colossus, Rhodes, the 'ill-Starred' Jameson and the fortunate Beit of the eponymous bridge, who had exchanged photographs with Queen-Empress Victoria, would now be

138

beyond the scale and mood of our present encounter. Yet, I found him 50 years on, down from Olympus, a fascinatingly complex man of the times, of any time. He had the charisma of Lucifer, the honey tongue of Nestor, the hardihood of Ulysses and the deviousness of Machiavelli, not to speak of the insidious and progenitive charms of Don Juan. He was old, but young; physically pleasing, but untactile; dominant, but not overbearing; gregarious, but alone. He was lavish, but ascetic, and told me with a self deprecatory chuckle, "I have no further needs; only a bottle of beer, a good cheroot and a toilet roll."

I had no personal involvement with Grogan's powerful influence as settler leader, in Legislative Council and in monetary policy, but his gems of mockery stayed in the memory. "The settlers are the pectin in the jelly of government." The Governor on seeking his advice was, "like a golf ball lost in the rough, requiring a 'mashie-niblick' to blast him out with a divot." He earned his enemies. His published opinions on the long litany of his contemporary figures ranged from encomium to execration. Of Delamere he opined, "D, as he was fondly called, was a loveable blend of puckish charm and unpredictable political orientation advantaged by a short-term hereditary title."*

Grogan took pride in having been involved in the location and first construction of Kilindini docks, in giving his name on 'Groganville' buses to the cleared swampland of Nairobi Bazaar Road, in cocking a snook at planners by having acquired title to the land which became Hospital Hill. Children he had and loved, if not all his own, and he conferred a wonderful gift on them by building 'Gertrude's Garden Children's Hospital' in honour of the wife with whose courtship it all began. He was not a man to whom you would raise a statue, but had made his mark on history and the witness in his book of Tutsi-Hutu massacres stood as a horrendous warning. He would rather build the finest hotel in Nairobi, Torrs, overlooking the seated statue of Delamere and giving life and sophistication to the city, with music and intimate lunches, cognac, cigars and conversation, spiced with caustic wit and words of prejudice such as 'mountebank', which some thought him to be. He planned that Girigan would develop by his bequest into an African Technical College for the Coast Province on the lines of Father Witté's school.

Before leaving the peaceable backwater of the Taveta I had two missions to perform in Moshi. One was to join in launching the Moshi Rugby Football Club and pit its full membership of thirteen, plus two borrowed, against Northern Province who were then to play the visiting South African Universities. The other was to be best man to my friend and team member, Len Bekker, at a full 'Moss Bros.' outfitted wedding; £7 for

*Rhodesia and East Africa; F. S. Joelson Ed., London, 1958.

the lot by air for two weeks! Len was a 6′3″ and 17 stone Gailey and Robert's hardware manager with a quiff of black curly hair and lips suddenly bloated with an allergy, or fear. His bride to be, Joyce Sugar, was a neat, mischievous, pebble-spectacled blonde, who was one of the only female District Officers ever sent out by the Colonial Office — to Tanganyika!

Len took his bachelor party and our farewell in the Pink Elephant bar seriously, to the point that he toppled like a leaning tower, complete with his high bar stool, across my waiting 'fireman's lift' and cracked my fourth lumbar vertebra for life. An infra-red species of paint-stripping lamp, wielded by Dr Hirschfeldt, melted the pain enough for Len and me to be seen, our hired Hudson Straight-Eight having shed its king-pins, running the mile with dignity, holding up our tails through the deserted midday heat to "get to the church on time". A patiently awaiting 'white' bride at the altar had cause to wonder at the lather of his expectations.

An hour's drive to Arushu, beneath olive timbered Mount Meru, capital town of Northern Province, with its Greek 'sisal Barons' and surviving German farmers, and where Hilda Tofte became Matron of the splendid Greek School, had enabled me to make an excellent deal at Subzali's Garage. My awful, but still unique, Standard-Vanguard, deceptively smart and silent on tarmac, was quickly sold in part-exchange for an imported Chevrolet ¾ ton pick-up, which I fitted with rear half-cab of *Mvuli* with windscreen-glass panels and roll-up canvas covered frame. The small difference of cost was covered by a United Dominions Trust loan arranged by the Kenya Government.

Swinging back to Taveta I handed over in great detail to John Hickson-Mahony, serious and fragile, paid a last visit to the Taita Hills and headed for my next posting with the more enigmatic Kikuyu of Kiambu. Ogoma bade farewell to his many Luo friends, though he conceded that Nairobi would be nearer home.

XV

KIAMBU DISTRICT – I
CENTRAL PROVINCE
MARCH 1950–FEBRUARY 1952

Before European settlement began the boundaries of the Bantu-speaking Kikuyu, within their steeply ridged forests, as of the encircling Maasai nomads, had been blurred and reduced by the coinciding plagues, of smallpox striking the Kikuyu, and Rinderpest fever devastating Maasai herds, which left great swathes seemingly untilled and ungrazed. By 1950 the Kikuyu people had been controlled and administered for barely fifty years within, first the East African Protectorate and then the Colony and Protectorate of Kenya.

Diminutive huckster John Boyes, self-styled 'King of the Wa-Kikuyu', and seconded Army Captain Richard Meinertzhagen, crack-shot pacifier, had come and gone, while Commissioner Ainsworth and Company Officers Hall and Smith had left their names on outpost, bridge and fort. The Kenya-Uganda Railway had thrown a spur north from Nairobi depot to Nanyuki (Maasai for red) at the foot of Mount Kenya (Kirinyaga to the Kikuyu, but with peaks named after Maasai heroes, Nelion and Batian). Box-bodies and garages had replaced ox-carts at the 'Outspan Hotel'.

Settlers, attracted by Delamere to fulfil the romantic dream of a 'white man's country' and hopeful 'demobbed' soldiers, had spread along and beyond the railway tracks. Irish, Dutch and Italian Catholic, Anglican and Scottish Presbyterian missionaries had introduced their different versions of 'Good News' and their soul-saving schools and services. The seminal Carter Land Commission Report of 1934 had apportioned rights of occupancy, albeit in jumbled and contentious fashion, as between 'native land units' (or reserves) and 'scheduled areas' (mistakenly referred to as 'the white highlands'), administered by a Highlands Board. Since the Harry Thuku led agitation and resultant deaths of 1922, the almost naïvely open Kikuyu Central Association had been initiated and then proscribed as secretly subversive on the outbreak of World War II. Jomo Kenyatta (with Malinowski) had published *Facing Mount Kenya*. The Kikuyu Independent Schools Association had been started.

Administrative control of the Kikuyu had shifted from the Kamba Province to a Central Province under a Provincial Commissioner at Nyeri, where they were grouped with the cognate Embu and Meru people around Mount Kenya, and with the adjoining 'scheduled areas'. The core of the Kikuyu land was in the shape of a long green lozenge squeezed within named topographical features. Opposite to Mount Kenya the western mountain wall had early been ennobled as the Aberdare Mountains. It was so named by explorer and writer of *Through Maasailand*, Joseph

Thompson, in honour of his patron Lord Aberdare, President of the Royal Geographical Society: strange irony that a Yorkshire coal baron who represented Lord Salisbury's Government in the 'Scramble for Africa' in Berlin, should have his escutcheon put on a Kenya mountain range! Its humped summit was called *Sáttima* (Maasai for a late-castrated bull) and its nose was the high *Kinangop*. The eastern side southwards was delimited by the crinkly foothills and dry alluvial plain of the Embu, to within sight of *Ol Donyo Sabuk* (Maasai for big hill).

The unwieldy length was divided by the Administration in southerly layers into three districts of roughly equal portions, respectively called Nyeri (Kikuyu name was *Gaki*), Fort Hall (*Muranga* or *Metumé* to the Kikuyu) and Kiambu (first located at *Kabété*, a corruption of the Maasai clan *Kaputéi*). Of these Nyeri, under the eye of Provincial HQ and near to settled farmers, such as former DO Peter Marrian at Mweiga, became the more closely attended: Muranga more aloof, introspective and traditional.

Kiambu District was the exposed salient of Kikuyu southerly drift. Through ground usage deals with the indigenous tree-top honey-gathering and elephant hunting *Dorobo* bowmen, they had gradually occupied, cleared and emerged from the forest fringe to face in the open their blood intermingled raiders, the Maasai, to be enfolded within the jig-saw puzzle of legally 'scheduled' white farms and exposed to the tentacles of Nairobi City (by 1950 Royal Charter).

There, inaccessible to them, Delamere's Muthaiga (Kikuyu for poison tree) Club looked down over *Engare Nairobi* (Maasai for cold water) where he was also seated pondering in stone over his own named avenue, written of caustically by Col. Grogan as a "shibboleth enshrined in a statue ... with no resemblance whatever to the original human model".*

Given large discrepancies between the baselines of calculations, the total population of Kikuyu had reached by 1950 about one and a quarter million, or one fifth that of Kenya. Increasing numbers, under pressure of land shortage, had spilled into the 'scheduled areas' as resident, useful if unlawful, labour and squatters, or in crowded Government resettlement schemes for the landless, such as *Olenguruone*, once in Maasailand, at the foot of the Mau massif in the Rift Valley, a sort of human drain from Limuru.

The Kikuyu and assimilated *Dorobo* population of Kiambu District itself was then around 390,000. European families in dairy, coffee, tea, pyrethrum, poultry, nurseries, social clubs, catering, professions and city occupations added many thousands, unevenly distributed and overlapping with the peri-urban Nairobi County Council services. Asian traders dominated the distribution, wholesale and retail trade.

*Rhodesia and East Africa; F. S Joelson Ed., London, 1958.

The statutory Native Authority of the District drew upon a wide field in origin and status. Although there was no tradition of rulers above local clan and ridge-based democratic units, there were outstanding and respected personalities who were sometimes invested with official rank and authority. Renowned among them had been Paramount Chief Kinanjui of Dagoretti, whose clan still held sway after his death. Higher up at Kikuyu was Senior Chief Josiah Njonjo, founder of 'Men of the Trees' and elder of the Scottish Mission School to which one Muigai wa Ngengi, to be called Johnstone or Jomo Kenyatta, had been sent early in the century. In the navel of Kiambu Kikuyudom was wily old Senior Chief Koinange wa Mbiu and his activist brood.

By contrast, at Githunguri Hill assiduous government service had fatefully raised Waruhiu wa Kung'u to be a wealthy Senior Chief, with Magugu Waweru, enlightened leader of the Mbari ya (clan of) Igi, raised to Chiefdom. Indomitable warrior Makimei of Limuru, blanketed and still robust in the odour of leprosy, was respected as a Chief, anointed or not. On the border of Muranga, potent and potatious Senior Chief Muhoho of Gatundu Division, home of Jomo Kenyatta, had such traditional clout as to bring powerful suitors for his daughter Ngina's hand, one of whom was to become her husband and Father of the Nation.

Kiambu political structures had not set in a single mould. Jomo Kenyatta's Kenya African Union, KAU, founded in 1944 but chaired in his absence abroad (until 1946) by usually capable and sobersides James Gichuru, ex Chief of Dagoretti, had so far made little impression beyond the Kikuyu. The gradualist Colonial Office approach to Legislative Council political representation had arrived at a total of four African M.L.C.'s of whom Kiambu member, Eliud Mathu, was first and foremost. The path of elective local government through the Local Native Council operated well within the limitations of powers and finance and under the Chairmanship of the DC. The Native Courts, in parallel with the Kenya Civil and Criminal Codes, blended customary and atavistic oathing practices with natural justice and imported concepts, again under Administrative supervision and appeal. The Court Elders enjoyed status, particularly in land cases, and public enthusiasm and huge expenditure reflected both land shortage and litigiousness.

Kiambu was a densely populated block of fertile land poised between the Crown Forest lip of the settled Great Rift Valley to the west, the Maasai escarpment to the south and the circumference of the spacious city, outside of which it was as full of loops and cavities of European land as Gruyére cheese. To the north was Muranga, a larder of the seething curds of Kikuyu tradition. There was little other than the localized cohesion of tradition and the shoestring of imported administration, including the understaffed professional departments, to hold in balance a vigorous people increasingly exposed to fragmentation within and every form of external intrusion upon the integrity of their land and way of life. My first posting to Kiambu coincided with a hiatus between outwardly calm 'control administration' with straitened resources and the inevitable turbulence of 'land hunger', development, growth and educated aspiration. Unease and rumour were rife, forms of subversive oathing were reported, but the fuse of insurrection had not been ignited and anyone could come and go without hindrance.

"I say old boy! I don't know if it may be of interest to you, but you have a flat tyre!"

The oddly arresting remark came from the only other customer who had mounted the wooden steps to Kassam Kanji's Kiambu Stores. It was couched in a fruitily seductive tone fit to smooth a military moustache across a moistened lip. Major George Norman Milne, misleadingly nicknamed 'Tubby', was all of a piece ex Indian Army, Bengal State Forces. He was impeccably accoutred at every point, and man of many parts. His physical presence was robust, deep chested and well planted. His luxuriant hair and brows were of vibrant white, with tawny undertones matching smoky eyes in florid unlined cheeks, and mouth held agape to bark expletives. He wore a loose khaki jerkin with poacher's pockets, 'Tattersall' check shirt, with silk cravat, sleeves rolled to show powerful fuzzed forearms and swelling over low-slung brass buckled belt and ankle cut cavalry twill trousers over chukka boots. Gold was the keynote, at tooth, cravat pin, wristlet watch and signet ring. 'He was the very model of a gallant hunting Major'. He once showed me a snapshot of himself, posed with gun and foot atop a huge bossed buffalo, sighing, "Old boy, in those days I was simply splendid." I believed him and we became lifelong friends. He was then the Kiambu Marketing Officer of the Maize Board.

Tubby's wife Jacqueline, called Jackie, was born in Madagascar, despite its secretly suppressed convulsions still a Colony of France, d'Outre-Mer. For her, and himself, he prepared a gilded 'chariot', the most perfect wartime jeep in existence. Yellow paint thick as butter, engine coppers burnished, chromed swivel action hunting lamp, custom built mahogany fascia panel with compartments for Zeiss binoculars, marine compass, altimeter, cartridges and silver flask. His Rolliflex camera declared his first profession *manqué*, when he had shared a flat with one James Stewart, renamed film star Stewart Grainger to avoid possible confusion with the other one! The family Milne, already with three tiny 'nymphets', were playmates with our *due porcellini* (two piglets) Kevin and Séan.

Before reporting our punctured arrival to the DC's office, we unloaded the prized Chevrolet pick-up at our neat 1930s bungalow set apart beside the last fairway of Kiambu Club golf course. Beside the porch there was a fragrant 'Yesterday, Today and Tomorrow' bush greeting succeeding dawns with its fresh blue and white petals.

Noël Kennaway, the District Commissioner, was a good man to work for. In his mid forties he was short, compactly built and balding with intensely blue eyes and few words, which he released slowly after what seemed like the click of a glottal stop. He had a Judo belt and hurled his otherwise astutely dominant wife, Nancy, over one shoulder and between his legs in a popular jitterbug turn at the club. He was humorous, trusted and rose to be a PC.

I again found myself outranked by the two other District Officers, to whom I was nominally senior as DOI and First Class Magistrate. Oliver Knowles, wartime Lt. Colonel, was red headed and raw-boned, his readily flushed skin emphasizing sandy-lashed, alert, sea-blue eyes. He was nicknamed the 'giant stride' after his determined ploughman's tread in heavy golf brogues towards an objective. He and his swan necked, golden blonde wife, June, another of the formidable Oscar and Olga Watkins' daughters, were somewhat highbrow fun. R. G. 'Bob' Wilson had the gruff, hunched shouldered, duffel-coated ire of a Naval Commander berating an idle watch, relieved by modesty and humour and the warmth of Jane, his wife. Our lunch hours at home were regaled with hilarious court anecdotes by David Christie-Miller, my Prince Albertian neighbour as DC Moyale in the NFD, now deploying his tolerant wisdom as visiting Resident Magistrate from Nairobi. Pleading before him were a notable pair of lawyers. Mervyn Morgan, ex-Resident Magistrate from Palestine had entered the new arena of representation of Africans. His still innocent junior was Philip Ransley fresh from National Service whose serial partnerships and our enduring friendship later began there.

I should pay tribute to the interim DC who acted for Noël on leave. He was Myles Edward Wentworth North, affectionately known as 'far gone'! He was neither young nor old, perhaps both at heart. His amiable head was shaped like a fairground coconut, with a cockatoo tuft at the top, and he lumbered a bit, surprisingly because he could clamber nimbly up a tree on climbing irons to watch any other rare bird. He was a world famous ornithologist and had a repertoire of recorded sounds, which compensated for an awesome stammer. He explained that in the Army he gave weapon training lessons in plain chant. When truculent old Senior Chief Koinange Mbiu, a forehead 'wen' agleam with pent-up rage, called with his henchmen quite reasonably to demand the lifting of the ban on coffee planting, they would totter out overwhelmed by Myles' inexhaustibly stubborn patience. "I've listened to *everything* you have to say and *n-now* I'm going to do it m-m-m-*my way*." He was sweet natured and kind to me and very possibly unhappy. He was not at all like a much earlier DC, Gerald Hopkins, whom he told me was perceptively called by the Kikuyu, *Koimbutho* or 'the bird which gets up quickly when startled'.

The layout of the Government *boma* was intimate to cramped, lining four sides of a grassy oblong enclosure divided by a bifurcated track from the DC's Office to the Native Hospital at the Kikuyu village end. All buildings, save a few scattered bungalows, dated from the First World War. The whole ran along a ridge directly over the main road from Nairobi, seven miles away, and on to the 'native reserve'. Below the road was a lavatory bucket washing plant, served by ox cart, past which was the road to the Prison, the Indian shopping centre, the Local Native Council Public Works yard and the coffee plantations of one island of the 'scheduled areas', managed by an exemplary Dane, Nils Fjastad.

Across the higher end of the compound the long single storey DC's Office deserved a listing as an undistinguished historic building. It began near the main road at an attached store, with a high barred aperture, which had served to hold overnight prisoners. The officers and clerks had their own thick walled cells in sequence as far as the DC's modest office. This was entered by the far elevation up concrete steps and overlooked a valley or grassy sump, drained by towering silver eucalyptus trees and flowering gums. On the opposite side was the rear entrance to the dressed stone and red Bangalore tiled Kiambu Club, guarded by a Faginesque caddy-master, assigning his ragged bag snatchers to arriving golfers, sometimes preferentially.

In a District of nearly half a million people of all races there was the practical problem of getting to meet scores of individuals, hundreds in the case of the Kikuyu people, Government Officers of every level and Department, widely dispersed settlers, traders and so on. I was struck by the quality of the meagre complement of underestimated and stingily paid employees of the Colonial Services on the ground. It might be best expressed that an idle, incompetent, ill-behaved and ill-intentioned one did not cross my path. Ambition, connivance, class feeling, cliquism, prejudice, insensitivity, lack of imagination or courage could exist in normal human degree, but the aggregation of team effort for service was remarkable.

Neither we nor our masters could have a foreknowledge of the unravelling of the Colonial Empires. There was no previous 'model' for Kenya of a multi- or mono-racial formula for an evolving African polity containing immigrant races. The southerly bastions of white rule and *Apartheid* stood firm, still with British involvement or recognition, while we were beset by the local ferments of actuality, conflicting expectations and the daily grind of matching practical needs to slender resources. The fulfilment of our personal lives and our ingrained *esprit de corps* could keep us together, but not expectably in full accord with the multiple opinions of the permanent occupants of the District, Kikuyu, settler or other.

There were religious and quasi-religious influences at work in conditioning behaviour. Whatever traditional, atavistic or deviant practices were used in controlling Kikuyu mass opinion or exacting their obedience, they were matched by devout adherence to Christian beliefs of Anglican,

L

Presbyterian, Catholic and other faiths, however absurdly or bizarrely they presented themselves in un-Christian conflict. While deep rooted conviction, fanatical belief, rage, hate, induced hysteria, even narcotics, could actuate hitherto unexpected fearlessness in the commission of terroristic acts, extraordinary bravery was also displayed in the calm acceptance of Christian martyrdom. "Faith of our fathers ... we will be true to thee till death" was lived out by many Kikuyu in the undeclared conflict looming ahead.

Affecting the Administration and other control departments such as the Police, there was a quite distinct sinew of conviction and behaviour, which seemed to have a discreet place in affairs. I had seen the influential and affluent Masonic Lodges in Nairobi and Kisumu, where I had gladly been a guest. I had observed a curiously jocular affection in Kiambu between the grizzled and loveable Revenue Officer, Rory Heard, with his sweetheart-wife Suzy, and the Chief Native Commissioner, Edward Windley. The bond seemed to be that Rory, of far junior position, had a formally established seniority in the Lodge over his service head. Democratic perhaps, but I wondered at the wider implications.

As a simple working microcosm within the complex apparatus of the Colonial Government, there was a District Team under the Chairmanship of the DC as king-pin, attended by his DOs. It had something of the character of a set of cards in Happy Families, representing the various avocations, with a recognized order of rank and status in the pack which extended to the dinner table and the spouse. To take an irreverent snapshot, there might be found seated:

> Brian Harris — Senior Medic., uproarious in mirth.
> Rena Angus — Matron, stern ruler of Wards.
> Harold Taylor — Inspector of Health, relentless on rats.
> Dick Lake — Educator, afire with scholarly zeal.
> Peter Gollop — Agriculture, nicknamed 'Manure'.
> Eric Peachey Wilkinson — Community man, devoted 'vox pop'.
> Ian Dundas — Police Super., too kind for the beat.
> 'Vic' Aubrey — A.S.P., true blue copper.
> Derek Foottit — Conservator of soil and culture.
> Ivor Brown — Music and the food of love.
> Rory Heard — Revenue and avuncular 'Master'.
> Jeremiah Nyagah — Teacher of elegance, hailing from Embu.
> Leon Fouché — 'Colonial Boy' from Bulawayo Ranches.
> 'Tubby' Milne (Major) — Marketer of Maize and Produce.
> Eustace Tapsell — Controller of Wattle and Bark*.

The DC wore another *ex officio* hat as Chairman of the Kiambu Local

*Father of Peter Tapsell, British MP to be.

Native Council, which had statutory powers of local taxation. Its committees mirrored as well as underpinned the specialist work done by the government staff on the District Team and were co-ordinated by a catch-all 'Finance and General Purposes Committee'. The Vice Chairman was Senior Chief Josiah Njonjo of *Men of the Trees* fame, whose son was a dapper, up-and-coming Crown Counsel, Charles Njonjo. There were both nominated (mainly Chiefs) and elected Members who met in a cavernous and rather ramshackle LNC Hall along the road past the last Golf Club fairway. It stood on a hummock overlooking a dry *vlei* (hollow) phonetically called *Kirigiti*, where European stalwarts had once played serious 'cricket'.

One day, when calling at the Secretariat in Nairobi, I was surprised to find Senior Chief Waruhiu of Githunguri Division, a sturdy be-suited figure, seated primly upright on a messenger's chair in the broad corridor outside the corner office of the new Chief Native Commissioner, Eric Davies. In the scale of his own society Waruhiu was at least a Lord Lieutenant and was nearly twice my age, deserving of some deference, but he was not a man to be put out of countenance nor take umbrage. He stood to greet me and said that he came there often to warn the CNC of the threat posed by a quasi-traditional oath sweeping through Kiambu District, then spoken of as 'Kula Muma', literally 'to eat a sheep': a goat would be even more potent. It was twenty years since the doyenne of African history, Margery Perham, in her *East African Journey*, had met him and described his shock at the murder of a missionary.

"Shall we go in together?" I asked.

Eric Davies was a gentle and charming Manx-Welshman, much liked in the service. He had a long wedge-shaped face with high carved nose and spiky, dark, silver-flecked hair, in no way suggesting the thrust of personality essential in a hinge position, which called for experienced leadership, while lacking direct executive or political authority. His tenure as CNC went on to straddle a long hiatus in Governorship, temporarily covered by the Chief Secretary, Henry Potter, when the once potent but over-extended old 'Lion King', Sir Philip Mitchell, ceremonially surrendered his sword to God at Nairobi Cathedral. His departure was followed only by rumoured names of eligible successors and inordinate delay in appointment.

To some wonderment, dynastic grandee, Sir Evelyn Baring, son of the great 'Sirdar' of Egypt and of the still mighty banking family ('The sixth Great Power of Europe') was sent up from the *Apartheid* south. After idyllic Indian Civil Service cut short by amoebiasis, youthful Governorship of Southern Rhodesia, and the British High Commissionership of the various 'Territories', including Bechuanaland (Botswana), he had been instrumental in the contentious banishment of Seretse Khama, heir to the throne of the Bamangwato people, for fear of tribal conflict if he took as consort his bride, a former London secretary called Ruth Williams. Apart from references to her race and work, it was widely reported in the press that her hair was red!

Baring's appointment appeared to run right across the prescient analysis by Colonial Kenya's great chronicler, Elspeth Huxley, in volume II of her *White Man's Country*, published seventeen years before. In this she rehearsed the sharp divisions in 'schools of thought' faced by Delamere on native policy as between the Union of South Africa, Rhodes' dominion, and the confused evolution of Kenya. Baring had much southern baggage to adapt swiftly to his new eastern command, already pre-destined since 1923 to be a 'black man's country', albeit with zebra stripes. It was unlikely that he could have been unaffected by his tenure of office in Rhodesia, founded by a flawed giant, who had been perceived by Grogan at the time as a "positive, pragmatic and ruthless sentimentalist", but yet the one outstanding historical figure, who had "conjured with men and bewitched a strange medley of Jews, aristocrats, roughnecks, statesmen, and tribal savages as his following in a then seemingly hopeless attempt to develop Darkest Africa".* I met Baring at very close quarters several times and was able from below to observe, if not comprehend, some elements of his enigmatic personality.

Eric Davies moved, with much regard but little reward, to be Chief Executive in the Isle of Man, no doubt relieved to hand over to the more worldly-wise Edward Windley. Naturally, these lofty clouds, flitting as if in cross currents high above our fields of work, did not filter much light onto our understanding of our part in the scheme of things, as we uneasily approached turbulence and disorder.

I spent many days in the countryside with Waruhiu, once clambering down the Rift Valley escarpment to the railway station and African Inland Mission at Kijabe, cut deep into the hillside, to hear a land case on appeal. As we ate sandwiches, he was distraught in his precise and measured way at the destruction of his society under the mass assault of un-Christian oathing. He already took the precaution of changing his sleeping place and bed position for fear of the planned murder of Chiefs, warned of by Ossie Hughes, the Nyeri DC, among others. He spoke out bravely in favour of peace for a year and more until he was ambushed and shot dead in his car off Redhill Road by hand of one of the 'Families'. Our friendship continued through his elder son, David, and Samuel whom we and the Education Department enabled to attend the University of Wales, the threshold of a very rewarding career.

There were several occasions on which I faced head on the Devonshire

Rhodesia and East Africa; F. S. Joelson, Ed., London, 1958.

Doctrine of Paramountcy in attempting to resolve disputes between European estates and Kikuyu lands. One such was between an influential coffee planter, called Dick Bellasis, and his Kikuyu neighbour, called Edward Kariuki, across a boundary stream. Bellasis had a fine two storey stone house, to which he invited me for lunch with two or three friends from near by, whom I also knew. It was both pleasant and politic for me to accept and warm the atmosphere for compromise, if necessary. We walked to the disputed stretch of water, which had in fact divided each side of a broken concrete weir for measuring normal flow. There was no longer a central stream. Edward Kariuki, a young educated man, sat waiting there and naturally claimed the deviation towards Bellasis. Likewise the other party. Honour was saved by accepting the weir with an agreement to dig out and line the original channel.

I found the coffee planters, who certainly enjoyed a position of privilege, both as employers of coffee pickers and with still exclusive legal rights to grow it, scrupulously honourable to deal with, if not penny pinching in setting their coffee pickers' pay, and they had no presumption that socializing went with bias. It would be unthinkable that the longer established planters I knew, such as Dick Bellasis, Ted and Eileen Belcher, Noel and Gillian Solly, Ronald Finlay, Tom Thumb, 'Mac' Mc'Lellan Wilson, John Warren-Gash, Ray Mayers, old Doctor C. J. Wilson of 'The East African Mounted Rifles', the perennial doubles tennis champion Gees, the Pitt-Moores, the enterprising Ellis family with Susan Richards, and others, would deviate from honest dealing whatever might be the basis of their views about land rights and the cause of the European settlers. It was up to us to hold the ring.

A different kind of land dispute involving both races was up along the windswept road to Limuru, where the delicate white pyrethrum flowers grew. It went back over seventeen years and appeared from the manuscript records to have come first on appeal before that very DC Gerald Hopkins, "the bird that gets up quickly when startled", known before the war to Myles North. The title of the case was 'Mbari ya Mwendwa v. Mbari ya Knight'. Mwendwa had been the clan leader or *Murumati* over a very large area of agricultural land, which was claimed in part from a European settler. His name was not only Knight but 'Wednesday' night because his initials were W.E.D. while his brother, an Anglican parson at far off Kitale church, was called 'Sunday' night.

This much being clear, I spent many a long session quartering the land and hearing evidence in the open to the point of exhaustion, which was often the determining factor in a land case. Scores of people attended; no witness was turned away; emphatic statements were delivered with simulated but seemly indignation, marked by the throwing down of sticks, dramatic advances and withdrawals, and final triumphant perorations.

Astonishing vigour was demonstrated by very old men and sometimes women. Litigation was impassioned and enjoyable. It remained for a record, a summary and a judgement with assessors to be made, in which a freshly sketched plan was viewed with satisfaction. The conclusion of a case had to be seen to be as watertight as possible to fend off any desire or demand for further appeal. It was difficult to avoid the temptation to wrap up a finding too tidily to this effect.

In Limuru I partially earned my first, and I believe only, Kikuyu nickname of *Karuga Ndua*. In checking the deplorable stews, which passed for workers' shanties at the back of the Trading Centre, and crawling through muddy entrances, I could detect the sickly smell of illegal 'rot gut' Nubian Gin stored in large *Kibuyus* (root vats), for sale and consumption. I tipped them all over, which was the figurative meaning of the nickname. The literal meaning, usually referring also to perceived character, was in the unlucky superstitious sense of jumping over the cooking pot in the centre of a hut, instead of going round it, thus indicating rashness, impatience and defiance of custom. If so, it was regrettably fair and never left me even as a friendly greeting to my face.

On the road to Limuru there was a hamlet and a European residential community of commuters, smallholders and coffee planters called Tigoni. It had been an island of Kikuyu occupation left within the patchwork of 'scheduled areas' after the Carter Land Commission, and as such was a bone of contention. A subsequent solution, implemented against strong protest, was to dispossess the Kikuyu occupants by compulsory purchase and compensate them at a place called Nyamweru, above Limuru, with excisions from Crown Forest marked out in favour of each dispossessed family in adjacent Biberioni and Ngararíga pine plantations. The basic arrangement was called 'the Tigoni-Nyamweru Land Exchange'. The Nyamweru land was however then formally cursed by a powerful local guardian of a '*Githathi*' stone (a meteorite) invoking death upon anyone who dared to occupy it.

I arrived at what was intended to be a late stage in the transaction. I rather enjoyed the days in the pine and resin-scented forests with Chief Makimei, husky in his pink shoulder blanket, cutting fresh red cedar corner posts and daubing on them with white paint the plot numbers of future owners, who would also have the benefit of cut timber. The benefit did not last long for acquisitive Chief Luka and his family after they had annexed the forbidden Nyamweru compensation for Tigoni. They were all massacred at Lari near Uplands in the most revolting manner, when it was taken to be an act of Mau Mau savagery, rather than the vengeance of a curse defied.

About this time there emerged an exotic species of European settler called the 'Tigoni Tigers', to confront what they perceived as the Kikuyu threat to the security of their land. Although they were on the political right and pretty ruthless in their professed attitudes, those whom I came to know and like, such as Quentin Cooper and Garth Roberts, as well as an old-timer District Commissioner, Clarence Buxton, of distinguished Anglican family, were people of some reason and restraint even in the worst excess of conflict. I had occasion to explore their convictions and those of their 'mates' in their lair, the Tigoni Club. I doubt they numbered more than a hundred.

At Limuru Township itself I was called urgently to the sprawling factory estate of Bata Shoe Company on its own railway siding beyond the central industrial area. The call came from the General Manager, Tony Carnecky, who was the Kenya head of the worldwide company set up by 'Tommy' Bata, son of the Czechoslovak founder Thomas, which was to separate from the huge domestic organization at Zlin when it was taken over by the Communist Regime of Gotwald after the brief 1968 'Dubcek Spring'. The Limuru factory and headquarters employed some 2,000 people, mostly Kikuyu, and reflected the paternal, if not autocratic, management tradition of the founder, to which the diminutive, prematurely silver haired, bespectacled Carnecky was well adapted in his precise and prescriptive way. The result was a very closely knit community in which the highly skilled and disciplined Czech technicians worked closely in every trade, from tanning to sales, with the work force to whom they communicated their expertise with rigour and enthusiasm. The close relationship was made the easier by the policy of recruitment, which favoured a high educational standard down to the lowest level so that even a menial job could be the opening to training, supervision or management. Living conditions for Czechoslovak staff and their extensive families, with a wide range of recreational facilities, were somewhat enclosed and brain-washed, but contributed to solidarity, output and a sense of loyalty and security. The labour force enjoyed good quarters and facilities with subsidized football teams in Bata 'strip', the first eleven including Luo stars competing in the Kenya championships.

It was in such circumstances that the request came to deal with a 'wildcat' strike at Bata. It also coincided with the May 1950 general strike called by Fred Kubai, incoming Vice President of KANU and Chairman of the EA. Trade Union's Congress, with the recently returned firebrand General Secretary, Makhan Singh, whom I was destined to 'entertain' in my next District posting. I passed by the Tigoni Kenya Police Station to pick up Inspector Peter Dodds, thickset, twinkling, blue eyed 'Angle', with whom ensconced and knitting I was delighted to find an admired friend from NFD days, Betty Cochrane, daughter of 'Cocky' Cochrane, Commandant of the Kenya Police Training College. They went on to great things in the Family Planning Field! I needed Peter to come along in case of formal crowd control or riot though he had few Police ranks available.

We found what appeared to be the entire labour force assembled on the football field and milling around outside the closed factory gates, behind which the management were uneasily clustered. I got up on something, perhaps the back of Peter's pick-up, and spoke in Swahili to the crowd from behind the main mass, attempting to persuade them to break up and choose delegates to negotiate any grievances.

I was rudely interrupted by a man just below me, who told me I was a f...... b...... On the spur of the moment and because of his words I jumped down to grab him, but he made off through the crowd towards the gates until I brought him down in a Magisterial Rugby tackle and sat on him spreadeagled. As the mass surged towards us I jumped up and asked them if they had heard what he called me. The element of surprise worked and when they were told, being normally well disposed and unused then to such abuse, they urged me to proceed with great good humour. Peter took him in charge and we debated whether he had committed an offence or I had. Since either way I was the local Court and the mood for a strike or disturbance had evaporated, honours were adjudged even and we called it quits.

From then onwards I found Bata's a welcome port of call at that end of the District and many exotic sounding friendships were formed with people such as 'Naughty' Emil Hatla-Patka, 'Jumbo' Frankie Vymetal, 'Gentle' Joe Chmelar, 'Hero' Jan Lazaar, 'Silent' Eman Chasak and their bird-caged spouses, who swaddled their babes into immobility "just like at home". Above all, my family became lifelong friends with Mirek Paseka, then Tannery Manager, and his English wife Betty, who lived out at Tigoni. He was short, strong and chucklingly bald, conjuring up thoughts of him in bonnet and kilt of the Cape Town Highlanders, fighting from North Africa to Monte Cassino, while she enlivened the ATS and mingled with the film world of Harry Waxman. Mirek made for me the first model Bata Safari Boots for fifteen shillings. They much later stood as wedding witnesses in the old DC's stone office in Nairobi, conducted most congenially by Roger Wilkinson, the best of men.

Senior Agricultural Officer, Peter 'Manure' Gollop's pungent reports to the District Team encapsulated the overriding problem tearing the heart and soil out of the Kikuyu land units of Kiambu. It was to be seen, as I had first seen it five years before from the train to Kisumu, in the chasms of erosion, the wretched crops, the rooting stunted livestock, the ramshackle habitations, the forehead grooving leather straps of women and girls bent under pelvis-rupturing loads of firewood and water. It stained and choked the tributaries feeding into the Sabaki River estuary by Malindi with the wasted tilth of peasant farms. It was dramatized by Colin Maher and others in warning pamphlets as *The Rape of the Earth*. Peter Gollop, a real 'Dungbeetle', sought tirelessly to restore to the Kikuyu lands at least the droppings of their own puny beasts. The problem arose in large part from pressure on 275,000 acres of potentially good land by as many people, of whom at least 40% were landless and a preponderance were women. Fragmentation by inheritance into absurdly uneconomic and scattered holdings compounded the disruption. To these factors must then be added the high population increase with lowered mortality, preoccupation with compulsory oathing, and the physical disturbance caused by road building, power and water supplies to Nairobi city.

The worsening congestion stimulated hectic individual litigation through the African Courts system over even the tiniest strip of usable soil, pursued to the Appeal Court and thence to the DC. For substantial disputes, such as that of the Mwendwa versus Knight saga, the fees at each level were relatively modest, but not for the space of a hut. Nor did proceedings stop at adjudication. There was the matter of ceremonially spreading 'tatha' (the contents of a sheep's stomach) on boundaries or of taking an oath of truth under pain of death for perjury within seven planting seasons (three and a half years), survivor take all or divide the land in half. It was no wonder that admission of advocates, without knowledge of custom or language, to such disputes was resisted by the Administration for reasons of equity, court delays and cost to poorer litigants.

Attention had been given since 1948 to the question of security of Kikuyu land title and agricultural credit. Chief Muhoya in Nyeri District and Chief Magugu of the Mbari ya Igi (clan) in Kiambu had consolidated local holdings by consent, but the general process of consolidation had to grind through its complex stages of practicality and popular acceptance. It did so under the inspiration of H. E. Lambert, the 'Thinker', Michael Evans, the 'Co-ordinator' as African Courts Officer, Ken Cowley, the 'Realist', in Native Affairs and not least the political support of Eliud Mathu, the first of the four African members of the Legislative Council and a Kiambu man himself. It had not turned full circle before the inexorable tide of subversion overtook us and directed all resources to the conflict. Meanwhile, there was always a backlog of appeal cases to hear, which afforded me the enjoyable and fascinating opportunity, on bicycle or foot, to get deep into the community and countryside and hear the unrestrained voices of litigants under croton trees or banana fronds, learning, disentangling and seeking elusive solutions.

I once had to conduct a well reputed columnist of the London Observer, Patrick O'Donovan, to Githunguri where he sat with the Court Elders and me on the platform of the stone tiered amphitheatre facing the pillared portico of the African Court and Registrar's offices (built by former Provincial Commissioner, Sydney Herbert Fazan, the apostle of classical democracy). My purpose was to warn about the dangers of secret oathing exercising Senior Chief Waruhiu, with whom we had lunched. I do not suggest for a moment that frequent recourse to his silver gin flask, without which Patrick assured me no gentleman could travel, gave a pink hue to a subsequently published article in which he described my performance in that bucolic scene as redolent of the splendours of ancient Rome. I hoped it was not, or perhaps a bit of Pompey was not out of place.

Back at Kiambu a more modern African Appeal Court had been designed by my predecessor, Neil Loudon, and was completed in the central grass triangle by the Junoesque Cecily Pitt-Moore and Gonellas Brickworks on the Ellis's estate, with knobbly dressed stone pillars and Roman tiles. Its modernity and the Presbyterian background of its initiator, a St. Andrews graduate, contrasted strangely with a public ceremony arranged with me by Chief Charles Karuga Koinange, youngest son of the last wife of the old Senior Chief. The venerable guardian of the 'Githathi' meteorite from Limuru set it up in a tripod, like stacked rifles, and put the elders through an elaborate ceremony binding them to faith and honesty under pain of death. Seven sacred twigs were thrust through the aperture in the stone seven times by each participant while circling the stone seven times to the accompaniment of the oath. Some alleged that such deaths as followed were in response to the oath. Many of the Kikuyu Court Clerks were of extraordinary efficiency and ability in the exercise of their culturally ambivalent role, in particular my friends and frequent advisers Stephen Thiongo, Chief Clerk at Kiambu, and John Ngugi, Court Surveyor at large.

The scarring of the countryside to provide for the fast growing needs of the capital followed a south easterly pattern downward from the raised lip of the Rift Valley beyond Limuru, and from Uplands and the Kinangop. First in sequence, a line of tall pylons bearing light and power cables reared up the escarpment on its long march from the distant hydro-electric installations at Jinja, the source of the Nile. To either side was a broad network of trunk and secondary road construction and widening, converging on Nairobi from Uganda, the prosperous west of Kenya, the Rift itself, the timber forests, the industries of Limuru and the vegetable growers of Uplands and the Kinangop. Further eastwards were two broad gauge water pipelines. The first issued from the recently flooded lake and dam at Githunguri where dying undergrowth drowned a Kikuyu school boy despite District Officer Bob Otter's brave attempts at rescue as we chanced near by. The shapely concrete wall was opened with unconscious absurdity by Nairobi's Mayor, Alderman Travis, with chain and mace of office, and the Warden's English country cottage entrusted to admirable Colonel Budd. It was soon to be backed up by a new Sasumua 'high dam' feeding off the larger catchment of the Aberdare mountains.

Each of these major intrusions crossed the chequer board of trim or tattered farms and holdings, without regard to their nature or ownership, whether fitting neatly within an orderly plan or ripping apart, even obliterating, small peasant holdings. The upheavals bore down most on the tenants or 'Ahoi', who had no security of tenure for their plots, and on the dependent landless people. For the Kikuyu so disturbed an elaborate system of compensation was agreed by the Administration with the main construction companies. One was W. and C. French, a world-wide engineering group, which happily co-operated fully and fairly, through agreements on the ground between the Branch Manager, Charles Livingston, the landowners and myself over every tree, shrub, banana plant, yardage of crops and vegetables disturbed by the pipeline, as well as all kinds of huts, dips, tanks and so on.

A curiously uniform and repeated feature of meetings held with landowners to pay out their compensation in the field was a harangue, sometimes impassioned, to the effect that Europeans were interlopers who had inveigled their way into Kikuyu land under false pretences. The metaphor invariably used was that of a camel and his master in the desert, not readily evocative of the altitude, fauna and flora of Kiambu. When halted for the night outside his master's tent the camel begged shelter from the cold desert wind and offered to stand inside with his hump supporting the apex of the tent and his legs conveniently straddling his master's bedroll. After standing a while he pleaded exhaustion and space to lie down, which granted his recumbent belly so bulged as to eject his kindly master! Once, near 'Redhill' road widening, the complainant was so clamorous that I had him restrained until each had received and signed for his due payment. He followed suit.

The process of disturbance and compensation led indirectly to the first of my many encounters in Kiambu District with Jomo Kenyatta, whom I had not met since his coming to Governor Mitchell's *Baraza* at Mumia's in 1947 to establish the presence of the Kenya African Union in North Nyanza. By this stage Kenyatta had emerged as the towering, if not unchallenged, figurehead of what had become known as Mau Mau. The name, never satisfactorily explained, had superseded the thraldom of the 'Muma' oath, which had caused such concern to Senior Chief Waruhiu. Circumstantially, it had been picked up by Charles Hayes as Provincial Information Officer of the Rift Valley, when in the Information Office Cinema van with his and my friend Eric Wilkinson at Rongai, and then passed to the PC. No doubt other gleaners such as Special Branch had presented similar reports.

A crucial, but almost laughable, encounter with Kenyatta was beside the Gatundu to Ruiru Road inside his home Division and fiefdom. Having had wind of a Mau Mau oathing ceremony near the boundary of the long settled coffee estates of the Mayers and Nordlingers, I had found before dawn the usual paraphernalia of sodom apples, impaled goats' eyes and banana fronds, wilted and deserted save for a dimly lit hutfull of 'fundraisers', like Rembrandt conspirators, their black iron cash boxes stuffed with aromatic notes and grimy small change. Having relieved them of their cash and registers, against receipts, and of their stated names and addresses, I repaired to Mrs Nordlingers' and her sparklingly diminutive daughter, so nicknamed 'Tikki' (like 'Sixpence'), for my own ceremonial breakfast.

The previous day I had spoken to a *Baraza* in one of old S. H. Fazan's amphitheatres at Gatundu Divisional Court, about a recent assault on a power line surveyor. He was appropriately called Tracey, although his elongated frame and agonized eyes turned dramatically to the light of the paraclete more resembled an El Greco Saint Peter. He had been cracked on his tousled head, his survey beacons uprooted and his staff scattered. As I spoke I was consciously distracted by the silent figure of Kenyatta, seated alone on the back tier in his leather jacket, beringed hands clasped over his carved elephant headed ebony stick or 'sceptre'. He slipped away quietly, but not unnoticed.

I then drove down to where the assault had taken place, where over a hundred local elders were assembled in a semi-circle some way back from the dusty road, the front row on bentwood chairs. 'Saint Peter' was present much repaired with sticking plaster. No sooner was I seated to warn against further attacks than a vibrant traditional elder leaped up to deliver the parable of the camel in the desert to the applause of many. As he finished along bowled a bulky, beige, nineteen thirties American limousine, a Hupmobile or a Hudson-Terraplane. Jomo himself emerged from the rear VIP seat with the benign assurance of the country squire. All stood up except for me, although I was in two minds whether to do so, and he sat next to me in a chair hastily vacated for him. Having enquired innocently what we were about, he rose to his feet facing outwards. In a thick, sonorous baritone he delivered himself in measured Kikuyu sentences, translated flatly by an interpreter, of a homily which began "There once was a camel ...".

No one can, at will, be more expressionless than a Kikuyu, with closed face and shuttered eyes. Although not a word of comment was uttered, by some form of subliminal agreement between us, Jomo and I went apart to his vehicle. We walked up and down the Gatundu road negotiating without touching on awkward facts some face-saving formula whereby popular protest could be expressed and Tracey's head protected from further battery. Back at the *Baraza* some golden phrase was ambiguously woven in Kikuyu and the matter closed, to my immense relief since I had risked much at my level in bluntly threatening to charge on slender evidence a personage of such power and menace, to whom I could not help being attracted as much as repelled.

It would be hard to convey the feelings engendered by this

extraordinary man more persuasively than writer Negley Farson, whom I had met at Kakamega in 1949. Atavism, anthropological lore, animal magnetism, deviousness, earthy majesty, all were there, with physical potency to match, including a head for drinking, to which I never saw him fully succumb. I once asked him in my office how he got on with Eliud Mathu, the sophisticated Kikuyu Member of Legislative Council. "Indeedy, Mr Gavaghan", he said in his quaint style, "Mr Mathu does not have the common touch. I have the common touch."* Indeed he had. Duck and weave as he did between the factions and forces and intrigues of subversion, I did not believe, as some accounts suggested, that he was subservient to the activist "Forty" group and the street bully-boy gangs of union leaders like Fred Kubai and Bildad Kaggia. I was convinced that he utilized them rather than otherwise and dissembled, when threatened, to his own agenda.

At a famous gathering of 40,000 at old Koinange's land, attended by British Labour MPs Fenner-Brockway and Leslie Hale, as well as sundry Special Branch observers, with me reverting to Administration despatch rider, he formally adjured Mau Mau to disappear down the roots of the magical *Mikongoe* tree. Underground or for renewed growth? Who could know for sure. A derisive view of the occasion was displayed by the Kenya Police Airwing which dropped a spare pair of woollen socks for Leslie Hale to wear with his open sandals, regarded as effetely symbolic 'Fabian' socialist attire. Such pranks were part of the jokey language of uncertainty in face of an unknown menace.

Another facet of Jomo's public persona was shown at a celebration and speech day at the Githunguri Teachers' College, the heart and soul of the Kikuyu Independent Teachers' Association (KISA), constructed by collection in 1949. The DC had been invited, but asked me to deputize, since I was familiar with the scene and was on good terms with both Senior Chief Waruhiu and jovial, cultured Peter (first son of old) Koinange, the Headmaster. On arrival at the entrance archway I asked some students walking by to open the gate, which they blankly declined to do. I did so without comment, but reported them to Peter who publicly upbraided them for shaming the ethos of the College. He asked me if I would like to make a speech at the opening, but I deferred to Director of Education, Patrick, who was present and clearly of the proper seniority and profession.

There was a palpable stir as Jomo Kenyatta drove up to deliver the principal address after brief and superfluous introductions. His escort was a strikingly handsome man in full Kikuyu warrior's garb of skins with traditional ornaments and a very convincing, if not burning, spear ('Burning Spear' was Kenyatta's sobriquet). He was the leader of the Age Grades and

*Reported by the author in his appreciation in the *Irish Times* the day after President Kenyatta's death in 1978.

chief fund raiser, Waira Kamau, a durably loyal henchman. Kenyatta's speech was of unrestrained passion, evidently intended to inflame and inspire, with explicit references to the spilling of blood for land and freedom. While the flow continued, I turned to Patrick and asked him quietly to rebut the violent tone in his own reply, but he excused himself discreetly for a prior appointment to play golf and left.

I then tugged Peter's sleeve and said that, in this case, it was my duty to accept his invitation to speak next, to which he concurred. I skirted Kenyatta's fulminations and praised the rapid development of the College and the inspiration and impetus it could provide in enabling the aspirations of their people to be attained in peaceful progress and co-operation with the Government, which shared many of their objectives. They would well understand that any unnecessary violence would waste resources and energy, as already explained so vigorously by Mr Kenyatta. No animosity was evidenced by any party and after an ample tea and sweet soda water I was able to make a circumspect escape and report to the DC. It was the last significant occasion on which I met Jomo Kenyatta before we had all become involved in a dark and violent phase.

Beyond the diverse strands of representation locally available to Kenya 'natives', including Government paid area Chiefs within the colonial 'scaffolding', semi-elective Local Native Councillors, Native Court Elders and converging leaders of protest, I found the role of the longer term representatives appointed to Legislative Council, MLCs, the most elusive. This was particularly exemplified in my frequent relations with Eliud Wambu Mathu. Other than Peter Koinange, he was about as formidable a candidate as it would have been possible to find to step in 1944 into a Legislative Council seat beside the Rt. Rev. Leonard James Beecher, last of a chain of European members, such as Harold Montgomery, former Chief Native Commissioner and brother of 'Monty', and Dr C. J. Wilson, representing 'native' interests. He lacked only Beecher's hot line to the divinity he invariably apostrophized as 'Gud'.

Born in 1910, Mathu was a confection of the Church of Scotland and Alliance High School at Kikuyu, Fort Hare University in South Africa, Exeter College in Devonshire, Balliol College Oxford, the Kenya African Union (albeit not an officer) and the Freemasons. He remained a Kikuyu through and through. We met first when he was about fifty. Although he declared publicly, in tandem with former agitator Harry Thuku become gentleman farmer, against Mau Mau oathing, I could not pick out any particular cause, other than his own field of education and individual cases, which he espoused, nor standpoint held. His manner was charming, melodious and conciliatory with a disconcerting habit of popping his eyes like headlamps for emphasis. As Kenyatta had told me, he lacked the common touch.

His bouncy ambivalence may have covered a deeper insecurity. He was way out ahead of most of his people in the formal Colonial structure, to which he was linked by education and religious affiliation. Below and around him was the dark mass of simmering discontent manifested increasingly through Mau Mau oathing. Was he, despite disclaimers, in some sense a peace wing of violence as some suspected? Insurance and double indemnity agreements were entered into by many Kikuyu out of fear and uncertainty. One oath might reasonably be regarded as a sign of one kind of tribal loyalty, support to the Government Chiefs as another, earning a Loyalty Certificate until the two loyalties came to converge or conflict in response to threat or reward. Mathu must have been acutely aware of such pressures in his dealings with ambivalent colleagues, and with junior functionaries such as myself who could offer little frank discussion of his plight. I liked him, but never came close to him. Notwithstanding, after negotiating the pitfalls through years of such lonely service, he both smoothed the way to a procession of nominated and elected African parliamentarians and, with Bishop Beecher, actively advanced formal African education and sought to make it more relevant to African needs and culture.

I was given an administrative part to play in an extension of European Secondary Education, which arose on the cusp of change in Kenya and was both politically eccentric and socially anachronistic. It came at the end of an era in which the Prince of Wales School, above Nairobi, had proudly carried the standard of local secondary education and leadership for several generations of Europeans, in some mutual antipathy with the product of overseas 'public' schooling. The election of Reggie Alexander, former pupil of the Prince of Wales School, to be Mayor of Nairobi City, was regarded as a local triumph.

The Royal Agricultural Society of Kenya had recently been granted a fine showground site, honorifically named 'Mitchell Park', excised from Crown Forest near Dagoretti Corner, where a clutter of Kikuyu dwellings faced across to Hurlingham Polo Ground and Nairobi Race Course. It was also decided to establish a parallel and equal institution to the Prince of Wales, named after the Duke of York and I was put to join a Survey Department team to walk the boundaries of a campus to be excised from the Crown Forest further along the Ngong Road towards Maasai. I did so with a will and was duly impressed by the stature and personality of the designated Headmaster, Dr James. A less promising and rather comic sign of how the times were out of joint appeared in a draft fragment of the proposed school song, attributed to the future classics master, of which I recall two snatches:

"The noble Duke of York ... nigh Dagoretti's fork".
and *"... neath Kenya's Afric sky shall hold imperial sway".*

Meanwhile a new cadre of field officers had appeared in the more populous African areas as members of the District Teams. They were called Community Development Officers and I found one already in post at Kiambu. He was Eric Peachey Wilkinson. His wife and kindred spirit was Chris. The seed nursery from which CDOs were planted out to districts was well known and long established as the Jeanes School on the Lower Kabete Road outside Nairobi. The school owed its name and inspiration to an enlightened initiative among the 'Negroes' of the southern states of America, which had been introduced to Kenya in 1924 by a visiting Commission, including the celebrated liberal West African, Dr Aggrey. The creative intention was to train African teachers in practical skills and produce leaders for their introduction into community life.

The Jeanes School complex had its own spacious and beautiful campus ideally suited to its purposes. It advanced, albeit limpingly, through the vicissitudes of war and temporary conversion to ex-service training purposes, into the last stages of paternal rule up to the Emergency clamp down of Mau Mau, and then ready to move into the broader fields of social welfare and rehabilitation of offenders. Although the European staff recruited to the new field service had no apparent common denominator, they differed markedly in background, education, style, conscious ethical standpoint, even in physical characteristics, from the generality of the regular Provincial Administration. They would probably have been glad to be so perceived.

A partial exception was Tom Askwith, my first Senior District Officer at Kitui, who had moved across in 1949 from being Municipal Native Affairs Officer, Nairobi, to take over from Horace Mason as Principal, Jeanes School. It was a happy example, as it seemed to me, of matching the qualities, temperament and experience of a man of dogged and insistently liberal attitudes to a task which brought the Administration into closer relationship with the people. Eric Wilkinson, who had already played a significant part in developing social and agrarian programmes at Jeanes School, was personally and at work an exemplar of the differences between regular DOs and CDOs. He did not wear the uniform of the lion and did not have a defined place in the executive structure of Administration. Without these labels he properly and wisely aligned himself close to the District Commissioner, the local source of authority. He and Chris, in fact, enjoyed a happy relationship with Noel and Nancy Kennaway who were, no doubt, glad of such informal relief from the restraints of rank.

Eric was of middle height and unobtrusive physique, neat headed with a trim double toothbrush moustache. He adopted a posture as well as a habit of reflectiveness, enhanced by Wilsonian tugs at a sharp briar, from which I seldom saw smoke come forth. He had a nimble and well stocked mind and contrived silently to convey an atmosphere of question, debate and

Old DC's office Maralal, 1952.
TG meets Senior Chief Lengerassi.

New DC's office, built 1953; photo with TG 1995.

DC's house, Maralal.

Caesar Cypriano Lobo,
District Clerk, at home.

Samburu District Team (Part: seven nationalities) at home of
John Ch. Cardovillis MBE (front left); (back) Tony Lavers/
Stan Kaminski/John Besson (between Jean & Garnet Seed/
David Brown;(front) Carter 'the Darter'/Una Stephens.

*Wamba 'Hospital',
1952.*

*Wamba Hospital, 1954,
inspected by warriors.*

*Baragoi Hospital,
1954.*

*Patient care by
Sister Giulietta,
Consolata Mission.*

*New District Hospital, 1955,
opened by Senior Chief Lengerassi,
with Dr Farnworth-Anderson,
Director of Medical Services.*

*Assistant minister
Jimmy Jeremiah
and Dr Trim Asst. DMS,
meet warriors.*

*Governor Baring
with Chief Commissioner
Windley (and TG) meet
Headmistress Edith Webster
at Bible Churchmans Mission
Girls School, Sirata Airobi.*

*Baragoi Chiefs with
Area Clerk David Adams
introduce first class
to Consolata Mission
School complex.*

Chief Yakáíné Lepuyapui
of Wamba Mountain Dorobo

and
Star in MGM film
'Mogambo'.

Moran Laigwenak
(warrior leaders)
Ramuré
and
Letikitik.

Corporal Lerogum, Interpreter Yole and Chiefs visiting Nairobi Show.

Samburu fertility dance;
'Ndorosi'.

Rendille widow visitor
with mud head comb.

*Impromptu dance chorus: **ingesting** and exhaling oxygen.*

Wamba monthly stock sale. Moran herding their beasts.

*Livestock Officers pricing;
Pat Grainger and
John Stephens MBE,
with Information Officer
Tony Lavers and TG.*

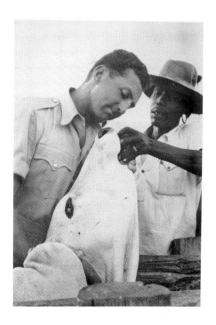

*Age check against size
by Chief Léakono/TG.*

Judging 'Supreme Champion',
TG, Interpreter Yole and winner Lekolol.

Joys of cash economy: Tax or Hospital contribution?

Dorobo hunters for elephant and dung.

Making fire with dung for smoking hives.

Leather bags for raw honey.

Testing chewed honey and wax.

Weighing for price.

Purified wax for export to Barclays Bank

*Governor Baring beholds the Great Rift
from Losiolo.*

*Meets Senior Chief Lengerassi with
Chiefs Siambu; Mfupi; Lepuyapui.*

Greets Turkana from across the Rift.

Samburu District Council Hall by traditional fig tree.

Governor (with TG) inspects Moran Guard.

Governor opens Hall with C N C. Windley, PC Wainwright,
(TG), Senior Chief, Notables and District Team.
Interpreter Paulo Rurumban, (later Assistant Minister).

Colonial Office Under Secretary Hugh Fraser, PC Wainwright,
(TG), Grazing Control Officer Brauer at Losiolo.

African Land Development Director, Paul Kelly, with TG above the rift.

District Assistant David Brown (later Chief Game Warden)
and regenerated pasture below Wamba Mountain.

Lava boulder 'road' to Lake Rudolf (Turkana).

"There is no rain."

Migration by camel pram.

*George and Joy Adamson (pushed off by TG in 1955),
to South Island to find traces of lost Fuchs
expedition members in 1934.*

Remnant tribe of El Molo (c.300) clinging to shore of lake.

Spearing perch and tilapia from dom palm logs.

MGM film 'Mogambo'; Director John Ford;
Chief Lepuyapui; (TG); Camera 'Skeets' Smith.

Film set at Ololokwe, Marsabit road. Clark Gable;
Ava Gardner with 'white hunters'.

evaluation as he sat semi-detached in District Team meetings. His interventions had a smilingly self-deprecatory cockiness which, if frustrated, could turn to a huffy show of stubbornness. He was well equipped to slip between and redirect the presumptions of control Administration and Departmental certainties handed down to the people. Our friends for life.

There was a loose and wide network of other individual personalities emanating from Jeanes School, in support of social welfare, information, marketing, soil conservation and so on, who somehow shared a common aura of 'Manchester Guardian' thinking, moral beliefs and self-perception, which both questioned accepted values and was sometimes suspected by those in authority who held them. Charles Hayes, vibrantly imaginative and compulsive Information Office disseminator, boyishly optimistic Mike Richmond with his very Mobile Cinema, kindly Colin Owen, Programme Co-ordinator, with his droopingly avuncular moustaches and Bunty Owen, famed for cookery classes, all spread their skills into the adjoining Kiambu district.

Two participants in the 1947 Course for African District Officers, supervised by future PC Desmond O'Hagan, were an ex Sergeant-Major S. O. Josiah, who took the orthodox Administrative path, and an outstanding Luo, Fanuel Walter Odede. The latter became suspected of extending Mau Mau influence in Nyanza and was restricted to the Northern Frontier District at Archer's Post abattoir. Pamela Odede, his beauteous and accomplished young daughter, caught many a settler's breath as she strolled the main street of Nanyuki, to be within 50 miles of her father, before she was captured by Tom Mboya — who had also attended a Jeanes School course — as his equally famous wife.

The Community Development outgrowth from Jeanes School was concerned in the spread of a nation-wide movement started in 1948 called *Maendeleo ya Wanawake* (The Progress of Women). This rapidly became of immense significance in both practical welfare measures of every kind and in bringing women into positions of social leadership on equal terms with men. It was unfortunate that these warm currents of human progress should have been temporarily engulfed in the chill waters of the advancing tide of Mau Mau.

A surprising outcome of the attention paid at Jeanes School to athletics, including encouragement to sports at district level and the installation of an internationally recognized track and timing arrangements, was the early flowering of two sprinters from the Goan community. One, Seraphino Antao was hailed as a national champion for his record breaking 100 and 200 yard victories which I witnessed. The groundwork of training was laid by the mercurial Archie Evans, but it was not until nearer independence that African athletic heroes sprang to the fore with the twin impetus of professional training (by a State Department assigned black American) and

162

a sense of pride of African race. One of the first was world famous distance runner Nyandika Maiyoro from Kisii, who became an honoured, if unqualified, member of Community Development.

I had a disconcerting experience in the educational field, when invited several times to give after dinner talks to the sixth form at the highly reputed Irish Catholic Secondary School at Mangu. On the first occasion my host was a Father Mackie, widely known as the 'singing priest' since he had sung duets on radio in California with Bing Crosby. After a trencherman's dinner in the refectory Fr. Mackie swept ahead of me into the classroom where some forty sixth formers and staff sat patiently to hear I know not what. "Boys, boys!" intoned Fr. Mackie in his ripe tenor. "Do you want to know why this is called a 'dark continent'?" Without waiting for the obedient murmur of assent, he cried at full throttle "Because of your blasted ignorance!" At any rate I shared my own with theirs, and happily their questions were equally barbed. It was the year before a State of Emergency was declared and less unctuously questionable sentiments were expressed by brave priests, such as old Father P. J. McGill, exposed to constant danger in isolated mission schools, who spoke directly and fearlessly against the excesses of Mau Mau intimidation.

Two years in Kiambu were not confined to the endlessly fascinating daily grind, the settler-official mingling at the Kiambu Club and the golf course, where I usually ran rather than landed on the fairway. There were endless semi-formal dinners within the 'boma' community, each leading to another, with overlapping guest lists, proper invitations by card and planned allocation of seats at table by perceived seniority, including wives, which could lead to silent umbrage, especially at the awkward settings for eight. A meal would start with 'first toasties', once enticingly called 'sucks' by a club waiter. There would always be sherry glasses and two for wines. Soup would follow, then a fragment of white Tilapia lake fish with a bland parsley sauce. Meat and many 'veg.' would be coarse and plentiful with roast, not chip potatoes. The sweet would be very sweet, leading finally to savoury 'second toasties' like 'devils on horseback', prunes rolled in bacon, or less creditably, sardines on toast. Tables decorated with family silver 'objets' were noticed and napkins would be linen and starched. The modest sequence would be assisted on its way by liqueurs in tiny glasses, mostly Drambuie, Van der Hum from South Africa, Beehive Brandy as cognac, or a Tusker beer for the manly. How did we afford it on our pittances? One did one's best.

Invitations from settlers, mostly coffee estate owners or managers, were more rare and represented something of a distinction in 'crossing the tracks'. Cecily came from Australian/Norwegian origins, and had stayed on her Uncle Cedric's mixed coffee farm near Kitale, or with her unassuming father Jack Tofte, a Chartered Accountant and her redoubtable mother, a

European School matron. There were many different 'tribes' and classes of settlers. Contacts normally came about at Kiambu club. I admired silver haired and parchment hued Colonel Ted Belcher, retired from the Indian Police and now guardian, with an invariable libation of pink gin, of access to a men-only select 'snug', known as Ted's Corner. Of an intellectual bent were Noel and Gillian Solly, he quizzically rubicund, she socially questioning author of *Turn But a Stone*. It was a marvel that such a variety of individual characters achieved a degree of social, but not political, solidarity which persisted in the run-up to the changes in their way of life as wider political events overtook them.

We became friendly with a prominent Sikh family in Nairobi, who owned British Furnishing House in Government Road and were proud that one of them, Kirpal Singh Sagoo, was a nominated Member of Legislative Council. His dignity was enhanced by a grey beard of venerable abundance making it hard to believe he was not yet forty. A younger brother, Dayal Singh, was a successful artist who had just returned from what would once have been called the Grand Tour of Europe. One night six of us went to the then tiny Donovan Maule Theatre near the old Bank of India. It had tight seating for 78, including the top of the bar at the back, but was already a triumph of the courage and tenacity of flamboyant Actor-Manager Donovan Maule and his equally determined actress wife, Molly and daughter, Annabel. Despite such humble beginnings it had achieved and retained something of a cult status among the resident European and diplomatic communities. There we sat without much common language; two turbans, two silk pyjamas and one suit and long skirt, midway to the right of the aisle, unmistakably distracting the attention of the audience from the play, who seemed more absorbed in surmise as to our presence. We in turn surmised that some of the interest might be connected with furniture accounts outstanding. Such awkwardnesses were in process of change even before Donovan and his many talented company including leading lady Jean Parnell, flame-haired guest 'diva' José Trevelyan, versatile Robert Beaumont, durable Kenneth Mason and the dependable Ollingtons, moved up a level to present such giants as the thunderous old Sir Donald Wolfit hamming Shakespeare on the larger and splendid air-conditioned stage next to new Parliament Buildings on City Square. A touchingly handsome leading man on contract from Britain, Ivor Earle, tragically developed Hodgkin's Disease, and I was able to attend his deathbed in St George's Hospital, then at the Hyde Park Corner site conditionally leased* from the Duke of Westminster's estate.

While movement by night was still secure we had the choice of a variety of hotel-restaurants around Nairobi. Brackenhurst Hotel was a lively

*Reverted and reopened as Lanesborough Hotel: 1990.

watering hole for pilots, actors and writers, many from overseas. The Njogu Inn was a wayside pull-in when drinking and driving were still the norm. At the Wattle Barns, appropriately located in the countryside and known for its cuisine, we met an extraordinary character lavishly entertaining all and sundry, giving the improbably upper class name of Rivers Atherston Royston, but hailing from South Africa. He was under thirty, indecently attractive, and so persuasive that he had 'sold' for cash, to the greedy, impecunious or gullible, shares in a large cargo of copper wire from Rhodesia, said to have been sunk in Dar es Salaam harbour during the war. It did not exist, but enquiry and prosecution were inhibited by the embarrassment that among his 'suckers' were counted the highest in and land, even Judges at court. Meanwhile, he lived and loved the heroic life style of his invented name, until the sad day when it was revealed that he had a previous conviction for stealing underpants from the O.K. Bazaars in South Africa. The denouement was a cause of ribald satisfaction to those whose buttons had not been undone. He long remained a sort of folk hero. In the words of Noel Coward's contemporary ditty "I wonder what happened to him".

As a physical and mental release from the teeming variety of work and people in Kiambu, I began one day to head for the rippling silhouette of the Ngong hills to the south of Nairobi, forming a natural boundary with Maasai country. On the way Cecily and Kevin with Sean, since born in the Bydand Nursing Home at Westlands, would stop off at Hoppy's ranch-style Ngong Inn on the fringe of the European green belt of residential holdings. Hoppy Marshall was a character. Retired on pension from the Prisons Department as Kenya's last hangman, he was nicknamed for his 'peg' leg which he would mischievously wield beneath a table to startle women, upon whom he doted, into fearing the worst. His inn was a favourite playground for children.

The Ngong hills could well have qualified as mountains, rising in dark blue undulations like Paul Henry paintings beyond the city, itself at over 5,000 feet. They had a visual and spiritual fascination for those blest to live in their cool shadow amid the forest glades of Karen, named after the enchanted Danish chronicler, Karen von Blixen Finecke. She had woven the spell of her native Gothic inspirations into the joy and sadness of her dreams and struggles for her altitude resistant coffee, her love for her elusive admirers and her devotion to her feudal fairyland of Kikuyu workers, under the all sharing eye of Farah, her Somali familiar. I had loved her *Out of Africa* long before passing through her 'realm' but found it difficult to relate the ecstatic prose-poem to the earthly preoccupations, the shabby petrol stations and stores of her suburban successors, although they revered her name and took pride in preserving her *Mbogani* (in the woods) Lodge in their midst. Perhaps Pliny, the Roman historian, had meant his full aphorism of *Ex Africa Semper Aliquid Novi* to convey this wonderment.

The story of Denys Finch Hatton, white hunter-lover, did not then strike any chord with me. He was the most elusive of Karen's three musketeers; the fickle, syphilis infected Bror, her husband; the gently cherishing, romantic Berkeley Cole and Finch Hatton himself, her noble 'Galliard' or 'Ariel', who crashed to death on the hills near Voi after abruptly leaving her home, his place of refuge. They all seemed to me, without knowing their own stories, as cherubs blowing wind from the corners of a masterpiece, or midges flitting around a bird of paradise. I would drive to the shelf below the first peak of the Ngong hills and stride the switchback path, passing the memorial where it was said that lion would rest in honour of Karen's fallen knight errant. At the last rise I reached a narrow track through encroaching bush, where buffalo had dropped huge, helically spreading pats and lurked cunningly to accost an unwary passer by. The air was intoxicatingly pure and only the sounds of distance echoed up from the heat haze of the vast Uaso Kedong valley.

It came as a wonderful surprise when, after two years in Kiambu, I was called to the office of the Chief Native Commissioner, Edward Windley, by the Secretary, Leslie Pritchard, and told that I was to be posted as District Commissioner at Maralal with the Samburu people, the separated cousins of the northern Laikipiak Maasai. Leslie was a trimly elegant man with thickly combed auburn hair, feathered over the ears, above a very deep collar and blazer suggesting ex-Army 'mufti', which indeed was so, as he was one of the 'baby Colonels' on Mountbatten's staff. His manner was modestly friendly and I was sorry when he soon chose to take a top position with Gallaghers' Tobacco in Rhodesia. I owed the next five years of work fulfilment to his commendation.

It was a parting of the ways. Cecily and I separated and Kevin and Sean remained with her in Kiambu, save for visits to distant Maralal. Ogoma Wakaya returned to his home and a teashop at Kendu Bay in Kisii District after years of good companionship.

XVI

SAMBURU DISTRICT
RIFT VALLEY PROVINCE
MARCH 1952–MAY 1956

"We see you, but we do not bid you welcome since we do not know you. When we have come to know you, we shall tell you what we think of you." Thus spoke Senior Chief Lengerassi,* as I was presented to the assembled Samburu Chiefs by the handing over District Commissioner, Jimmy Butler. It was easy to accept young anthropologist Paul Spencer's** current analysis of the Samburu that I was entering a 'patrilineal gerontocracy', (Government by old men: OED), in which the grade of Elder stood at the summit of tribal hierarchy, not to be down-graded as 'Elderly' in the British honorific of Senior Citizen. The xenocracy of Direct Colonial Rule cut across the disciplined structure of grades, leaving open the path to unregulated autocracy.

Lengerassi was a last exemplar of the old tradition confronting the new, in me!. His withered frame still flickered with the flame of authority. Somehow it did not leave him, even when signalled only by his double *wildebeest* tail flywhisk waving from the red oat grass where he might lie prostrate, a bottle of beer and sweet brown sherry to either hand. Was he not head of the El Masula, most numerous of Samburu clans, and had he not sired an infant by his recent child bride?

Accounts of the origins of the Samburu were varied and confusing, both as to the meaning of their collective name and their ethnic roots. One version of 'Samburu' was taken to derive from a sort of tanned hide Gladstone Bag, the 'Samburr', used to carry loose harness and personal effects. Another was an uncomplimentary nickname meant by their more potent Maasai cousins to convey that they were like 'Samburimburr' or butterflies, both in disposition and decoration. They more usually called themselves 'Il Lokop' or the 'people of the world', implying their right to appropriate cattle in others' hands, who might call it stock theft.

Their ethnic descent, if indeed they were concerned with such an exotic concept, had three possibilities; namely 'Nilotic', positing arrival from the west; Hamitic, favouring provenance from the 'Horn of Africa', or Nilo-Hamitic, assuming a conjunction of the two. The first, put forward by individual explorers and some anthropologists, seemed to be contrary to the logic of facts. If they had moved from the lower Nile basin only one jump

---

*'Ole' or 'son of' used in the 'Maa' tongue of the Maasai was compressed into a prefix 'Le' in Samburu usage.

**The Samburu: A Study of Gerontocracy in a Nomadic Tribe: Paul Spencer, Routledge and Kegan Paul, 1965.

ahead of the demonstrably uncircumcised Nilotic Turkana, across the scorching '*suguta*' (salt flats) south of Lake Rudolf (renamed Turkana), how was it that they emerged with circumcision an essential part of their culture and with a tradition of mutual hostility with those pressing behind them?

On the other hand, the south-westerly thrusting eastern Hamites like the Somali exhibited similar refined facial characteristics and total commitment to male circumcision as well as female clitoridectomy. Furthermore, the Samburu were, to an extent, bonded and fused with the more numerous Maasai, whose dominance already extended through the Rift Valley and deep into Tanganyika. Over centuries of warfare and proximity some blending of disparate races was inevitable, even if not so dramatic as one case brought to me in court when a trespassing Turkana herdsman, under the pressure of a Police patrol in hot pursuit, was arrested triumphantly circumcised for all to see that he was a true Samburu.

All explorers concur that a great swirling, mingling and skirmishing took place during recent history in the vast zone contained between Mount Kulal looming over the south eastern shore of Lake Rudolf, the floor of the Great Rift Valley, the savannah then occupied by the Laikipiak branch of the Maasai before their scattering or annihilation by the Purko clan; and the eastern plateau occupied by the pagan Boran, driven south and converted by the Islamic Somali.

Place names also defined boundaries as occupied, at least seasonally, by Maasai or Samburu nomads. *Donyo* applied to mountains; *merti* to a plateau, such as that towards Marsabit mountain; (g)*uaso* and *engare* to rivers and water; *aibor* to anything white; *soit* to rocks, often defined by colour. Even where explorers or their patrons' names were attached to significant landmarks, such as 'Teleki's Volcano', dedicated by his companion and chronicler, Von Hohnel, to Austro-Hungarian Count Samuel Teleki de Szék, who himself gave names to lakes Rudolf and Stephanie in honour of his own Royalty, and to the Mathews Range as a tribute to General Lloyd Mathews, Chief Minister and Army Commander of the Sultan of Zanzibar and provider of his lifeline; all had their local appellations, although the foreign ones might be assimilated into usage. There was even a certain snobbery about this and I often heard the mountain Dorobo Chief Lepuyapui refer to his own '*Ol Donyo Lengiyo*', in the choicest Chelsea accent as 'General Maychoose'.

The slender boned, dark to copper skinned, loop-lobed Rendille peeled apart from the Samburu to the east of Mount Nyiro and the Ndotos. The Samburu, scattered by constant fighting, harried by the Turkana, and their herds depleted by rinderpest fever, had for a generation taken refuge with other tribes and in the mountain fastnesses of Kulal and Nyiro. Their associated client tribe, Suiei or Dorobo, had mustered in isolated groups of hunters in the forests and on the boundary of the Laikipia plateau, depopulated and undergrazed. When first recorded by the succession of explorers from the 1850s, the Samburu had been referred to in rather derogatory terms as *wakwafi* or *burkeneji* (*il aibor kineji*, the 'white goat people'). They only gradually reassembled and recovered their morale, numbers and livestock under the protection of Kings African Rifles patrols and Colonial Administration within defined boundaries in the 1930s.

Meanwhile, the prophesy of a great serpent coming to divide the Maasai land had been fulfilled on an epic scale, albeit with a deal of writhing in the process. The practical purpose of what became known as the 'Maasai Move' was not much in dispute when it was embodied in a 1904 Treaty between the panoply of the Colonial Government and the great *Laibon* (rainmaker) Lenana representing all the Maasai groups. In fact the local signatories of it, Governors, Maasai and Lord Delamere, showed goodwill, good sense and mutual trust, despite some lack of these qualities on the part of the distant Colonial Office. Basically, it was intended to separate on fair, agreed terms the quite different needs of pastoral nomadic people, who depended on livestock for everything and did not kill game for meat, from the more intensive and disease controlled farming practices of a very few Europeans with established 'rights' of occupation.

A series of technical delays and misunderstandings, with some broken promises and policy differences, caused an extraordinary mass to-ing and fro-ing of Maasai people and livestock from south of the railway line to the former Laikipiak Maasai grazing grounds and back, which tried the trust of the remarkably resilient Lenana and exasperated the settler farmers. The process was strung out for more than ten years until it was largely reversed with the main body of the Purko Maasai accommodated between the Mau massif in the Rift Valley and the Loita plateau in a settlement regarded later by the Carter Land Commission as unduly advantageous! The number of Maasai on the move was once recorded as 10,000, with one million small stock and quarter as many cattle.

The significance for the Samburu was twofold. On the one hand the occupation of the near empty Laikipia plains by settler ranchers left them apart from the depredations of the Maasai which had largely confined them to small stock. On the other they had secure access to the 800 square mile Leroghi plateau, with its forested slopes and springs, which enabled a rapid build up of cattle and human population. Elspeth Huxley noted in 1935 that by "1928 there were 115,000 head of Samburu stock (largely cattle) owned by 6,500 people on the Leroki Plateau" alone. The uprooted Europeans with some camp followers regarded Laikipia as only part of the 'promised land' and cast envious eyes on the Leroghi plateau, setting up a border tension which was heightened by clashes over stock theft and attendant spearing of herdsmen. The ranches leased nearer to the border were called the '50 or 30 cents an acre' lands to reflect the increased element of such risk.

The focus of Samburu District Administration, in terms of settler border relations, stock marketing, disease control, policing, communications and other services, was to the south. For these reasons the District was administratively controlled from Provincial Headquarters at Nakuru, the settler Township and railway depot on the main line bisecting the former Maasai grazing, and only 100 miles distant via Rumuruti and Thomson's Falls. Legally it remained an Outlying or Special District within the Northern Frontier District, requiring permits for entry via Isiolo or Rumuruti.

The District, as so formed, was over 9,000 square miles in the shape of a plump tilted pyramid with the apex at the south eastern tip of Lake Rudolf. The 800 square miles of the 'promised land' adjoining Laikipia was a high plateau rising to Poror summit and the Karissia hills, often referred to as 'breeding bulls' of the land. The barren and sparsely covered remainder was loosely termed the 'low country', descending from 4,000 feet near Wamba Sub-station and Trading Centre towards Isiolo in the NFD, and to Baragoi Trading Centre on the track to Lake Rudolf in its wind blasted volcanic sump at 1,800 feet. Within the low country, forming a protective crescent to the east, were forested mountain ranges, from flat topped Ololokwe on the Isiolo to Marsabit road, to Uaraguess above Wamba in the Mathews range, north to the Ndotos and Nyiro, as far as Kulal beside the lake. The climate was equably hot and dry at 70 to 90 degrees maximum, with seasonal rainfall below 20 inches down to 10 or less, or none.

In this vast territory lived a largely nomadic population estimated at between 35 and 50 thousand, nearly all of one tongue and tradition, and in both akin to the Maasai. They were divided vertically into eight mainly exogamous clans, variously spelt, and horizontally into whatever number of age sets or circumcision age grades were living at any one time:

Clans	Status	Age Grades	Circumcision
El Masula		(Marikon	c. 1880
Il Pisigishu	Elders	(Terito	c. 1893
Lorogishu		(Merisho	c. 1912
Longieli		(Kiliako	c. 1922
Lokumai			
L'ngwesi	Marriageable	Mekuri	1936
Loimusi			
Nyaparai	Moran	Kimaniki	1948
(plus)		(initiates)	
Suiei/Dorobo	Indigenous		

Despite the vicissitudes of their recent history, the Samburu remained much
preoccupied with the minutiae of their traditions and ceremonial, including
the coiffure, adornments and ochre paint of the Moran, and their close
relationships with each other and with 'familiar' steers. There was a useful
tradition of personal leadership by which exceptional Moran were appointed
to the style of leader or *Laigwenan* (plural *Laigwenak*) which was adapted
for administrative purposes to provide a sort of cadre of clan prefects,
entitled to carry spears.

To serve the peculiar needs of Samburu District there was a polyglot
team of individuals, hailing from over ten different countries. Without cross
correlation they were:

Positions	Staff Serving (1952–1956)	Origins
District Commissioner	T.G./G. Hill (leave relief)	UK
District Officer	Antonin Gregoire, 'John', Besson	Ireland
District Assistant (2)	Fritz Brauer	South Africa
District Clerk	David Brown	Kenya (born)
District Livestock Officer	Mike Cooper	Uganda (born)
Livestock Officer (3)	Hector Douglas	Poland
Land Development Officer	Denis Doyle	Germany
Forester	David Edye	Greece
Game Warden	Rodney Elliot	France
Works Officer	Frank Englebrecht	Czechoslovakia
Ranch Manager	'Harry-the-Gyppo'	Goa
Abattoir Manager	Jack Fairhall	Romany
Health Assistant	Pat Frère	
Locust Officer	Pat Grainger	
Mayor (Hon)	Jock Green	
- J. Christos Cardovillis	Colin Hill	
	Jim Howard	
	Stan Kaminski	
	John Kidner	
	Peter Lepelley	
	Caesar Lobo	
	Sandy Munro	
	Pat Patrick	
	Garnet Seed	
	John Stephens	
	John Wreford-Smith	

Less than half were married but all lived well and were settled in their jobs
and homes. Wives participated as team members in every aspect of District
life from livestock sales accounting, to sports days, to 'happy hours'. There
was no Medical Officer, save Doctor Lowi at Thomson's Falls. There was
no Education Officer and the DC was Chairman of a District Education

Board, including the UK Bible Churchman's Missionary Society and the Italian Consolata Catholic Mission.

Jimmy Butler walked me up to what was to be my only home for most of the next five years, from the age of 29. He was in his thirties, comfortable rather than muscular, with thick locks of dull blond hair met by upwards darting eyebrows, which he waggled quizzically, in time with the heaving of his shoulders, as he emitted ecstatic wheezes of laughter, punctuating his repertoire of mischievous comment on people and events. He was quite unpompous, tolerantly perceptive and very instructive to a newcomer. Pam was shiningly dark, violet eyed and graceful, keeping her own smiling counsel with the stillness that hints at deeper waters. They both eased the practical problems of introduction, as did their staff with James, my new factotum, who had taken over from much missed Ogoma.

The DC's bungalow was the uppermost of the widely dispersed cedar offcut and corrugated iron houses of various other members of the District Team, each enjoying its own eminence on the hillside overlooking the village and, sometimes magically, as far as Mount Kenya 100 miles across a misty carpet to the east. A curving, gravelled ascent ended at a fork, the upper prong leading to kitchen quarters and water tanks, the lower by a flagged path to a rockery girt terrace, on which the house was set above a murrum surfaced tennis court. A pergola afforded a moment of privacy as visitors shouted their arrival or switched off engines. The front garden was mainly of orange flowering aloes, jagged desert succulents and shrubs, from behind which at dawn an old soldier-gardener would lurk to leap to attention and salute my extensive morning libation.

The bungalow itself was of mud and dung plastered withies set between cedar posts with a cedar shingle roof. It was entirely surrounded by a cedar railing verandah. There was a living room large enough to entertain the District 'scrum' if upstanding, with a spitting fire of gnarled red cedar for the cool nights. The central dining room inside the main door barely sufficed to seat six and opened on to front and rear double bedrooms, as well as the back verandah, with a larder once raided by a civet cat, and a bathroom with a senile trickle of a douche, fed from a wood burning boiler replenished by my garden admirer. James' kitchen which produced simple miracles of colonial cuisine, was skirted by a pathway to a splendid look out post and 'thunder box' latrine, recently demolished by an enraged buffalo being savaged by a lion. The same buffalo had casually walked through the tennis net, and sometimes heaved a sigh as its rasping hide reclined against my bedroom wall. One day he went too far in greeting villagers and my guests and had to be shot.

The guest accommodation consisted of a thatched rondavel down rough steps which tripped the overindulgent, and a disabled, iron wheeled caravan, which an earlier DC, either 'Sharpie' or 'Daddy' Cornell it was said, had 'liberated' from an Afrikaner Road Foreman while he was away. He then took the precaution of 'losing' the rear wheels to secure possession and level the cab against the back slope. It was much in demand by the amazing turnover of guests of every kind, from film star to borehole driller, to Colonial Office bureaucrat, some thousand in my five years.

A few hundred yards below was the DC's Office near the T-junction, where the main gravel road from Rumuruti turned off to the Trading Centre. It consisted of three rooms in line, with partitions up to wall height under a gable roof, and was of the same material as my house. One office was mine, entered by the District Clerk's central room, which opened on to the Tax Clerks. All conversation was audible so that I could hear Caesar Cypriano Lobo's warning to a visitor, "He is angry this morning," followed by a fat chuckle. From the T-junction a worn footpath led through a grassy dip past a magnificent umbrella shaped flowering tree, said to be 'Ekebergia Rueppeliana', which emitted such an intoxicating smell, just like orange blossom, that I always looked forward to inhaling it. We built the first Samburu District Council Hall near by under a huge wild fig tree.

On the corner of the one broad, dirt street, divided by a straggle of pepper trees, there was a large general store of the inevitable cedar offcuts under corrugated iron, together with its godowns and a bungalow at the rear with a unique diesel electric light generator. The notice across the fascia read John Ch. Cardovillis, the Greek merchant who was known to the Samburu as 'Giriki' and to us as the 'Mayor of Maralal'. Across the street were the galvanized iron, petty trade shops of two alien Somalis, that is from British Somaliland, who were also links in the chain of livestock traders and butchers which extended deep into Tanganyika. One was the uxorious but ingratiating Issa Mohamed, whose compound fencing was regularly hung with voluminous 'Mother Hubbard' attire. Of a different kind was 'Effendi' Farah Rageh, formerly of the KAR, ramrod and soldierly, ready in his seventies to leap nimbly to the high pommelled saddle of his caparisoned and snorting pony for a neat exhibition of 'bending' between ochre daubed, spear carrying loiterers.

Over a drainage depression, set apart from the shops, was a crudely constructed beerhall, owned and presided over, dourly but very profitably, by a powerful elder, Lekalja. He would deposit wads of toxic notes and cotton bags of blackened shillings on 'J.Ch's' front counter, leaving them, unreceipted, to set against all his requirements for months ahead. When exhausted, he would silently replenish without demur. Transactions would be recorded in a school notebook by lovable shop assistant 'Nikko' Angellopoulos, happily cheeping and twittering. Trust was complete. The store was a bank without charges, which came from goods sold or transported. It was also the Royal Mail. One day Lekalja came to me with a packet of 10,000 shillings, at 20/- to the pound sterling. He instructed me peremptorily to tell the Government Doctor in Thomson's Falls to cure his son of TB, which had caused him to be invalided out of the Kenya Police. No expense was to be spared in treating him exactly as a European; accommodation, drugs, food and all. Dr Lowi, who was an open minded Czech, undertook to do his best, including experimental treatments as an in-patient. To my knowledge the son was taken back by the Police, the attack having been arrested in time. Lekalja and I never felt the need to speak of it again.

Next to 'J.Ch' was 'Bhola's Wagon Works', established long since for the ox-wagon halt at Maralal, which corresponded to the Outspan at Nyeri on the eastern route to the NFD. Bhola himself was a Pakistani, trim, grizzled and open faced. His *dhoti* style trousers were protected by a mechanic's apron on which, with sprightly courtesy, he wiped his oil grimed hands to usher wayfarers to his spotless family quarters, to wash and share a meal served by his gentle, handsome son Siddiq.* Bhola's was the only and reliable repair service for 100 miles each way. It fortunately coincided with the Land Rover revolution, which changed the nature of field administration and development, as well as slipping many a spinal disc on the original 'torturous', shield-backed seats. The remainder of the flat area within the corner of the Karissia Hills was taken up by the 'lines' of the Tribal and Kenya Police, the Station Hands and, not least, the primitive, rickety Government Hospital supervised by one Hospital Assistant, which we had perforce to push over before we could secure funds for its replacement. There was a Government Primary School beyond the village and a small Detention Camp providing extra labour.

Such was the hub of my bailiwick, from which to extend the 'benefits of progress' to the distant rim of Samburu land according to many a plan drafted hopefully or launched by those before and now serving with me. All fell into a clear pattern of need. The be-all of existence was livestock, mainly cattle, though in the low country the Samburu still kept to the tradition of 'white goat people' and to the north made great use of camels for migrating with the upturned frames of their mushroom huts, like swaying galleons under sail, infants peeping from hide cabins atop.

The constant task for us, if not for the Samburu, was to keep the livestock population within the variable carrying capacity of the land, both by disposal of surplus and by upgrading of pasture and beast. Each aspect was complex. The carrying capacity, in terms of bovine units (equivalent to 5 ovine), was rarely better than 10 acres, often not even 40 to the unit, and the cattle were generally poor and stunted. By any reckoning both land

*Years later I lunched there with explorer Wilfred Thesiger who had retired to Maralal and wrote in Siddiq's upper room. Siddiq kindly remembered me as quoted in *We Came in Dhows*; Cynthia Salvadori; Kul Graphics Ltd., Nairobi, 1998.

and livestock could only deteriorate without some practical control and remedy. Hitherto, the low country herds had relied in lean times on seasonal access to the Leroghi Plateau and some control had been exercised through the provision of floodwater pans and boreholes, financed under the post war renewal of a pre-war 'Dixey Scheme' for the NFD, although such points tended to concentrate overgrazing and trampling around them.

In planning any controls, it was of primary concern to have understanding and acceptance of the part played by livestock in the psyche, the ceremonial, the pride and prestige, the security and insurance, the nurture and well being, in fact the survival of the whole fabric of the Samburu tribe. For a largely illiterate people, without even the Somalis' daily use of Arabic script in bush schools, branding the 'Suras' of the Koran onto wooden tablets and lively minds, cattle were not only food, clothing and shelter, they were objects of sensual beauty, the music, poetry and song of herding, the blood and milk of sustenance and sacrifice, lonely company and affection, stimulus and entertainment and the proof of bravery in protection against lion or marauder.

Their preoccupation was not as complete as that of the warlike Nilotic Dinka, beyond the Turkana, whose crooning infatuation with their beasts was recited stork-fashion on one leg in the silence of the Nile *Sud*. It was qualified by the hard experiences of survival. They had a shrewd and stubborn calculation of the merits of retaining a system which was not seen as destructive and appeared to guarantee its own continuity through product and increase, not to be matched in sterile unproductive coinage. A balance had to be found in which the benefits of the past could be sustained and improved while providing for the needs of the future, such as education and health, by means of a partially cash economy with material goods to buy, which would encourage culling of useless stock and marketing of improved surplus steers.

Solutions were complicated by several extraneous factors; the uneasy border relationship with the vocal and influential European ranchers in Laikipia, who coveted the adjoining Leroghi plateau and feared disease and stock theft; the onset of the Mau Mau emergency and the increasingly manipulative influence of the Moran soldiers concentrated into an anti-Mau Mau Company, and the inevitably conflicting needs of game and the new National Parks with the introduction of controlled grazing area and water supplies. On the positive side we had the inestimable support of ALDEV, the African Land Development Board, under, in my time, two imaginative former DCs. The first was inspirational and cultivated Richard Hennings. His successor was tireless Evangelist of the harmony of man and nature, Paul Kelly, he of the wartime Mobile Cinema.

Their hydraulic engineers, who worked with our team on the ground, were led by 'gentleman' George Classen, whose monocled eye, dowser's fork and drilling rods would strike water from Biblical rock and his theodolite entice from catchments into dams water which would run to waste. Every device was used to spread the supply up to giant bulldozers and graders gouging out a 100 million gallon reservoir and dam across the watercourse at Suguta Marmar, a Dorobo enclave on the Laikipia boundary. We smugly contrasted this with the 44 gallon steel drums still propelled by calloused feet uphill from the river to Jack Forrester's Stores at Rumuruti.

The authoritative structures and democratic traditions of the good natured Samburu helped continuous consultation and action by the able and enthusiastic young expatriate field staff already in post. Apart from the District Livestock Officer, at the Veterinary Improvement Centre, who was responsible for the entire District, first John Stephens, then Denis Doyle and Hector Douglas, there were three Livestock cum Grazing Control Officers for Leroghi plateau alone.

The Leroghi trio, all around thirty, could hardly have been keener or more suited to the work. They were Garnet Seed, Fritz Brauer and Jock Green. Garnet's given name was after Dublin born Field Marshal Viscount Garnet Wolseley, whose astonishing career in Africa, from north to south, and in Army reform, was capped by the huge, inverted boat-shaped helmets since imposed on Colonial Officials on parade. I wore my two thrice; khaki for the re-interral of a preceding DC; white for the Queen's coronation parade and for a gubernatorial visit. Garnet, who would never have been seen dead in one, was stocky, tough, complex and volatile with a winsome smile and a dangerous eye. His romance was hunting and the wilds, about which he knew much and wrote a visitors' guide. He was blessed at his home below mine with warm hearted Jean, little Colleen and Robin. There was a rift in the lute for a while involving his threat, reported to the Governor, to shoot me for curtailing an invidious domestic affair which upset our close community morale and endangered his own career. It burnt itself out without casualties, but had its moments.

Fritz was crisply blond and cocksurely handsome, deploying discipline, logic and sure knowledge in his dealings with the Samburu. He married Jill Skinner, mercurial artist daughter of a Laikipia ranching family and I was proud to be their 'best man'. She painted huge wall panels of us all in our own clubhouse, which were appropriated by a mean spirited successor DC. Jock was of a similar mould thrown in Devonshire clay, but with a modestly persistent and conciliatory style of securing clan agreement to our strange innovations. They worked closely with each other and with the Samburu Grazing Guards, in sharing out grazing and water between the clans with rights on Leroghi.

Usage of grass varieties required skill and method. The swaying red oat ('themeda trianda') and the various delicate star types ('cynodon dactylon') were to be encouraged, while the coarse 'pennisetums' were to be hammered, particularly the knotted, bamboo-like 'mezianums', which drove out the sweeter grasses like bunchy 'hyparrhenia'. The Samburu liked to burn the dried ranges seasonally and move about freely, competing with teeming, white rumped, flick-tailed Thomson's and Grant's gazelle and yapping Burchell's zebra for the green shoots springing from the ash after rain.

Range management and livestock control* were introduced in overlapping phases after mainly good natured consultation. First, blocks of land were agreed for the various clans, taking into account human and cattle numbers and the distribution of water. Within the larger areas smaller ones were flexibly marked out for intensive grazing by concentrated herds. If they were put to advance in mobs shoulder to shoulder, shoving and jostling in a given direction, they grazed down broad swathes of grass like some animated mower. Willy-nilly they ripped and munched whatever stood in their path, coarse or sweet, trampled the crushed residue and plopped great pats of homogenized manure behind them to enrich the new growth.

Better livestock management meant finding markets for excess and increase, by way of sale or other disposal. We had already at the western exit from the district a crude corrugated iron structure rather unheroically called Archer's Post Field Abattoir (Alas Sir Geoffrey Archer!). This crude Veterinary Department Animal Products facility, stood upon the scorching rocks over the Guaso Ngiro, inscrutably watched by marabou storks awaiting their bony feast and beak painting their scrawny leather legs with pure calcium excreta in a grotesque travesty of white stockinged can-can dancers. It was managed, in turn, by a gentle Voortrekker with pebble glasses and Boer bush hat, Frank Engelbrecht, and a slender, lubricated bronze, salamander, known only as 'Harry the Gyppo', who hailed from the Thames Valley caravans and disproved the aphorism that 'you can't put 20 bottles of Tusker beer daily into a pint person'... The evidence lay in ten thousand crinkly beer caps neatly carpeting his compound paths.

The abattoir annually slaughtered, hung, flayed for hides, stripped for *biltong*, drained, rendered and dried for blood and bone meal, several thousand camels from the NFD and such emaciated cull cattle from Samburu as could straggle into its portals. Access to a better class of beef market was from Leroghi plateau along the fenced side of the Laikipia ranches, where there was a Veterinary Department Quarantine and holding ground, called Kirimun, managed by a massive, taciturn young Pole, Stan Kaminski, which could filter through 'clean' cattle direct to railhead at Thomson's Falls for onward despatch to the huge concrete Kenya Meat Commission Abattoir on a railway siding above Athi River beyond Nairobi.

---

*A negative version of this fully documented programme is at page 159 of the "Investigative Account" entitled *No Man's Land*; George Monbiot, Macmillan, 1994.

The diseases most feared by the ranchers were bovine pleuro-pneumonia, which often lurked unreported in the nearby Seiya Valley, and the more widespread foot and mouth. The latter hardly troubled the Samburu, who dealt with an infection by wiping a smear from the nostrils of the first detected animal and spreading it by hand across the remainder of the herd, so that all had the feverish symptoms together. When blisters appeared on their feet, the herd was walked across rocky ground to burst them so as to encourage scab formation and healing. Since outbreaks were not rare the fever tended to be light, and I was shown shaggy coated beasts at livestock sales indicating that they had passed through it. Another obstacle to sales was the prevalence of measles, resulting from defecation around *manyattas* (nomad village) and shared grazing with the pretty but heavily infested gazelle, which showed up as multiple cysts in slaughtered beef carcasses, grading them unfit for human consumption or reduced to manufacturing or canners grades. The prospects for improvement and marketing were bleak, without a series of incentives and controls, amounting almost to a social revolution, at least on the Leroghi plateau.

First, we asked the elders to set aside, but still within tribal ownership, an oblong strip of some 40,000 acres along the Laikipia boundary. This was initially to serve as a *cordon sanitaire* against disease, stock theft and violence. It was to be a cleansing and fattening ground for the most promising steers and queen cows bought at stock sales. It was the first African ranch in Africa, established by the local Samburu Council and having its own staff and budget. It proved an essential element in acceptance and participation by the Samburu in the complementary processes of improvement in living standards.

The search for a Ranch Manager lighted on a demobilized Armoured Cars Captain, Nick Carter, whom I met while visiting the Samburu soldiers at Nanyuki. The post being unique, I had looked for an unusual candidate. Nick was over thirty, red bearded, field experienced, competent in Swahili with a little Samburu. He was broadly self-educated with a literary bent and had been a hand on J. B. Priestley's farm on the Isle of Wight. Above all he was independent, stubborn and fanatical but with a humorous twist. He became as famous as his book, *Carter the Darter*, for initiating the programme of saving rhinoceros by stunning them with narcotic darts from a crossbow and uplifting them to safer environments. He had an excessively boisterous young motherless buffalo, from whom one rasping lick was enough, and a floppy Pekinese called *Siambu* (roan) who trekked in superior fashion on muleback. Nick proved ideal for the task and was a cultural buffer between settler and Samburu. He recruited a small cadre of Ranch Guards and trained a tall copper-hued Dorobo borehole operator, Joseph, to cement his relationships with the local Dorobo under their shrewd Chief Leratia, whose ample person plied across the border on a

o

Vespa, illegally carrying bags of maize flour from the mill of skinflint Andrew Dykes, the Scottish bane of my life.

The Samburu Ranch could carry up to four thousand cattle with ample water and good grass. This number was to be built up from stock sales held once a month at Maralal, Baragoi to the north and Wamba to the east. There were already minimal cattle quotas laid down for the Chief of every clan in the area to bring to the crushes for estimation of value on the hoof by a Livestock Officer, who purchased on behalf of the Kenya Meat Commission. Vouchers were scribbled out for the owners to take to the payout desk in a wooden lean-to where a Livestock Officer's wife (unpaid) would count out notes or cash, less any tax due and offered, for which a receipt would be issued by a Tax Clerk. I frequently took part in each activity, learning a great deal during direct handling or valuing of several thousand beasts of every age, size and condition. A particular discrepancy in valuing was that of age related to size. In females this could be ascertained by lifting the tail and checking the teeth. Worn out, late cut bulls called *Sattima* could be quite deceptive. Runtish elderly gents, whose furrowed, lustful brows and aggressively bunched up humps gave the lie to their small stature were paraded under the pretence that they were tender young steers (*Mungo*), never to be bulls (*Laingok*) at all.

What was now needed was a system of upgrading and incentives, leading to markets and usable cash income. This was where the ranch and the new controls came in. We began with more selective pricing at stock sales. The previous best price of 150 shillings (about £7) was trebled for young steers for fattening and selling on as clean standard beef for the Nairobi market, thus realizing valued added profit for yet higher purchase prices. Competition was further stimulated by awarding an improved breeding bull from the local Veterinary Department Centre to the person who had already secured the highest price. Response was immediate and enthusiastic, notably by shrewd trilby-hatted Chief Lekolol of the Longieli clan who started to stabilize their cattle on permanent, managed holdings. Some splendid steers were offered and the judging ring was packed. After fattening, inoculation against tick borne diseases and precautions against measles, the Samburu Ranch began to supply Nairobi in quantity on nearly equal terms with some of the Laikipia ranchers.

The next phase in progress towards overall de-stocking was the introduction of choice in the selection by the people of things like hospitals and schools, for which voluntary deductions could be made at stock sales, but all was not yet sweetness and light. Mutterings in opposition to strict grazing controls coalesced in the person of an elder of the Il Mekuri age grade and the Nyaparai clan, one Lesilélé, who had persuaded a Samburu Company in the anti-Mau Mau forces at Nanyuki to threaten mutiny. It was not a traditionally acceptable posture for Moran to adopt but the circumstances were unusual and serious enough to send me up to talk with them. In consultation with their Company Sergeant Major, Mick Rowlands, we decided to play it formally, standing easy on parade to inhibit any agitation such as 'the shakes' to which Moran were prone in tense moments. After a very frank but good natured exchange I undertook to carry their views back home where I understood that Lesilélé had offered to spear me. I co-operated by having a spear-maker fashion an exceptionally fine wood and iron haft with a leaf blade which was honed to gleaming perfection. At each gathering of clan elders, who always left their spears outside, I asked Corporal Egelai, a steady, half Turkana Tribal Policeman, to thrust his *Excalibur* of a spear into the ground in front of the squatting Lesilélé. It became known with mocking ribaldry as 'Lesilélé's spear', but he never attempted to draw it and we almost became smiling friends.

After this problem Senior Chief Lengerassi decided to let me know what conclusions about my stewardship he had reached. Through interpreter Yole Learmogo, often ambivalent and hesitant in delivery, he told me in the time honoured phrase, once addressed to Queen Victoria, that I was a "blanket", without extending the metaphor to bugs. He then said that I was like an "anthill", or a termites' red soil tower, upon which the rain fell without impression, and from which the flying ants flew safely. So far, so good, but then came the teaser. I was indeed the "big nose", which evoked a murmur of assent. Yole reassured me that this was entirely satisfactory as the function of a nose, the larger the better, is to keep the eyes from knocking against each other. I felt a sense of mutual recognition and acceptance of my role, which was confirmed by the conferral of a nickname by which I was addressed directly in Samburu and Turkana and spoken of thereafter. It was *Édera* with heavy emphasis on the 'E'. It was said to mean the sort of withy without knots or kinks cut from a bush to make a walking stick. No one greeted me in any other way.

The passing of these hurdles encouraged me in two further directions. The first was to link desire for social benefits like hospitals with voluntary deductions at stock sales. The other was almost visionary and certainly politically risky; no less than the collection of contributions to build up a fund to buy additional land in Laikipia within the scheduled areas of the highlands, where the 1920s Laikipia Farmers' Association was open "only to adult farmers of purely European descent", although many descendants were visibly not eligible in those terms.

In the complicit and well founded hope that we would secure funds before long to replace the tumbling-down Government Hospital at Maralal, we turned to the needs of Wamba, the eastern Sub-District HQ. It was only a tiny village, with a few alien Somali petty shopkeepers cum livestock dealers, but it already had a Bible Churchman's Missionary Society School, run by two brave English women. The Government was represented by one of two remarkable Kikuyu Sub-District Clerks, the other at Baragoi to the north west. Leonard Waithaka from Kiambu had become more a citizen than an exile. He was an inscrutable, slow spoken man in middle years, his skull like face rarely lit by a smile, but his quietly formal manner had gained the ear of the clan elders who would heed his opinion. I could never tell whether he was in any way influenced by Mau Mau.

He and the elders expressed the unanimous wish for a decent cottage hospital to replace the present, thatched shack. After alternative sketches and careful costing in relation to monthly stock sales, we agreed a plan of action. There would be a permanent building with 20 beds each for men and women and a furnished dispensary. The walls would be of nearby rocks, to be bound by anthill mortar. One would be carried in by each Moran bringing an animal for sale. The roof would be of corrugated iron with a hardboard ceiling to reduce heat and rain noise. The cash requirement would be met by an automatic deduction of 20/- from the price of a single beast (in addition to any tax due), with on the spot exemptions for poverty granted by the clan elder present. The District Works Foreman, John Besson and the Kikuyu Master Carpenter, Obadiah, from Maralal would supervise and construct with voluntary labour provided by clans in turn. The Wamba Hospital was completed within months and was a huge success, rating a Hospital Assistant, and encouraging a similar project at Baragoi. The more ambitious project for purchase of Laikipia ranch land was deferred for cross border consideration.

Although the Wamba chiefs came from the same clans as those on Leroghi, notably El Masula, Lorogishu, Lokumai and Dorobo, they operated quite independently in controlling their part of the low country and the mountains. Their cattle needed at least forty acres to the beast competing for sparsely seeding grass with ubiquitous 'harvester' ants, and they traditionally depastured fat tailed sheep and white goats which browsed in the scrub between the few boreholes and dugout pools in dry river beds. They clashed frequently with Boran raiders on the NFD border. I was never at ease with the Lokumai Chief, Lenyakopiro, who seemed to have some direct information line to the PC's office in Nakuru and was, without anyone's apparent recommendation, alone awarded a 1952 Coronation Medal. His plump cheeks under a round pork pie hat, glinting steel rimmed spectacles and tubby body encased in khaki bush jacket, sat oddly on smooth tubular legs with schoolboy socks and shoes. He exuded a sense of being rather above any discussions I had with his colleagues. Perhaps he was and we never directly conflicted.

Contrariwise, Chief Yakaíné Lepuyapui, of the Dorobo people in his General 'Maychoose' mountains, was a heroic figure by any reckoning. His towering presence and personality pervaded many later happenings. He was well over six feet, of lithe build, muscled like a steel spring. His cranium was perfectly formed, with cheeks and forehead as deeply etched as a Leonardo drawing, showing determination without anger and awareness unlimited by lack of formal education. Every movement was vigorous and graceful and I walked behind him through the bush for many hours without ever mastering the hinged thrust and pace of his tireless and economical stride. We could communicate about any subject as far afield as Egypt or Burma. His was the energy behind the implementation of an ALDEV design for piping water from the long arrested flow off the forested Uaraguess mountain down to Wamba village, which had depended on camel and donkey supplies once the seasonal stream nearby had dried to a trickle.

Under Lepuyapui's guidance, with ALDEV technicians, 'Brookie' Brookland and 'Wally' Argent, able young District Assistant David Brown,* and guarded from elephant by my orderly, Letengen, we set about the task. We each carried two interlocking lengths of light, red, resinous pipe up a steep path worn smooth by elephant, despite their forays and trumpetings, laying it a few inches below ground or clamped with stakes to any side fixings. We made small cement break-pressure tanks at intervals to prevent the rush of water from the boxed spring at the top from jerking the pipes apart. It was a wonderful moment when at a collecting tank in the village the first bucket of clean cold water was ceremonially drawn from a tap in the middle of a reclaimed cover of star grass.

Just above Wamba Village, on the way to the Archer's Post Abattoir and Isiolo, the Samburu Honey Refinery was set up for the mountain Dorobo honey gatherers and elephant hunters of Chief Lepuyapui. They were mostly old and grizzled with surprising agility and skill, as well as poisoned arrows. A hardwood stick twirled by hand, with gut tautly stretched on a small bow, into a softwood matrix quickly produced fire, upon which they lit dried twigs and elephant dung to smoke out a swarm from within a suspended wooden honey drum. They then shinned up the tree and milked the drum as if an udder, scooping out mingled raw comb and floral matter in a delicious white pulp. This was put in a leather shoulder bag strapped across an empty one on the opposite shoulder. The mobile honey separator would scurry through the forest masticating dollops of pulp until it yielded mouthfuls of wax to be placed in the other bag. Arriving after many hours at the corrugated iron refinery he would sell the wax and liquid by quality and weight to the operator, with evident delight. When purified by boiling in an old baker's vat the wax would be set in aluminium bowls into moulds of pure orange hue which fetched a good price from Barclays Bank as sealing wax. The purified honey, dark and tangy, would go to the bulk trade in four gallon tins.

Directly responsible for this enterprise was 'Igo' Mann,** the

*Later Chief Game Warden of Kenya.
**The Times (London) Obituary, 1 November 1986, 'Polish refugee who devoted his life to Kenya".

Veterinary Department Adviser on Animal Products, including the Archer's Post Abattoir. Indeed Ignacy, often referred to as Igor or Ego, did nothing indirectly or without éclat. He fought his life through from being 1920s Polish Olympic canoeist, graduate of Lvow and Brno University Veterinary Colleges, wartime refugee in Rhodesia, to ever expanding expertise in livestock and meat production in Kenya and abroad. On the way through Romania he found Erica, his brilliantly beautiful wife and indispensable sparring partner. Their home and obsession became rooted in Africa. If you did not detest him you joined and loved him, as I did with all his budding genius brood. As often as I drove up to stay at his unrivalled domestic 'museum' of Africana in the heart of Nairobi he would appear like some carved eagle in floppy shorts through a wrought iron portcullis and greet me. "Terry, bastard. Come at once and read my draft paper on Hydatid Cysts to be delivered in Kiev next week." I did and, over the years, never escaped my duty of minor English adjustments to papers on such impenetrable matters as Cystocercosis and Kwashiorkor in children, delivered finally with cacophonous clarity. Erica, meanwhile, planned African Townships and Trading Centres throughout Kenya and, with indomitable precision and social involvement, stimulated every kind of cultural and productive idea and artifact.

My happiest mule and foot safari along the Mathews and Ndotos ranges was spent in company with Johnny Wreford-Smith, our Forester. Although younger than me, and with a swivel hipped ploughman's walk from a youthful accident, he was sturdy and bushwise. He had been born in East Africa of a famous Provincial Livestock Buyer father in northern Karamoja, who had once been equal partner in farm No's 112 and 121 on the Uasin Gishu plateau (Maasai for striped cattle) near Eldoret, (where he also built the first mud Standard Bank), with Denys Finch Hatton, fated flier and intimate of Karen Blixen. Their partnership contract styled the one as 'gentleman' and the other as 'farmer'. How could they play cricket together? Johnny quite rightly took me in hand. He saddled my reluctant black mule, saw off charging rhino, charred the goat, caught yellow barbel, gathered wild honey and helped brew our nightly chocolate with goatsmilk and Martel brandy, as we recited a wartime radio comedian Syd Walker's catchphrase "Ee, if ever a man suffered!" Our campfire entertainer was huge ex-KAR Sergeant Simba, hewn from oak. He would heave a full 14 gallon copper camel baramil to his knee, then to shoulder and straight arm stretch, while bragging that he was not allowed to enter Company Orderly Room lest his salute caused the windows to shatter. We saw 13 rhino grazing openly like cows within sight of our camp and watched at night a vain lion clamber onto a high rock overhanging a deep pool called Mewa which phonetically echoed the sound of his amplified and terrifying roar — May-Wa! Along the forest tracks carpeted with elephant droppings the dung beetles did their silent cleansing work.

No visit to Wamba was complete without calling on Jack Fairhall, the resident Livestock Officer, and mine host at his offcut and corrugated iron house set high on the hillside. The panorama of the low country was the inspiration for his favourite cowboy ballad, "Oh, bury me not on the lone prairie, in a lonely grave just six by three." Jack, now in his thirties, was a former Sergeant-Major in the Royal Scots Greys. His neat, spare, person did not carry an ounce of excess 'condition' from top to toe. Thin, carefully combed, dark hair and trimmed beard set off an earnest expression in keeping with his serious west country burr. He wore only carefully pressed shorts and pipeclayed gym shoes. His entire safari equipment was contained in a small homemade matchwood case with a tin clip fastener. It consisted of a spare vest for company, a white cotton face towel, steel comb and scissors, a Mason Pearson oval hairbrush and a small bottle of Vaseline Hair Tonic. His toothbrush was a splayed bush twig. The case with a saddle blanket served as a pillow. Tireless and competent in his work, he misguided the English and Swahili languages into gems of quaint precision. I never saw him with any weapon save a jack knife, which he called a 'kiss you' in his rendering of the Swahili Kisu (Keysoo), spiked on which he would courteously proffer a chunk of salted ox tongue as 'first toastie' with a bottle of Tusker beer. This would be followed by a bubbling, butter fat brown skinned, rice pudding, soused in Tate and Lyle's Golden Syrup, a dish he referred to as Cockie's Delight or Bullockie's Joy.

Jack was a card. His saucy anecdotes of life around the world were unforgettable, including an account of the police in Georgetown, British Guiana who carried boat hooks at night to haul in inebriates, who fell into the numerous canals and were required by law to wear Mae West life jackets with neck rings to rescue them from being washed out to sea. One day he overstepped the mark when delivering mail to the ladies of the Mission. The formidable Miss Ruby Grindlay greeted him guardedly from the top step of their verandah and assured him she was well. And how, he asked, was her younger, still comely, companion, Maud Parsons. "She's in bed with malaria!" *Horrible dictu*, Jack asked with the most sincere concern after 'his' health! Utter dismay and near diplomatic incident, requiring the DC's immediate assurances of innocent intent! Happily, perhaps even for blushing Maud, Jack was forgiven and I remained well received at the Mission House near Maralal.

Education on Leroghi plateau had not yet reached the level of Christian rivalry described by Mark Twain as "snatching a soul right out from underneath your nose." The Bible Churchman's Missionary Society's mother mission was located at an idyllic spot a few miles from Maralal called *Sirata Airobi* (cool breezes), which also had sweet water springs and cannabis growing wild. There was an excellently conducted school for girls at primary and intermediate level in good buildings of local materials. The whole establishment gave the impression of being as spotless as its staff, giving girls a head start over boys. The Mission head was the sturdy and Reverend Richard Hacking, flying buttressed by Grace, his wife. My special favourite was violet perfumed and gracious Jessie Scudder, prematurely white haired widow, with her son John, who must have been lonely without a chance of normal mischief. The third teacher was Edith Webster whose modest spinster address could not possibly have excused my ex-army Persian clerk, Ahmed Khalil, his war medals wickedly dangling in a plastic envelope on his lapel, as we all celebrated the Coronation at my house, enquiring bibulously as to the number of her children. When invited to the Mission for high tea we would take care in slipping away to our vehicles for additional refreshment.

At the boys' Primary School across an open sports field beyond Maralal village, the splendid, javelin throwing, Teacher-in-Charge, Paulo Rurumban, of the Kimaniki age set and the El Masula clan, emerged with near 200 feet as one of two Samburu athletes of international standard. He graduated into national politics. The other was Jonathan Lenamiria, who came up from BCMS Wamba to compete in the high jump and won a medal in the Vancouver Commonwealth Games, despite being under 6' tall. Sporting events, often held after regional stock sales, at which many Moran gathered, were prodigiously popular and regulated with difficulty by all members of the District Team. Entry was open to all comers and sleek red body cloths were the only strip, ripped off and carried for sprinting to free flailing limbs, tossing ringlets and testicles, for maximum power output. Defeat or humiliation sometimes set off the palpitating frenzy known as the 'shakes', which I encountered in other contexts.

Rather grandly, there was a District Education Board of which I was Chairman. Grace and Edith were members, joined recently by a distractingly handsome Italian priest from the Consolata Catholic Episcopate at Nyeri, Fr. Barra. His presence as their Education Supervisor was to obtain clearance for a Catholic school up the fertile Barsalinga re-entrant near Maralal and for a full Mission Station and school at Baragoi, both being the first Catholic ones permitted in the NFD. After some decorous wrangling between two entirely well intentioned seekers after souls, Edith's gentle inflexibility gave way to the extent of agreeing to "submit to this contagion", at which my own early Jesuit bonding led me to ask, "As one disease to another, Fr. Barra, are we all agreed?" He responded smoothly, as if it was he who had been converted. Both projects went ahead to the lasting benefit of the Samburu.

The first of many safaris to Baragoi, several hours north by lorry or Land Rover, revealed new wonders, large and small, some of which I have compressed into one account. Quite unavoidable were the drainage runnels dug across the track by French Works Foreman, John Besson, to whom I shall return. They were universally known as 'buggerjohns', as being the instant ejaculation jerked from those whose lumbar discs were impacted. The track wound upwards through blackened skeletons of cedar trees, relics of successive forest fires, interspersed with promising saplings born from their heat burst seeds. They gradually gave way to blasted but living survivors festooned with silver haired lichen or 'old man's beard' serving as sponges to absorb the mountain mists which trickled down to moisten the crushed forest mulch.

Approaching the 7,000 foot summit at Poror there were intrusions of Podocarpus timber trees with crisp, delicately pointed leaves spread in pale green fans from silvery trunks, as if to herald emergence on to a 'high place' from which to be seduced by a vision of 'the kingdoms of the world and the glory thereof'. It was possible to make our way even higher along a grassy plateau to the very lip of the Great Rift valley, called Losiolo. This always evoked for me the *Los Patios de la Mañana* (Courts of the Morning) in John Buchan's romantic description of the terraced descent from the *Mato Grosso* (great forest) highlands in Brazil. From Losiolo it was possible to peer into the echoing Rift 3,000 feet below, and past ranges of distant mountains on the far side, dappled by scudding cloud systems discharging their slanting rainstorms.

Another time, escorting the gallant Sir Hugh Fraser, Under Secretary for the Colonies, we passed near a courting pair of ostriches. The cock, whose neck and thighs were empurpled with arousal, swaying and swooping like a male Tutsi dancer, displayed his billowing feathers of basalt black and glacier white, just as seen from afar by the Kamba to resemble Ki'inyaa, the peak of Mount Kenya. The demure, modestly dressed hen swooned at this encirclement and sank submissively beneath his enfolding wings. After a long silence the entirely human knight errant, not yet allied with the luminous 'Longford girl', reputedly known at Oxford as 'hot-lips' Pakenham, asked me "Do you find, Gavaghan, as you get older, that you become more and more obsessed by sex?" I was stymied for an answer. It seemed unreal, much later in 1956, to be his guest in White's Club amid the extraordinary hubbub of powerful men responding to Nasser's seizure of the Suez Canal.

Back on safari at Poror, we camped and feasted our wind sharpened appetites on a giant black mushroom plucked by Letengen, my orderly. It was flat and rippled like a sinking buffalo pat, from which came its power, but was quickly tamed by James into a pungent mixed grill. Off again at chill dawn, we turned north towards the desolate Elbarta plains. Bucketing at ten miles an hour down the rocky track with cedar forested hill slopes to our right, we were fortunate to glimpse a single Kudu bull. 'Lesser' it might be graded in its species, but not in the noble poise of its challenging head with powerful, twirling horns and delicate white lines of concealment stippled down its smooth, slate grey, flanks.

As we came in distant view of the first expanse of the Elbarta, the surface appeared to be shifting and dancing over the dull grey gravel. It was formed of wind blown clusters of dried sage, no longer held to ground by withered roots. Between tangles of low thorn bushes, mediaeval, unicorn-like, Oryx condescended a casual stare at the sound of our vehicle. The neatly turned lances of their dangerously couched horns were balanced by flowing black tails and their silky dun coats were stencilled, as if with the outline of caparisons. Each time we came close enough to draw a bead on one selected for the pot, the group would toss their heads with a contemptuous huff and trot off just far enough for a repeat performance, which could continue for miles.

Half way over the Elbarta plain a black volcanic ridge ran across like a raised scar, through which the road passed. On the Baragoi side there was an open quarry yielding cut stone blocks. It had also attracted the attention of an American plutologist, Professor Haddascheitter, who was excited by signs of pitchblende and the possibility of a deposit of uranium oxide. His search extended to Baragoi itself after a new hospital, being built by the people through stock sale contributions, produced buzzing reactions on Geiger counters. We were happy enough that the traces had been carried unwittingly from the quarry.

Apart from such earth shattering prospects, there were excellent mica deposits being prospected in utterly primitive fashion by an Afrikaner share-farming family called Van der Merwe. I never saw a settler habitation like theirs, which consisted of a tarpaulin, drawn across a square of oil drums, held down by rocks but flapping incessantly in the desert wind. Husband, wife and two barefoot, teenage daughters, hardly clothed in shifts, had nothing but tools, utensils and a rifle for their biltong hanging in the sun. Despite their gaunt and slatternly condition they were kind, friendly and hauntingly optimistic.

I visited Baragoi many times over the years, on foot, by Land Rover, jeep and lorry. Changes were so numerous that I can only touch here upon selective experience of people and things, centred upon what was both an isolated Government Sub-Station and a trading outpost with cash flow generated from monthly livestock sales. The Clerk-in-Charge was David Adams, the counterpart of Leonard Waithaka in Wamba, who had achieved a similar status, even further from his home and despite a congenital limp restricting his mobility. He took part in everything with energy, pleasant demeanour and absolute reliability, although his service loyalty might well have been tested by the fact, which later emerged, that my Kikuyu driver, Mwangi, young, frank, open faced, whom I had trusted implicitly, doubled as a Mau Mau intermediary and oath administrator.

This did not matter much until a large number of Mau Mau prisoners suspected of involvement in the Lari Massacre, who had been severely mistreated by security forces during interrogation at *Kampi ya Simba* (camp of the lion) in Laikipia, were sent to me for restriction and recuperation, away from public exposure. I made the mistake of having horrific published pictures of Mau Mau brutalities pinned inside the lorries carrying them but visible reaction there was none. We constructed a Detention Camp at Kawop, beyond Baragoi towards Turkana, and communications with Kikuyu country were increased for food supplies and Prisons Administration. The camp achieved a certain notoriety in Mau Mau mythology for severity and isolation, which I found difficult to hold in balance, particularly as the Turkana indulged in night-time transactions through the wire, in tobacco and sex, while the Samburu offered to hunt down any rash escapers.

The two meeting places for visitors to Baragoi were the relatively large, one-counter, mud plastered shop of Mohamud Ismail, the principal trader, and the DC's safari camp of thatch and branches on a small hill above the village. Mohamud was an Isaak from British Somaliland, sophisticated, handsome and hospitable with a gift for friendly relations with all and very sundry. His ever ready lubricant for this was superb curry and rice with Black Label whisky, served at a benched table in a narrow, perfumed, chintzy room behind the shop.

A not entirely spiritual dynamic in Baragoi educational development was the arrival of Fathers Carlo Andrione and Michael (Michele) Stallone of the Consolata Catholic Mission to build their new school. I could not speak in the same breath of their relieving priest Father Facchinello, who astounded visitors by the mincing Italian enunciation of his name as if an Anglo-Saxon oath. I could not resist introducing the American professor and the Italian priest, name to name, at dinner in my rustic pavilion. Carlo was a huge smiling peasant, with the strength to manhandle his BSA 500 motorbike through mud, his tiny feet encased in soft black home stitched shoes, to shoot game for the pot with his shoulder-butt fitted Luger automatic, and caress a chicken gently to a painless dinner. With falsetto innocence he would accept "two drops" of refreshment and would contribute sweet, unblessed Muscatel altar wine to our celebrations up the hill. We called it '*Mungu* Juice' in thanksgiving. Carlo could move mountains in the service of God and Dionysus.

Michael Stallone was only 28, with glossy black curls, rosy cheeks, and happily gleaming spectacles. His short, plump body was hoist on braces up to the chest in grey flannel trousers, topped by a labourer's wincey shirt, worn without dog collar. We affectionately dubbed him 'the little stallion' or '4 x 4'. 'Michele' came direct from his priestly ordination in Italy to teach in the first three primary classes to be opened. He picked up several local languages and produced a lexicon in three. He investigated the prospects of schooling for nomads in South Horr, below Mount Nyiro, and went on to the starveling El Molo fisherfolk beside Lake Rudolf. Much later, in the steps of their Bishop Carlo Cavellera, formerly head of the College of Papal Propaganda in Rome, he celebrated mass at Loiángolani camp, a palm girt oasis in the wind blasted volcanic pit. Not far away, in company with the Seychellois camp manager, Guy Pooley, this most loveable of men was shockingly done to death by '*Shifta*' bandits from the north.

A far seeing school complex had been pegged out on a spacious campus, granted by the Samburu Council and Baragoi elders, between the DC's camp and the village, adjacent to the site chosen for a hospital. Dressed stone buildings for the Baragoi Primary School went up at a great pace, despite every 44 gallon drum of water used being dug out of the Baragoi lugga and hefted by Carlo in his battered short wheel base Land Rover. The enlistment of pupils flowed less smoothly. I had difficulty in persuading the elders, anxious for their goats and calves, that an educated lad would be just as much an investment in their future as a herded kid. The first such entrant in 1954 was the son of Tribunal Court Elder, Leiton Leparlein, of the Lokumai Section. He was given the propitious name of Patrick* and his rise to be Chief Executive of the Samburu County Council was long after retailed to me by my proud, illiterate old friend. Patrick's uncle was my orderly, Letengen.

The 'radio-active' stone Baragoi Hospital went ahead with equal speed as an informal joint enterprise between the Government, the local people and the Mission. It was opened by Dr Trim, Acting Director of Medical Services. When completed, with wards for twenty men and women, divided by dispensary and stores, it was pleasingly set in a perimeter of drooping pepper trees impervious to goat nibbles and giving shade to waiting patients. Roof tanks at each angle captured thousands of gallons of precious rainwater. Before long we also secured refrigeration equipment and an ambulance as part payment in kind for film extra services to Metro-Goldwyn-Mayer, a novel transaction for both sides, to be described later.

A great blessing was the arrival from the Consolata Order of Sister Guilietta to be nurse and midwife and, in no time, matron and mother and an inspiration to us all. Her calm face, forehead deeply lined, was framed in an immaculate white wimple and she turned her healing hand and gentle smile to every person and task that needed her skill, myself included for an ulcerated lid.

There was a side effect which we had not foreseen, but welcomed. At Baragoi there was a significant spill-over of Turkana from west of the Rift, living side by side with the Samburu, but remaining distinctive in every

*Patrick Leparlein: Director of Personnel and Training, President's Office, 1997.

respect. Paradoxically the Turkana Chief was called Mfupi, meaning short, some six inches shorter than most of his people, but he made up for any lack of stature in shortness of manner. The monthly stock sales took in cattle regardless of tribal owner so that contributions to the hospital were shared, as were the beds for circumcised and uncircumcised alike.

Baragoi became a place of some note and pride, as well as rest on the road to Lake Rudolf. On the day of our departure north in company with District Assistant, David Brown, I had a unique experience outside Mohamud's shop of a fertility ceremony by the very independent Samburu women. It was called *Ntorosi* and was a housewives' jamboree, with ribald song and dance designed to cure barrenness. At its most blatant climax it could involve a surging mass of mature women enveloping a lone male and, in the other rather unsuitable word of my anthropologist friend, Paul Spencer, "manhandling" him. It was thought to be effective, which I could readily believe as I stood in their midst and admired the unforgettable leader of the dance. Naked to the waist with clinging hip skirt of softly tanned skin, and countless necklaces to mark her triumphs, she was the epitome of fecundity. Her swelling breasts with dark, distended nipples, her softly pouting lips and inward looking eyes spoke of complete absorption in her own fulfilment, which communicated its excitement to the others. She was the most woman I had ever seen and needed no cure that I might offer.

On the way to North South Horr we turned off to climb Mount Nyiro, some nine thousand feet high, more than half of which loomed above the surrounding terrain at Tum. A thigh and lung tearing climb up an unrelentingly steep and narrow footpath at last emerged into a large, well grassed glade in magnificent rain forest with springs of delicious clear water. There was a sense of being in the verdant realm on top of Olympus, where the gods looked down on earthly creatures.

To the east, between the blistering salt flats and the lake, was the turbulent volcano named after Count Teleki by his chronicler Von Hohnel, whose name the Count in return gave to the bay beneath. Before my next safari to the lake an unexpected group of visitors to my house in Maralal was led by the formidable Haroun Tazieff, volcanologist extraordinary, and later Disasters Adviser to the Government of France. His granite visage and commanding presence blended easily with Gallic charm and grace. A subsequent illustrated account of his pilgrimage to view the glowing cauldron was published in 1954 in a scientific 'collection' entitled *L'Eau et le Feu*. A copy was kindly inscribed to me, the text rather oddly describing me as *Ce grand gaillard ... type parfait de colonial servant*. What would the other buccaneering, perfect types have said?

In the sheltered pass of South Horr, between two shoulders of Mount Nyiro and Ol Donyo Mara, was the neat spiky-hutted Forest Department outpost manned by smart Rangers in green jerseys with leather shoulder pads and bandoliers. There was a crude little shop for tobacco, salt, sugar and suchlike, much frequented by Rendille nomads from Marsabit District, their children not having the look of future Consolata pupils. There was a cluster of women, some widowed mothers marked out by high combs of mud, smoothly caked into upswept hair, rather like the curved tufts on ancient Greek helmets. They were reluctant to be photographed by our intrepid and resourceful Government Information Service companions, who brashly proffered cotton bags of sugar. One woman, of quite exceptional beauty, stood proud and glaring, with light goatskin cape, in a pose of magnificent contempt which almost defied description, except on film and in the admiring barrack-room Swahili exclamation of Tribal Police Sergeant Lerogum, '*Matité fixi bayonets kabisa!*' If pointed breasts could kill!

Across a limitless expanse of rock strewn gravel, cut by sandy gullies in which we sank to the axles, we saw little save swaying files of slender camels heading on softly padded feet for distant water, some carrying inverted hut frames with babes ensconced. There was an occasional scampering *gerenuk* antelope weaving like a whiplash across the rocks to stretch vertically on lithe and sinewy legs to nibble a spindly thorn bush. It was said they had no need of water save the morning dew. At one deep crossing between exposed basalt cliffs we were shown ancient rock graffiti with the outline of long necked antelope and geometrical patterns, believed to be of the same era as the burial tumuli of the mythical giant Madhanle in the NFD. Such spear carrying herdsmen as we came across were emaciated to the bone with shaven skulls, their dun cotton garments streaming in the wind, which tore across their ears rendering them insensible and silent. When startled by our approaching engines an identical trio turned as one, striking a biblical pose with free hand upraised in salute and Samburu supplication. "There is no rain; there is no water; there is no grazing".* We left water and tobacco and drove on.

From the lip of the gigantic depression containing Lake Rudolf, which stretched north to the border of Ethiopia, a fantastic litter of giant volcanic cannon balls spread down to the water's edge. There was no sign of a track, except for the re-arrangement of rocks by occasional passers by to reduce the fall at the steepest steps. It took six hours wrestling with the wheel to reach the small beachheads of the El Molo fisherfolk and the palm trees of Loiangolani. We spent time with the El Molo Headman whose dignity, if not his condition, deserved the title. He had gathered most of his 300 or so people, refugees from many tribal conflicts but now homogenized by deprivation and exposure to the elements. They depended almost entirely on tilapia and perch harpooned with skill from craft of lashed palm logs. Their flimsy leaf shelters survived the crushing winds only because they

*We were pictured in the BBC publication, *Ruling Passions*, taken from the TV series in 1995.

could pass through. Their diet left many with mottled skins and teeth, some with scurvy distortions of face, eyes and limbs. The Headman had one fine eye and two ornaments. We left them fish hooks, line and chewing tobacco, which was always prized.

By a lucky chance we encountered George and Joy Adamson on the very edge of the lake near Loiangolani, where the Game Department had an established camp site. They had come in from the back of Mount Kulal in the NFD, where George and brother Terence were Game Rangers. Joy had joined him to undertake the hazardous crossing to South Island, which had been his ambition since his first safari to the lake in 1934, before the ill fated (Sir Vivian) Fuchs Expedition came to grief, when two members, Dyson and Martin, crossed and never returned. The Adamsons had made careful but discreet arrangements, without letting anyone know in case of official refusal, to keep in touch by signal between his lorry headlights and their Verey Pistol. Their boat was a fourteen foot, flat bottomed wooden dinghy, with one 4 hp outboard motor for speed and a 1 hp back-up inboard for safety. The heavier allowed only two inches freeboard in flat calm; the lighter, having jettisoned the other, offered some control in the heavy water whipped up by ferocious gales. I felt quite as anxious as George's driver, Ibrahim, when we pushed the tiny, overloaded craft into the water, defying the local tales of a demon inhabiting the island from which no one escaped.

Some days later with no news of George and Joy having returned to base, I had no option but to let my old DC, Myles North, now acting PC NFD, know of their situation. Happily they were spotted by the Kenya Police Air Wing back ashore. George forgave my splitting on him and sent a fascinating account of their week's adventure: no demons, but an eighteen foot crocodile, huge spitting cobra, herds of healthy wild goats, dense shoals of fat tilapia scrabbling up rocks to gobble pink plankton slime. Of Dyson and Martin no trace save tidily gathered camp debris. I was to meet both George and Joy separately many times and was then glad to have been a witness of her redeeming qualities of courage and endurance.

In the relative safety of the shore near Loiangolani we saw within a few hours both faces of the lake. Wailing banshees had nothing on the screaming, raging wind at night. A tarpaulin securely rigged between my Bedford three tonner and the Land Rover, held down by the heaviest rocks we could carry, could not prevent our camp beds from being buffeted to its limit. A fire when finally lit saw its flames blown in tongues ten feet long, offering no hope of cooking or boiling water. We huddled miserably till dawn determined to leave at first light when miraculously the wind dropped and we decided to dispel our torpor in the calm lake.

In our party was Mirella Rocco,* Kenya born elder daughter of a

---

*Mirella Ricciardi (née Rocco). *Vanishing Africa*. William Collins and Sons Ltd., London, 1971.

flamboyant and brilliant Italian family, settled on Lake Naivasha, whom I had recently met. Her father, Mario, had been an Italian Air Force ace and was a smouldering force of nature. Her Franco-Belgian mother, Giselle, who had been a pupil of Rodin, was herself a gifted artist and was staying behind in my caravan at Maralal. Mirella was already embarked on a career as a photographer, but came to world attention long after our safari through her magnificent collection published as *Vanishing Africa*. Her unadorned, barefoot beauty, musky as burnt honey, enlisted the Moran as eager camera assistants, who posed and participated in early photographs for publication. She and I tested the lake's reviving properties in our underclothes and found it strange that the lukewarm and oily water gave no trace of sensation as it crept up our limbs to which our garments clung like skin. Our whole circuitous journey was splendidly photographed by Kenya Information Services led by Alastair Matheson, with Tony Lavers and cameraman Ted Mullis, whom I found jousting at midnight in the dry sands of the Serolevi *lugga* south of Marsabit. A duel of honour apparently.

Back in Maralal, having gained some perspective on the District as a whole, it was time to attend to local matters. Funds for the District Hospital had been voted in the annual recurrent medical budget, we having caught on to the subtle distinction of seeking an 'extension to existing buildings', which involved none of the red tape, policy and siting problems of new 'capital' works. In no time at all the rather dignified looking Director of Medical Services, Dr Farnworth-Anderson, came to conduct the ceremonial opening, hand in hand with old Senior Chief Lengerassi, who brandished his fly whisk with procreative vigour.

Before this we had been fortunate to be visited by Ophthalmic Surgeon, Dr McKelvie and his wife, a former Surgical Nurse. They had recently retired from the Sudan Medical Service and gave their practical experience of nomadic eye diseases free of charge to Kenya districts most affected. The Samburu, their children's eyes often glutinous and stuck with feeding flies, suffered grievously from still notifiable trachoma with its awful ravages leading to final blindness, as well as leukomas and cataracts. Not-so-old Chief Lekarsia of the Il'ngwesi clan could scarcely see through his rotting lids, grimacing between pain and desire to continue in service. (It afflicted me later in Somalia).

During three weeks in Maralal and Wamba the McKelvies tirelessly performed miracles. While I watched them operating on a scrubbed wooden table in the sunlight with only local anaesthetic, he showed both how tough and how fragile was the eye. He sliced and teased and painted and sutured gussets into lids, swabbed and bandaged, handed the patient to a family guide standing by, patted him on the shoulder and told him to come back in days for removal of stitches before returning home. The drug of choice at the time was Aureomycin 1%, a golden ointment. We devised an optimistic scheme for inducing at least the young Moran to use it protectively. Hitherto only their *laigwenak*, or 'prefects', were allowed to carry spears in order to reduce stock theft, tribal fighting and lion killing: otherwise a special permit had to be carried. Dr McKelvie had small tubes of 3% bovine ointment made up with a label depicting an eye with a simple caption in Samburu *Ol dawa longonyek* (Eye medicine). The increased strength was intended to make up for probable infrequency of application, and a freely replaceable tube, containing a residue of ointment, had the same validity as a spear permit. Since the Moran indulged in hours of *maquillage* a glistening golden sheen was thought to be quite the thing, but I knew of no medical evaluation of results. I sent Dr KcKelvie a leather bound set of Rudyard Kipling's works, to which he was devoted, as a gift from the Samburu Council.

The increased tempo of activity made the old DC's Office obsolete so we built a new one. This faced over the incoming road from Laikipia, just below the side track past our houses, across a deep old watercourse called 'elephant walk', 100 or more on many evenings, then to the Livestock Improvement Centre and onward to the Bible Churchman's Mission School. It was of cedar offcuts on dwarf walls of brick, with red heartwood corner posts and lined corrugated iron roof. It was built to last for the future and did, with a roll of DCs on the wall.

We also needed some kind of meeting place to bring together such Chiefs and outside visitors as wished to mingle with staff, and to spread our enjoyment and the cost of hospitality, sometimes burdensome, more evenly. Once again the skills of John Besson and Obadiah were called upon. This time it was our turn to contribute in cash or kind towards the considerable cost of five hundred pounds. We who did so were Founder Members and the first Committee of Maralal Club, of which John Cardovillis, Honorary Mayor, kindly allowed me to precede him as President. We each donated an identical pewter beer mug inscribed with the member's name to be hung over the bar. Among many others who responded to an appeal for funds it was enjoyed by chief Siambu with his huge beam at both ends; by beershop owner Lekalja with a friendly scowl; and copiously by the current Maasai Member of Legislative Council for the Rift Valley, Justus, or John, ole Tameno. Situated in the trees below Lion Rock it preserved a magic place of quiet resort and became the nucleus of a National Parks Lodge. Those who later paid to stay there owed much to our investment.

I must pay tribute to our John Besson, baptized Anton Gregoire at Lyons in France, which he had not revisited in thirty years. I called on leave to take news to his bristly, diminutive mother, and at Nice, to his frugal, sun bleached sister, divorced from a professor. He had come to Nairobi as a French Consular official and was an ardent collector of stamps and women, still indulging both pursuits in his retirement to

P

Maralal. A famously full breasted Samburu widow, known as the 'Guinea Fowl' cared for him. In his career as Works Foreman neither Samburu loafers nor Turkana labourers failed to grasp the import of his Maurice Chevalier accented abuse of their tongue and characters, delivered with garlic pungency. He was a bon viveur to the core and brought the sauce of life to us all.

After the concentrated activity on permanent buildings all over the district; three hospitals, a school, a Council hall, DC's offices, ranch housing, a social club and more, my Annual Report from the Provincial Commissioner arrived. The Code of Regulations laid down that praise need not be detailed, but any fault, within the power of the recipient to correct, must be communicated. The first part was short and favourable, but the second said that I "should pay more attention to maintenance of temporary buildings". Could he have heard of my use of station hands to assist the leaning of the old Government Hospital, thus emphasizing its temporary nature?

I now felt ready to beard the denizens of Laikipia in their hinterland with some comprehension both of long-standing causes of friction between our Districts and of potential common interests. The ranchers combined personal individualism and a collective sense of unity to a high degree. Many nurtured a lurking memory of the unsolved mystery of the spear blooding murder in 1931 of young Theodore Powys, Ranch Manager of Lady Eleanor Cole, at a time when the settlers' claim to Leroghi plateau was hotly disputed. To the Samburu, whose suspected Moran were tried and acquitted, it brought also a painful memory of the imposition of a punitive Levy Force so severe that it entered their language, in English. A recent complication was the infiltration of the whole area by Kikuyu squatters and employees, many being both trusted friends and active Mau Mau adherents, making isolated homesteads into armed defensive posts with weapons constantly at hand, night and day.

On the way to Rumuruti, via Nick Carter's Samburu Ranch house, I passed the 50,000 acre border ranch, which had been given as a twenty first birthday present to, unsurprisingly cocky, John Dykes by his father, Andrew, the influential and wily Scot with a finger in any lucrative chink in the laws concerning butchery, maize milling, squatter acreages and crossborder deals. Behind the roadside cedar post and barbed wire fencing of well controlled paddocks were orderly herds of beautifully presented de-horned steers. They were run in groups of fifty or more, differentiated by each six months of age and by colour; a pleasure to behold. Their slaughter value was quite disproportionate to the wages of their mainly Samburu herdsmen, who were themselves at risk of attack by their fellows.

A respected rancher, whose name was painted on a harrow disc by a cedar gateway, was Hugh Collinson, a former Lieutenant Colonel, whose civilized and fair-minded style characterized many of these lonely men. A more volatile type was Dermot Paton-Kerr, known as Der. Kerr, a small but explosive and fearless Celt, who brooked no interference in going about his lawful occasions. He had just escaped death in his canvas covered Land Rover, when instinct told him that a farmhand in the back had raised a *panga* (machete) to split his head, only to be shot dead by Der's firing under his armpit.

In Rumuruti I dropped in on warm hearted Wally and Leonie Kibble, he being now in charge of the District Sub-Office serving the widely spread ranching community. The District HQ had recently been moved to Thomson's Falls (Nyahururu)), the railhead and hub of general population, by enterprising Neil Loudon, the new DC whose reputation had preceded me at St Andrew's as golfer and graduate. Turning left at Forester's Store, he of the rolled water drums, I went directly to the cedar slab on stone Rumuruti Club set beside a crystal stream lined by splendid podo trees, along the same curving drive that led to the Governor's Camp. There was a hump of rock between on which teams of little ungulate hyrax wound their wooden football rattles through the night. The club was the social heart of the community and the meeting place of the Laikipia Ranchers' Association, whose documented customs were both arcane and strict, to the extent that only tinned milk was to be used for their tea, lest fresh milk be diverted from the nourishment of calves.

As a generous courtesy the DC Maralal was allowed access to all the facilities of the club, tennis, library, bedrooms, outside bar etc. Beside the bar entrance there was a tall window frame set with five vertical iron bars which proof of *machismo* required should be seized and bent apart. One night I found seated alone at the bar the powerful, beetle browed Major Tom Mills, whose appearance of an eighteenth century ostler belied his minuscule copper plate script and skill as manager of his cousin Brian Curry's ranch. Scholarly Brian, with his avuncular deputy, Colonel Bill Marsden, was the acknowledged master of the art of beef production, regularly turning out prime Boran steers at an average of 400 lbs cold dressed weight.

"Bloody DC Maralal, take your bloody tie off!" Tom greeted me warmly with clear intent. After some more nose to nose ritual abuse he bought me a compulsory drink served imperturbably by barman/procurer Manji. Sometimes there were bare-knuckled fisticuffs with female incitement in which I escaped involvement. Tom met a tragic and sordid death at the hand of a newly hired assistant manager who had slipped the net of the Immigration Department on arrival from the UK, having a criminal record for forgery and theft. The newcomer unwisely forged a will in Tom's inimitable handwriting leaving everything to himself, putting it about that Tom's Kipsigis mistress had administered a fatal dose of strychnine to him in a fit of jealousy at his homosexual attachment supplanting her own affections. An extraordinary CID Inspector 'Big' Bill Dent, six foot five and eighteen stone, followed the suspected murderer with relentless tenacity, appearing everywhere he went with his amiable bulk and gentle Gallic concern for his prey, until at last his nerve broke and he drove off wildly, anywhere. When he came to the end of his tether and his fuel, Bill was there with comforting arm and steel cuffs. His name was Huxley. He was hanged.

Despite the distances between ranches of up to 50,000 acres with several thousand cattle, I was able to meet, and often admire, many of these educated 'wild west' stockmen. Dick Jennings, with curly russet hair and smiling blue eyes, was stone deaf, but an intrepid monoplane pilot and motor racing driver, who monosyllabically fathered a clutch of russet 'scuttlers', as he called them. He often flew to the airstrip near Maralal and once, when flying me over Lake Rudolf, pointed down to say in his flat drawl that we were going backwards, driven by the lake wind. Major Gerry Edwards MC, gallant survivor of the World War was crippled with arthritis, but still burning with honest zeal, depended upon his nephew David, who somehow seemed the lesser. Tommy Tomlinson was a vast, moon faced old reprobate, with a bawdy turn of phrase about women and a fair product of vigorous sons therefrom, whom the Farmers' Association rules debarred from inheriting his farm, which was left to Dick Jennings, who himself had sired a similar problem. John 'Cookie' Cooke was more professional hunter than smallholder and served with Dulcie Wedd, but not wife, and son John as social mixers between cattle ranchers and the famous game ranching and capturing enterprise of Carr Hartley. A hero figure of Laikipia was Ken Cunningham, a dashingly handsome man of long established settler family with a calmly beautiful wife, Nan, and a contrasting pair of lovely daughters (of whom fair Clare married Stan Kaminski of the Kirimun Veterinary Quarantine, while dark Katherine came to marry John Wreford-Smith, our Forester). Ken would sit up alone at night in the forest towards Thomson's Falls to stake out Mau Mau gangs.

Less heroic, to my mind, was a relative newcomer, retired Major Fred Day, who bought a ranch near the salt springs of *Suguta Naibor* (white salt) on the Maralal Road. He had personal and political plans which clashed with any I was hoping to promote for land purchase by the Samburu, which would both gain in cogency from the fact that several ranches would pass to half African heirs, circumventing Highlands Board controls, and encounter political opposition from 'white highlanders'. I was told that Day and Dykes were trying to gain support and collect evidence to have me drummed out of the service. A well attended meeting in the Club, to which I was invited, debated the perennial subject of stock theft over the border by Samburu Moran and I was, as expected, given a rough time for not putting a stop to it. There was no great comfort in being told by Andrew Dykes, in his whinnying, lowland Scots accent, "Ye know, Gavaghan, we're no' *entirely* dissatisfied wi' ye," to which I could only reply that I wished I could reciprocate.

A much larger assemblage took place near the administrative boundary of Laikipia comprising ranchers, Samburu leaders and the Maasai entourage of the greatest rancher of them all, Gilbert de Préville Colvile; a gathering which was to leave me in no doubt of the seriousness of feeling against border stock theft. Since his taking up land in 1913 at Ndabibi and Lariak, Colvile had painstakingly built up vast herds and earned a high reputation among the Maasai whose language he spoke. Though narrow shouldered, with a domed elfin head, at nearly 70 he was tough as a whip. He exuded a sense of calm confidence in his status with the Maasai and that of his own Norman-French forebears, smoothed by Etonian sang-froid. The adventurous Lady Diana Broughton, mistress of the murdered Earl of Erroll and widow by suicide of his alleged killer, Sir 'Jock' Delves Broughton, had then openly sought out the wealthiest available suitor and married Colvile in a mutually affectionate and complaisant arrangement. This included the constant presence of dashing Jack Hilton, Deputy Director of National Parks, under Mervyn Cowie. Jack's gallantry was unkindly said to be the cause of a pronounced twitch of the head when Colvile tried to shake off his horns. That cause was to be removed by amicable divorce and another marriage for Diana to become Lady Delamere.

Ironically, the Samburu themselves fell victim to attack in defence of ranchers' cattle. We heard late one night, through John Cardovillis' mail lorry driver, that six cattle herds near Rumuruti had just been knocked up in their huts and their bellies ripped open by Mau Mau. Police Inspector Sandy Munro at once called out his Guard and with Interpreter Yole Learmogo, Tribal Police Orderly Letengen and several Moran spearmen, we returned with John in his lorry to Rumuruti. There we found that the Mau Mau gang had been pursued by a regular British Army 3″ mortar platoon into the fifteen mile long papyrus swamp nearby, which they scatter bombed. I saw with horror a young Lieutenant throw petrol from a jerrycan straight at a blaze they had also started on the dry papyrus fringe. The back draught of flame knocked him flat and he was lucky only to lose his eyebrows and lashes in a badly singed skin. Our Samburu posse hacked through the matted papyrus which formed a lattice floor over the swamp water and reared up to ten feet. I crawled along a tunnel into the legs of a Moran with raised spear ventilating with anticipation. Some excreta and blood further along, to our intense relief we found five bodies of the gang stunned to death in a camouflaged hideout. A hand was taken from each corpse for Police fingerprint identification.

A different kind of denouement to my visit to Laikipia was a sharp summons to present myself forthwith to the Chief Native Commissioner, the redoubtable and choleric Dick Turnbull, formerly of NFD fame as PC after 'Uncle' Reece. I had just imposed an arbitrary collective fine on a border clan for failing to hand over culprits in a recent stocktheft. As his secretary ushered me into that familiar room, Turnbull exploded at me from the back of his neck as he looked at the serried array of the Laws of Kenya on his book shelf. "What the hell do you think you are doing, Gavaghan? You know bloody well you can't find a section in the Ordinance to cover you!" I think a little dumb insolence then followed on my part as I asked with extreme respect and politeness if I could go back to the elders concerned to sort the matter out. I was able truthfully to convey to them the CNC's anger, if not its target, but assured them that I thought we still might avoid a much feared 'Levy Force' being imposed. They asked me to assure the CNC of their co-operation in punishing the thieves and signed a paper to this effect. On my return to his office Turnbull accepted the arrangement sardonically, as well he might. He had been a DC himself.

In Maralal we made careful preparations for a widely spaced succession of important official occasions; the Coronation of Queen Elizabeth; successive Provincial Commissioners' visits and a full blown Governor's Safari, but not in that particular order. My first PC was Carruthers Melville Johnston, generally known as 'Monkey' from his attractively prognathous features. He was a fine figure of a man of immense style, disciplined charm and grace. His courtesy hardly ever failed, his script was clear and shapely, even in his black flickover Police notebook with elastic band, in which he sedulously recorded on the hoof numbered notes and promises, which were faithfully followed up or redeemed and stroked off with a determined snap of elastic. I succumbed to his qualities and enjoyed a stay in his house, alive with classical music and banter with his delightful wife 'Barbie'.

On an otherwise happy safari the Johnstons brought along one of the well bred young ladies who passed through Government House, sometimes connected with the incumbent Lion of Empire. They were socially a cut above what used in India to be called the 'fishing fleet', scanning colonial horizons for a likely catch. This one was landed on me as my guest and was seated in my Land Rover as we searched for elusive elephant on the hillsides towards Wamba. I recall I was bold to point over her shoulder at a distant dun coloured rock, which I had seen was an elephant. It was as near to a touching encounter as we got, but not, so I came to hear in campfire gossip at a Government House party on safari in Uganda brought by their White Hunter, Frank Poppleton, to Garnet Seed his relative in Maralal. Hugh Fraser, apropos, had warned me to take care not to be vulnerable. I was innocent of all but passing attraction, but the smell of it in that circle persisted in more important contexts. Johnston went on to be CNC, having been honoured with a CMG (popularly known as "Call Me

God"), which provoked Douglas Penwill, the DC from whom I later took over at Kiambu, to exclaim "Permit me to congratulate you, Monkey, that the channels of promotion are no longer constipated."

Johnston's successor was Robin Wainwright, a decent and proper man, whose orthodoxy was leavened with a perfectionist dedication to beautiful joinery. This hinted at a more tactile and sensitive side than that which was clearly irked by me, tending to the headmasterly and twitting rather than the encouraging. Apart from my reported "neglect" of temporary buildings he privately told me that I was "the most amoral person he had ever met" and, publicly, at a formal DC's meeting of his "irresistible urge to clip my wings." Since I liked him as a person but could not do much to alter his opinions, an easy working relationship was sometimes inhibited. Robin's wife, Bridget, had no side at all, but a companionably humorous touch, which countered any misapplied use of a chilly nickname. He also went on to be CNC.

Meanwhile, there had been an odd exchange of civilities between the Samburu people and Buckingham Palace. Caesar Cypriano Lobo and I, on behalf of Senior Chief Lengerassi, prepared a Loyal Address to Her Majesty on the occasion of her Coronation. I had some thick cartridge paper for sketching and Caesar's ancient manual office typewriter had red as well as black ribbon. By judicious use of red capitals and sundry "wherefores" we produced a modestly portentous document rolled in pink ribbon and humbly forwarded it. Weeks later we had a stencilled, cyclostyled page addressed to "Dear Sir/Madam" acknowledging our "communication". On behalf of the Samburu I remonstrated in writing and was moved up a couple of notches in the Royal Household with an appropriate acceptance of the Loyal Address on crested paper. The negligent gaffe was atoned for during the Governor's safari by his inauguration of the Samburu Council Hall, wherein we hung a framed colour photo of the Queen, mounted side saddle, cockaded and in a red tunic much approved by the Chiefs, together with a white flag, embroidered in silk with a steer's head, presented by the Consolata Sisters.

It was the first time I had met Sir Evelyn Baring, described in John Gunther's *Inside Africa* at the time to be "one of the most aristocratic aristocrats (he) had ever met." Gunther's 1953 summation of Baring's uneven political impact, his ambivalent character and the rarefied atmosphere of his Court seemed to me scrupulously balanced and fair and reflected the man and the Governor I met at my level on this and on more fraught occasions elsewhere. Sir Evelyn came accompanied by Edward Windley, Chief Native Commissioner, by Robin Wainwright newly taken over as my PC, and by Government House staff. Windley and Wainwright stayed in my *banda* (hut) and the Governor chose the caravan. I had been briefed to supply bland food, including marmalade without coarse rind to avoid upset to his amoebic liver, but Robertson's Golden Shred still required the teasing out of slivers of simulated peel at verandah breakfast. While concentrating on this he engagingly referred to Andrew Dykes as "a sairtain pairrson", relieving me of some anxiety on that score.

Over the next few days I lived in a state of suspended reality and, I suppose, sycophantic parading by me of what had been done in the name of his Government. I was uncomfortably aware of the tolerantly amused gaze of Edward Windley whose own credentials, including courageous forest confrontation with Mau Mau and long experience as DC Maasai, as well as closeness to Royalty in the prickly esteem of visiting Princess Margaret, were secure. They soon led to his Governorship in The Gambia, of which Douglas Penwill remarked ineffably to him, "... should be a piece of cake, Edward, after DC Tana River," then a one motorboat coastal sinecure.

Although Baring — could I dare have spoken of him so? — was said in his immediate circle to have a boisterous, galumphing humour, with a honking guffaw, I did not see that side of him. Rather I saw the grandeur of the Golden Lion, radiating the magnificent condescension of a bygone era, among people of an even earlier one. For the ceremonial address in the new Samburu Council Hall the Administrators all turned out in white Colonial dress uniforms with engraved, toothpick swords, gloves and Wolseley helmets. The Governor was further decked out with helmet feathers, breast orders and bootstrapped buckskin breeches and spurs. The breeches, which were skin taut over his substantial thighs, presented a problem of flexion when easing him sideways into the front seat of my Land Rover. All in all, he cut a splendid figure, drawn to full height, with monumental head, sculpted features, hooded lids over slumbrous eyes and full lips curling slowly over his teeth in lisping but ponderous utterance. Having studied Swahili, he enunciated carefully chosen phrases, such as, *"Ninafurahi sana kuonana na wewe"* — 'delighted to meet you' — and, *"Umefanya kazi ya serikali miaka mingapi?"*— 'How long have you been in Government service?' The cadences were rhythmical and precise, with underlying plosives, as if coached by Professor Higgins to Bernard Shaw's *Pygmalion* at the ball; "How kind of you to let me come."

Stilted mannerisms seemed curiously suited to the pomp and circumstance of both Colonial hierarchy and Samburu patriarchy at their stage of evolution, as the Governor first addressed the extraordinarily varied assemblage and then mingled with the throng. Lengerassi and his elders indulged in lengthy, undulating hand clasping, meaningful looks and assurances that all was well, except for a passing list of needs. The Turkana Chiefs led by Mfupi joggled their head-dress pom poms above direct, man to man, looks from under white daubed, Hallowe'en-like make up. The Guard of Honour of Moran spearmen looked bravely straight ahead, as if we were not there, but stealing glances like Guardsmen everywhere.

Dressed country style we visited the Veterinary Department farm and admired the prospective breeding stock, an occupation that in no way reduced formality, which only marginally relaxed at the Bible Churchman's School among the delighted gaggle of girls in their white kerchiefs and blue cotton frocks. We made the routine, but always exhilarating, journey to Poror and the yawning Rift, where Baring, at the very edge of this phenomenon of nature, revealed his interest in botany, by cradling some non-conforming daisy in both hands and asking, "I wonder who you are?" It was a question we might well have asked of each other.

One of the three 'away' roles currently played by the Samburu, the others being in the anti-Mau Mau forces and as spearmen/guards at the Mawingo Hotel in Nanyuki, was the annual appearance of spear toting and ochred Moran on the Veterinary Department *Beau Geste* fort at the Royal Agricultural Society of Kenya (RASK) Show. It was a popular outing for a selected few, including a Chief, a Headman, a Tribal Police NCO, an Interpreter and my Orderly. On one occasion I took Chief Siambu of the Leroghi Lorogishu section. He spoke neither Swahili nor English, but had an ample, blanket clad, senatorial dignity which carried him everywhere and was given voice by direction signals from eyes and lips which could point round corners. The party was eager to see Nairobi, fascinated for a day by the show and the city elevators, and longing to return home by the third, as indeed was I.

Beside the Galton Fenzi Memorial globe and distance guide and the AA headquarters was a wine merchant, evidently discovered by Siambu whose body language on the Land Rover seat urged me into the kerb, where he said firmly in Samburu (phonetically) "*Kaiyu* (I want) *kalabar.*" So clear was his direction signal that we entered the shop together and his lips rounded the corner and settled on a shelf containing brandy bottles. Although by law spirituous liquor was not sold to Africans, I invested in a goodwill bottle, which Siambu clasped like a baby, crooning with content, his lips at rest. I found that the law and liquor represented the Samburus' only seriously felt manifestation of a racial 'colour bar', which had thus entered their language. We later shared a drop of *kalabar* at the Maralal Club.

In 1953 Garnet Seed, being a manly fan of Clark Gable, bet me five pounds that I could not get MGM film company to come to the District while they were making the safari film *Mogambo*, which was named not for the jungle sound but after a New York night club. Scenting interest and advantage for the Samburu and hearing that the film party were making their plans at the Mawingo Hotel in Nanyuki, I headed there directly to inspect our Samburu guards and investigate opportunities. Mawingo had first been a private house built as an emotional snare for an elusive Belgian,

Gabriel Prudhomme by his rich American wife and adorned by rare and beautiful plants, only later becoming a glamorous hotel. The Manager, Brian Gotto, and his wife Liz, both Irish, were already good friends and they introduced me to the film company in the bar, presided over by Benedict Anampio (later a Manager at the Nairobi Intercontinental), and at dinner to the stars and directors.

There sat the towering and anti-British Director, John Ford, Clark Gable, 'the King', Ava Gardiner, 'the Queen', Grace Kelly, still on the way upstairs, and a young Donald Sinden, surprisingly fruity and facetious after his film heroics in Nicholas Montserrat's film, *The Cruel Sea*. With Brian's backing, the Samburu spearmen as superb crowd models, the proximity to the District as both convenience and saving, I pressed the case for entering at once into an agreement. We would offer a significant actor/Chief with up to 1,000 warriors armed with spears on location near the humped mountain of Ololokwe on the Marsabit road. MGM would provide 3½ yards of best quality red silk cloth per man present on site, plus twenty five shillings each for the 1,000 spears made by our metal workers and 7 pounds of meat per man per day, based on 300–400 Samburu steers, the hides to be retained for cash. In addition two refrigerators would be left for the new hospitals and a Willys 4-wheel drive station wagon ambulance would be imported and coach built locally. The agreement struck was unwritten but faithfully adhered to without difficulty, thanks to quicksilver, baseball-capped Production Assistant, Eva Monley (now film producer) and Barbara Allen who with Murielle, her mother, wife of Bunny Allen, Chief White Hunter, saw that the Samburu had everything supplied.

The filming episode of some three weeks, based upon a tented camp at crystal clear Buffalo Springs near Archer's Post, was replete with enough cameo adventures to fill a book. John Ford so took to Chief Yakaínné Lepuyapui that he gave him his honorary, wartime Rear Admiral's white dress tunic; Grace Kelly bewitched us all, noticeably Gable, who accepted female adulation in general with equanimity. He was 54 and in splendid shape, but with a curiously strangulated voice, lacking percussion.

Ava was perfection of beauty, often fully revealed. She was fortunately not beset by Frank Sinatra, then at a low ebb but much flow. After taking her once to the pool to swim in her usual nude, I asked why she besmirched her loveliness with her foul language. She shrugged it off by saying that filming was just a job at which she was a professional. On set she would chew gum right up to a take, when out it would go as she launched into her lines. Her undulating dove grey silk slacks evoked a universal growl from the warriors, eliciting an unprintable offer from the Director, while she gasped to me in her turn at red silk revelations among squatting spearmen, which were hastily contained with kilt pins by Murielle Allen. My only inheritance after our brief encounter was her folding, full length, canvas bath. Such fantasies! After a surfeit of Donald Sinden's "Jolly Japes", I met the two stand-ins for the stars, each of comparably stunning beauty; Lorette Bauaraschi for Ava and, for Grace, 'Pippa' Bruce-Smith, daughter of the piratical Colonel in whose quarters as Manager of the Kyanite mine near Voi I had seen her photo. All our paths crossed again elsewhere, although Pippa died sadly young in a flash flood in Maasailand.

Less beauty and more beast were the overweight white hunters; sinister film villains Francis de Wolf, Laurence Naismith, and surly shaven headed Eric Pohlmann, whose casting reflected John Ford's aversion to things English. The warriors had fun experimenting with a spear prod or two as the monsters puffed heavily up the natural rocky steps between them. At a curry party in Caesar Lobo's house at Maralal two of them staged a corner to corner jousting match, arms behind, bellies to the fore, colliding full tilt with a mighty thunk, centre stage, while Caesar wailed "Please, gentlemen, this is temporary building!" Shades of my PC!

While the warriors were being assembled near Ololokwe before filming, Joy Adamson came to me from Isiolo and demanded to have a selection to sit as models for her series of paintings of tribal regalia. I referred her to MGM as their paymasters. Later she turned up again at Losook, a favourite elephant watering spring past the Mission school, where a small species of wild cannabis grew profusely and was chewed by Samburu when walking distances without food or water. I called at Joy's camp to discuss her needs, taking care to leave her lair safely before 'sundowners'. Meanwhile George Adamson and his boon companion and counterpart, Isiolo National Parks Warden, Gerry Dalton, took time away from their spouses' scrutiny to pass a rollicking evening at my place. Perhaps fortunately George's Maralal equivalent, Game Ranger Rodney Elliot, was away in hot pursuit of the usual suspect Italian trophy hunters, weekending from their Naivasha farms and riding the noble eland down to exhaustion. Such tales of game aroused passions which needed no fuel. Rodney's passion was of an intense nature, rooted in an innocent naïveté, disturbed by the fidgety suspicion of a gazelle scenting lion. To my and our shame we would set him off on a chase simply by pretending not to want to upset him about some offence which was not happening. His stiff greying pompadour and long neck with sloping shoulders accentuated his sinewy height through long body to agile legs, the ideal stalker. When 'his' game were at rest, so was he; modest, amiable, kind and much respected for his utter integrity.

The Samburu became something of a cult for photographers and Hollywood film makers. Victor Mature, overripe and far from intrepid, came also to Buffalo Springs to star with too perfect Janet Leigh, not at all the dramatic murder victim and always with mother, in a pseudo safari film called Udongo (Did they know it meant 'mud'?) His biceps were uplifted by leather armlets and I saw his white, crease-marked underbelly hanging over a Public Works Department mirror like dripping toast to reflect the sun's tanning rays. I was also invited to meet glorious redhead ‑Rhonda Fleming in full bloom, with her co-star Macdonald Carey, ex US Navy Commander, in a slight, but clean-cut, film called *Safari* on set beside a waterfall on ex Police Inspector David Partridge's farm near Rumuruti. David gave me a full size, framed portrait of a Samburu Moran. It faded but not the memory. He became faithful retainer and friend to Lady Delamere.

A Kenya financed film unit, set up by Alan Tarleton, then came to Maralal to make a semi-documentary to be called *No Rains in Timburi*. The Director, a straggle bearded, maverick, travel writer called Alastair Scobie, gave me kind tongue in cheek mentions in two books, *Animal Heaven* and *Paradise Precarious*, from which I stole the sixteenth century introductory couplet about the lion. To strengthen his B movie, 'Clark Gable' lookalike hero, Peter Dakeyne, Alastair had secured as his leading lady Carole Raye, star of Australian musicals, now married to a strikingly handsome Vet. at Naivasha. My relieving DC, Geoffrey Hill, and I did our best to help the most congenial crew, but I never saw the finished product. No matter: warm friendships arose with such as cameraman Eric White and Sheila Massada (unhappily professionally renamed Storm Mallory), enchanting folk singer of *Greensleeves* by the camp fire outside our new club. Closest of all was with Sylvia Storey, partner of Polish Bernard Kunicki in Mercury Film Productions, winner of the All Africa Film Festival Award, the African 'Oscar', then held at Mogadishu. Sylvia arranged everything, including a photo album for my memory. She was as gently spoken as a governess but her surface calm contained, like her luxuriant snood-held bun, a perceptive and sensitively elemental woman. Free of spirit and independent of things, she gave her all to friends in need and went to work in a Retirement Home in Nairobi, living in a two-decker London bus rescued from a settler's barn. One night her car crashed head on into an unlit steamroller outside the Swiss Grill near Westlands. Her face was broken but not her spirit.

The list of my often self-invited house guests was quite beyond recounting, but they were marvellously varied and there was never one who did not fascinate with the unexpected revelation. One such was a Falstaffian character called Sir Harold Mitchell, who regaled me with stories about his own Caribbean island, where he was wartime host to Winston Churchill, when secretly meeting the President of the United States, Franklin D. Roosevelt. One day he came to breakfast splendidly attired in *lederhosen* shorts of true chamois skins with embroidered braces sustaining them over his fine belly. "So glad you like them," he roared, "shot them myself." Contrariwise, the Government Auditor surreptitiously knitted himself a pullover while ferreting out from the service log and fuel consumption that

I had borrowed the MGM Willys ambulance to go to Malindi while its body was made in Nairobi. As luck would have it, I had spotted in the Malindi bush the crashed light aircraft of Lofty Whitehead, who carried shellfish to the Lobster Pot Restaurant in Nairobi, and the ambulance entered service to deliver Lofty to Dr Zoltan Rosinger's Hospital.

One day I found seated on the corner of John Cardovillis' shop, swinging her khaki skirted legs and holding joyous court, Lyduska Hornik Nordis, known to all as Lydushka. Of Austro-Hungarian birth, at Gorizia near Trieste where the border was bent towards Italy, she came to Kenya to join her father Hornik. In 1929 her uncle Dolfin Boldu bought 'Slains Farm' in the Wanjohi valley west of Aberdare Mountain, a resort of the 'Happy Valley Set', from a hard-up Lady Idina Soltau. After wartime sequestration it was recovered from Custodian of Enemy Property H. B. Sharpe (DC) and when, as she blithely put it "my poor dear uncle pulled his last breeze," Lydushka became the proud owner. The full family name was linked with the 'Committee of Ten' of the Venetian Republic through the great sixteenth century swamp drainer and canal maker, Doge Hieronimus Dolfin Boldu, whose crest was three dolphins. Lydushka was all of a piece, glowing with full bodied country health, perfect teeth and gorgeous Adriatic blue eyes. Silence was not natural to her generous temperament, which engaged all outspokenly and without distinction. Her Manager and constant companion was Nani Piotto. Her major domo, in Kenya as in visiting her Gorizia palace, was Italian and Samburu speaking Nyongo. She had a small string of retired thoroughbred race-horses of which one, Donino, a once celebrated winner, was her treasure. To stay in her quadrangular farmstead of many rooms with its baronial salon and cavernous hearth and dine like a trencherman on beef and polenta amid a company of loved hounds, was a symposium of warm and lasting friendship.

An unique and involuntary guest at Maralal was Makhan Singh, General Secretary of the East African Trade Union Congress, who had close links with Kenya trade union and Mau Mau leader, Fred Kubai. He was legally restricted to Maralal where we were required to provide secure family accommodation for him and a precise circuit of movement to my office, to the rear of John Cardovillis' shop and back during daylight. His mail was to be censored by me. He was a short, prickly Sikh positively bouncing on his self importance and his rights, which he would tick off on a meticulous list as often as he could get at me. Item: "Your office boy says you are not in his pocket!" Item: "Why must I go in Mr John's backside?" Item: "When I am climbing to my house, I whistle and my wife whistles to save us from buffaloes; nobody comes!" I liked his spirit and fortitude and passed all his letters and annotated books, save only to underline passages which seemed to balance his more extreme views. A bizarre encounter took place outside my office, linking Makhan with one of my next visitors. This was Hugh Fraser, Under Secretary for the Colonies, accompanying William Gorrell-Barnes his official counterpart. Somehow, Makhan Singh had expected a Labour party House of Commons 'pair' to be with them and, bristling like a terrier at Fraser's ankles, demanded to know "What has happened to Labour MP?" From his lordly height and in full voice Fraser responded with feigned surprise. "Oh, I shot him!" The rest was silence.

The Colonial Office pair made a fascinating contrast. The one, as already met, was a red rather than blue blooded aristocrat; the other an outwardly proper and astute bureaucrat, securely at the peak of a brilliant service career, having once been Private Secretary to labour Prime Minister, Clement Attlee. During a quiet evening over whisky and crackling cedar fire, I hazarded a question above my station. "...You seem to have a very high opinion of Michael Blundell's place in the scheme of things?" After a Mandarin class pause for silent osmosis of thought into shared solution, one or the other said, "One makes use of the instrument to hand." It mattered directly to me since Dykes and Day of Laikipia were said to have brought to Blundell's attention as Member of Legislative Council for Rift Valley my floating of the idea that the Samburu might offer cash to buy border ranches.

Another Governmental pair were part of the East African Royal Commission, appointed in January 1953 to examine land development and usage in general, which had a particular relevance in Kenya to the environmental plan of Roger Swynnerton, Director of Agriculture. The two Commissioners, also Privy Councillors, referred to engagingly by the Queen in the Royal Warrant as "Our trusty and well-beloved", were Rowland Skeffington Hudson and Arthur Gaitskell. The latter was the eminent brother of Hugh, the blazing comet of the Labour Party. He was the inspirational General Manager of the world famous Gezira Cotton Scheme in the Sudan. Their report was influential in releasing African Land Development funds for Samburu dams. Gaitskell handed over to a charismatic Sudanese Administrator from the Sudan Political Service, Essayed Mekki Abbas, who when later invited to tour Kiambu chided me paternally for not dressing like a proper DC.

In May 1955 my guest book recorded that for no very clear reason, Walter Fleming, 'Wally', Coutts and 'Bones' came to stay. The name resonated to me both from St Andrew's student folklore and from the confrontation between Wally and Jomo Kenyatta over the 1948 riots in Fort Hall against soil conservation terracing. From 1949 Wally had been Administrator of the West Indian island of St Vincent where his mastery of Kikuyu language and custom languished unheard. Now he told me he was to undertake a revision of the electoral system in Zanzibar until a new post came up.

A visitation from the glittering European realm of power, finance and Château 'Mouton' was that of Baron Alain de Rothschild. He was co-Director with his cousin, Guy, of the French branch of the Rothschild banking dynasty, which had once financed the European powers since the Napoleonic wars. By this century they had achieved unchallenged leadership of the '1,000 Names', the select few known as 'Tout Paris'. An employee of Rothschild's rose to become known as President Pompidou. Baron Alain now came to Samburu District from west African business ventures to enjoy the less dangerous pursuit of hunting wild animals with a camera. Having local responsibility for his presence I spent a pleasant evening in camp near Losook Springs where I met his charming partner. I was unversed in family arrangements at their sublime level, but found the Baron the soul of discretion with an offhand use of Anglo-Saxon profanity.

In any event I was invited, when on leave in 1954, to lunch at Alain's Paris home. This he described modestly as number one in the Avenue de Marigny off the Champs Elysées. The only such establishment proved to be known as the Hotel de Choiseul, opposite to the Palais de L'Elysées of the French President. It lay within a high wall with a black iron gate operated by a buzzer and a butler in a small inner 'temple'. He conducted me to the presence of the remembered ravishing personage reclining on a leopard skin chaise longue. She greeted me with a wave of an ivory cigarette holder. She took me through several salons to the large walled garden shaded by flowering horse chestnut trees where Alain was talking with a robust looking guest, a beef baron from Algeria. I did not register his name. We were served an exquisitely simple lunch from a gilded chariot. Attempting intelligent conversation in my one and only Donegal tweed jacket and trousers from Maralal, I asked casually if they shared what seemed to be the British good opinion of their new, young, Socialist Prime Minister, Pierre Mendes-France with his patriotic sounding name. The men exchanged glances and Alain remarked coolly: "Let him extricate us from Indo-China within six months, as he has undertaken, but let him not touch our interests in Algeria." The evacuation of Dien Bien Phu, where French forces under General Navarre were hopelessly entrapped by the Vietminh, followed shortly after. In February 1955 Mendes-France's intervention in Algeria may have precipitated his fall from power.

On the local political front a sensitive matter arose, in which it was difficult to avoid involvement. Justus, or John, ole Tameno, Maasai, was the current elected member of Legislative Council for the Rift Valley constituency, which included Samburu. He was understandably disgruntled, as an Edinburgh University qualified Vet., at being placed on the very low 'C' African salary scale. He had a reputation for drink which posed a problem, both as political member of Leg. Co. and guest in the Maralal Club. With national elections coming up, an opportunity arose for the non

Maasai districts of the Rift constituency to combine on a single alternative candidate, who would be sure to win the seat. A process of informal discussion followed between the electorates of desirable characteristics, including age, education, family, good reputation and non-contentious tribal base. The choice and the seat fell to a young, personable, married, Christian headmaster, of the small Tugen group, one of the virile, intercommunicating, congeries becoming better known as the Kalenjin. His name was Daniel Torotich arap Moi.

Some special tributes remain to be paid. When I went on home leave, altogether another story, Geoffrey Hill took over for a spell. It could not have been a happier appointment for the District and for me. He left everyone and everything in better shape than before and his departure was much regretted. He moved to General Management in a plantation company of the Mitchell Cotts Group in Ethiopia and in the Middle East, where sadly he was killed in an accident.

John Christos Cardovillis, general merchant, has been referred to as Honorary Mayor of Maralal. From his first arrival from Ethiopia at the age of 18 to join his uncle George he became an indispensable contributor to the administrative and social life of the district. In his discreet and sensitive but straightforward way he steadied and advised many a DC as well as others, in an often stressful existence. He invented the evocative term 'buffalados' to cover the mood of depression, a sort of 'cafard' which overtook many of us, enabling it to be used lightly to cover or excuse ill-humour. He had four boys and four girls with his wife Njeri, a connection of Kenyatta, some of whom I used to drive to the White Sisters' School at Thika. Later he was godfather to our third son, David. A recommendation for an Honorary MBE was successful and the honour conferred by Governor Baring. He was much more than a 'Member': He was a 'Companion'.*

It was in the nature of Colonial rule that it should be authoritarian and intrusive, even if benevolent. It has been castigated by opponents as sterile, exploitative and frustrating. Whichever may be so, it was sure to vary at local level in response to external policies and personalities and to the changing character both of the District Commissioners and the people over whom they had charge. This was demonstrably so in the case of the Samburu. They had had wildly fluctuating historical experiences, through which they had emerged into the Colonial period with their structures and traditions stubbornly intact. The question ahead of them was how they would further adapt their own needs to the influences of the developing world around them. As I came to be with them the Samburu were a gerontocracy without power based on a warrior tradition without function.

*The Times (London) Obituary, 30 May 1989: "When ... Jomo Kenyatta was released from prison and sent to detention in Maralal in 1960-1, Cardovillis was informally entrusted by the Government with his general welfare ... their good relationship continued into ... Kenyatta's Presidency."

I felt some identification and sympathy with the current *Kimaniki* age grade, the 'loafers', spanning in part my own years from 29 to 34. The frustrations on both sides of the coin of rule were considerable and I sometimes felt the explosive urge of the Moran to find release in *Ikirikir* and *Ipush*, the so called 'shivers' and 'shakes'. On occasion I only half jokingly apologized to the elders for my own repressed ill humour or 'buffalados'.

The course open to me, as District Commissioner, seemed to lie between the extreme of what was pejoratively called 'Maasai-itis' and the energetic and just detachment required by the Colonial policy of Trusteeship, as varyingly interpreted by our masters. The keynote seemed to me the enlistment of the character, traditions and resources of the Samburu to participate in their own self advancement, to a point where they could hope to survive as a distinct people. Whatever happened thereafter, they would have a platform from which to determine their future with pride and confidence. And so it fell out for a time, albeit with a degree of intrusiveness on my part!

During these remarkably amicable processes I formed a number of friendships which extended across the age grades. In the nature of things all were with men, although laughing mutual flirtation without words was quite usual with women. In only one such case did I experience publicly a sense of mutual sexual attraction displayed by a woman seated on a railing at a stock sale in a trance-like movement and gaze. Foremost of men friends was Lepuyapui of Wamba, followed by old fixer Leratia on the border, Lekolol the yeoman stock farmer and Siambu the mischievous but dignified toper of 'Kalabar'. I should add tough, plain spoken, Sergeant Lerogum and, with some reservation, my constant companion and Interpreter, Yole. I had a feeling of group pride in the Moran Laigwenak, but individually for serious and thoughtful Ramure, for lively Rukaruk and laughing Letikitik. There was an odd asexual closeness, as if of customary fellowship, to one Moran, not a Laigwenan, the beautiful, languid Molu, who draped himself over my Land Rover bonnet before my departure and asked, "What shall we do when you are gone?"

When that time came, the Chiefs presented me with a number of heifers which inadvertently caused a bureaucratic hassle.* Punctilious District Assistant and Accountant, Colin Hill, arranged sale and encashment into a presentable cheque drawn on his account. The puny cheque form was not pleasing to the Elders, who in turn freshened it in the office with the spittle of sincerity. When ironed it was credited to a suspense account pending the requisite government authority for me to receive a gift of value. After mounting to the highest levels of the Colonial hierarchy, formal permission

*Elspeth Huxley, the great chronicler of Kenya's evolution, appropriately recorded the episode in *Out in the Midday Sun*, published much later.

Q

was received for me to retain £5 for the purchase of a modest commemorative gift, the balance to be held on deposit for ultimate disposal.

The Chiefs were not amused. The gift of heifers was intended for me to remember them well, not as paper skinflints. They had no call to remember me. When on leave I spent the permitted sum at the Medici Gallery in London on a framed glazed print by Petrus Christos of an almond eyed girl with beads, reminiscent of a Samburu maiden, to hang by my bedside. Years later Major Charles Chenevix-Trench,* a successor DC and former cavalryman in Hodson's Horse, wrote to ask if the long-standing deposit could be used to mount a Tribal Police section. I demurred on the grounds that the heifers were surely not given to enable a Sheriff's posse to pursue stock thieves who might be the sons of the donors. We settled on a circular thatched shelter for people waiting outside the new DC's office, to be known as the house of 'Edera'.

The question had arisen as to whether I should continue at Maralal beyond the five years already served. Happy as I had been, I did not think such an unusual length of tenure would be to the good of the Samburu, or of myself as a 'typecast' bush Administrator. I was warned frankly by Ken Cowley, fair minded but caustic Permanent Secretary in the CNC's office, that Districts were at a premium in what he called 'the cold world outside", but I chose to take my chances in Central Province, where the Mau Mau emergency was not yet ended and I had not done my stint. It was arranged that I hand over to Philip Jones, coming from Kakamega District Court, in a most convivial and whirlwind circuit of Baragoi and Wamba. His black-lashed, blue eyed and smiling self-possession masked a perceptive sensitivity and an intense desire to acquit himself in the best traditions of the service. There was no knowing how Philip and the Samburu would respond to each other, he having a more pleasing 'big nose' than mine to keep harmony between the features of their life, but he was himself soon to leave them to the quite different perspective of the mounted Major.

*Chenevix-Trench chronicled the story of the Kenya Administration: *The Men Who Ruled Kenya*. Radcliffe Press, 1993.

XVII

CENTRAL PROVINCE
NYERI DISTRICT — JUNE 1956–MARCH 1957
MAU MAU DETAINEES — MARCH 1957–APRIL 1958

NYERI

My first exposure to the "cold world outside", after the five golden years with the Samburu, was at Nyeri, where the mist shrouded, forested hump of Nyeri hill, detached from the Aberdare massif, reared up alone and visible for miles around. I had skirted it many times on my way to Mandera ten years before and, latterly, to and from eastern Samburu, mainly to pull in at the welcoming old Outspan Hotel in time for their famous buffet lunch, with incomparable brandy snaps. A hotel log cabin was to be my home or my refuge during the next two years.

The early pioneer Township, become almost the capital of Kikuyudom, served both as Provincial Headquarters for the whole of Central Province, which had included Kitui when I served there, and as Nyeri District Administrative HQ, to which I was now assigned as Senior DO under Brigadier Pat Hughes as DC. At first I was cast down at not still having charge of a District, the more so since I had asked that, when the post war anomaly of our inverted seniority in Kakamega in 1946 was properly reversed, it should not place us together, as a matter of good sense. Happily, no-one could have been more sensible than Pat, whose amiable nature, modesty and sportsmanship made him always a good companion. He was considerate both of my enthusiasm and my impatience during our months in harness, although I was kept personally on my toes ducking barbed shafts of wit from the formidable 'Ronnie' (née Watkins). I had to thank our office secretary and general ray of sunshine, Barbara, for her lovely soothing presence.

My indeterminate posting to Nyeri, without the burdens of command, proved valuable in other ways. It was late in the day to share in the fears and dangers of the active campaign against Mau Mau, bravely conducted by many in all services, some done to death, but there was creative work of reconstruction in hand to give some meaning to the sacrifice of lives. It was necessary to switch thinking and planning away from the traditions and needs of forty thousand socially cohesive pastoral nomads, spread across a mainly arid expanse of nine thousand square miles, to the totally different circumstances of seven times the number of peasantry densely packed in a tenth of the area, relatively educated, inclined to secrecy and introversion, used to living in small homesteads on narrow forested ridges, and recently crammed artificially into regimented defensive villages. The papers I had written for Samburu and put into practice on range management, grazing control and destocking were in no way relevant. I had to adjust to a huge expansion of still mainly European, staff and services available to all Departments on a scale far greater than the simple, intimate District Team, undermanned on a shoestring budget, of pre-Emergency Kiambu. The Kikuyu population of Nyeri District was now divided into definable segments: the static, serried ranks of peasantry in protected villages: the diminishing groups of forest gangsters; the considerable number of so-termed Loyalists adhering to the Colonial services, the Tribal Police, the Kikuyu Guard, and the Chiefs' henchmen; the stalwart Christian Mission communities and the dammed up flood of detainees in camps and Prisons, from Manyani through to District Works Camps.

There was a unique separation of functions at the head of the Provincial Administration. The regular Provincial Commissioner, heading the various Districts, was partially overshadowed by a Special Commissioner who had both extra and supra-Provincial powers in respect of Reconstruction, Community development and Rehabilitation. He was not only 'Special' within Central Province, the main locale of Mau Mau, but was Minister for African Affairs, above all PCs, as well as Minister for Community Development and Rehabilitation. Tom Askwith, my former Senior DO at Kitui, was his Permanent Secretary for both functions. The Special Commissioner was effectively a 'supremo', with three converging lines of approach direct to the Governor. He was the same Carruthers Melville, 'Monkey' Johnston, a former DC of Meru in Central Province, who as PC in Rift Valley Province had been my guest at Maralal and my host in Nakuru. He seemed to me gracefully unchanged by his Gilbertian status.

The regular PC was Frank Loyd, who had exceptional experience among the Kikuyu, having been DC for six years in all three Kikuyu Districts. His Provincial responsibilities were orthodox and clear cut, except that his remit did not extend to the Mau Mau Detention and Rehabilitation network, which was the exclusive preserve of the Special Commissioner. I saw no sign of strain between them on this account, other than jocularity masking the difference of proximate rank. My duties around the District leant towards the Special Commissioner's concerns of Community, Development, Rehabilitation and returning detainees, while also liaising with the Divisional District Officers on behalf of Pat Hughes on regular administrative matters.

Karatina Division was centred upon Karatina Trading Centre, the second township of Nyeri District astride the main Nairobi to Nanyuki Road. It was a muddy shambles of clamorous, clapped out vehicles and disorderly construction, with shabby, teeming Kikuyu released from the constraints of fear. Long before Mau Mau it had been the scene of riots against terracing for soil conservation and bulk supplying of a vegetable factory. The dynamic Divisional District Officer was John Campbell, who carried the weight of reputation for gallantry in Popski's Private Army in the Balkan imbroglio during the war. This put me somewhat in awe of him recalling that three of my own former comrades in the Royal Ulster Rifles had been captured by Germans on landing by parachute to join the mountain guerrillas. John exuded an overwhelming charm and conviction accentuated by the hunching forward of his shoulders to sustain a fine Thespian head. His lowered jaw, with mobile mouth urging his case, raised his heavy lidded eyes to fasten hypnotically on his listener. Utter certainty, meticulous argument, disarming frankness guaranteed agreement, which was noted down with copperplate precision. His plans for development gained public support and swept ahead on a tide of enthusiasm and some financial optimism, so that Karatina became a hub of frantic activity lifting the resurgent populace away from sterile violence and the paralysis of fear.

Othaya Division was in the charge of Hugh Galton-Fenzi, younger and much smaller brother of the ruddy, robust Tony, who ten years before was my neighbouring DC at Wajir, two hundred miles south of Mandera. Hugh was brisk, astute, efficient and a stickler for discipline, not least in the conduct of Othaya detainee Reception Centre, through which were filtered hundreds of detainees, who had been deemed fit to return home from the main detention camps after rehabilitation. (Our initial meeting became significant two years on, after my own stint as Officer-in-Charge of Rehabilitation, when I became DC Kiambu. I was approached privately by Hugh's mother, then the much respected widow of a former Chief Native Commissioner, Harold Montgomery, brother of Field Marshal Sir Bernard Law Montgomery, 'Monty'. She had retired to a residential plot on a bend of the Kiambu road, marked by towering eucalyptus trees. Hugh was apparently under the scrutiny of the CID in connection with allegations of mistreatment of detainees. They were believed not too secretly to regard the Provincial Administration with suspicion and were said to be about to prevent Hugh from taking off by air on home leave. I went at once to the office of the sympathetic Secretary for African Affairs, Leslie Pritchard, and said in confidence that, if action was taken against Hugh, it might result in my offering myself for the defence as witness in regard to character and circumstance, which might also require my resignation. I heard no more and Hugh went on his way, but my rashness may have had some part in a subsequent oral accusation of disloyalty, with other sins, which nearly did for me.)

North Tetu Division, with South Tetu, lay between Karatina, Othaya, the moated forest edge of the Aberdares and the settled areas of the coffee estates of Mweiga and the ranches of Nanyuki. It was also adjacent to Nyeri Township and the panoply of Provincial Headquarters. The community was widely known for maturely handsome, enlightened and subtle leader, Senior Chief Muhoya, who had pioneered a pilot scheme of consolidation of fragmented peasant farms before the Emergency. The Divisional DO was John Nottingham, a recently joined Oxford politics graduate. Like Johnston and Peter Marrian of Mweiga he had been at Shrewsbury School. Marrian had also been a pre-war Cadet with Frank Loyd before departing for active service. He had returned to farm at Mweiga with his "lovely child-bride", American Susan, entered liberal politics and became a nominated Minister. Of another kidney, Nottingham had a rather 'uptight' manner which then left little imprint other than of intensity of commitment to his local community, which attracted both applause and unease.

Campbell's enthusiasm at Karatina and Nottingham's commitment in North Tetu also fitted into Johnston's remit for Community Development centred on Jeanes School, where its programmes had been advanced under Tom Askwith before he moved to the Secretariat as Permanent Secretary to the Ministry for Community Development and Rehabilitation. A lively and innovative husband and wife team, Robin Short and his distractingly lovely wife Jenny, were the District Community Development Officers with whom I toured the area in Monkey Johnston's truck, he driving dashingly, silk scarf at throat. I became fascinated by the potential of the programmes for solving the problem of the 18,000 Nyeri children who were not in schools and submitted a Memorandum on Community Development Services and Youth Training Centres (CD 36/10/131). The memorandum extended from village, through Location, Division and District up to a proposed Ministry of Social Development and Information embracing an information branch, youth activities and women's movements. Unfortunately, from my future career point of view, it not only trespassed on the responsibilities of existing Departments but recommended the possible use of vacated detainee Works Camps with which I was later to be involved.

The Public Relations and Information aspects of my draft paper also brought me into frequent touch with the Provincial Information Officer, a delightful naturalized Austrian called James Bonninger. He was a fastidious miniature of the wartime cinema idol, Anton Walbrook, (in the film 'Dangerous Moonlight') but had a magically mobile front tooth which he wiggled disconcertingly under his pencil moustache. His caustic and witty sensitivity, cuisine and '78' records of songs of the Auvergne made an oasis of civilized enjoyment. His devoted wire haired dachshunds added to my vocabulary, evermore known as 'Bonningers'. He used to borrow my small savings to pay his debts before the bailiffs came and to take my wife-to-be to dinner in Nairobi!

A harsher part of my duties was to inspect the main District Reception Centre for returning detainees at Aguthi. The Officer in Charge was Terence Price, a young Kenya-born man who was intelligent and efficient in a humorously robust way suggested by a macabre welcome on the entrance arch. He was not believed to overstep the disciplinary mark in terms commonly accepted, even applauded at the time, when there was little enthusiasm on the part of many DOs for the return of detainees, lest they upset the balance of stability at home and the process of land reform and consolidation. (His successor, Emergency DO Sam Githu, George Medal, was much later held criminally guilty of a death of which I learned when I was DC Kiambu.)

A sudden flurry of excitement and a reversion to the tensions of the silent forest campaign against the surviving Mau Mau gangs occurred in 1956. It was reported that the top forest leader, known as 'Field Marshal' Dedan Kimathi had been shot. For months Police Superintendent Ian Henderson and his 'pseudo' gangs, consisting of 'turned' Mau Mau captives, had been staking out the forest trails in hope of capturing this final prize. A lone Tribal Policeman with a .303 rifle spotted and fired at a figure creeping through the sharpened stakes in the perimeter trench dug around the forest to keep both Mau Mau and game animals from marauding the protected villages. The wounded creature was found to be Kimathi himself clothed in animal skins with leopard headdress. He was carried on a rough litter to the Nyeri court house to be charged pending trial. By chance I was there to witness the reality of the published photograph of a man celebrated in song by the detainees and destined to become a national hero. After lengthy proceedings he was finally convicted and hanged the following year from a shuttered gibbet to avert public heroics.

A greater contrast could not be imagined than the visit to Provincial HQ of Daphne Vandepeer and Elizabeth Usher, the only two women expatriate Colonial Civil Servants in the Administrative class to be assigned to Kenya, where they were Secretariat and Treasury officials. It was a new and somewhat disconcerting experience for a male service to be under their authoritative scrutiny in project planning and expenditure estimates. Of course no such thought was voiced! I recall Daphne as a dark, composed, fastidious and intellectual woman in the style of a Virginia Wolfe beauty. Elizabeth was the Kismayu born daughter of the elected member for Mombasa in Legislative Council who had served as a DC in Jubaland when a British Protectorate. She had frisky blond hair on a challengingly tilted head with a direct, confident manner and quizzical glasses. At a dance her shapely marble shoulders rose daringly from a black velvet, strapless dress.

Social life in the mainly Government enclave of Nyeri was in fact both lively and stratified. Nearest to the Township, with only the old stone prison between, was the Provincial Commissioner's sprawling bungalow of clapboard and corrugated iron in the traditional sub-India style. The superb garden with purple Jacaranda and Nandi flame trees sustaining towers of blazing bougainvillaea and cascades of golden shower above tall, bluebell agapanthus, orange to scarlet canna lilies and a profusion of smaller flowers was tended lovingly by Kath Loyd. On the next and similar rising plot was the DC with marginally less splendour, while above again was the senior DO's house, assigned to me when my authorized stay at the Outspan Hotel next door ran out. Since this layered arrangement had not envisaged a Special Commissioner-in-residence, a fine modern house was secured for him off the very summit of the avenue leading to the Kikuyu cultivation. It enjoyed a magnificent view over the Cottage Hospital and nine hole golf course, and my running track, which stretched down to the White Rhino, the less classy Hotel cum Club House on a bend towards the Indian shops. A great number of European civil servants and families centred on this elevated town land, as well as neighbouring settlers, visiting officials and a re-emerging trickle of tourists braving the forest track to the world famous game lookout Treetops. Groups of them were conducted by the doyen of such adventure trails, Col. Sherbrooke-Walker, who had escorted Princess Elizabeth there, to become Queen overnight.

More vulgar public entertainment was offered at the Outspan where a weekly film was shown in the hall opposite the bar and such amorous assignations as were feasible could be negotiated between all comers. Between the car park and a steep path to the stream below was a squash court where I would get up a sweat playing such as Tom Preston, cleft chinned and worldly wise young DO and, fatefully, Donald Hodge, Personal Assistant to the PC who was himself son of a famous former PC, 'S.O.V.' Hodge. In a long match Don's steady skill stretched my energy to the limit, and in a frantic lunge on the squeaky, resin coated floor my ankle gave out such a crack that I fell on my back clutching at the heel and telling him he had not hurt me. He assured me he had not struck me from behind so I felt the floppy, gelatinous mass above my right foot and realized that my Achilles heel had indeed been found out. By better fortune across the road at the Cottage Hospital there was a young Irish doctor, Donagh Hurley, who had surgical experience in a Uganda leper colony, where he had sutured a similar total break of a tendon. After a lengthy operation I awoke to find myself encased in plaster from below the metatarsal arch to mid thigh at a knee angle of several degrees. A long haul lay ahead on crutches, which almost became an enjoyable and uninhibiting skill, until the gelatine at knee and foot had to be painfully restretched in hot baths, and the banana shaped calf restored.

During this disjuncture in stepped 'Monkey' Johnston. Every detail was imprinted on my mind as I lay in a small private ward on a plumply stuffed mattress in a white enamelled iron bed, ironically facing Mount Kenya. A charming friend, Sue Pugh, a District Officer on leave from Aden, had just left me flowers. Monkey carried a well chosen gift, one volume of *The Men Who Ruled India* by Philip Mason (a.k.a. Philip Woodruff), a tribute to the Indian Civil Service, in which my father had served and into which I had been born at Allahabad, Hindu holy city on the Ganges. My admiration for

Monkey was enhanced by this solicitude which left me vulnerable to persuasion. Seated casually on my bed he quickly explained his purpose.

Of over 80,000 Mau Mau suspects detained since the Emergency Declaration in 1952, overwhelmingly Kikuyu men, equivalent statistically to about one third of all male heads of families of the Kikuyu people, some 60,000 had, one way or another, been released to their homes. A great number of them had been let go, either because there was no longer cause to hold them, or possibly because they had been clever enough to slip easily through a wide mesh. A solid residuum of more than 20,000 now remained. They were distributed in a number of detention camps throughout Kenya, and still posed enough of a security risk to be considered in need of further rehabilitation before release. The enlightened, humane and Christian based procedures of Rehabilitation introduced into the camps, with an early Moral Rearmament input and utilizing Community Development staff, trained at Jeanes School, appeared to have run their course. The largest accumulation of so called 'hard core' detainees were held in Manyani Camp near Voi, who were not in any sense deemed amenable to peaceful approaches. The Government faced a dilemma of action in that both political and economic progress towards independence was inconsistent with the stagnant incarceration of such a mass of future citizens of Kenya in such conditions.*

Without further ado, Johnston told me that it had been agreed by Government that an officer of the Provincial Administration should be charged with the task of unblocking and invigorating the progress to release, with the objective of bringing the numbers down towards 6,000, if at all possible. It had been decided to offer me the new post of District Officer in Charge of Rehabilitation. There was no way in which I could assess the magnitude and nature of what was being asked of me since there was no precedent for it and no guide book to the way out of the impasse, apart from which I was unable to walk properly. I had only that most dangerous thing, an irrational and unjustified belief in my ability to face the challenge of the impossible. There was also a conscious need to make up for having agreed to accept release from the Ulsters to the Colonial Administration, and for not having been exposed to my share of the worst dangers of the Emergency. In this special role I could perform a service to Government and the Kenya people, while 'being true to mine own self'.

I accepted at once, lest the offer be withdrawn, and then attempted to elicit from Johnston some sort of briefing. For staff there would be the same two main elements as currently available. One was the Kenya Prisons

*Caroline Elkins' Harvard University research (unpublished 1998) revealed that Baring was already negotiating with the Colonial Office for the indefinite detention of Kenyatta and top Mau Mau 'Politicals' if the Kenya Administration reduced detainee numbers to a few thousand. cf Colonial Office 822/836, 822/888, 822/1034 and 822/2093.

Department complement of Camp Commandants under a Senior Superintendent, with some hundreds of non-Kikuyu warders. The other was a team of European Rehabilitation Officers, under a Senior Community Development Officer, with three Kikuyu Rehabilitation Assistants and a considerable number of Kikuyu Elders as screeners or verifiers of evidence. All of the latter were on the payroll of the Ministry of Community Development of which Tom Askwith was Permanent Secretary. This duality of command proved important and was brought together by Johnston holding three posts, namely the Ministries of African Affairs and Community Development as well as being Special Commissioner for Rehabilitation. There would be no separate budgetary requirement but additional finance would be available without difficulty. No legal constraints were envisaged. Reporting would be direct to him and through him to the Governor. The Provincial Administration had no responsibilities nor authority within the camps nor for rehabilitation generally. The briefing was minimal to the point of folly or negligence on both our parts, although it did not seem so in that safe and clinical bedroom.* My relationship with the Special Commissioner was one of trust, without question of the reasons behind my selection for the task, which was endorsed by the Governor and made known to the Secretary of State.

*I was given no information at all about an unimpeachably documented and highly relevant episode in Manyani camp three years earlier, when scores, possibly hundreds, of detainees had died of typhoid occurring in disgraceful conditions there. I only heard of it years later when accused out of the blue by a Catholic priest, Peter Esmonde, seeking support in fund-raising for Action Aid and when first hand evidence emerged in medical memoirs sent to me.

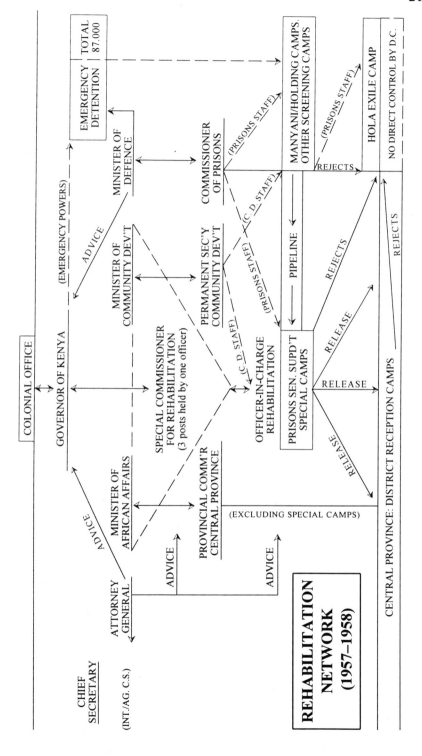

REHABILITATION
NETWORK
(1957–1958)

DETENTION CAMPS
Diagram of Locations

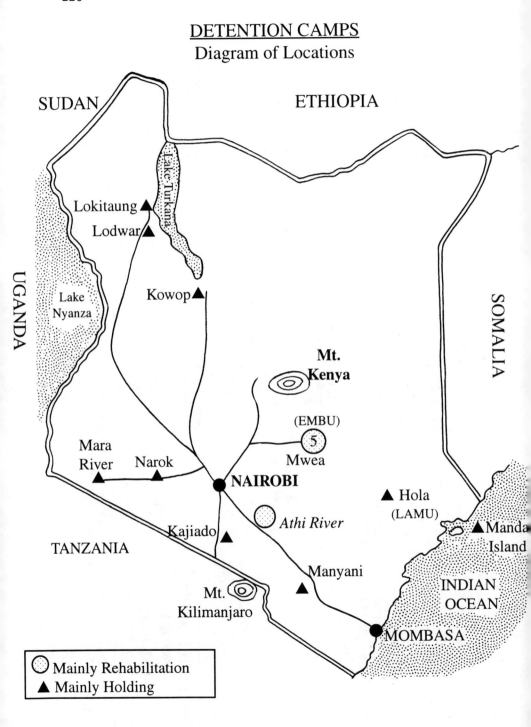

SUDAN

ETHIOPIA

UGANDA

SOMALIA

Lake Turkana

Lokitaung

Lodwar

Kowop

Lake
Nyanza

Mt.
Kenya

(EMBU)
5
Mwea

Mara
River

Narok

NAIROBI

Hola
(LAMU)

Manda
Island

Athi River

TANZANIA

Kajiado

Manyani

Mt.
Kilimanjaro

INDIAN
OCEAN

MOMBASA

○ Mainly Rehabilitation
▲ Mainly Holding

MWEA*

As a first step in establishing the extent and nature of my remit, I set out from Nyeri, limpingly, for the Mwea plain in the Embu District of Central Province. The main so-called 'filter' camps had been grouped there, through which the flow of rehabilitated detainees to their home district reception centres had hitherto passed.

The plain was a flat and unprofitable expanse of Crown Land, which had been tacked on to the Kikuyu Land Unit in 1934 and administered from Embu. It covered an area of some 100,000 acres at between 3 to 4 thousand feet, with an average 20 to 30 inches of rainfall. The whole was bordered to the south by the great, in Kenya terms, Tana river and to the north by the interlinking Nyamindi and Thiba rivers. Arid and overgrazed, the northern part had since 1954 been chosen by the African Land Development Board, ALDEV, my old friends in Maralal, for their largest project, the Mwea-Tebere Irrigation Scheme. In 1955 Government had decided to utilize the irrigable area for rice and cotton to provide useful employment for thousands of Mau Mau detainees. Fenced accommodation was constructed in Works Camps at Thiba, Mwea, Kandongu and Tebere (also called Gathigiriri). A separate camp at Karaba was used for administration and transients. Another at Wamumu was for Mau Mau juvenile offenders, for whom the Ministry of Community Development retained direct responsibility.

There were three separate control points for me to call upon before considering how to approach the detainees, each having extensions into other camps. The first was the Senior Superintendent, also called Staff Officer Works Camps, SOWC, at Prisons Department HQ at Karaba. The second was the team of European Senior Community Development and Rehabilitation Officers centred on Thiba works camp, holding detainees from Kiambu District; Mwea camp being for Nyeri and Kandongu camp for Fort Hall (Murang'a) detainees. The third was the trio of Kikuyu Community Development and Rehabilitation Assistants, of whom one operated at Gathigiriri camp, mainly for detainees from the distinct Embu and Meru people of the Province, another at Thiba and the third at Mwea.

Beside Thiba Camp was the fine thatched office cum residence of the Chief Executive of the Irrigation Scheme, while along the road nearby was the sub-office of the local District Officer reporting to the DC at Embu, within whose District, but not responsibility, the complex camp system of Rehabilitation lay. In order to explain it, at least to myself and our staff, I drew up the preceding chart, which illustrated it tolerably well for our purposes and placed our work in a context quite lacking in any recorded

---

*A full but partly fictionalized account by the author of the circumstances, process and outcome of rehabilitation of detainees was published privately in a limited edition in 1994 under the title of *Corridors of Wire*. It is available direct from the author.

definition from on high. The next stage was to establish clear and firm relations and common approaches with the personalities concerned, since we would have to share the burden of the days ahead. I was fortunate to an extraordinary degree.

Senior Superintendent John Black Templer Cowan was the same age as myself. I had been friends with his parents at Kisumu twelve years before. His mother was related to General Sir Gerald Templer the 'Tiger' of the Malayan Civil War, later touted optimistically for the Governorship of Kenya. Although of middle height and light build he had been victor ludorum at the privately owned Kenton School in the Rift Valley, widely reputed for its blend of intellectual rigour with discipline, from where he went on to Kenya's foremost European boys school, the Prince of Wales. After war service he joined the Kenya Prisons Service and found himself assigned to the Mwea group of detention camps in 1957, shortly before my own arrival. We both came without preconceptions or burdened with past action or inaction. John was immaculately turned out at all times, quietly in command of himself and his men, a full battalion of them. He had a self deprecating sense of humour, laced with pith and irony and a quiet seemliness which concealed great tenacity. Different as we were and from separate services, we were never at cross purposes. This unity was the bedrock of the co-operation of a thousand staff of all kinds, which communicated itself to the many thousand detainees who never tried to divide us. John had at Karaba a Camp Commandant appropriately called Hoy and an angular, rather Dickensian accountant, Reginald Potter, for whom the familiar 'Reg' did not seem proper. He commuted from Nairobi with his accountant wife Barbara, and safely delivered Deirdre, John's discreetly attractive and venturesome wife, herself daughter of an Irish Senior DC, for conjugal visits in that dreary place.

John and I, as an early demonstration of the intended closeness between the Prisons and Rehabilitation, drove together to Thiba camp escorted by his Sergeant Major and Chief Warder, Ahmed Dabasso, impeccable, inscrutable, faultless of bearing, a man of intuitive command. We went straight to meet Camp Commandant Jim Brackenborough who took us to take tea with his shingled blonde wife, Marie, who made us at home as we all prepared to move across to the Rehabilitation Team still under the Ministry of Community Development. We found them at the house of Ivan Hook and his wife Glacie. The Hooks were an endearing, devoted and somehow quaint pair. He was of the eccentric, intellectual family of Nanyuki settlers, one half brother Raymond combining mule coping with the classics and another, Commander Logan Hook, Silverbeck Hotel-keeping on the equator under the codes of both British Navy and British Israelites. Ivan loved mankind, adult education and hydroponics and seemed unperturbed by the stress of our task. Indeed he later published in the

Prisons Department Magazine a witty parody of Kubla Khan by himself, 'Kooh Navi', casting me as 'Kava Khan' in a mêlée with the detainees, a work which I include later since it hardly suggests a brutal regime at work.

Don McInnes, the Senior Rehabilitation Officer was also there, a gentle, handsome Scot with a soft Highland burr. He was courteous and tactful in the informal handing over of his team to me prior to returning to the Ministry of Community Development. I then learned that Tom Askwith* had expressed mistaken umbrage when the responsibility for Rehabilitation had been withdrawn from him and had impugned an assumed new policy of force to secure confessions by someone more amenable! Don wrote to me of his acceptance of the need for a new approach to Rehabilitation and his agreement with it, which he conveyed to both Ivan Hook and Emile Hawley, as well as to the Kikuyu members of the team. Emile was at first sight a rough old Africa hand, but proved to be a well read thinker with shrewdly robust views. He wanted vision, purpose and action, to which he contributed fearlessly. The remaining European Rehabilitation Officer was at Kandongu Camp. He was David Bais from Malta with a Cypriot wife, but they spoke and acted as one sincere and kindly unit, he burly and hesitantly smiling, she petite and supportive. The Camp Commandant was Paul Wood, with the unmistakable, independent spirit, free carriage and straw hair of a Kenya born youth. He was accompanied by his comely buxom wife and three children.

The trio of Kikuyu Rehabilitation Assistants were all outstanding, but quite unalike. They had separate control of a group of paid elders in each District camp. Wilfred Thimba had been right hand man to Don McInnes and Ivan Hook in Thiba, screening the incoming detainees to establish their involvement in Mau Mau. Wilfred was about fifty, immensely respected, rotund and dignified with a constant smile betokening both goodwill and imperturbable determination. Isaiah Mwai Mathenge in Mwea camp was tall, gangling and handsome as were many of the people around Nyeri, who might once have shared boundaries and blood with the Maasai. His personality was confident and engaging. Few detainees could resist his firm left hand on shoulder, holding a man to man gaze of genuine concern and frank interest in any sinner. His qualities balanced the successive Prisons Department Commandants of Mwea camp, sharp witted Ronald Spottiswode-Bush and rugged Ken Brogan who resembled a professional boxing trainer. At Gathigiriri Jeremiah Kiereini, slender, subtle and well balanced, was a thoughtful counterpart to Camp Commandant Bill Halsey, manly, powerful and a professional butcher, whose off duty

*Askwith's tendentious 1995 version of being relieved of responsibility for Rehabilitation in 1957 is at p.118 of his Memoir, *From Mau Mau to Harambee* published as Cambridge University Monograph No.17; 1995. In it he cites *The Men who Ruled Kenya*; Charles Chenevix Trench; Radcliffe Press; 1993; p.276.

skills we all enjoyed.   Such was the motley array of the Mwea community outside the barbed wire. Haphazardly brought together in time of Emergency it comprised, varyingly, of seven hundred uniformed Prisons Department staff, the seven Community Development and Rehabilitation Officers, one hundred or more Kikuyu Elders, the unified whole under the joint direction of a Senior Superintendent of Prisons and myself as Administrative Officer-in-Charge answerable directly to the responsible Ministers. An integral and invaluable part was played by the many wives, who alleviated the strains and discomforts of a thankless existence. We were all to be involved with each other in the unresolved problem of how effectively to reach the presently inaccessible five thousand detainees already in the Mwea camps, so as to resume the flow of rehabilitation at a rate of about one thousand a month and make space for periodic replacements, enabling the release of another fifteen thousand from the 'hard core' holding camps, principally Manyani. We needed a consistent and coherent plan, which would engage the co-operation of the detainees with our own commitment, secure Government participation, and gain the trust of hard pressed District Commissioners called upon to feed back thousands of possibly disturbed and disturbing exiles into recovering societies.

On the face of it, there appeared no reason to suppose that such a haphazard accumulation of ordinary people, even if weeded through, would be any more likely to achieve progress towards release of thousands of detainees than the previous worthy and well motivated charitable bodies and workers, whose efforts had reached sticking point. Indeed many were the same. Clearly new staff were not the answer. We needed a new forward dynamic to be generated between us and the detainees. This suggested a switch away from attempts to 'confess', exorcise, purify, rehabilitate within the disciplined confines of detention, according to values and concepts abhorrent to a congealed residue of fanatical Mau Mau adherents. Such an approach might have seemed to them like a kind of capitulation without compensating advantage. Whatever the analysis, for which there could be no direct proof, inaction was not on anyone's agenda and would only let matters worsen.

John Cowan, Don McInnes and I proceeded on the basis of a formula which we called 'convergence' in place of stalemate. It had many contributory aspects. We devised a pragmatic schema based on four main tenets, namely control, convergence, co-operation and community. The first, 'control', was and is vital to the orderly functioning of any lawful institution holding people captive, albeit in this case mainly on long standing Emergency Detention Orders. 'Control' is much related to physical factors, such as the number held in a single area, compound or hut, who can be managed without serious risk of conflict and harm, or even death.

Thiba camp held over 1,000 men in a single compound in A-frame huts holding fifty each. A determined core of five per cent of such a number could in ordinary human terms adversely influence the behaviour of the remainder. Quite apart from the political validity of detention, there was no great moral principle involved in remedying this situation by subdivision of accommodation.

'Convergence' was really a re-interpretation of earlier approaches to rehabilitation, designed to remove what might be construed as patronizing attitudes by foreigners inculcating their own moral concepts, and to redirect the conflict of ideas towards a common objective. In this I posited that declared emotions amounted to facts to be taken into account. Mau Mau's stated aims included national independence and occupation of alienated land. Colonial government policy had long foreshadowed the one, inevitably leading to the other. Why then fight on those issues rather than bring the parallel lines of aspiration into convergence? Why obstruct progress by retaining a mass of vigorous younger men in sterile confinement, where they were denied a share in the current, highly advantageous, consolidation of land and registration of title at home? The detainees themselves were increasingly alive to this!

'Co-operation' proceeded from the acceptance of convergent interests. Manifestly and in logic they could more rapidly be achieved by creative use of the energies and resources of both sides of the equation, including the participation of detainees in persuading their fellows along the path of 'co-operation' and a positive attitude towards the prospect of release to life and freedom. Emphasis on so called cleansing from the Mau Mau oaths would be made less of a ritual and more a cross check on past records to make it clear that the examining elders had a shrewd idea of everyone's past activities, their place in the movement and possible influence in the camp, for better or for worse. Sometimes those with the worst records proved to be the most effective proponents of 'co-operation'.

'Community' was an essential characteristic of the traditional structure of Kikuyu life. Its disciplined recreation in the artificial arenas of detention, where differential age grades scarcely existed, where there were no families and where identity was not tied to land, offered a poor and sterile alternative society. The nostalgia for tradition was defiantly displayed in the frequent claim by Manyani inmates to have been born there and to have no other name or home. Undoubtedly they were nostalgic for their traditional life, without which they were isolated and lonely despite the solidarity of their Mau Mau profession and a few callous and violent rejections of their own families come to visit. 'Community' was a magnet of normality.

We now had a provisional plan. Next we had to ensure full commitment to it among ourselves before securing access to the closed compounds and minds of obdurate detainees in the Mwea camps as a preliminary to the

R

phased infiltration of the main mass held in Manyani. Always in company with John Cowan and his various Officers I put our proposals to fully attended meetings at which any who were not in agreement or who had hesitations of a moral nature were invited to apply for transfer. None did, though there were a few movements of individuals not considered safe or suitable for the task on their disciplinary records.

We then decided to apply the first control operation to the subdivision of the Thiba camp compound containing 1,000 men into four of 250, leaving a fenced cruciform access corridor between. This required advance preparation of tall posts, deep holes and rolls of barbed wire, with implements. We also recruited from eager volunteers a 'Praetorian Guard' of over 100 educated young Kikuyu of good physique and address. They were quickly drilled in simple unarmed combat and equipped with short wooden truncheons slung from leather belts binding judo style heavy cotton tunics over calf length trousers. Their heads were shaven for effect as well as protection.

John Cowan, Jim Brackenborough, Wilfred Thimba, Ivan Hook and I with Sergeant-Major Dabasso formed up outside the high double gate of the undivided compound to the uneasy interest of 1,000 watching inmates. The young volunteers were fallen in to the rear. It was mid morning and quite silent. With the gate opened I went forward slowly to address the detainees, who had taken up the squatting position in serried lines to which they had become habituated in years of detention camp routine. Apart from industrial strikers in Kiambu in 1950, it was my first experience of facing at close quarters a thousand potentially violent men and with a message likely to be met by rejection. There was an atmosphere of expectancy and tension. If they were nervous, I was certainly so, though with a frisson of exhilaration that this was a moment of truth which would determine the future course of events for all of us.

I put it to them firmly, but in a low key, that we intended them no harm and proposed only to divide the compound into four so as to have opportunity to tell them of new circumstances which could lead to freedom. This would entail vacating the camp through the passageway leading to the adjacent playing fields, where they could see a number of elders from home seated on a bench. Within a few hours they would reoccupy their existing accommodation. I would return after an hour to give the instruction to move, which they would carry out peacefully and at once. I left to join the others waiting outside for the next fifty five minutes. We chatted uneasily: the detainees remained silent. The control group then entered the gate together and I formally repeated the order to move out. No one stirred. On the hour the young Kikuyu volunteer contingent filed in barefoot, dividing along each flank in extended order. The high perimeter wire was manned outside by armed Prison Warders as were the watch towers at each corner.

We began to close in slowly.

Outnumbered by five to one, we had prepared against resistance of some kind, but did not expect any concerted attack. The options open to either side were limited by space and weapons to hand, if not by hours of daylight. The front lines and outer fringes did not so much crumble as concertina, scrambling awkwardly into each other until no inch was left. We could not have imagined the hysterical crescendo of a convulsion which imploded within their ranks. Limb intertwined with limb in a tangle of bodies, squirming upwards into a living mound. From inside arose a wild ululation, soaring and waning like some banshee's dirge multiplied a thousand fold. It was a horrendous and unnerving glimpse into the inferno, which shocked us all into a moment of pause. The scene gave rise to the trivialized expressions 'Mau Mau howl' and 'Mau Mau pyramid', which were loosely applied in reports on later crises, including the 1959 Hola débâcle.

John Cowan and I, with one voice, gave the order to separate the bodies methodically, seizing any available limbs and dragging them to the exit corridor, where Warders formed a chain to propel them onwards. The young Kikuyu contingent kept the central mass compact, grasping those who cut loose and bundling them out. Fists, nails, feet and teeth were engaged. Truncheons were not drawn except in defence. How long it lasted I could not tell, but in about two hours, singly or in clusters, frog-marched or stumbling loose, the whole thousand sat slumped on the grass outside in several large rings, within which stood one or two elders. From the centre of the field I reminded them all of the order and my promise. They would return to their A-frame quarters shortly to wash and have the usual evening meal. The fruitless struggle need not be repeated. At this the elders intoned traditional Kikuyu songs and catches, leading the dispirited company in a monotonous but somehow calming refrain. In response to our phone call, the Embu Medical Officer of Health had sent an African Doctor to examine any injured detainees or Warders. The tally was one suspected fractured skull, several fractured limbs and multiple contusions, scratches and bites, evenly distributed. John and I submitted our separate formal reports of the incident to Prisons Department HQ and to the Special Commissioner. There was no response.

A quick circuit of the other camps revealed that news of the action at Thiba had preceded us and a certain lightening of the atmosphere was noticeable. This was essential for the next phase which was the introduction of an experimental intake from the main depository of long term detainees at Manyani. A local build up of momentum was needed to exploit the degree of control gained before positive hope subsided into sullen inertia. A flying visit to Manyani by John and myself was thus indicated to take the measure of our potential guests and calculate the numbers that might initially be taken into each Mwea camp with a fair prospect of dilution through persuasion by their erstwhile fellows, whose own hopes of release would also be advanced.

The first sight of Manyani camp from a single engined Kenya Police Airwing Plane, was not encouraging. A regimented array of glistening corrugated aluminium A-frame barracks extended within barbed wire compounds along the baked earth flats at the foot of a low ridge of weathered rock. The site was reached from the gravelled Mombasa road and by a railway siding a few miles before the Voi–Taveta branch line to Tanganyika. At the Nairobi end near the airstrip an unfenced line of large timber frame quarters was shaded by a green fringe of pepper trees. Every compound seemed alive with scuttling figures, resembling disturbed and angry nests of soldier ants, until revealed as men rushing hither and thither wielding batons stripped from tattered aluminium huts and smashing at anything within reach in an orgasm of undirected fury. As we wavered in to land the frenzy petered out and there was only heat and overpowering silence in which a small group of Prisons Officers stood awaiting us. Among them were Colonel Terry, the Commandant, and the same 'Reg' Potter who was assigned, with his wife Barbara, to the Accounts Office at Karaba HQ in the Mwea.

From a discreet distance, to avoid exciting notice, we were shown the outward evidence of a tightly controlled camp with contacts between detainees and Warders limited to heavily guarded stone breaking and lavatory bucket disposal gangs. Food was passed over or into compounds for distribution by the Mau Mau cells which maintained internal control by fear and favour. Individuals' names and places or origin were not known and identification was by numbers inscribed skilfully on link bracelets fashioned from aluminium pieces. It was a place of violence contained by truce. We saw the railway siding and armoured carriages, with their glassless window frames bolted over by heavy expanded metal screens, in which transfers would be effected to Sagana Station in Embu district.

There was no cause for us then to be told by the Manyani officers of the raging typhoid epidemic in 1954, which had carried off scores of detainees. It had only been halted by a new experimental drug, Streptomycin, flown in at great expenditure of scarce dollars authorized by the Governor, and by an emergency medical team which rapidly controlled contributory abuses of culpable negligence and conduct. The whole affair was quite at variance with a statement made to Parliament by the new Secretary of State, Alan Lennox-Boyd, which was far more open to Opposition questions than they realized. This 'sleeper' mine lay beneath the surface to emerge years later, but knowledge of it and its residual effects was of first importance to my present responsibility for coping with detainees who had survived both the abuses and the epidemic and were about to be transferred to the Mwea camps.

Consolidating hope and confidence within the quiescent Mwea camp populations involved introducing, or resuming, every kind of practical inducement and activity. They included renewal of personal identity and home connections; adult literacy classes; constructing temporary churches; re-assembling old lorry engines; making wooden suitcases; sewing civilian clothes from used blankets; even Ivan Hook's favourite hydroponic gardening! Work done on these things and on camp chores, as well as in the irrigation scheme paddies, earned a small wage for extras or savings for their return home. All this was in preparation for the next complex stage in our four part plan now ready to begin; the introduction of 'hard core' detainees from Manyani to join with their fellows in a controlled flow towards release.

Co-operation between Prisons and Rehabilitation staff and my own co-ordinating position was secure. We saw good signs of it in the busy and settled receiving camps. We had no inkling of how men 'reborn' of Manyani would respond, after years of stagnation of their humanity, to a complete change of environment. As yet we had no clear mandate or direction set out in writing, nor a proper chain of command between us and our various superiors. It was time to define authority for action in the light of attendant risks and to fill in any gaps in co-operation. I requested the Special Commissioner, Monkey Johnston, to bring together the other heads of relevant Ministries and Departments to monitor the first experimental intake, both to ensure their full understanding and to obtain their formal clearance of what they saw. The SC agreed, in that capacity and as Minister both for African Affairs and Community Development and Rehabilitation.

We selected Kandongu Camp for the first intake from Manyani. It was the closest to the Sagana Station siding where the carriages would be off-loaded. Near by lay Fort Hall (Murang'a) District from where most, if not all of, the present 1,000 or so inmates came. As earlier described they were the most closed in of the Kikuyu people, with a strong sense of community. The Camp Commandant, Paul Wood, being Kenya born, had broader understanding of African circumstances than other officers and had established a surprising relationship with a formidable Mau Mau oath administrator called Hezron, who had earlier come from Manyani breathing fire. He was known to us all as 'toothy' from the overlapping fangs of his calcium rich incisors which he twisted through his lips into an oddly mild and seductive smile with the manner of a benevolent scoutmaster. He had contrived to alter his power base to that of a persuasive leader of 'convergence', from both his slant and ours! He was to be a trump in 'turning' the belligerence of new arrivals.

Since we were concerned to treat the initial intake as a model for future action, full co-operation and the endorsement of authority, we pitched the numbers very low, though we could well have been more cautious. Sixty should have been twenty; one lorry load instead of three, dealt with in a single group without a build up of tension between. Otherwise preparations at railhead through to admission were drilled meticulously, including the arrangements for observation by the Government representatives.

The handling of departures from Manyani in the barred railway carriages was not within our local control, which operated from arrival at Sagana, although the Manyani Commandant was made aware of our needs and one of his Prisons Officers with an escort was Officer i/c Train up to formal handing over. John Cowan and I waited nervously over sweet tea in the perfumed back room of an Indian trader and provider of detention camp supplies until a telegraphed signal confirmed the time of approach.

The loading yard of a siding leading up to a pair of huge buffers had been cleared of timber, wire and corrugated iron and cordoned off by armed warders. Two Prisons dog handlers held back trained Alsatian dogs on leashes. As the old fashioned steam engine blasted to a halt, the Manyani Sergeant-Major called the peering detainees to come out slowly. This they did without urging, shackled hand and foot, stepping awkwardly down to the platform, and looking about wildly to see what might befall them and what they might do. At this point Sergeant-Major Dabasso took command and ordered them into lines of six abreast in the direction of parked lorries, gates open, beneath which they squatted, hands on heads. Meanwhile the Officer-in-Charge train presented his nominal rolls for signature. In complete silence the arrivals were ordered into the open lorries, twenty to each, facing the cab. Hezron and his chosen colleagues in the other lorries were the first exposure the incomers had to known intermediaries between their past condition and what lay ahead.

Meanwhile the group of our superiors sped by saloon cars from Nairobi, bypassing Sagana, directly to a rendezvous near to Kandongu, where we hurried to meet them ahead of the lorries from the station. After brief and businesslike introductions John and I conducted them straight into the camp where they were positioned by Paul Wood to the rear of an A-Frame hut in a compound directly adjoining the intake entry. This was some 40 feet long by 12 feet wide measured from the gate and had been prepared with ten spaced out piles down each side, consisting of a mat, a blanket, white tunic with shorts and a bar of yellow soap. I handed to each Nairobi observer a named buff file containing an identical résumé of what was to follow. None was ever acknowledged.

The three lorries then drove up, the first stopping with its tailgate level with the entrance to the wire corridor, where the reception kits were laid out. The other two lorries waited spaced well away to the rear. Old Hezron moved through his troop urbanely and dismounted to take control of proceedings. He instructed the twenty men to get down in pairs to have their shackles removed by two of the existing inmates equipped as armourers. When all were squatting free, Hezron led each separately to one of the neat piles beside which stood two unarmed Warders and a camp barber. He then took up position at the head of the defile. He told them to look through the barbed wire on each side into the compounds full of their former companions from Manyani, urging them to co-operate in being shorn of their matted hair and changing into their clean cotton outfits. Paul Wood then gave the Swahili order to proceed in an orderly fashion.

At first it seemed that Hezron's homily, persuasive voices and the familiar faces through the wire had taken effect and the shaving of heads began without fuss or resistance. Suddenly a remembered howl sounded from the rear and a man was thrown to the ground thrashing about wildly, followed instantly by several more, and a general mêlée took place. The warders had been trained for just such an outbreak. One took their man in an armlock, tripped and forced him to the ground, head pressed sideways against the angle of the body, astride which the other sat while the barber did his work. Within moments violent resistance collapsed, except during removal of dirty Manyani garb to enable camp clothing to be donned. At once the first batch was turned loose among those in the compound where they were to be housed, who engaged them in excited persuasion and reassurance. The next two batches followed much the same pattern, though we wished we had not risked handling as many in the experimental intake.

It was now the turn of our superiors to speak their mind or minds. We could count on Johnston's triple vote, since we were the instruments for carrying out his special task. The Commissioner of Prisons, 'Taxi' Lewis, John Cowan's service chief, was unlikely to step outside orthodox Prisons Regulations. His mild temperament and health weakened by facial surgery rendered him unsuited to the rough and tumble of mass detention, which had fallen to his lot after he had been transferred from the Provincial Administration to enjoy a stable career up to retirement. He was in any case answerable to the Minister for Defence. The Minister, Jake Cusack, was a personality of some style and consequence. After a vigorous and exuberant pre-war career as a DO at Maralal and then on the northern frontier he had been transferred with military rank to the highly irregular Civil Administration of occupied Italian Somaliland. He served as deputy to the Administrator, Brigadier Denis Wickham, at the irreverently dubbed 'cockroach castle' in Mogadishu. During the 1952 Mau Mau Emergency he returned to Kenya to become Secretary and then Minister for Defence. Urbane, effortlessly brilliant and detachedly self-indulgent, his sympathy was not likely to be engaged by the disciplining of recalcitrant detainees in his Prisons Department bailiwick.

One step sideways and higher in the pecking order was the Minster for Law and Order, Attorney General Eric Griffith-Jones, the Governor's

232

principal adviser in matters such as the treatment and handling of persons held on Emergency Detention orders. He was lean, of middle height, with straggly dark hair across a broad forehead, black framed spectacles and a busy stoop as if carrying a brief to court. Nervous and nimble he conveyed agility of mind with a rather tortured charm. He now assumed the role of spokesman for the group of invited onlookers in terms which I took care to remember. Almost verbatim, he told us of his own wartime experience of confinement in the hands of the Japanese which had taught him painful lessons about violence applied to the underdog. Boots should not be worn; any blows to the body should be to the front, which could be curled or covered up against serious harm, and never to the back where damage to organs could be fatal. "I saw you, Gavaghan, strike a good blow which was within bounds." He described others which were not.

The Attorney General went on to distinguish between 'punitive' blows struck in anger or impulse to cause hurt, and the proportionate degree of force required to restrain, or 'compel' obedience to a lawful or reasonable order. Thus was promulgated by the highest legal and executive authority, having witnessed planned and recorded events, the clear distinction between 'punitive' and 'compelling' force. It ruled, guided and limited all of our considered actions to achieve and maintain control for the next year. (Two years later ill-considered and misdirected compelling force became the crux of national and international enquiry into its fatal misapplication at Hola.) The visitors departed for Nairobi leaving us clearer as to our practical, moral and legal position in carrying out the thankless task set to us. The ruling was never conveyed to us in writing nor were the named folders setting out the intake procedures acknowledged or referred to again in any enquiry. My confidential files were few and I did not think it correct to retain them.*

John Cowan and I at once did a circuit of the other camps, which had received equivalent intakes and found nothing more serious than the happenings at Kandongu. Wilfred, Isaiah and Jeremiah were quite satisfied that the newcomers would be shaken down within two weeks, when such regular intakes could be assimilated fortnightly. This would mean a full scale reception of 120 at Sagana station every week. Our rough statistical calculations, based upon intakes of 60 twice a month to each of 4 camps, produced a total monthly intake of 480 or 5,800 in a full year to add to well over 5,000 already in the Mwea. We had good hopes of building up momentum to at least 10% of the combined total ready for return in weekly batches to their District reception centres, leaving a few thousand releases

*Caroline Elkins (Ibid.). Baring letter to Secretary of State; Colonial Office 822/1251 of 25 June 1957. "Gavaghan has been perfectly open with us.... The hard cases are dealt with on their first arrival in a rough way. We have instituted careful safeguards, a medical examination before and after the arrival of the intake, the presence of the Officer-in-Charge all the time, the force being used by European staff only."

still necessary to attain the human and political objective. In following the sequence of 'control, convergence, co-operation and community' we had to ensure that a cumulative sense of optimism was fostered and that the balance of influence in camps, compounds and huts was never in danger of tilting back to the fear and solidarity of Mau Mau allegiance. The initial practical safeguard against this was the evening assembly of the whole camp population, the much smaller phalanx of the day's intake being placed to one side between the co-operating majority and the Elders seated at a central table symbolizing the lure of their home communities.

In Thiba, where my own zinc lean-to adjoined the compound wire, Wilfred Thimba conducted the next act of a staged performance designed to reveal publicly to everyone who among the newcomers had what status in Mau Mau, or who sought to deny or deceive. Only in this sense was a form of public confession elicited by each moving forward a few yards in response to Wilfred's gentle enquiry as to how many oaths they had taken. Every unspoken declaration was greeted with bursts of applause. Known evasion or deceit met cries of derision. When the rather popular and revivalist proceedings were over the newcomers were allocated between huts, the worst to the best. In the morning detailed individual interviews began again, in what had cosily been called 'screening bowers'. Each in turn sat on a wooden offcut bench facing three Elders, often for hours. Statements were recorded and correlated in great detail with those in other 'bowers'.

There is nothing like the tedium of routine for keeping the peace or, as Churchill put it more succinctly, jaw-jaw is better than war-war. So the peace of routine set in, briefly interrupted once a week by the intrusion of a new intake from Manyani. Work on the irrigation scheme was a great solvent, in terms of physical and mental well-being, enhanced by a small pay packet and the philosopher's dream of a stake in the soil so tilled. Football and basketball outside the camp offered normal enjoyment and innocent violence. The first time I heard a laugh it was a sort of revelation of hope.

There were, of course, resisters who in a way defined the genuineness of those who were not. Camps dealt with them in different ways. The Mwea regime was one of a 'square bashing' exercise called 'bucket fatigue', which meant carrying on the head buckets full of building or brick-making mud. I watched it once to be sure that its severity was not excessive. Fewer than ten men were involved. The same day I brought a number of letters of complaint which had been returned through the Government from such varied addressees as 'Queen Elizabeth' or 'Lake Success' (United Nations). I read them aloud inside the full compound, explaining that they had been delivered, taken into account and sent back. I then tore them up publicly saying that, if they felt that they had scores to settle with me, I promised that after 'freedom' and Independence they would find my name board outside my house in Nairobi, which I would buy with my Kenya earnings. This promise was meant also to signpost the end of our journey to 'convergence'.

In Thiba camp we had only two impenetrably stubborn men with whom no acceptable level of punishment would have been effective. We made do with public exposure, isolation and a degree of humiliation designed to offset any fear or adverse influence. One called Kimani I rather admired, even liked. As he sat alone, ankles shackled, in front of a pile or rocks with a lump hammer at hand, I felt we could respect each other's position. No attempt was made to compel him to lift the hammer, though he did so in a desultory manner to ease the construction of his limbs. I only once witnessed routine Prisons Department punishment in Gathigiriri for a breach of Prison Regulations. Six strokes of a rattan cane across wet cloth covered buttocks was administered by the camp Sergeant-Major. I lost control of myself once in 'Mwea No.1', when Isaiah and his Elders were attempting to reason with a man who adopted the 'Plasticine doll' technique of falling about if pushed and adopting postures resembling the lava encrusted Roman soldier at Pompeii. Partly to associate myself with the frustration of the others I hit him back-handed across the face, ripping my knuckles on his teeth. The gash caused our resident and revered Quaker lady Missionary, Miss Margery Reid, visiting my office to sympathize until I told her the cause, when she wished we could find a gentler approach. I told her she and her young male assistant in the camp were welcome to take over the task, which she was honest to declare impossible. When I was taken by the Special Commissioner to report to the Governor on progress in what he termed our 'moral crusade' he did not enquire why I presented my right wrist in greeting, above my bandaged hand. In such circumstances our 'crusade' kept the power of the disaffected below the dangerous 5%.

The procedures in the Mwea rehabilitation camps had attracted a good deal of notoriety and comment resulting in a number of fact finding visits to which no kind of objection was raised. One visitor came with the blessing of Secretary of State Alan Lennox-Boyd and with the onward recommendation of the Governor to Thiba camp and myself. She was the fiery and outspoken labour MP, Barbara Castle,* noted for her penetrating Parliamentary Questions about conditions of detention and abuses of human rights. We received her with due formality and offered to show her what she wished. She demanded private talk with detainees to whom, at that time, I judged it too risky, both ways, to expose a woman. She bridled at this strikingly visible distinction and asserted her gender-neutral status as an MP which I begged leave to doubt. Then, with an unashamedly feminine volte-face, she swept through the camp, keen eyed, practical and down to

*The encounter is exactly recalled with humour by (Lady) Barbara Castle on p.270 in her Autobiography, *Fighting All the Way*, Pan Books; Macmillan; 1995.

earth. I think we all enjoyed ourselves and she departed amiably, replete with first hand material for a Parliamentary Question.

I had previously been questioned in careful detail by Dame Margery Perham, revered '*grande dame*' of African history and liberal thinker, at whose feet I had studied during the post graduate Devonshire Second Course at Oxford in 1948-9. She comprehended the whole nature of our task without condoning its severity, about which she had been informed by one Josiah Mwangi Kariuki,. formerly detained at Kawop in northern Samburu. He was later to achieve fame and brief political fortune after his book, *Mau Mau Detainee*,* was published with a magisterial and definitive introduction by Margery. His charismatic leadership potential, recognized by Ministerial office, incurred the jealousy of the political gods and cost him his life by assassination.

Of comparable stature, and as worthy to be dubbed 'Dame' was Elspeth Huxley, redoubtable champion of Kenya settlement in her seminal 1930s books *White Man's Country* and *Red Strangers*, as well as in her fascinating, hammer and tongs debate with Margery Perham, published in 1945 as *Race and Politics in Kenya*. Elspeth, always open to new experience, came with her formative and formidable mother, Nellie Grant, to visit us in Thiba camp, where John and I vied for the courtesy of collecting the spilled contents of Nellie's reticule from the office floor. Elspeth had a natural gift of felicitous phrase, delivered with pith and wit, about people and affairs, perceptively observed but rarely debunked unkindly. Her parting comment inscribed in John Cowan's office log read as "a shattering experience", one that long after she did not care to recall. It may well have been repugnant to her concept of the society in which she was raised.

Professional and humanitarian visitors were not confined to distinguished women. We were very happy to be scrutinized by the Delegate from the International Committee of the Red Cross in Geneva, the very sanctum of investigation and protection of human rights. Phillipe Junod was the son of a famous philosopher, a humanist and a poet. Small and crab-apple cheeked with quiffy snow white hair, his brilliant blue eyes sparkled with insight. He did not attempt to impress his Red Cross Mission or his own compassion on anyone, but quietly left me more determined to avoid abuses. "Do not distress yourself" (*"Ne vous inquietez pas*), he said; "Compared with the French in Algeria, you are angels of mercy."

There was continuous interest and concern expressed on the part of the Protestant churches, notably Archdeacon, later Bishop, Leonard Beecher and the Reverend, later Bishop, Stanley Booth-Clibborn. We assumed they were kept informed by our visiting pastor, Reverend Obadiah, who

*Oxford University Press: Nairobi; 1963.

regularly roared in and out on his motorbike, goggled like Mr Toad, destination unknown, without ever a word to ourselves, save civilities exchanged outside the Anglican church built for him by the detainees. His reports may have caused the most angelic of Assistant Bishops, Canon Langford-Smith, to materialize like a paraclete inside Thiba camp. There was clearly no harm in him, though a little vanity may have prompted him to ask me to guess his origin from his modulated '-strailian' accent. He was certainly no mover or shaker, perhaps being chosen for that benign quality.

Two visiting colleagues from Tom Askwith's Community Development and Rehabilitation Department, working in Athi River Camp, caused us, I hoped unwittingly, some awkwardness in regard to the changes we had thought necessary to clear the choked pipeline to release. They were Major Jim Breckenridge, of an old Kenya settler family, and Mike Seaward. There was no outward tension between us, but I sensed unspoken moral comment, as well as some understandable resentment at changes implying criticism, in which their colleagues working with me had concurred. (Two years later, in the aftermath of the Hola affair, they may have taken comfort from the Report's findings.)

Not long after I was delighted to welcome an old friend from Maralal days, Tony Lavers of the Information Department, who had been with our idyllic safari to Lake Rudolph. Tony was uncertain whether he would be free to cover in detail our Rehabilitation procedures, but we urged him to do so, not least because we trusted implicitly in his experienced judgement and that of another friend, his Chief Press Officer, Alastair Matheson. In the event no report was published, Alastair having been seriously and admittedly misinformed about our 'crusade' from an outside sniper. It was not surprising that there should have been a climate of opinion among some well and some less well motivated people, who judged from a distance what they thought we were doing to be without moral or intellectual content. Others were frankly sceptical of Rehabilitation and opposed to return of 'unreconstructed terrorists' to their homes where 'loyalists' held tenuous sway. We had to steer a course between them all in the wider concern.

During the next, seemingly endless and repetitious year, a significant but unremarked factor contributed to our own morale and to the atmosphere of the camps. This was the presence inside every camp of the wives of the majority of our staff, uniformed and civilian. It was accidental and did not take into account either the moderating effect, emotionally and physically, on ourselves or on our relationship with the detainees. Their presence could reasonably be held to render less likely any possibility of the camps becoming brutal or inhumane places. Both John and I also benefited from periodic visits from his wife and mine to be. So it went on week after week, intake upon intake, month after month, lightened by an extraordinary feeling of fulfilment upon hearing regular chanting lorry loads of those deemed ready to return home without risk or disruption. After a gruelling year we began to allow ourselves to think that there would come an end. It was towards the spring of 1958 and the beginning of the long rains after the long drought.

Meanwhile we did not fail to make our own enjoyments and relief from the two way tensions of confinement. Apart from a snatched weekend with James Bonninger at Nyeri, reporting to Monkey Johnston on progress, I joined happily in whatever pleasures our Mwea community offered. They mainly centred on Gathigiriri Camp, where there was a Prisons Department 'mess', and the comfortable homes and lush gardens of the Irrigation Scheme staff. At Gathigiriri there was Commandant Bill Halsey's pork butchery and buffet dinners with dancing. Isaiah once laughingly told me I had intervened when a European officer had refused to allow his wife to dance with him, but I did not recall any such racial friction among us.

Successive Irrigation Scheme Managers, living and working in a fine thatched house the other side of the wire fence from my corrugated hut, entertained us generously. As professional Hydraulic Engineers they commanded far better pay and conditions than ours. The first was Laurie Bion, swarthy and well nourished with an exotic background in Indian jute plantations. He was followed by Douglas Taylor, a more orthodox and plain spoken irrigation expert. When invited to sundowners and canapés to meet guests from outside we felt rather out of touch with such gracious living and wore ties — until things warmed up.

The Field Manager at Tebere, near Gathigiriri, was Major Ted Calvert, a giant, husky voiced, cuddly bear. Adele, fashionably shingled, generous of spirit and bosom, had a bawdy wit, a roustabout son and an asking to be locked up nymphet of a daughter. Their spacious thatched house looked over the perfect sward of a bowling green, flanked by a clear water furrow gurgling through blazing canna lilies. The lawn was overhung at one end by bougainvillaea, shading a constant supply of refreshments for exhausted bowlers. A Sunday passed happily with them cleansed us to face the week ahead.

A most lively and regular guest was 'Tiger' Wilde the District Officer, Mwea Plains. Much decorated in the war, Tiger had distinguished Provincial Administrative service in Equatoria Province of the Anglo-Egyptian Sudan, though he was not admitted to the élite Sudan Political, which considered itself a cut above the Colonial Service! Laden with retirement honours and 'lumpers' (compensation), he had a go at farming in Kenya, but lost all in a dud partnership. This brought him back as a 'retread' to his present modest post, to which he lent the undiminished fire of his old age and adventurous spirit. He also brought a charming pair of most attractive nieces, whom he presented as his wards. They were from the family of Roses Limejuice.One whom I particularly admired was later to marry an Embu District Officer, John Tennant, scion of the house of Tennant's Lager. Whisky in my tin lean-to with Tiger and Margaret, stink beetles from the marsh crunched underfoot, still contrived to be a fragrant occasion.

At last in March 1958 we came to the point where the Special Commissioner, Monkey Johnston, declared the job sufficiently done to cope with the remaining few hundred. The onset of relief was held in check by anxiety that something could yet go wrong, symbolized by the silent crouching bronze figure of Kimani, who remained adamant and impenetrable, though I had long come to respect a certain dignity in his defiance. He stayed on until final and for him terminal detention in Hola.

A farewell party was organized by Wilfred Thimba at Thiba on behalf of all Rehabilitation staff. It was quite an emotional occasion for all of us because of what we had come through together. I was given a copy of a speech delivered with precision by Wilfred. I reproduce it because some have commented that Africans, particularly the Kikuyu, tend to say pleasing things. Let it speak for itself. The signatories went on to higher positions than mine in their own independent Government. I was especially touched to receive individual letters from the Community Development Officers, who had worked with me on Rehabilitation and would soon return to their substantive Community Development Department under Askwith. Each fully endorsed the changes and procedures we had introduced. John Cowan and his staff set up a complementary occasion at Gathigiriri signalized by a salver inscribed to mark our collaborative effort.

With a residuum of under one twentieth of the previous total of detainees, the question of handing over did not loom large, until I learned that District Officer John Nottingham had declined the job offering moral objections. As he could have used his undoubted talents and sympathies to good effect I questioned with Monkey Johnston his right to refuse to undertake the duty, since he knew nothing at first hand of our or my actions and was not called upon to continue with any which might be repugnant to him. If he believed that it was Government policy to implement unlawful or immoral procedures, he should either require changes or offer to resign. At this sensitive time in the programme of releases he was diverted to another posting without controversy. Happily, in his place an officer of less confused pretensions and attitudes, not shared by the Kikuyu staff in the Mwea, came unencumbered with such pharisaism. He was Denis Lakin, dashingly handsome, his black waves, violet eyes and shy smile covering the mettle that had won him an Emergency MBE. He, and later Hugh Galton-Fenzi, cleared away to Hola not only the remaining detainees but also hard-core prisoners from Nairobi who passed through Karaba camp, where I heard of one fatality.

Two letters of thanks came from Monkey Johnston's office, one handwritten in his graceful script. He asked me to give thought to my next posting and I took the opportunity to request an 'A' grade district, Kiambu or Machakos or, with some temerity, the Department of Community Development. I had a strong inclination towards CD in the field, although the top post was still held by Tom Askwith, who had superior qualifications and experience at the centre. The lot fell on Kiambu District where I had been DOI six years before.

There was little time to take stock between leaving the Mwea and taking over at Kiambu, only an hour but another world down the road to Nairobi. Behind me lay the single purpose, disciplined and intensely stressful period spent on freeing the minds of thousands of men imprisoned in violence. There was a sense of huge relief that not one life had been lost and no severe harm had been done, save perhaps to myself. Lifelong friendships had been formed and enmities wittingly incurred.

Ahead lay an administrative responsibility of great complexity and countless pitfalls, some of which could be foreseen. One of the first was the reintegration of the thousands of 'rehabilitated' detainees sent home from camps within the vast mass of the population living in 'protected' villages guarded by 'loyalist' elements. Neither the District Administration nor the influential coffee growers, many of them 'soldier settlers', were of a mind to regard the contagion of former 'terrorists' with equanimity. The District Administrative apparatus, the 'Native Authority', the African and European District Council, the African Courts, as well as educational, agrarian and political developments, had burgeoned during and since the Emergency years, 1952-7, to an unimaginable extent compared with my previous experience in Kiambu. As first time DC in an agricultural community there would be much to learn on the job.

Personally, I was at 35 younger than the norm of Kiambu DCs. Having been separated during five years at Maralal, there would understandably be some local reaction to my remarriage to whomever, among the conventional, mainly British, society. I might have had well founded misgivings, despite 14 years of reportedly good service, seven as a pastoral area DC, but the euphoria of recent achievement and kind accolades blurred my judgement sufficiently to "summon up the blood"! No one else could have approved more warmly than my fragile and long suffering cook, Ndungu, who had faithfully accompanied me from Nyeri to our wretched tin huts and stink beetles in Thiba camp. With gentle insistence he had urged me to acquire a wife and a proper house in Kiambu — which was his home.

A valedictory message from the Governor, Sir Evelyn Baring, saying he had been ill overtook me in Kiambu. It was a personal, hand written, letter on blue Government House notepaper congratulating me on being appointed a member of the Order of the British Empire, in which John

240

Cowan shortly joined me. He wrote that *"Your accomplishment there was one of the outstanding successes of the Emergency".* *

*Caroline Elkins (Ibid) Baring to Secretary of State, letter of 26 February 1958, Colonial Office 822/1252:
"I recently visited the Mwea camps and was enormously impressed by the remarkable work done during the period of exactly one year by Mr Gavaghan. It is his work in these camps that has been the key to the flow out of detainees. It is due to this work above all else that we are no longer faced with the danger of having tens of thousands of people on our hands, who would be dangerous to release but whose retention would gradually become a political impossibility."

Later:

*Baring Papers held at Durham University; Random notes by Baring; GRE/1/97: 6 x 4 Black Notebook, 1958–1959; Extract:

"...Gavaghan as adviser to roving Commissioner".

WILFRED THIMBA'S SPEECH

Ladies and Gentlemen, although we are doing our best to put happy faces on today's proceedings, it is no use our pretending that our happiness is not rather forced.

It is always pleasant to have an occasion on which we can pay tribute to one whom we respect and admire and in this case I may say whom we love, but although today by no means marks the end of our esteem and affection, it is sad to remember that henceforth Mr (T.J.F.) Gavaghan's presence among us will no longer be a present reality, but kindly and treasured memory.

Mr Gavaghan was seconded to Rehabilitation in the Special Camps at the time when the rehabilitation process was almost at a standstill due to the obduracy attitude of the oath fanatics.

We needed special power to deal effectively with the ever annoying but essential task of rehabilitation; this power came in the person of Mr Gavaghan. When he took the office he initiated most of us in our duties; frankly he "told off" many of us for our early mistakes, and then with unfailing kindness and courtesy and good humour helped us to put them right. He secured complete co-operation of the Prisons Department which was vital to rehabilitation.

Owing to his indefatigable effort and keenness, great achievement has been made and to prove it, the biggest special detention camp known as Manyani is almost empty through following and applying the methods initiated by him. Our words of mouth cannot express our gratitude and appreciation for his effort and love of our tribe for he has saved many souls which would have been declared and were actually declared irreconcilable and condemned in toto.

Now that he has been called to the position of greater responsibility, we all wish him from the bottom of our hearts all success, good health, happiness and comport in the years to come. We have been very proud of Mr Gavaghan's connection with us and we will miss him a great deal as we shall no longer have his cheerful smile and loveable personality among us.

On behalf of us all, I ask him to accept the following gifts:

1 Dining Table: 1 Book-shelf: 1 staff.

It is a very inadequate token of our feeling for him but it will perhaps sometimes remind him, in the new life to which he is going, that the Rehabilitation Staff in the Special Camps would still like to be remembered as his friends and well-wishers.

S

KAVA KHAN
A Fantasy, after SAMUEL TAYLOR COLERIDGE
by KOOH NAVI (IVAN HOOK!)

In Mwea Plain did Kava Khan
A Rehabilitation Plan decree,
Where fast the Thiba River ran
Through Shambas measureless to man
Down to a sunlit sea.
So many plots of barren ground
With poles and wire were girdled round,
And there were gardens bright with brilliant flowers
Where laboured many a Y2 Detainee,
And here were fences, churches, screening bowers
And whitewash dazzling for the eye to see.
But O, that vasty compound, wind bombarded,
Which 'neath the view of towered guards lay spread,
A savage place! As closely locked and guarded
As any plot whose dusty soil was larded
With tears and sweat of many a hardcore 'Z'!
Within whose bounds, with frantic turmoil seething,
With shouts and grunts and sounds of laboured breathing
A mighty battle fortnightly was warred
Between askaris and the intake horde.
Great men of valour these, replete with tricks
To Rehabilitate reluctant Micks,
They stand together: S.O.W.C.,
Oft kicked but still undaunted, smiles to see
The foemen overpowered, their war-cries gagged
By CDOs or OICs, and those
Who try refusing to remove their clothes
Being relentlessly, remorselessly debagged,
And ever in the forefront, in the van
Of trouble, strides the stonefaced Kava Khan!
The path of Rehabilitation
Following these drastic ploys
Leads to ball-games recreation.
Song and dance and other joys,
It is a miracle of rare device
That Rehab is so nasty — and so nice!
A Y2 plays a concertina
Neatly dressed in Prisons clothes.
He's a softcore young Kikuyu
Who, until last month would do you
In, to serve his horrid oaths.
He has now revived within him
Desire for an employer:
Treads the path that soon must bring him
To the arms of Tom Mboya.
He builds his castle in the air
On Rehabilitation's plea,
And you who read should see him there
His manner meek but debonair:
His flashing teeth, his growing hair
Mark him fit to face S.B.
So keep your fingers crossed 'tis said
For he on honeyed words hath fed
And drunk the milk of M.C.D.

XVIII

KIAMBU DISTRICT – II
APRIL 1958–AUGUST 1959

My reversion to a relatively normal officer of the Provincial Administration had implications at the tugging end of the chain of command. I was no longer answerable personally to the Special Commissioner for Rehabilitation, trebling as Minister for African Affairs and for Community Development, with his hotline to the Governor, nor did I have charge of Community Development staff seconded to rehabilitation. The too close for comfort links with ministerial levels fell away. Instead I came directly under the command of the Provincial Commissioner at Nyeri, Frank Loyd, who had been insulated from any responsibility for rehabilitation in the detention camps. Reversion to the orthodox hierarchy was clear-cut and congenial, especially since Frank Loyd had been DC at Kiambu and knew its ropes. The return to Kiambu via Thika and the Muthaiga roundabout was at once exciting in its challenges and familiar as to a home revisited. The quadrangle of District Headquarters was unchanged in layout, but much congested with prefab. extensions, 4 wheel drive vehicles and scurrying people. I went at once in my battered Volkswagen Beetle to the DC's house, which was off the driveway to my old DOI's quarters overlooking the fairway.

The departing DC, Douglas Penwill, and his wife Pat were welcoming hosts in the rambling stone bungalow with its small brick guest annexe. There were no government supplied comforts or modern fittings, but their own furnishings and ornaments were of a style that reflected his entrepreneurial and horse racing flair and her Scottish family fortune in South African media. Their posting to Kiambu had lasted little more than a year and evoked Douglas's wry comment that planting roses was sure to lead to transfer. He had and I did. Douglas himself was a formidable man from whom to take over, even without his war record as a young Lieutenant Colonel with a DSO. He was tall and deliberate of movement with limited vision in one eye. His manner appeared aloof, even superb, with what I had earlier described as the "gift of ineffable condescension to his superiors", which also affirmed equality of status. Ambition, self-esteem and selective arrogance, were offset by an inner modesty, quirkish wit, perceptive intelligence, vision and a capacity to inspire admiration and loyalty. It was clear during the handing-over that Douglas had achieved an immense amount in stimulating post emergency development of every kind centred upon land consolidation, agrarian improvement, township planning and construction and plantation crops. Pat had complemented all this by her maternal support of *Maendeleo ya Wanawake*, the new women's movement.

It must have been quite galling for them to leave so much creative team work to someone younger, with less experience and less credentials by any measure. I felt it, even if they and others did not show it.

After Douglas left there was no available position in Central Government large enough to hold him. He was appointed acting Permanent Secretary for Housing, which kept his links with the model town projects he had started at Riruta and Kangemi near the city and county boundaries with Kiambu, as well as being handy to the Nairobi race course! He was also able to live rent free and, as he told me, almost tax free on the small Beacon Ranch he had acquired astride the Athi River road looking across the National Park to the rolling Ngong hills. How I envied him! His Housing Ministry duties caused him to send to me the Deputy Governor-General of the Belgian Congo in the care of a benighted senior Colonial Office Official. Douglas referred to our guest on the phone as *Monsieur le Noir*, by which title I naïvely greeted him, to my later extreme discomfiture. The conducting Official in riposte called Nairobi "the biggest confidence trick (he) had ever seen". Douglas, being frustrated of his ambition to be Provincial Commissioner, Nyanza, left the service for Northern Transvaal, to carve out a fortune in plantation crops and on the golden turf. A gifted Governor was lost.

The rigging of the colonial government in the District had been extensively redesigned and refitted during and since the Emergency to carry the dense proliferation of staff and function in every department. The DC led a central operational group including the DOI, the officers in charge of Land Consolidation, Revenue and Community Development and the District representatives of Produce Marketing Boards. With the heads of specialist departments we made up the District Team. We also had enjoyable weekly visitations for Court and lunch by Resident Magistrate, Harry Oulton, who would bowl up in a vintage Rolls-Royce family pantechnicon, fully populated.

Field administration had been devolved to five geographical Divisions each with a Divisional District Officer working closely with a Divisional Senior Chief and the panoply of the 'Native Authority', exercised through paid Chiefs of Locations, Headmen and so forth. Divisions could contain as many as a hundred thousand people and were managed through Divisional Teams on the same model as at District Headquarters. Of necessity and variable human nature Divisions developed a measure of individuality and autonomy related to the circumstances of the area, including proximity to European settled land, and to the distinct personality, enthusiasms and abilities of the incumbent DO, which embraced DO's wife!

I was fortunate to have inherited from Douglas' regime, Alan Simmance as DOI, in a role become more complex and varied than mine had been six years before. Alan was a twin born in India with a Brigadier father who had suffered as a prisoner of war. He himself was ideally suited to a demanding staff function. He was a barrister, master of any brief, a convincing raconteur of the absurd and an amateur actor of note in the mode of Rex Harrison, whom he was pleased to resemble. By way of emotional release he would play original recordings of the soaring coloratura of Amelita Galli-Curci at stupefying volume. Phina, his wife, was named after Napoleon's Josephine, widow of General Beauharnais, from French Martinique in the West Indies. Her formidably fragile mother, Mrs Phyllis Shand Allfrey of Dominica, was Minister of Education in the abortive British Semi-Self-Governing Federation. Phina exuded a sense of the exotic warmth of her mother's literary gem, *The Orchid House* (1953) and felt a close empathy with the few Kikuyu women Mau Mau acolytes placed under her charge in a camp near Kiambu. They were quite unsuitably described by the Governor in a letter to me as 'St Trinian's girls'. She revelled in astonishing dinner party acts like inhaling nasal drops flat out on the floor in mid conversation. Her zanily brilliant mind and flashing smile earned many admirers including the ascendant political star, Tom Mboya. She and Alan came together while she was at Oxford and formed a twin-yolked partnership of equals. They adopted Diana and Stephen.

In the place of shaggy old Masonic Master, Rory Heard, as Revenue Officer in 1950 was smooth pated young Scot, Alastair Anderson. Brisk, efficient and charming he upped and married the comely daughter of Graham Clark, Managing Director of the powerful Metal Box Company. I found as Community Development Officer, following Eric Peachey Wilkinson, a demobbed British Army Captain from Malayan forces, Barbara Rigby. She was a most winsome cat who walked alone but loved people and company including that of a red headed Irish District Officer, Peter Dempster. She was single-mindedly devoted to the *Maendeleo ya Wanawake* women's movement. After my own re-marriage I was honoured and sad to 'give' her away when she married Major John Harper-Nelson of the Uganda King's African Rifles, under whom had served one Sergeant Idi Amin, a champion boxer and a tyrant in the making. Barbara remained our friend, wherever.

The job of John Golds, District Officer Land Consolidation, was new and developing into the most challenging and far reaching one in the District, if not the Province. Apart from its beneficial ramifications, consolidation of their confined and precious land went to the very heart and hearth of the Kikuyu people. It was the foundation of Government plans for recovery from the dead period of the Emergency and of introducing a better way of life. Its side effects ranged from arresting the flow of red silt from the Kikuyu highlands down the Sabaki River to choke the sparkling beaches of Malindi, to the relief of peasant women from plodding under their pelvis cracking loads of water and firewood, and the clearing of land for tea and coffee plantations. It also made possible the securing of bank loans against individual title for capital improvements.

Consolidation was not a new idea. It drew its inspiration from land reform in India and had been mooted as early as the 1934 Kenya Land Commission, which had parcelled out the Highlands and the Kikuyu Land Unit. A procession of Administrative Officers had noted the evils of fragmentation and the solution by fragment gathering and consolidation had been advanced by such 'seers' as the revered social thinker H. E. Lambert and crisply decisive Desmond O'Hagan, guru of African courts. It was reluctantly put on one side in face of the complexity and cost of redistributing a rural slum absolutely unprepared for the detailed processes and social disturbance involved, but overripe for the Emergency that arose in part from that wretched condition of life. Ironically the violent upheaval of Mau Mau brought about the changed circumstances which opened the way to rapid consolidation.

The entire peasant population was withdrawn from the land by Frank Loyd when DC into tightly controlled and 'protected' villages. Thousands were in detention camps as Mau Mau sympathizers. Thousands more were employed in the Government security forces, a discipline and education in itself; scores of young white settler farmers became DO's Kikuyu Guard, later released to become Land Consolidation Officers. The conjunction of arbitrary control, available resources and agrarian reform was at last conducive to success. The idea had found its time.

My own minor preparation for taking part dated from 1951, when I had been asked by Miles North, my acting DC, to submit outline proposals from Kiambu to the Chief Native Commissioner, Edward Windley. In 1956, after Samburu, I had been sent, while on leave, to attend a major International Conference on Land Consolidation at Cambridge University. This was set up by Andre Cohen of the Colonial Office, later the Governor who dismissed the Kabaka of Buganda. It was chaired by (Sir) William Gorrell-Barnes, my former official guest at Maralal. He very tolerantly invited the plenary session to adopt my oral submission as a syndicate rapporteur, which I had impertinently if accurately expressed in topical blank verse, having drafted it in the Earls Court basement flat of my wife to be. It was printed in the Conference Report.

The practical task facing Kiambu from the outset was intimidating. Even in loose estimation, two hundred and eighty thousand acres were owned by nearly forty thousand peasant farmers, divided into half a million scattered fragments, averaging eight each, adding up to a potential five acre unit. These rough calculations had to encompass the division of clan or common land and space for population centres, services and social facilities. In all the African Land Development Board posited at least two million topographical measurements before reconciling a 5% discrepancy with the very popular aerial photography which 'flattened' the ridged terrain. The solution was found in a combination of human wit and ingenuity applied with extraordinary unity of purpose. Chief Muhoya of North Tetu in Nyeri District had shown the advantages of fragment gathering as had Chief Magugu and the Mbari (clan) ya Igi in Githunguri Location of Kiambu. The conjunction of Douglas Penwill as DC Kiambu, with Provincial African Courts experience in Nyeri, and of John Golds, a volunteer District Officer in the Kikuyu Guard at Githunguri, provided an ideal administrative base for launching a campaign which was to sweep the District, lead the Province and provide a model for the country. It was Douglas' recognition of this timely opportunity which inspired him to appoint John as 'supremo' of a land consolidation task force.

John Golds was the son of a Shell Marine Captain and had settled as a young farmer and commercial cheese maker at Lessos on the western wall of the Rift Valley towards Eldoret. He was full bodied and robust with the dark curls, firm, plumped features and lips of a Goya portrait, or a bucolic Dylan Thomas. His engaging smile, black olive pip eyes, and attentively penetrating gaze presided benignly over great and small as they painlessly succumbed to the simple thrust of his plans and methods. He at once inspanned a dozen redundant Kikuyu Guard officers as field supervisors, with hundreds of trainees fired with enthusiasm for the recreation of their land. The inseparable partnership with the Agriculture Department was headed by solid, smiling Gary Yates of the butter blonde hair, pale blue eyes with slanting lids and calcium rich teeth. He was assisted by German, Lud Kolbe, and Rhodesian, Leon Fouché, who jointly wrote a manual on consolidation farm planning. Not least was the enthusiastic backing of durable Leg. Co. Member, Eliud Mathu, who had ridden out the Emergency storms.

Two guiding principles affecting both present and future society had to be decided. Both were concerned with respect for popular choice and traditional institutions. The first was whether to introduce consolidation systematically and arbitrarily across the board, utilizing a brief quiet period of Administrative dominance, or to do so sporadically, area by area, in response to the expressed wishes of the people. As it was, both proved to be the answer since initial rejection often turned into fervent requests, anguished at losing place in the queue. The Kikuyu always knew a good thing about land when they saw one. The second was the application of local democracy in the whole process with maximum consultation and minimum opportunity for corruption.

This was achieved by placing decisions as to ownership and relocation of joined fragments at the level of a typical ridge between two streams, where everyone knew each other and where a committee of thirty elders, or 10% of the adult male population, would encompass all interests and be almost impossible to bribe. There were levels of appeal reaching to John Golds, but spurious ones got short shrift. The quasi legal grass roots system of adjudication was not open to legal representatives since it was held that, as for African courts, they would, without expertise or understanding, complicate and delay decision to the disadvantage of poor claimants. That the legal provision for consolidation was so effectively set out in a few quarto pages was a tribute to the remarkable skill of the Legal Draftsman, Anthony Webb, which Alan Simmance tested scrupulously at every point.

This 'grass roots democracy' spread across to pervade all the other technical and social elements of development in the area. It afforded a hearing to claims by returning detainees, convinced the people that they were getting a fair deal and that a land title so publicly established was secure, even worth paying for. To top it off a title, visible and verifiable in the imposing Kalamazoo Land Registers locked in fireproof rooms, was negotiable as a source of bank loans. Both in terms of willing payment of consolidation costs and punctilious repayment of loans, acceptance and confidence were enthusiastically demonstrated on both sides. It was a heartening sight to find a traditionally clad elder, without Swahili, English or letters, clasping a Title Deed with clear understanding of what it was and prepared to pay the small fee for verification by beating the bounds. The glint in the eye reflected the pure joy of secure ownership of land.

An inevitable but serious result of putting together what were called in the jargon 'discrete parcels' of land out of tiny fragments was the squeezing out of tenants, squatters and landless people. This could extend to wives, widows and paid labour who had scratched a living on or between the parcels. The resultant sense of insecurity and deprival was a ready recruiting sergeant for disaffection which spilt over into nearby Nairobi where there was already a wretched mass of landless unemployed. In fact a recruiting agency was standing by in the shape of the People's Convention Party which had started life in 1957 as the Nairobi People's Convention Party, N.P.C.P., a Nairobi electoral base for Tom Mboya in his tussle for national political influence with his senior, Gem Argwings-Kodhek, who had sounder Luo roots in Nyanza Province. Shorn of the N the People's Convention Party, at first fortuitously, came to be seen by many as one with a new Kikuyu society, *Kiama Kia Muingi*, a perfect cross translation which brought Mboya closer to the Kikuyu. I once tested the possible connection between them by sending an undercover Tribal Policeman, shoddily attired, with some crumpled notes in his tobacco twist, to offer a modest subscription to the K.K.M. at the office of the P.C.P. in Nairobi. A receipt with the stamp of the latter was returned. It was no proof, but alerted us to the possibility of joint action along the city boundary with Kiambu and left open to question some expressed anxiety lest K.K.M. might prove to be a recrudescence of Mau Mau and connected with the return of detainees from the rehabilitation camps.

An all-party Parliamentary Committee of unofficials was appointed to examine on the ground the whole policy and practice of consolidation and I was willingly assigned to take them round Kiambu on the first leg of their Provincial tour. They included up and very coming politicians Tom Mboya, Doctor Julius Gikonyo Kiano of Stanford and Kiambu, future Deputy Speaker Jeremiah Nyagah of Education and Embu, long-serving member Bernard Maté of Meru and the University of Wales, with Mkamba activist, Muimi. This vigorous and able young ginger group contrasted amicably with two much older European members and one Indian. Shirley Victor Cooke was an Irishman who had been a notably unorthodox Colonial Administrative Officer between the wars and had moved into Legislative Council as Member for the Coast. Humphrey Slade was an Eton King's Scholar, dyed in the gown lawyer, risen to be deputy Judge Advocate General, after which he turned ardent right wing settler and anti terrorist hard-liner. He was outwardly an ascetic and monkish man who blended severity of moral conviction with decent compassion. Of another kind was Mr R. K. Travadi, a rather crusty and rigidly upright man with a painful limp and a stick. While driving to a meeting near Dagoretti we passed leaping and laughing urchins to whom I waved. Mr Travadi told me of his surprise that a DC should do this and when we dismounted he took me firmly by the left hand and we continued to hold hands while seated in the 'Baraza'. The Kikuyu elders evinced no surprise at a DC, known simply as *Karuga Ndua*, enjoying such intimacy with a visiting Indian MP.

We had started the tour of investigation at John Golds' command post consisting of a linked cluster of Kikuyu thatched rondavels on an eminence beside the 'Banana Hill' road to Limuru. He and his officers served a picnic lunch of bread and butter with cheese and strawberries and cream from his Lessos farm. My eye lit on a large roulade of his mature Cheddar in a wrapper topped by a label with a map of Kenya and the brand title 'White Highlands'. I offered the platter and a cheese knife to Mr Mboya and asked if he would care for a slice. He helped himself liberally and later got his own back. (John gave us a cheese knife and board for our wedding present).

Hour upon hour we tramped the fields and heard endless representations, often relating to land case appeals which I had adjudicated as DOI six years before. At sunset on the third day we came to the small country estate of retired agitator, gentleman farmer, Harry Thuku, once mentor of Jomo Kenyatta. The entrance pillars were of white stucco topped by impressive balls between trim macrocarpa hedges. Harry, his corduroy trousers tucked into Wellington boots, proudly displayed his triple stem coffee bushes, laden with roseate berries, planted in orderly ranks along perfectly scarified contour terraces. With Tom Mboya standing on the contour above me, silhouetted against the falling sun, I shaded my forehead with my hand to pay attention to his questions. Next morning the popular Swahili newspaper *Baraza*, edited by respected Boaz Omori, carried a photograph, blown up top centre front page, over the caption "The DC sweats while interrogated by Mr Mboya"!

With the best of Administrative motives I had been informally encouraged to take the sharp edge off the committee's enquiry before they visited Fort Hall (Murang'a) and Nyeri, who were behind in the inter-District race for completion. Committee attendance did fall off and no adverse effects were reported on the Kiambu programme. On the contrary the very open investigation by known political independents served both to restrain undue arbitrariness and to encourage faster progress. It did not solve the human problem of the dispossessed nor dilute the poisons of unrest simmering within their wretched plight.

After this essentially political diversion in support of land consolidation, it was time to attend to the home front, preparatory to calling on Divisional DOs in the field to learn about both administrative and departmental activities. I had yet to assess the atmosphere and prospects among the people, many of whom might have opinions about me from earlier land litigation and from Thiba detention camp, as well as to become better acquainted with the adjacent settler communities some of whom were flexing their political muscles in varying degrees of defensive alarm.

New District Commissioner's offices had been authorized by the Treasury in capital expenditure estimates and put in hand in Douglas Penwill's time. They were designed and built by PWD engineer Jim Graham, as an elongated bungalow in the English 1930s country style of warm red brick under Bangalore tiles. The whole was set below and at right angles to the fifty year old former office, where Miles North had held court, and hugged the slope facing over the vlei to Kiambu Club. I was able to move in at once to a long room at the quiet end 50 yards from the back of my house. Between me and Alan Simmance was a double reception area with Frances Crag, our incomparable secretary and, for a time Ann Shields, her eager learner. It would be hard to overstate Frances' place in our functioning. She cared for the office as we for her. Our only anxiety was lest she succumb to restless overwork since normal retirement age had long slipped by. When respite came she allowed a girlish smile to flit across her harassed, still pretty, face. She lived in genteel simplicity at the early settler home of the McLellan Wilsons, affording a respected bond with the Office. Ann, not yet twenty, was the nubile daughter of 'Bertie' and 'Connie' Shields, leading coffee growers now enjoying the hard earned prosperity of rising prices, who were most generous in hospitality and fresh vegetables which then seemed to sprout on my verandah. Across the passage behind his counter in the Revenue Office was venerable District Cashier Mr Almeida, whose dogged pursuit of a receipt or a missing shilling would end in a mischievous chuckle.

The quiet of the gum tree copse below the office was disturbed by construction of the new African District Council building which was sited down the slope to one side. It had been designed for Douglas by a Nairobi architectural partnership, Hughes and Polkinghorne (Dorothy Hughes of Ford Motors family, not Richard Hughes of his own practice). The architect's impression had the look of a horse chestnut shell split open to reveal the 'conker' within a spiky carapace. It was so 'ultra-mod' in concept as to be sure to become dated. Nothing was traceable to the inspiration of Kikuyu customary building or their environment, although functionally it was an improvement on the previous corrugated iron cavern down by *kirigiti*, the old settlers' cricket pitch. Despite its oddity I noted for future reference that I ought to be the last 'ex officio' DC Chairman of the Council, possibly handing over to Senior Chief Josiah Njonjo, pillar of the Church of Scotland, and that inauguration might be concelebrated in the Christian rite together with the traditional holder of the Githathi Stone, the heaven sent meteorite. It did not happen so in my time and a wall plaque later recorded the opening by Governor Baring. A lost opportunity in the transfer of power.

The Kiambu Council had considerable executive powers on behalf of its large electorate and enough resources from taxes, fees and grants to employ a qualified European Works Foreman, Jim Knight, for road maintenance and delivery of piped water to every consolidated holding above 4 acres. We achieved a valuable coup in putting a tarmac road through the settled coffee estates linking the Kiambaa location near Kiambu with the Banana Hill trunk road to Limuru. This initiative earned the surprised respect of the Nairobi County Council of which the DC Kiambu was 'ex officio' member. It afforded me in turn opportunity for comment and intervention in matters affecting both intertwined council areas, as far as Karen 'garden suburb' south of Nairobi, where the water supply, privately owned by Rolls-Royce borne Remy Martin, was an undiluted source of contention.

In this capacity I was exposed in turn to public protest and censure about some odd conflicts of interest. One was the siting of a Roman Catholic Seminary for African Ordinands on the southern side of the Karen to Langata road, which was held to be in contravention of the Highlands Order in Council. The Chairman of a meeting in Karen Club was none other than my old Provincial Commissioner in Nyanza Province, Kenneth Leggat Hunter, now in retirement. Another complaint raised in a County

Council meeting was about the bedraggled ribbon development of dormitory and petty trade shacks along the side of the Ngong road opposite to the Royal Agricultural Society of Kenya (RASK) showground, the élite Hurlingham Polo Ground and the Nairobi Racecourse with its bright bougainvillaea laced fence. The substance of complaint was accurate but, however understandable, was hardly consistent with the spirit of 'paramountcy of African interests'. The *bijou* architect designed villas at nearby Riruta and Kangemi model townlets for the middling affluent were no answer to the need for sanitary 'doss houses' for low paid city workers to be located within walking distance of any sort of livelihood, starting long before daybreak.

Up among the 'Tigoni Tigers' I was unsuccessful in supporting an application for a site for a roadside petrol pull-in for rental by a suitable Kikuyu with backing from an oil company. There was at the time great competition between the oil majors, Shell/BP, Caltex, Esso and some new entrants to the market, for strategic sites throughout the District. I had regular meetings with their English 'rugger' type salesmen to sort out rival applications. Dagoretti Corner, for example, was hotly contested being on the main road fork to Karen and Limuru and was won by Caltex. The condition of final allocation of a site leased from the Kiambu Council was a rule of thumb undertaking by the company to construct for an approved tenant a petrol station and apron to the capital value in pounds (20 shillings) of an estimated month's throughput in thousands of gallons of petrol. This worked well at any level and the Dagoretti station, at least, was not unsightly.

The heads of the companies exercised considerable business power and sometimes beneficial social influence at a higher level through golf clubs, Rotary, Lions, Freemasons and patronage. Two were Kiambu Club members. John Francis, elegant chief of Shell, financed the foundation of an inner city college for boys, called *Staréhé* or 'be at rest', under the direction of Geoffrey Griffin, formerly Deputy Headmaster of Wamumu Approved School for young Mau Mau adherents in the Mwea. Attendance at Staréhé was initially entirely voluntary for two weeks, after which a commitment was expected to make planning of classes possible. Ironically the centre gained such a reputation that it became fashionable for privileged and powerful African parents to seek places for their children. (My eldest son Kevin later did a pre-Oxford stint there teaching sports, maths and French with his salary reimbursed by me.) John Grant, bustling clubman, Managing Director of Caltex, had access to every part of society and charitable movement. American bald eagle, Bob Belknap of Esso, had links across the increasingly active American involvement in Kenya through the Consul-General Dudley Withers, the US Information Office and US Aid (first called International Co-operation Administration) under Bob Powers and Gavin Lawson, with whom I was later to work closely.

In the densely populated, hectically regenerating and politically charged District of Kiambu, intricately affected by the stimulus and contagion of Nairobi, the specialist departments of Government were of a scale and professionalism outside the umbrella of the Administration, sometimes held over them in smaller and less complex districts. The heads of departments neither needed nor accepted involvement in their work, other than in consultation over District policy objectives and good order.

Oscar Killen, trenchant Ulster born Medical Officer of Health, with diminutively dominant Matron, Peggy Timms; gently adroit Paddy Doran, my old friend from Kisii, for Education; blandly competent Gary Yates for Agriculture; Assistant Superintendent John Sherrard-Smith, most regular Police Chief, with socially mobile courtier Robin Marshall of Special Branch and his celandine wife Marian; these and other departmental peers were not colleagues to tangle with or call in question. Their responsibility was independently exercised through Divisions. As a rule there was easy camaraderie at all levels between the separate branches and the Administration. This was not to say that the old chestnut of the 'heaven born' Administrator, 'knowing a little (or nothing) about a lot', versus the trained Specialist 'knowing a lot about a little', was entirely buried, any more than was the settler versus official 'myth'. As a close community we worked together, played together, and dined together, albeit with unwritten, inherited service etiquette governing order of precedence, which could cause heartburn to either sex and any rank! I once took a chance in arranging with the Kiambu Club Committee a structured question and answer session between a panel of departmental officers, including myself, and the mainly settler membership, no holds or questions barred. It seemed to go well, though I was tipped off by a friend that my facial reactions were sometimes unguarded at awkward moments!

The first of regular forays into the field was to Githunguri Division in homage to Senior Chief Waruhiu, my old friend from my earlier tour in Kiambu, who had been murdered by Mau Mau while I was in Maralal. His sons David and Simon remained in the division. Simon was now Location Chief, solid, dependable and quietly firm. David, the older and weightier, who had been involved in Moral Rearmament during the early stages of rehabilitation of detainees, rose to head the transformed Kiambu County Council. Waruhiu's successor as Senior Chief, Magugu Waweru, was a well educated, serene and devoutly Christian man, an early environmentalist who, with his brother Wanyutu and surveyor John Ngugi, pioneered the land consolidation experiment of the Mbari (clan) ya Igi. Magugu's daughter was making a name for herself as a pianist, on the path to whose country wedding I ripped open the trousers of my good suit climbing over a barbed fence to circle round the throng.

The Githunguri Council, whose permanent offices I was invited to open on 19 July 1959, generously gave me *Permanent Way,** Mervyn Hill's splendid historical record of the Kenya-Uganda Railway which had laid tracks upon which Kenya and the Kikuyu developed. They may have adopted it as a symbolic milestone of their own progress. The new cottage hospital on Githunguri Hill had installed an odourless methane gas emergency lighting system for the operating theatre, harnessing the past to the future. It depended upon recycled cows' manure of which the energy source was mobile, regular and renewable, while remaining fertile when the gas consumed had generated light. I had first seen the technique with Zakayo Opondo in Kisumu District ten years before.

The Divisional DO was Johnny Rowlands, an unique member of our service. He had an earlier career on a vineyard in France, evidenced by a dark blue beret and comfortably rural garb, which might once have been uniform, set off by a reflectively aromatic pipe. His warmly husky voice appeared diffident, almost apologetic, but not when the gentle mockery of his gaze lifted to reveal a serious perception based upon careful study. His Spartan government bungalow was partly furnished with stacked beer crates, indicating hospitality rather than consumption, seated on and at which he spent hours with elders delving into Kikuyu custom for which he had great empathy and controlling the hostilities between the hilltop camps of convivial Catholic Missions facing pure 'Coke' Americans of the African Inland Mission, vying for school sites.

There was nothing authoritarian about Johnny and he tended to an eccentric view of life with a derisive, if respectful, attitude to Government. He chided our masters for being 'tardigrade' in a slender volume of Edward Lear style poems entitled *A Nosegay of Cacti* privately printed in Mombasa. He dedicated it by initials to an admired DC, Denis Hall. Our personal copy was inscribed, "May your lives be toujours merry, Nicole, and *quasi beau-père Terry*", to mark my giving away his also not so young bride, Elsie Posner, who came out from Austria and was affectionately renamed by us as 'Allsop's Pilsener', his favourite tipple and she a culture match. He wickedly gave my schoolboy sons a furtive puff on a forbidden cigarette at the window of the Mombasa train and became godfather to our daughter Sarah. He was a lovely man, but I could not recommend an extended tour for him at Githunguri in a period of radical Government intervention in traditional life. Johnny went on to be DO in charge of Mukogodo, an adjoining District to Samburu and a repository of the Laikipiak Maasai remnant.

Kiambaa Division took off directly behind the Kiambu District Hospital

Permanent Way: Published by East African Railways and Harbour: Nairobi, 1959.

towards Githunguri. It was hemmed in uneasily between settled coffee estates on either side and was the densely populated home area of the Koinange family, whose rambling homestead sat above the road from Kiambu towards Banana Hill. It was there that the crowd, said by Special Branch to be 40,000 strong, had heard Jomo Kenyatta's sibylline speech just before the 1952 Emergency, urging Mau Mau to disappear down the roots of the sacred *Mikongoe* tree (underground?), an occasion when I had acted as motorbike messenger for the DC. I could never pass old Senior Chief Koinange's home without imagining the angry susurration of soldier ants disturbed in their questing path. His son by his youngest wife was Chief Charles Karuga Koinange, tall, direct in manner, well educated and broad minded. He was widely respected as a conciliator between the ferments of the past and the rapid pace of new development. He was as able to support the activities of the African Courts, established by law, as to endorse the swearing in of Elders by the holder of the sacred Githathi meteorite under pain of death for corruption. It was noted that some court Elders met an untimely end. Charles himself was a tower of strength behind the Divisional DO and was strongly tipped to become in time a Provincial Commissioner. Sadly his wife died young and he and the DO went together to her funeral near to what the DO described as the 'rural slum' of Banana Hill.

That DO was Carr Newton who with his wife Minkie arrived in the District in April 1958, almost at the same time as I did and as their own son Charles appeared. Carr, dark, clean cut and alert was of sterling stuff, coping without fuss with the endless problems of his congested area, ranging from overt and covert political unrest like KKM, to boundary disputes with the scheduled areas and the disturbing impact of his assistant DO Theo Pike, son of a British Somaliland Governor, upon the nubile pupils of Limuru Girls School. Minkie, of Irish Belleek-white skin and Rosetti hair, was a figure of calm, soft of brogue, unobtrusive in precise arrangement and firm belief. They took over from Johnny Rowlands when he moved from Githunguri, which they called an oasis of peace after Kiambaa. (We kept in touch through to Mandela's South Africa.)

Gatundu Division lay alongside Fort Hall (Murang'a District where the southerly border Division of Kandara had long been embattled with Mau Mau under the charge of doughty DO 'Tommy' Thompson. The nature of the upper terrain was altogether wilder, descending in steep spines between rivulets emerging from the dark forest edge. Further down were wattle plantations providing fuel, building poles and dry stripped bark in huge cigar rolls for the Ruiru and Thika tanneries. Beneath them were neat rows of tufted pineapples planted both to rot down the stubborn roots of exhausted wattle with their tenderizing acids and to supply the prosperous canneries of Thika, marketing their delicious golden rings. Expensively safari suited, pineapple 'Baron' was Bobs. Harries, smoother brother of Songhor mixed farmer 'O.C.' with whose family I had romantically convalesced ten years before.

Also across the Ruiru border were the Mayers clan of many talents. Rusty and Erica were in retail trade, hotels, tennis and athletics. Ray Mayers had been Civil Affairs Officers at El Carré in British administered Somalia when I was DC Mandera in the Northern Frontier District. Beside them was feisty 'old' Mrs Nordlinger and her diminutive Nairobi florist daughter, 'Tikki'. Near by lived brilliant surgeon Lesley Neville, irrepressible founder of a hell-raising group known as the Balls of Fire Club. At Mitubiri, towards the cluster of European settlement at Makuyu, was Colonel 'Paddy' Merritt, irascible but hic-laughing warrior with flaming white hair dipping over hot blue eyes and high complexion. Acknowledged as a coffee expert and adviser to the Governor, he was said to exert undue influence on the Kiambu scene.

Gatundu was the traditional family home of Jomo Kenyatta, whom I had often met around Kiambu District before his lengthy 1952–3 arraignment in the Special Court of Mr Justice Ransley Thacker QC, held at Kapenguria, for 'managing' the 'unlawful society' of Mau Mau. The then DC was Dick Wilson known as a safe pair of hands needed for keeping tight control of local and international interference. Interest in the Trial was deliberately provoked by Communist Defence Advocate D. N. Pritt, QC, whose failure in defence of Kenyatta had the successful effect of enabling his imprisoned client to grow on the world stage. Jomo was nearing the end of his prison sentence at Lokitaung, where he had come under the wise supervision of Leslie Whitehouse,* known as 'Wouse', formerly of the Education Department, and by an inspired turn of fate, transferred to be Officer in Charge of Turkana. He was to move under a follow-up detention order to restriction at Maralal, where he was to be confined to the direct distance between his special habitation above Maralal, near where Makhan Singh had been detained during my time as DC, and the rear quarters of my old friend, general merchant John Cardovillis' store. It was another well conceived arrangement in which John was allowed *carte blanche* by Government to supply Jomo's needs. A bond of respect grew between them, the stronger that Njeri, mother of John's eight children, was a family connection. During uncertainty about his future constant care had to be exercised lest the embers of local Mau Mau cells might be re-ignited by infiltrators from the new Nairobi based PCP/KKM, in support of which secret oathing was reported.

The Senior Chief of Gatundu Division was Muhoho, a very dark,

*Whitehouse's biography by Elizabeth Watkins, with a foreword by Elspeth Huxley, was published as *Wouse. Jomo's Jailor* by Mulberry Books, 1993.

hulking man with softly fine aquiline features, a taciturn, if sometimes warmly befuddled, demeanour and self conscious dignity. His regally tall daughter, Ngina, was married to Kenyatta. After four years spent herself in emergency detention she joined him in Turkana and then Maralal until his final release. She was already a consort of significance with deep roots in her society. A dark horse hailing from across the border in Kandara was the huge eyed, beetle browed Bildad Kaggia, said to be with Fred Kubai — trade union leaders both — a baneful influence among Nairobi hard-liners on Kenyatta's political stance. My own conviction from personal encounters with him, recently reinforced by experience among thousands of Mau Mau detainees, was that he towered above them in stature and guile, however they might snap at his heels.

The Divisional District Officer responsible for this fractious area was Jon Wainwright, younger brother of Robin, previously my PC in Rift Valley Province, but somewhat older than me. After a Cambridge degree in French he had served as a Major in the Indian Cavalry and while retired to farm at Sotik had joined an irregular mounted group of settlers before signing on as a regular DO in 1954. With curly brown hair and a rakish inward smile he was in the mould of Royalist Prince Rupert, dashing and full of initiative. He was concentrating on rooting out *Kiama Kia Muingi* and walked me up hill and down dale with dawn raids on remote villages, often backed up by Inspector 'Van' Rensburg, a surprisingly gentle giant and South African head of the Kenya Police Dog Section, with his trained Alsatians. Jon enthusiastically found employment for idle hands on dam and road building, encouraged by 44 gallon drums of local beer after work and discretion could sometimes go overboard in financing such large beer through 'ghost' payment vouchers receipted with identical thumbprints. It was a device which could be brought by an ill disposed functionary to the attention of CID, ever watchful for Administration's indiscretions, but we could in difficult times rely on Frank Loyd for rescue with a sharp caution against such innocent short-cuts to a useful end. Suzanne Wainwright had the composed charm of a Colonel's lady in an Indian hill station, maintaining a meticulous style in their isolated and exposed situation, closer to the Mitubiri social scene of Paddy Merritt than to the hub of Kiambu '*boma*'.

Limuru Division presented an entirely different mix of problems, although still not returned to secure conditions. From the upper end it descended from the high forest reserve plantations and chilly Kikuyu cultivation near Uplands, overlooking the railway track gouged out of the wall of the rift, past the Uplands Bacon Factory and pioneer settler 'Morson's Plot', through the congested farmlands of Senior Chief Makimei, down to the model dairy farm of bluff Tom Brown, with his showground champion Friesian herd, nestling in the re-entrant above Limuru Township.

The name of nearby Lari still evoked the horror of the 1953 massacre by Mau Mau of Chief Luka's entire family as retribution for his defying the curse put on Nyamweru land in compensation for surrender of the isolated Kikuyu enclave at Tigoni to European occupation.

Limuru Township was in a deep hollow at the hub of divergent spokes of activity. At one end of the flat built up area was Bata Shoe Company, much as I knew it before. The centrally placed railway station handled vast array of cargo including footwear, hides, chemicals, trade goods, agricultural produce and tea from the neat company estates spread close above on the road from Nairobi. Behind the roadside Indian shops was a sprawl of primitive dwellings packed with labourers, Nubian gin bars, brothels and throw-outs from the Olenguruone settlement scheme in the Rift. It was where I had earned my Kikuyu nickname 'Karuga Ndua' six years before, while impetuously upending vats of ruinous Nubian gin.

The so-called Tigoni-Nyamweru land exchange with its attendant curse and bloody exorcism in the Lari Massacre had left a curious aftermath. Possibly arising from a residual sense of insecurity of tenure, a 'pride' of settlers had sprung up, fiercely resistant to any local African land pressures. They were dubbed the 'Tigoni Tigers'. The males were very male and the females, young or old, deadlier, but they were mainly good hearted and fair dealing people, defending what they saw as their birthright. Their waterhole was at the lively Tigoni Club, where I was invited to speak in tandem with a new African Assistant Minister of Housing and other services, Musa Amalemba. Musa was a North Nyanza man of great modesty and charm, with an already outstanding career in social service, education and on Nairobi City Council. Quite at odds with his Humpty-Dumpty shape and soothing, open vowelled, speech, he had in 1944 been a Sergeant Major in the Army Education Corps. Here in the Tigers' lair Musa addressed a packed house, as taken aback at his standing before them as he was to be in such a place. "My wife," he said in Biblical tones, "warned me to beware of entering under your roof and does not expect me to come out alive." He wowed the meeting, captivated the Tigresses and was the toast of the bar.

The European community in the scheduled areas adjoining Limuru was a lively mixed bag containing every sort of society, high and lower. There were the tea, descending to the coffee planters; bucolic mixed farmers; commuters, city, civilian and local; retired officials from Sudan, Ghana and India; live-out managers from Bata factory like our friends the Pasekas; ardent golfers and other odd balls; writers and Thespians. I remembered in particular a rambunctious young farmer, Garth Roberts, a D'Artagnan in the Service of the Crown; the Dalgleishes, gentle George of stage villainous mien, formerly of the Government of Ghana, and both now involved in Nairobi cultural life; the elegant Lindsays of Brooke Bond, conveying that sense of style inseparable from the tea companies; Quentin Cooper, politically inclined farmer; John Hillard, CMG, heavyweight businessman politician, formerly head of Sudan Railways, with his young wife. There was the inevitable smart set.

In sharp contrast with what had been a lotus land in peaceful times, was an arid series of overgrazed terraces to the south of the Nairobi–Naivasha road branch-off to Limuru Township. This windswept expanse called the Ndeiya spread down to the Maasai plains beyond the *Ewaso* (river) *Kedong* valley, with a scattering of enclosed villages, mainly given over to goats and scrawny cattle, and supplying labour to the Nairobi poverty pool. There was some interchange of blood with Maasai through border raids and relationships and much land grabbing by powerful Kikuyu interlopers. There had been extensive Mau Mau oathing before the Emergency, apparently now transmuted into *Kiama Kia Muingi*, through the daily labour link with the Peoples Convention Party. Wall eyed old Kungu Karumba, Kenyatta's disciple and fellow prisoner was an Elder of the Ndeiya, with whom I later waltzed down Bazaar Road in Nairobi to celebrate his freedom.

There were two successive Divisional District Officers in charge of this jig-saw puzzle during my period as DC. The first was Roger Goldsworthy who was already in post when I arrived. Roger had all the carefree *élan* of a former RAF officer and was described to me by Barbara Rigby, our noticing Community Development Officer, as 'gig lamps' because of his widely spaced and luminous blue eyes. He was cheerfully unfazed by any obstacle and proved such an effective land consolidator that he was sent to sort out problems being encountered in Fort Hall District. His seemingly imperturbable wife, Margaret, was his 'air traffic controller' but I had no chance to get to know them well. After an interval Keith Shaw came with Maureen and two small children to reoccupy the vacated DO's house on the hill above Limuru Township. It was set apart and still unsafe for Maureen to walk abroad. Keith was a dapper and orderly man, both physically and in his well arranged, methodical mind. He was quite unflustered, with a precise melodious voice, and was well suited to deal logically and persistently with the bewildering array of immediate tasks facing him. He identified the restoration of order in the Township as a focal point of many other problems and got so far as to establish a proper shopping centre with Kikuyu merchants in place of the impoverished shambles which survived the Emergency. This was opened by Frank Loyd, PC Nyeri when Bill Raynor took over the District during my overseas leave. Both Keith and Roger were blessed with the wise and humorous presence of retired Wing Commander, Bill Knowlden, bald, middle aged but youthfully beshorted. No task was beyond or beneath him. Every DO and DC needed such a guide, philosopher and friend, detached from any constraints of service

260

rank, to speak up frankly and keep him on the rails.

Kikuyu Division was the fifth and by far most complex of the arbitrary Administrative Divisions of Kiambu District, sharing the eponym with the Township and Kenya Uganda Railway Station at its centre. The Division was roughly outlined in a long quadrangle south west of a line drawn from the Limuru settled area to Dagoretti corner on the edge of Nairobi city. From that point its shorter base line skirted the green residential belt of Karen towards the Ngong border with Maasai, returning north west along Maasailand back to the Limuru boundary. If the outline was simple, the interior was not.

It was difficult to comprehend that, within a Division of less than two hundred square miles, a rural population ranging up to one hundred thousand should, over the span of a lifetime, have been involved in continuous intrusion, land acquisition, disruption, redirection and redistribution, not to speak of Evangelization, and yet emerged with their fibre largely intact. In his Introduction to Fr. C. Cagnolo's *The Akikuyu*, 1933, Colonel S. H. La Fontaine of the Colonial Administration had described them as "quick witted, progressive and intelligent people, destined to play a prominent part in the development of Kenya". Twenty five turbulent years later, the traditional ten Kikuyu clans or *Muhiriga* still retained their identity.

Always wary of Maasai raids they had burrowed their way with silent burning and shifting cultivation and furtive goats, under the indigenous forest cover, clinching shrewd land deals with the honey and game hunting *Aathi* or *Dorobo*, in persuasive but impractical upstairs, downstairs arrangements, until they had either chopped down or emerged from the edge of their forest shelter, exposed both to the Maasai and the incoming white men. They had suffered a devastating plague of smallpox in 1894 called the year of *Motongo*, that sent them reeling and depleted back from their forward outpost of Muthaiga, above Nairobi. In the van of explorers, Missionaries, soldiers of fortune and land surveyors came the Maasai's mythical iron snake that lay up at the cold waters of Nairobi to gain strength before coiling onwards and upwards through the Kikuyu fields to the shoulder of the Great Rift Valley. This 'permanent way' was laid by myriads of Indian tracklayers, who peeled off to become traders, and brought Administrators, soldier settlers, missionaries and entrepreneurs, aristocrats and adventurers.

Through the initiative of the Irish, Holy Ghost Mission of Teita Hills and St Austin's,* Nairobi the introduction of coffee attracted hundreds of European planters, soon exporting a crop valued in the records of the Italian Consolata Mission at Nyeri at over one million sterling before the world

*Said to be an abbreviation of Augustine of Hippo who prayed for purity "but not yet"!

market crash. Such inter-Missionary praise was as rare as truth! The
Kikuyu were not trusted to grow so precious a plant as coffee and keep it
free from berry disease, though women and children were gladly employed
in picking the berries. Barely twenty years apart, came the two world wars,
mainly external to Kenya but cutting deeply into local life in manpower,
conscript labour, meat supply quotas, and financial stringency. The Kikuyu
were not thought suitable physically or temperamentally for recruitment as
line soldiers and were assigned to clerical and communications work which
ironically gave them pervasive influence later, for good or ill. Peace
brought further eager arrivals of soldier settlers.

Increasing population pressure set off peasant hunger and political
demand for return of their land among the Kiambu Kikuyu. Articulated in
1922 by young firebrand Harry Thuku in open conflict, followed by the
passionate advocacy of Jomo Kenyatta, it led to the 1934 Carter Land
Commission's judiciously unworkable Report, interleaving European and
Kikuyu land. There were successive waves of more secretive unrest,
notably the Kikuyu Central Association, which was banned as subversive
in the Second World War, and in 1952 the Mau Mau Emergency which
brought the detention of one in three adult males and the concentration of
the remaining population in planned protective villages. The current
recrudescence of Mau Mau type oathing seemed to run in parallel with the
growth of the People's Convention Party of Nairobi which exactly
corresponded in name to the *Kiama Kia Muingi* of Kiambu.

The Divisional District Officer in charge of Kikuyu Division was
Douglas Johnston, who could have been hand picked for the particularly
demanding job. He was a Scot, about thirty, with a St Andrew's University
degree and a light furring of accent. He had the spare frame for marathon
rather than sprint, with a fine boned face and sandy hair. He conveyed
clarity of mind, nicety of judgement and fixity of purpose and appeared
cool and controlled, with powers of concentration and moral conviction. He
was the obverse of flamboyant and eschewed display, which he could prick
with pawky humour. Having myself been a scholar at St Andrew's, a
lambasted private at the Black Watch Initial Training Centre at Perth and
an Assault Course instructor in the Ulsters slogging between Roxburgh and
the Inner Hebrides, I could remember my chagrin at being unable to
emulate the Scots' capacity to combine high jinks with hard work. I felt that
Douglas noted my deficiency, as perhaps did Janet, his wife, who was kind
and hospitable when I was invited to their 'home' above Kikuyu, but whom
I did not get to know well enough.

I once sat in at a land case appeal conducted by Douglas with a
knowledge of African customary law and a meticulous testing and recording
of evidence which put me to shame. We went together to a gathering of
hundreds of people doing voluntary communal labour on the same lines as

262

with Jon Wainwright at Gatundu and I took the opportunity to speak generally about consolidation, development and the dangers of *Kiama Kia Muingi* oathing. In the Rehabilitation Camps I had been accustomed to and preferred speaking without amplifier and perhaps used a more dramatic style than the more seemly Administrative approach, although many in the audience would have been with me before release.

It was an exciting experience to visit the sprawling new town of Banana Hill where 'luxuries' such as electricity were being installed and then admire the two flagship border towns of Riruta and Kangemi. Douglas Penwill and John Golds had initiated a pilot scheme to provide fully equipped, good quality, low cost, permanent housing at these strategic points for middle rank Kikuyu commuters to Nairobi on a direct bus route. A forerunner in occupation was Bethuel Mareka Gecaga, Crown Counsel, who climbed steadily to the heights.* He was married to Jemima, sister of handsome Doctor Mungai Njeroge** who with Peace Corps support had built the Riruta Clinic nearby, and daughter of influential local Headman Njeroge, with whom my wife Nicole gave prizes at the local sports stadium.

Returning from Kikuyu Division to Kiambu on one occasion I was correctly dressed in bush jacket with brass belt and buttons, decent shorts and long khaki stockings, as urged by the visiting General Manager of the Gezira Cotton Scheme in Sudan, Mekki Abbas, himself a very proper former Provincial Commissioner. I had official reason to listen to a Legislative Council debate on land consolidation and took a seat in the public gallery outside the roped Speaker's enclosure. I was intrigued to observe the Sergeant at Arms leave the Speaker's side and come purposefully to the rear of the house. To my mortification he ordered me summarily to withdraw as being improperly attired, despite my brief protestation that I was in regulation uniform, on official duty and there was no conscious disrespect. One does not question Speakers and my personally delivered letter of apology followed swiftly, humbly explaining my misapprehension. The occupant of the Speaker's Chair was Humphrey Slade QC, earlier a member of the Parliamentary Committee visiting Kiambu to investigate land consolidation. It was said that I had cut short a question he had posed!***

Elspeth Huxley came to stay with us in early 1959 while she was writing *A New Earth*.**** She was a bubbling spring of wit, wisdom and historical lore. She wrote at length of John Golds' magnificent work on land consolidation which Kiambu finished ahead of other Districts in August

*As Chairman of the University Council, Chairman of British-American Tobacco Company (BATS) etc.
**Future Foreign Minister.
***Sorrenson: *Land Reform in the Kikuyu Country*: Oxford University Press, Nairobi, 1967; p.246.
****A New Earth: An Experiment in Colonialism: Chatto and Windus: London, 1960.

1958. She referred to *Kiama Kia Muingi* and to the fact that one third of all Kiambu men had been Mau Mau detainees and quoted me as saying "Now that the consolidation is over, a tremendous surge forward in farming is about to begin — if only we have peace". She encouraged me over the years and letters or cards from her home 'Green End' in the Cotswolds were an art form.

There was local political manoeuvring on all fronts. Animating everything was land: hunger and acquisition on the part of the Kikuyu and retention with security on the part of settler farmers and planters. Regular reports came in of the disturbing oathing ceremonies by *Kiama Kia Muingi*, while on the European side a number of vociferous new political factions burgeoned. An obstacle to Kikuyu recovery was the, to my mind, outworn distinction between 'loyalists' (with certificates) and terrorists, given impetus by the return of the 'rehabilitated' detainees to participate in land consolidation and by continued uncertainty about the future release of top Mau Mau leaders. A cross current was the redistribution of the people from tightly controlled villages to small consolidated farms, and planned urban communities which needed some kind of representative Local Government. At a DC's meeting in Nyeri I was in a minority of one in proposing unrestricted adult voting and eligibility for the new Townships' councils, regardless of electors' and candidates' past activities. Continued direct use of the Native Authority was preferred.

James Gichuru of Thogoto Village epitomized the uncertain public mood. Educated, like most of his contemporary leaders at Alliance High School, under the great headmaster, Carey Francis, and at Makerere University, he had been appointed Chief of Dagoretti Location before the Emergency. He changed track to become first President of the Kenya African Union, KAU, and caretook the Presidency of the renamed National Union, KANU, while Kenyatta was in prison and detention. It might be said that Eliud Mathu, four years Gichuru's senior, also of Alliance and Makerere, but with Fort Hare University South Africa, Exeter and Balliol Colleges added, plus fifteen years Legislative Council membership, was the peace front of Kikuyudom. Gichuru, having followed both the orthodox administrative and the political path, was a handsome, widely respected, if puzzlingly ambivalent and sometimes charmingly befuddled, fence sitter. As with many others, courage was required of him to straddle the factions.

The incoming wave of younger Kikuyu politicians was led by Julius Gikonyo Kiano, whose education in America after Alliance High School encompassed Antioch College, Stanford University and the University of California, which brought him back to Kenya in 1957 with a Doctorate in Economics and an African-American wife and astute businesswoman, Ernestine, who found the cultural change perplexing. In the 1957 elections to Legislative Council he ousted Eliud Mathu, for all his meritorious national service, and became the Kikuyu member for Kiambu. With lively, mocking eyes, professorial spectacles and slack, open lips, he affected an elder's style with a symbolic stick. As counterparts in the system of colonial Kiambu he and I achieved a certain rapport in which he would address me in public as "my favourite enemy". As invited guest we could not tell when, or if, or with whom, he would turn up for dinner.

The election for the European seat covering Kiambu was contested and won by Air Commodore Leslie Howard-Williams, MC. He was eccentric almost beyond the limit of centrifugal force. From being a Yorkshire volunteer private soldier in 1914, with honours degrees from both Oxford and Cambridge, in maths and in engineering, he headed the Air Force in Sudan, and in Iraq as a Pasha, flew across Africa and back in 1930, and initiated and organized just about every movement in support of flying in peace and war. He had a coffee farm in Kiambu and aligned himself with a wacky, right wing, die-hard settler party, headed by dead straight Group Captain 'Puck' Briggs, of far less stimulus and charm. I was bedazzled by him over the hustings at the club where he cut a self consciously Churchillian figure, squat, neckless, one dark lock teased across a broad forehead, half glasses slipping down his nose and giving out an honest flow of gravel-voiced bombast on any subject. His younger, blonde wife, 'Ducky', was in public relations, a subject which, for all his romantic, adventurous life, he never quite mastered. He and Briggs later attended London Constitutional Conferences without altering history.

During the first months after taking over in Kiambu I was not free to remarry, until August 1958. In September Roger Wilkinson, who had first met me on arrival at Nairobi Station in 1944, now as DC Nairobi benignly intoned the civil marriage service over Nicole and me in the original grey fortress like office. Mirek and Betty Paseka from Bata were both our witnesses and our honeymoon hostel at Tigoni. From then on the DC's house was properly conducted and social life was hectic, widely spread and happy. Our 'David to be' served notice of intended arrival early the following August. Kevin and Séan moved up from Catholic schooling at Soni in Tanganyika.

We continued to be much taken up by the hospitable Shields with their lovely pink stucco *hacienda* which Bertie, who designed it, quaintly described to me as "merely the intelligent application of efficiency". We saw a lot of Alan and Phina Simmance next door though their black spaniel, 'Highgrade', once helped himself to Nicole's leg on arrival for dinner. Our superb young ridgeback lion dog Sindbad was not on the job. Perfectionist photographer Tubby Milne and Jackie from Madagascar were in and out, as were my old friends Leda and John Farrant, he being by chance Kenya agent for Nicole's father, Richard Goldstein's, firm 'Flexello Casters and Wheels' of Slough. She was a budding writer admired by Robert Ruark, famous for his lurid 1954 historical novel *Something of Value* about Mau Mau, of which he averred unconvincingly that the hero was not modelled on white hunter, Harry Selby.

Nicole being horse and stage mad and a regular performer, we saw much of the famous Donovan Maule Theatre Club professional crowd and mingled with the separate National Theatre enthusiasts, next to the Voice of Kenya studios. At the National were the impossibly handsome DO, now Secretariat official, Teddy Eggins and Nicole's friends, zoology lecturer Malcolm Coe and Charleston dancing architect Zbish Trzebinski, who married neophyte actor-artist-writer, Errol. At the studios under seconded BBC Director, Patrick Jubb, ballad singer Roger Whitaker was already a star. No African yet trod the boards unless at the adjacent Royal College. It was not easy to keep up with the social pace, especially within the so called '£1,863 Club', the top of the DC's annual salary scale.

Frank Loyd came on his first PC's visit of inspection before we took some overdue home leave. He was compactly built, firmly planted and quick footed as a 'southpaw' boxer. He could never be caught napping even by a Kikuyu. After touring briskly and knowledgeably around what was still his own beat he spent a night in our guest quarter. His management style was a well aimed fusillade of penetrating questions, delivered without opinion and punctuated by quick reflective draws at his briar pipe, often empty. After thorough interrogation over late night whisky, he had a habit of saying with a quizzical twinkle, "You know my form Terry". This left some doubt as to exactly what it was in terms of judgement of oneself, but he was a good man to work for because he knew what he and you and it were about.

Frank had arranged for Bill Raynor to move over from Meru District as leave relief. Bill was a very affable and companionable person with a pragmatic and understanding approach to Kiambu Kikuyu needs, despite the Meru people on the northern flank of Mount Kenya having distinctive structures and customs and, being at a safe distance from European coffee, not precluded from planting their own; old Koinange's still unbroken hobbyhorse! Bill had won an MC and was a popular soldier's man without vanity or pretence, although twitted mildly as to the Grecian source of the jet camouflage of what might be prematurely grey hair. He handed back the District at the end of 1958 in steady progress and good heart, except for stealing that of Frances Crag's young assistant, Ann Shields.

Home leave was also our honeymoon in Italy and Denmark, staying between times with Nicole's father near Maidenhead. Our Alitalia flight from Nairobi to London allowed a stopover in Rome and the chance to visit my old friends the Valles, a once Senatorial family with the northern branch of which I had previously stayed in Rosá del Grappa in Vicenza Province. Their palazzo, formerly the summer retreat of the Doges of Venice, had been taken by Hitler's Field Marshal Kesselring as his southern command headquarters, bombed by the Allies and refurbished to its past magnificence out of war reparations. This time we were guests of the Roman branch, headed by the last Italian Governor of colonial Eritrea, in their white stucco bungalow residence off the Via Vigne Nuove, at the far end of Mussolini's broad Via Nomentana. It overlooked a stud farm outside the old city wall and warm apricots could be plucked in the orchard garden for black coffee at dawn. Access was through convent land donated by the Valles as a 'holy green belt', where once lodged the lovely and lively Principessa Maria Theresa Adelaida, a last spriglet of the Habsburg dynasty, of which a giant Prince von Windischgrätz had retired to live in Nairobi. On my last visit Maria Theresa had given me a protective St Christopher clip for my VW Beetle steering wheel, guided me round the catacombs to see the sacred loaves and fishes, and saucily tipped up the flat black hat of a worldly Monsignor, whom we took to lunch al fresco near St Peter's. Francesca Valle had then taught me, once a despatch rider, how to enjoy riding pillion on her zipping Lambretta. Now her handsome brother, 'Avvocato' Giorgio, racing driver manqué, fitted in twenty coffee and phone stops on our death defying return to the sensational new Leonardo da Vinci Airport, spreading its skeletal black wings according to the drawings of the old master.

In Denmark at the Angleterre Hotel we were so charmingly treated by the newsvendor at the entrance that we felt bound to enquire one morning why he was glum and shifty and could not supply our London paper. He confessed to his shame on our behalf at the headlined allegations of a Conservative Junior Minister of Foreign Affairs, John Belsher, being discovered *in flagrante delicto* with a guardsman in Hyde Park. '*O tempora! O mores!*' We marvelled at the Danish Royal Ballet with Erik Bruhn, the epitome of the masculine *danseur noble*. On our way to Elsinore to meet Hamlet's ghost we sadly decided not to call in at the house of Karen Blixen whose Kenya farm was still the lovely sanctuary overlooking her beloved Ngong hills. She was too ill and old to disturb. We toured the Carlsberg Brewery, where the daily food ration was 12 bottles of beer per man. We helped consume towards the national cultural fund created from the profits. Nicole's father's agent, Kai Skov, was the proud owner of the first Italian designed Karman Ghia Volkswagen, known as the 'lover boy' from its convenient shapeliness, which also won him as his bride Gitta, air hostess of Scandinavian Airlines. Before return to Kenya for the New Year we were generously invited to a last dinner by the holidaying Shields at the fashionably American Westbury Hotel off Bond Street.

Sailing slow boat by first class, to which the Administration were still entitled, in the *Warwick Castle* liner, we found ourselves honoured to sit at the Captain's table. He was an extremely garrulous, not to say bibulous, Scot, continuously afloat, whose watchword was "not to worry".

Fortunately we did not need to as he narrowly failed to chip the rock on approaching Gibraltar, a feat which he accomplished on his next voyage. Our onward port of call was Genoa, whose port Captain, Enrico Levi, I was to meet again at Eilat in Israel. We took on board a honeymoon couple who became our firm friends. They were parasitologist Dr Ronald Heisch of the Kenya Medical Department and Eliane Dominici, a former United Nations conference interpreter. Ronald, whose past I knew was not unblemished, was cock-a-hoop at having captured at nearly fifty such a comely and cultured younger bride of a family so distinguished in Geneva history. They settled in Ngong where of an evening he might slip out to address the forest, or sometimes me, about how to change the world. Sadly depression later overcame him unto death, but he had also a wickedly joyous spirit. Eliane moved on to happier times with their children.

On 17 February we were summoned to Nyeri to be presented to the Queen Mother (*mama ya waingereza* was heard shouted in the streets) who was a marvel of grace. As she walked down the reception line her feet were placed with the economy and precision of movement of Victor Sylvester. When her wrist-hung chiffon kerchief fell she swept it up so swiftly that two courtiers' heads collided over where it had touched the ground, and never a shadow on her smile. Perfect composure and command!

Soon afterwards Frank Loyd paid another welcome visit, having also since been at Limuru with Bill Raynor to open Keith Shaw's proud creation, the new Limuru Shopping Centre. This time it was on a farewell tour of the Province, which he followed up on the 18th of February 1959 with a manuscript letter of such lasting importance to me that I must quote from it:

> ... *I am writing now to thank you for all the very hard and good work you are doing in your most difficult and exhausting district. I think you are doing an excellent job and it has been very reassuring to me to have you as DC at the other end of the Province ...*

The incoming (acting) PC during March was F. R. 'Dick' Wilson, moving from Embu where he had succeeded Roger Wilkinson, and whom I had met in DCs' meetings at Nyeri. Dick had joined the Administration in 1947 with a military OBE and a great reputation as a young Colonel on Mountbatten's staff. This experience had been of particular value in controlling as DC the excitements of Kenyatta's trial in Kapenguria and in National Security liaison. Personally he cut a willowy figure with a tow of blond hair over pleasingly irregular features and firmly pursed lips. His wife 'Dottie' was the life and soul and irrepressibly outspoken.

I had been attempting for some time, in discussion with Alan Simmance and others, to understand the course on which the Administration in the field was set. The principles of trusteeship and paramountcy were clear and valid but the methods of approach to them were beset by a great deal of uncertainty and lack of policy guidance. Physical development was pounding ahead and concomitant social change was so great as to be vulnerable to simmering or explosive reactions. We needed to know, particularly in Kiambu, Kenyatta's home, whether sustaining his original detention order or allowing his controlled release to Kiambu were contemplated. No political pronouncement on the subject had issued from the Government since Baring's 1954 forecast of 'perpetual detention' and administrative blunders could at any time arise from misunderstandings, misjudgements or risks taken in a vacuum. No timescale was being floated for the run up to Independence. Orthodox administration through the loyal Native Authority was still viable, but its time was running out. There were understandably divergent views on this and a certain creative tension generated between different experiences and loyalties. Divisional DOs had borne the brunt of the long days and nights in facing the active elements of Mau Mau on the ground. By the parallel design of the Governor and Johnston as Special Commissioner, I had been put to work on clearing away the hard core of those withdrawn from the fray into detention during the Emergency, necessarily and speedily declared by Baring after the period of indecision preceding his arrival in Kenya. The resultant staged mass release of the detainees to their homes could easily be regarded as an added complication in adjusting to planned economic and political progress.

With new development and increased funding prosperity was also coming back to the Indian shops. Popatlal Hansraj from across the valley had constructed a fine brick building of several storeys with a central hall, which he wanted the PC to come and open. Young 'Popat', smiling but humourless, consulted me in the office about a suitable gift and was crestfallen when I told him emphatically that the PC would not wish to receive a presentation silver salver that he showed me, backing up my assurance in his presence by a phone call to Pat. Mowbray-Thomas in the PC's office, requesting confirmation. On the 7th of June came the day, a fine reception for all the neighbourhood, and the very salver. "Poor Popat" said Dottie, which he was certainly not, and the salver was held overnight in my safe. That evening at dinner Dottie, on my right, said in the most amiable way, "You know, Terry, all my other DCs I can put labels on like hats on a shelf, but I can't make up my mind what label to put on you. I think you must be the biggest poseur I have ever met." I did not reject the 'palpable hit' and liked her the better for her honesty. Their entry in our guest book showed the date as the 7th of June 1959.

After Frank's departure from Nyeri, news filtered through of up to eleven unexplained or violent deaths in the detention camp of last resort at the remote Agricultural Development Scheme at Hola in Coast Province, to which had gone an adamant residuum of detainees from the Mwea camps augmented by some hundreds of convicted Mau Mau prisoners from elsewhere. It was well over a year since I had left the Mwea and the news did not at first impinge on the hurly-burly of Kiambu preoccupations. In fact it did not come home to me until I read and heard the dramatic press and radio coverage implicating names I knew including my comrade John Cowan.

To the media the beating to death of eleven detainees at Hola was an atrocity or massacre crying out in banner headlines for blame. To the responsible political leaders in Kenya and London it was an inexcusable, tragic occurrence arising from nobody's or everybody else's fault. Tom Askwith, when relieved of responsibility for rehabilitation of the last 20,000 recalcitrant detainees, had taken care to warn that the use of force in obtaining confessions would be unacceptable to him and could lead to disaster. The Attorney-General of Kenya, Eric Griffith Jones, had then enunciated to us on the spot the distinction between 'punitive' and 'compelling' force. John Cowan and I had, with our Kikuyu and other teams, including Askwith's, kept well within these bounds in releasing thousands of detainees without death or maim, under the close scrutiny of the churches, politicians and humanitarian agencies. Any link between Hola and what Baring had called the 'moral crusade' of Rehabilitation was specifically discounted by Enoch Powell MP* while also exculpating the Secretary of State of blame for Hola.

What shocked me particularly, amid the welter of conflicting accounts, cross accusations, evasions and multiple dissipatory official enquiries, was the misleading use, by Mombasa Senior Resident Magistrate Goudie, in a much publicized inquest-cum-enquiry, of a Prisons Department confidential internal memorandum on control of detainees at field work. Goudie gave this the title and status in capitals of 'The Cowan Plan', imputing to it a share of the botched failure of management and the fracas which ensued. In fact, John Cowan, the writer of the memorandum, had advocated extreme caution to the Commissioner, who had sought his advice, and urged that no compulsion to work should be attempted without the close supervision on the ground of himself or an officer with direct experience.

In later personal correspondence Elspeth Huxley, who had visited us in the Mwea, described it as incident "monstrously blown up out of all proportion". My own view, from a distance but with exceptional

*The Rt. Hon. J. Enoch Powell, PC, MBE, letter to author of 11 May 1995. "Thank you for sending me your book (*Corridors of Wire*). I do not think I have ever suggested that responsibility for what happened at Hola rested anywhere than at the top."
  Parliamentary Debates. Commons. Vol.610. 27 July 1959; Kenya (Report); Hola Camp; Mr J. Enoch Powell. (Praised by Mr A. Wedgwood Benn in his Eulogy of February 1998 as the finest Parliamentary speech he had ever heard).

experience, was that the object of the exercise proposed at the Hola irrigation scheme, the weeding by hand of vegetables, was trivial and unnecessary, its effective performance minimal and refusal virtually certain. Furthermore there was no pay-off in terms of rehabilitation and release. The attempt made was hardly more confused and disorderly than the fumbling Government and Colonial Office investigation of the tragic result, which then went through a series of changes of public explanation convincing no one, inviting derision and provoking demands for heads to roll.* My cumulative interpretation of what followed was that, at the highest political level both locally and in London, it was decided that damage limitation required a cut-off point of direct responsibility to be established at the level of the Attorney General, who held most of the strings of enquiry and legal definition. Below that level disciplinary measures could be taken openly, and were. Several heads fell discreetly, were bundled off the scene, or had a change of career.

It did not seem to occur to the Public Relations chief, Bob Lindsay, nor indeed to the Governor and Secretary of State, that the misdirected, inadequately supervised and final frantic beatings by fearful warders leading to eleven deaths could be frankly acknowledged and atoned for within the context of the huge exercise of incarcerating and releasing over 80,000 men during five years of an Emergency authorized by a Governor accountable to the British Government. I would willingly have put my own neck on the line for an explanation and defence, but was with John Cowan inexplicably precluded from giving evidence to the later 'independent' Fairn Commission and was not then aware of the implications of the deathroll at Manyani in 1954 which might have been disinterred and connected.

Without consciously regarding the Hola shambles as a relevant factor in the limbo of Government policies affecting public stability in Kiambu, I began to formulate in my mind a letter to the Provincial Commissioner setting out my doubts and fears and need for guidance. I had given vent to some in DCs' meetings on particular topics such as the criminal trial for murder before an imported 'green' judge of District Assistant Sam Githu, George Medal, without official defence evidence being offered by us as to his character, his duty and the circumstances. Instead, after his conviction and sentence, we collected 'conscience' money for his family and to buy a bus for his future release. I had spoken about my policy misgivings to Kiambu DOs separately and in meetings, but did not presume on their sharing them. I addressed a personal and confidential memorandum to the PC, Dick Wilson, setting out my anxieties. Incautiously, if not rashly, I referred to the pre-Emergency reluctance of Government to heed the many

---

*Borne out by Viscount Boyd in his address to the 1978 Symposium at St. Anthony's College, Oxford on the *Transfer of Power*, University of Oxford; Inter-Faculty Committee for African Studies; 1979; pp.2–9.

warnings by colonial officials and settlers of all kinds, by Chiefs and churchmen, of the danger then posed by the rapid growth of Mau Mau, which might now be a model for recurrence in the *Kiama Kia Muingi*. Unfortunately, if correctly, I did not retain a personal copy of my letter, which never resurfaced and was never acknowledged or referred to.

Subsequent to its despatch I did not discuss the letter further with Alan Simmance since we, his brother officers, were preparing in the mock secrecy of such occasions, a farewell presentation to mark his impending transfer. I did not know during those informal meetings that or when or whether he had been told of the postponement of his transfer. I was neither told nor consulted, but was orally instructed by telephone message, at two days' notice but with no details, to attend at the Minister for African Affairs office on the Saturday morning. It did not require imagination to connect the unusual and peremptory summons to go directly to the Minister with my letter. It so happened that Nicole and I were invited formally the same Saturday afternoon to a reception on the grand scale at Bertie and Connie Shields' coffee estate to celebrate the marriage of Ann Shields to Bill Raynor.

I anticipated a difficult interview with 'Monkey' Johnston, under whom I had worked so closely through hard times, but no premonition could have prepared me for what followed. The Secretariat floor in the stately old Law Courts building was nearly empty, but I was ushered into the Minister's room by his secretary, 'Bunty', the repository of many secrets, whom I knew and liked. The Minister rose as I entered with his usual mannered courtesy. We sat alone facing across his desk. There was no preamble; only a measured pause. "I have sent for you to tell you that you are to be moved from Kiambu at once. Your District Officers cannot stand you. Your Departmental Officers cannot work with you. You are disloyal to the Government."

I was stunned into silence by the brutality of the statement and gutted by the spelled out personal implication of others which brought tears to my eyes. I asked if I might have time to consider and discuss, not least because Nicole's first child was due on the eighth of August and it was already mid July. The response was that there was nothing to discuss, that we should move without delay to the Ministry of Local Government in the Secretariat and that Simmance had been told to delay his transfer briefly until a new DC was installed. With that the Minister somewhat jauntily left the room, perhaps out of some consideration for my upset, although I was told he alluded to it disparagingly. There were no witnesses, no record and no written confirmation. Dick Wilson personally did not appear in the matter at all and I remained in the dark as to why as PC he failed to assert his line authority over me. Dottie's label had not yet been pinned to my hat!

That afternoon we drove through the beautifully tended Shields' plantation to our ticketed parking place in a vlei below the grassy area prepared for the reception. We did our best to put a bold face on it, joining the happy throng in applauding the whole occasion, including the witty speech of best man, Douglas Penwill. There was no one to whom safely to direct our greetings, since we could not now know who or if or what might reject or respond to us. It felt as if everyone must know that something was afoot. So we took part in the merriment, regardless, and carried our private misery home.

I tried coolly and honestly to assess the basis for what Johnston had said and any reasons why he had said it in the manner chosen. In fifteen years service I had never heard of the like being done to anyone. The very fact of it depended only on the word of the two of us, making it impossible for me to ask anyone else to say true or false or maybe. It had been deniably said but manifestly done and could not realistically be unsaid or undone. The only sensible choice open to me for survival was to maintain composure and self respect, family included, to hand over my position creditably, and to proceed positively in my next assignment. It would have been against my nature to suppress a certain defiance in the face of widespread rumour about my plight. Meanwhile, there was a gauntlet of pretence to be run, while a *deus ex machina* was lurking unsuspected in the wings. There was an element of the absurd in what at other times would have been a normal succession of farewells. Fare well! The largest was a gathering organized by I know not whom on the terrace in front of the office facing across to the club. A whole company was foregathered from every quarter. There were valedictory speeches and I suppose I made one, at least to give thanks for a fine cine-camera hung in a pale pigskin case which I could never bring myself to use. Cameras are for commemoration!

Another occasion was with the African District Council whose unanimous motion of regret was later forwarded to me in the minutes by Peter Derrick, my successor as Chairman. The most poignant was a private dinner given in my honour by the senior District Officers at a long table in the Wattle Barns restaurant. I remembered the swallowed pain washed down by a robust Falernian style wine in earthenware goblets. At least that was how it tasted. On my own account I called a meeting of Chiefs and DOs in my office where I said my farewells, but had to turn to the window away from proffered handshaking as I could not disguise my confusion and my emotion. Some at least were friends. During what could well be called our pregnant parting arrangements and the dulling of pain by business, there came a spontaneous flow of letters from many quarters, some rather surprising in that the writers had somehow had wind of my precipitate departure from Kiambu. In the absence of any protection of my rights under the Code of Regulations, I must perforce take the liberty of briefly citing some of them.

John Golds, one of the most creative District Officers of any time, wrote *"The name of Gavaghan has reached new heights with all your officers and settlers ... regretting that it has now ended in such an unpleasant and unfair way"*: Barbara Rigby, ex Captain and Community Development Officer (W), wrote *"I have worked for a number of men, but I have never found one so interested and inspiring as you"*: Julian Spence, CDO; *"Under your inspired leadership I cannot see anyone but trying to give of his best ... (with) many of the attributes of my boss in the Sudan, Arthur Gaitskill"*: Eliud Mathu, MLC, was reported to have said in a meeting, *"Kiambu District has made greater strides in development during the past twelve months than during the previous twelve years"*.

Letters expressing regret came from Sir Godfrey ('God') Rhodes, Boy Scouts Commissioner; Chairman J. A. R. King of both Red Cross and Kenya Meat Commission; Chas. Livingston, Manager, W & C French, Civil Engineering Contractors throughout Kiambu; the Nairobi County Council; the Limuru District Association; the African District Council, again, unanimously adopting a motion by Vice Chairman, Senior Chief Josiah Njonjo. Father P. J. McGill, doughty priest in charge of embattled Kiringa Mission, wrote twice, *"I was shocked ... that they should transfer you when you were so much needed ... There must be some very powerful people behind your move and I don't think it has anything to do with your work"*. He could not resist the mischievous dig, *"Was it the Protestants?"*

The Kiambu Club Chairman's written aside was interesting. *"We are all very sorry to see you go and those of us who know a little of the circumstances not at all amused"*. I was welcomed as a club member. John Hillard, CMG, of Limuru, ex Sudan Political Service, Director of Sudan Railways, Chairman of Portland Cement and President of the Federation of Kenya Employers, made a point of taking me to lunch at Muthaiga Club, where Jews were not yet admitted as members! He asked me whether I thought our situation was connected with that prejudice. I had not. Ronald Findlay of Migaa Estate wrote me in a personal letter, *"It is not often that one gets a DC who is liked and respected by both Europeans and Africans, but you have managed this and, while being firm, have gone out of your way to help bring both closer together ... I think that your leaving Kiambu is a great tragedy"*. Frank Loyd, on much later reading Findlay's letter wrote of him as "a splendid, upright and sound man, enormously respected and liked by his fellow coffee barons and by the 'watu' (people)".

A number of letters urged me against any thought of resignation from her Majesty's Oversea Civil Service, in which I had recently received an honour at the hand of her Majesty for service performed under the direction of her Governor and under the close personal supervision of his Special Commissioner, Johnston. Who could have made the writers aware of any such intention to resign or of the cause of it I did not know. I received no written official criticism, appreciation, explanation or instructions of any kind, but at least I felt clean, if stripped of esteem. It was a great comfort to be handing over to Peter Derrick, my next door desert neighbour at Wajir in 1947 and, with Meg, our landing mates in South Parks Road on the 1948-9 Devonshire Second Course in Oxford. A more sensitive pair of friends as successors we could not have wished for.

Before I left the Kiambu stage in a medley of confusion and applause the *deus ex machina* swung out from the wings to help the gods decide my fate. Out of the blue I was invited to be Chairman of a Steering Committee to bring the separate European, Asian and African Civil Servants Associations into a single non-racial association. This absorbing voluntary task formed a good part of my next chapter in Nairobi and opened the door to a totally different future.

XIX

NAIROBI
LOCAL GOVERNMENT AND TOWN PLANNING
SEPTEMBER 1959–SEPTEMBER 1960

It was a pleasant irony to receive a personal letter from Wilfred Havelock, the Minister for Local Government, welcoming me in advance to his Ministry, which he "understood I was joining". I had known Havelock, officially and personally both in Kiambu and Samburu where he had come to open a hospital. I had found him mild and courteous, but politically adroit and durable. He was tall and slender with delicate features under rippling black hair. By background and conviction he was in the multi-racial camp, aligned with Michael Blundell, Leader of the European elected members, having once been a Prisons Officer.

Havelock's Permanent Secretary was Charles Farquhar Atkins, who had been my DC at Kisumu fifteen years before. From being a lusty Brasenose College, Oxford, oarsman he had gained ballast and beam as Commodore of Kisumu Yacht Club, in which he was known for his expertise at luffing, or taking the wind from one's sails. He had once been a DO at Maralal, the DC of Tana River District, where the Hola irrigation scheme and detention camp were later situated, and had recently been Permanent Secretary for African Affairs, so he was familiar with much of my own background.

I presumed that Atkins was privy to my posting to his Ministry and was somewhat taken aback to receive my regulation Annual Report for 1959, of which one third had been under Loyd, one third under Wilson and one third under him. I had never before had an adverse report, save one separate and specific disagreement by letter with Reece at Mandera in 1949, and comments from Wainwright in 1955 about "dictatorial manner" and "neglect of temporary buildings" at Maralal! The rest were as complimentary as could be wished above the line, as was Atkins' current one. Below the line he added, "I have felt bound to say that you are doing yourself no good by nursing a sense of grievance over the circumstances surrounding your transfer from the Provincial Administration". The word "circumstances" stuck in my craw, as it had with the Kiambu Club Committee. Atkins was neither unkind nor untruthful, but his comment was lacking in specifics and heavily qualified in expression. "Grievance", yes, since contrary to procedure I had had no official censure or warning to account for the circumstance of summary transfer, other than the callous sentence pronounced in private by Johnston. "Nursing", perhaps, in the sense of a viper in the bosom, but not wallowing. I was too constructively busy for that. But there seemed to be an elusive blend of warning and concern in "doing yourself no good". He had spoken to me in neither

276

sense, nor about any precipitant of the circumstances such as my confidential letter to Wilson. Wilson himself now called unexpectedly at my Local Government office seemingly to mend fences in respect of his unseen part in the matter, with a conciliatory reference to our future relations. I told him that on my side no question of forgiveness arose.

Charles Atkins also had been a member of the main Commission of Enquiry on the Hola incident chaired by R. Duncan Fairn, Head of the UK Prisons Service. As noted at the time, I had not been called as a demonstrably relevant witness,* having been privately alerted by a friendly Secretariat Staff Officer that this would be so. John Cowan was likewise not called. In the absence of complete evidence the Fairn Commission had effectively detached the Hola Enquiry from the Mwea rehabilitation procedures based on the Attorney General's distinction between punitive and compelling force. It had commended the earlier 'tutorial' approach, which had been superseded by Baring's 'moral crusade', and had appointed an outstanding and fearless DC, Bob Wilson, to overall charge, although the rehabilitation course was by then almost run. Bob and I had served together as DOs in Kiambu in 1950, but no communication passed between us during this 'limbo'. The Commission's findings also closed off the trail back to the multiple deaths in Manyani camp in 1954, which had occasioned a joint visit by Baring and Lennox-Boyd, followed by an incomplete even if not misleading statement to Parliament.

There followed two further top level interviews, one admonitory the other inquisitorial. The first was alone with Baring in the rarefied atmosphere of Government House, so brilliantly brought to stately life by John Gunther.** It was brief. There was no direct reference to letter or circumstance, only an acknowledgement of my competence and the prospect of a good future once I had learned to accept and conform to the disciplines of the service. There was no place on which to stand my ground and Johnston's words, possibly not known to Baring, might never have been said.

The second interview was along the corridor in the corner of the Chief Secretary's wing. It was with Eric Griffith Jones, the substantive Attorney-General who had devised, promulgated and witnessed in my presence his own doctrine of compelling force. He asked me to review the responsibility, as I saw it, for the processes of rehabilitation in which I had been involved. I replied that, if he was recording my statement, which I would wish to sign throughout, I should begin at the top. I listed the Governor, the AG himself, the Special Commissioner, the Minister for Defence, the Commissioner of Prisons and, of course, myself. I could not speak for John Cowan. Any others would only be involved in specific instances, within the ambit of their duties. I heard no more of my statement to the Attorney General, but it served notice of the sort of evidence I might give later if called upon. (The lid was lifted on me again, once by Baring as Lord Howick, Chairman of the Commonwealth Development Corporation and once when Lord Caradon [Hugh Foot], my honoured 'patron' at United Nations asked if I knew of any blackball against me in London.)

Atkins' Under Secretary was Bobby Tatton-Brown, in whose company it was impossible to feel ill-used. His emollient voice, pleasingly owlish face and genuine warmth conveyed humour, interest and open mindedness. He was also a great frequenter of the Ngong hills with our zany parasitologist friend, Ronnie Heisch. They had served together in the NFD, Ronnie in Wajir as Doctor for the whole frontier and Bobby as DC at Mandera, where I had found our disreputable Head Station Hand, Osman Muslim, to be his fervent admirer. Next in the pecking order was Jack Tasker, Senior Assistant Secretary, the epitome of the Dickensian Head Clerk, precise in work and deed, saturnine and cerebral, his dryly courteous mien concealing a kindly family man with a sparkling sense of fun. Jack had crossed from West Africa with an MBE for his service there and went on to the perfect appointment for his talents, as Chief Executive of the pioneering English 'New Town' of Milton Keynes. We were joined by Krishna (though not 'dark as a cloud') Sondhi, of whom it could be said that she was a rich blend of the cultures; Kenya Indian professional and English ladies' college. She was quite small and leisurely, with ropes of jet hair falling behind her spectacles down a habitual sari. Her full lips and vowels and slightly mocking Roedean drawl dealt humorously and efficiently with the oddities of our trade. Her calm grasp of affairs and independent spirit marked her out for rapid advancement. We shared a delightful secretary, Rose Ali, daughter of the most senior and respected Asian Executive Officer, Ayub Ali, OBE.

A branch of the Ministry provided a service of the greatest importance, in financial management, audit and general advice, not only to the Ministry in supervising more than 40 African District Councils but also as trainers and change agents available to the Councils in the field. The Chief Local Government Inspector was Fred Altorfer of rock hewn Swiss ancestry, honed in Yorkshire. A problem brought to Fred was subjected to wry scrutiny, merciless dissection and what always seemed the only practical, commonsense solution, delivered with a chuckle in his flat northern accent. I asked him once to tell me his guiding principle in audit. Without hesitation he replied "The test of the reasonable". He had indeed applied it when he had audited me in Maralal. In my next job I returned to Fred and to Senior Inspector Joe England as invaluable guides in framing unique and unorthodox national estimates. Another Inspector was Jack Followes, whose sunny disposition and adaptable skills made him a natural for field attachments to big African Councils, who came to regard him as an organic part of their rapid and complicated growth. His success with the councils marked him out as the ideal candidate for Local Government training for Independence.

Meanwhile, we settled in to our Public Works Department standard furnished quarter in Elgon Road quite near the old zebra frequented house of 'P. Wyn' Harris, with whom I had stayed on arrival in Kenya before he went off to be Sir Percy, Governor of the Gambia. We had a garage for our grey battleship of a Peugeot 403 station wagon and a shady pepper tree over our tiny brown lawn, green dappled with plantain weeds. The unused garage housed a colony of hungry fleas which instantly invaded the Peugeot and had me abandoning it down the road frantically peeling off to the buff as I ran home to duck under a cold bath. As I knelt to pluck them out with calloused thumbs the plantains offered a handy therapy for misery in suffusing my brain with blood. The Ngong hills beckoned calmly from across the Nairobi Game Park below.

Magically I was soon immersed in the arcane mysteries of civil service representation which I had been invited to undertake. There were in existence a European Civil Servants' Association, an Asian Civil Service Association and a Kenya Civil Servants' Union. Broadly speaking they represented the ten thousand or so senior grades, mainly European, the senior clerical and junior executive grades, then mainly Indian or Goan, and the junior clerical and allied, nearly all African.

As self government under African majority rule began to assume the shape of reality, it became obvious that service representation should be rejigged to give impetus to the grinding processes of successive Commissions of Enquiry into the public services of East Africa aimed at achieving more equitable treatment as between the races. The Lidbury (Sir David, KCMG, CB, DSO) Commission of 1953-4 had noted the actual if unwritten racial discrimination of the A, B and C salary scales and the 3/5 rule applied to the few Africans admitted to the top grades. It had concluded that "grading by race rather than responsibility should disappear". More than five years later the Flemming (Sir Gilbert, KCB) Commission of 1960 provided for new basic scales A, B, C and Z, which gave further effect to this process, although the entry of Africans to the senior scales was still regulated by the invisible filter of "maintenance of standards". It was this very disparity of racial treatment which had been applied, demoralizingly, if not intoxicatingly, to Edinburgh University qualified Vet, Justus, or John, ole Tameno, the Maasai member of Legislative Council for Rift Valley.

I had neither expertise nor experience in such matters, except touching my own personal interests, and had been surprised to be invited by existing racial Associations to chair a Steering Committee to agree and to recommend joint representative and negotiating structures, which would also have regard to employment status and terms of compensation on Independence. We quickly recommended the formation of a new non-racial Senior Civil Servants' Association, SCSA, (separate from a Civil Servants' Union) to a packed meeting convened in Nairobi City Hall where it was authorized with acclaim. In a primitively mechanized ballot count I was elected first Chairman, with which went the Chairmanship of the Staff Side of Central Whitley Council. It was the greatest and most timely honour I could have been accorded by my fellow civil servants, not least because we were the only non-racial association of its kind and scope in Colonial Africa.

Among the widely representative elected committee of SCSA was a nucleus of regular workers. They included the Deputy Chairman, Eric Prince, a stalwart from Education; Fred Eddleston, a football fanatic from Works; Christopher Mlavu, Uganda born entrepreneur; Aquil Quraishi, Senior Immigration Officer and later Alan Simmance, Barrister, and my former DOI and friend from Kiambu. Our Organizing Secretary was graduate career woman Betty Annesley, supported by Joyce Jones who made it all run without fuss.

There was no idle time for regrets what with local Government duties and the Association work, mainly out of hours and at weekends. Recruitment of members was no problem since future uncertainty affected us all. Wide consultation was essential and involved open meetings at Kisumu, Nakuru, Mombasa, Nyeri and other gatherings of civil servants, who established links with Local Government officers in the Municipalities. Positive enthusiasm was fuelled by our determination to achieve the best advantage for the individual and for the service of Kenya during transfer of power. Shock, horror, we even applied to be registered as a Trade Union!

SCSA was fortunate in the arrival in 1960 without fanfare of Sir Patrick Renison from British Guiana to take over from Sir Evelyn Baring. He was known as a 'service' Governor, which came as something of a relief to me after having been brought so sharply to heel by grandee Baring. Contact with Renison came about quickly through a visit by Colonial Office Under Secretary Philip Rogers to discuss compensation terms for loss of career and related matters. We invited him to address a full committee meeting of SCSA in our offices. He appeared both conciliatory and accommodating in his opening address, which was standard 'Yes Minister' stuff, but when he asked to go off the palantype record, we pressed him first to explain, in view of a lack of trust in previous Colonial Office emissaries of lower rank. Nothing useful emerged except a complaint about me from Rogers to

Renison, who judged from his own early experience on behalf of the British Honduras service that I must be doing a good job. Rogers wrote me most courteous thanks for a sundowner party we laid on for him "when we could express ourselves more freely"! Renison then sent for me and enquired in his homely way, knee to knee, how I had come to be in my present situation, about which he had spoken to Wally Coutts, the Chief Secretary, who was also Chairman of the Official side of Central Whitley Council. I told him everything that I knew, to which he responded that, in fully accepting my account, he must assume that there was a Government position in the matter. He would not revert directly to me, but I might draw my own conclusions from my future progress. A series of events justified my trust in him.

Meanwhile the SCSA 'nuclear group' was invited formally to Government House to meet across the table the formidable Conservative Secretary of State, Ian Macleod, and his Colonial Officials beside the Governor and his senior officers responsible for the Civil Service. It was really only a preliminary, possibly placatory, locking of horns, but it was very significant to us in recognizing the facilitating role of the senior and expatriate functionaries of the public service in effecting governmental changes. It was arranged that an SCSA delegation should call at the Colonial Office in London.

Sir Patrick Renison came across as an innocent and almost naïve man in political terms. At 48 he was already a consistently successful career civil servant operating in a bear pit of political power and expectation, for which he lacked the talons, the cunning and a killer instinct, as well as African instinct and experience. If he had a natural vanity or pride, it was in his achievement without advantages. One day in our Elgon Road 'remand' home I exclaimed aloud "that's the end of Renison" when we heard him on the radio pronounce against Jomo Kenyatta's release in the fateful phrase "a leader to darkness and death". The drama of the long delayed pronouncement, which for the moment slammed the jail door without a clear alternative political exit, was compounded by the finality of the biblical sentence drawn from Job 10:20. It seemed to me out of his character, except for a certain stubbornness, and was more likely a distillation of the advice of his chief officers who had personal Kikuyu experience and fundamental religious convictions. (I knew nothing of Baring's earlier part in the matter.)

Our SCSA mission to London, to culminate in the call at the Colonial Office, included Betty Annesley, Aquil Quraishi and Fred Eddleston. We were ushered into the presence of Iain Macleod, who was with Philip Rogers. He was a difficult man to assess or confront, whether in his political persona or his formidable reputation as a world class player of contract bridge. His blunt features, high bald forehead and trenchant mouth, eyes aglow with perception, combined to present a concentrated force of argument even before its utterance in rasping tones.

"I recognize that in Kenya you have a special case," he began without much preamble, slicing across the final vowel sound in the diction of the ruling class of the day and clutching his torso evidently in pain. I knew Macleod's Kenya employed brother, 'Roddy', slightly but doubted that his political attitudes as opposed to his information would be affected by that link with Michael Blundell's multi-racial group. I asked cautiously why our case was special. He went on that "one must look after one's own." I tried again to clarify what that might mean to a non-racial delegation in the context of the Commonwealth ideal as currently espoused by Prime Minister Macmillan. Rogers smoothly deflected further discussion, but we had had our high level audience and could proceed with our mission on that plane.

We hit the national broadsheets with a couple of favourable second leaders and were contacted by reputed columnists who recognized that our contribution to a stable transition should be secured by fair treatment. I was invited to attend a Conservative Party committee in Parliament, where I was questioned by Sir John Tilney, Dame Joan Vickers, a senior back-bencher called Morrison and others, as well as, at his Cheyne Walk house, by Major Patrick Wall VRD, a right wing Conservative MP who was continuously concerned in London and Kenya. I took issue with an injudicious statement put out by a Mr Cuthbert Alport, Minister of State, Commonwealth Relations Office, opposing continuity of career between the Colonial and Commonwealth Relations services. After seeing a headline press statement advocating "a clean break" with the past, I enquired whether the colonial period under the hand of Parliament was now seen to be dirty? My rhetorical question was not well taken, but former colonial officers were later to cross the divide, which became irrelevant with Ministerial amalgamations.

On our return to Kenya, the Chief Secretary, Wally Coutts agreed to address a full public meeting of SCSA in the Nairobi City Hall to set out Government's position in our regard. It was extremely well attended and Leader of the European Elected Members Michael Blundell, from the 'royal circle' shouted a humorous Swahili quip in the middle of my reply from the stage. I was able to respond in kind. Relations with Coutts could be a little fragile, although I had enjoyed the Coutts' private stay with me at Maralal on his mid career return from the West Indies. He did not find it entirely congenial to have a subordinate pop up from across the table as Co-Chairman of Central Whitley Council in negotiation for the Staff Side, nor did I find it easy to be both equal and unequal over his office doorstep, but it worked well enough because of his decency and courtesy and my genuine respect.

Regular Local Government duties placed various and continuing demands in dealing with 40 African Councils' affairs and drafting by-laws. One such was a proposal that the Samburu Council might derive revenue from the export of naturally growing cannabis, used as a hunger averting stimulant over long distances, which might displace the ruinous and costly trade of chewing 'khat' in the Yemen as well as in Isiolo for licenced old Somalis. I minuted that I thought this a disreputable by-law to recommend to the Samburu. We dropped it. A very satisfying job was to take part in a field mission under Director of Education Bromley and produce the 'Report on Educational Expenditure by African District Councils in Nyanza Province', serving nearly two million people. This was a fascinating study of thriving education among both sexes in Government and Mission schools of every kind from the Elim Missionary Society of Massachusetts to Seventh Day Adventists and Pentecostal Assemblies of Canada. There was not a tumble-down school nor a slovenly pupil to be seen among the eager phalanxes of young warriors and budding Amazons. While the Councils were not strapped for funds nor niggardly in expenditure on their favourite subject, the burgeoning of education owed much to popular enthusiasm canalized sedulously through the intensely competitive soul hunting of the Missions, whose expatriate staff were often well funded and lavishly transported in comparison with ordinary mortals. A Chevrolet sedan imported on permit and resold once a year would provide for its successor and leave a handsome surplus for Mission school expenses.

The 'Nubian Village' at Kibera was only two miles from our Elgon Road house, along the Langata tarmac to the Wilson Civilian Airport, the Army Headquarters and the heartening Animal Orphanage, run by elegantly toothless old Bobby Caid, once Family Remittance Officer and my breakfast forager at Kitui. The Nubians, deriving from southern Egypt and Sudan, enjoyed a formidable historic reputation as porters, guides and armed askari without whom few safaris of whatever intent would venture into the interior. They were strikingly tall and fearless as mercenaries, but fiercely proud and not above mutiny if given cause. They kept to their own Islamized society and congregated in small pockets for rest and retirement at main caravan halts. Their Nairobi settlement was one of the largest, set out in orderly ranks of hammered *debbie* (petrol can) roofs over square wattle and unwhitened mud walls with many private rooms. Their Elders enjoyed dignified status as if a cell of Local Government under Nairobi City Council. The Nubian village spread along one sloping side of the original Nairobi dam, a small oval of fresh water still so clean that European children splashed safely and parents rowed dinghies or tried to fish, although water skis were frowned upon. We sometimes picnicked there with the Polish Veterinary Manns, the Rumanian Architect Roszas and the Advertising Dunfords, Cleo a statuesque Alexandrian Greek United Nations interpreter, and Michael Nicole's employer.

One day we planned that Oscar Mann, Leslie Rosza and our Kevin and Séan, all around 10, and our David 3, should safari in the battlewagon Peugeot to the rapidly developing Tsavo East National Park under famed Warden David Sheldrick and his elephant tending wife, Daphne, assisted by young Peter Jenkins my friend from Taveta days. Thence, living off the land or cadging, we would cut across to Malindi and a cavernous communal hut called the 'hangar'. Our first night stop was inside the park across the bilharzia snail infested Galana (which means river locally), at the tented camp of two young Zoologists, Ian Parker and Tony Seth-Smith, both Kenya born. They were funded by a Nuffield Foundation Project of great simplicity and imagination. It was designed to convert the indigenous Waliangulu bowmen/poachers into licensed hunters with full bellies and pockets from their own efforts and the motive to see off outside poachers for which they were well able. They were allocated quotas of paint daubed elephant to cull with agreed arrangements for apportioning meat and trophies. An excess of elephant population ringbarking trees could wreak havoc on the environment while unchecked poaching could decimate the herds in the tourist attracting National Park. Unhappily Ian and Tony were just off on two weeks leave but they left us the freedom of their camp.

Our route south east lay along a bush survey boundary cut straight as a hair parting for some 30 miles to intersect with the main Mombasa highway near the wartime Army camp at Mackinnon Road, then razed to concrete plinths. We had two spare Michelin tyres but I had not heeded 'uncle' Reece's NFD lesson about destumping bush tracks. Before morning heat every tyre had blown and the rims could not sustain rubber stuffed with dry grass. There was nothing for it but for me to perch Nicole's straw hat, secured demurely under my chin, put a few dried apricots and prunes into a plastic bag and set forth, however far. I disciplined myself to halt five minutes in the hour, shoes and socks off, feet up a bush stump, but I could not push aside the dozen elephant who lumbered and rumbled across the track taking no notice of this odd intruder, nor could I shoo away a hunting pack of wild dog who did notice me with whimpering anticipation. There must have been ten or more but they formed a loose cordon constantly exchanging positions in the scrub about thirty feet away. They were so graceful and delicately poised as they rose on hind legs to get a smiling look from silvery, black tipped masks that I almost forgot having seen a pack in Mandera rip apart a wounded comrade on the run. At least the silent terror kept me from feeling tired until they vanished as suddenly as they came.

After some seven hours to my intense relief I heard the friendly howl of a Mombasa train soaring above the savannah a few miles ahead. I almost trotted straight into the Mackinnon Road campsite, nearly opposite to which

I recalled a remaining Indian shop whose Coke supply I lowered until I gurgled. A quick lift got me to Voi where I was able to engage a truck from the garage, well stocked with the popular Peugeot Michelin tyres, to get me back to our marooned family. They had eked out a Jerrycan of water and a gallon tin of pineapple juice from 'Bobs' Harries' Thika cannery, with the radiator as reserve, but Nicole had them like angels on their knees as we roared in before sunset. Delivered back to the main road we headed straight on to Malindi, where the 'hangar' felt like heaven beside the pearly, mica dusted sands.

Local Government provided few other excitements but much interest during early 1960, enlivened by the precipitate departure from the Belgian Congo of the colonial power and the ensuing frantic exodus of large numbers of the 100,000 mostly Belgian settlers. Being near at hand I was assigned an administrative task in the reception of the influx by road, rail and air, and their accommodation in railway bungalows and lodgings. Most of the hard and sometimes frustrating logistical work fell on a calm, competent and attractive Kenya educated assistant made available to me, called Angela Bell. My long felt lack of sympathy for the Belgian colonial regime was not lessened by some bizarre selfishness on the part of a few arrivals with parrots, pets and paraphernalia from their lotus eating lives, who demanded and complained continuously. They were refugees and our guests and the wave soon subsided. I was later to be more constructively in touch with Congo convulsions in the new Democratic Republic in formation, and in the involvement of UN.

In October my guardian *'deus ex machina'* again showed his hand when a new post of 'Localization and Training Officer' was created and advertised at senior level in the Treasury.* I at once applied, was selected against stiff competition from Denis Hextall and others and soon moved over from Local Government to the traditional power house of Finance, even in a Colony.

Daily Nation, Nairobi; Saturday 3 October 1998. Today in History, "Mr T. J. F. Gavaghan takes charge of training African Civil Servants to prepare them to take over jobs held by Europeans in Kenya."

XX

NAIROBI
AFRICANISATION AND TRAINING
OCTOBER 1960–NOVEMBER 1961

The Treasury had two effective heads, the Permanent Secretary for financial matters and the Director of Establishments for personnel, the former being more equal than the latter. John Butter from the Indian Civil Service was a classic exponent of the aphorism 'silence is golden'. He had a calm bony face, clenching an elegant cigarette holder while he chaired finance meetings, with scarcely a word or a puff, to a conclusion usually congenial to himself. His wife, Joyce, painted splendidly in oils. Tom Skinner was my enigmatically able Director, smilingly detached from the passions of personnel. His apparent inscrutability and fine olive features attracted snide comment about his mixed descent from the founder of the élite Indian cavalry regiment Skinner's Horse. I felt well seen by him especially when he later wrote below a favourable report that "Mr Gavaghan should learn to be more tolerant of the shortcomings of his superiors". No fairer word was written!

Between Tom Skinner and me was Cyril Claude Ricketts, naturally known as Peter, in the position of Deputy Secretary, having previously been Headmaster of the Arab Coastal Academy at Mombasa. Peter had the well rounded cut of a bon viveur. He was professional at his work, without false pretence, and a boon companion on tour overseas. I was assigned two outstanding co-workers, Elizabeth Saldanha and Nisar Mir. Elizabeth was an experienced Goan secretary, a perfectionist, assiduous, tireless and imperturbably demure in manner. Sometimes a quietly feminine smile behind her spectacles revealed inner thoughts about the turmoil of our small office. Only once did she slip up by locking me securely in my adjoining office, when she went out for lunch, leaving me with a Squadron Leader Fletcher, who then revealed himself to be an Encyclopaedia Britannica salesman. He could never before have had such a chance to vociferate a captive customer into a purchase. Nisar was a very manly Moslem, dignified and deferential, who revelled in designing and researching detailed analyses of every nook of the senior civil service. He and Elizabeth were of veneers apart, but they blended perfectly.

It was natural enough that the new post of Localization and Training Officer was established by Government at the same time as the non-racial reform of Civil Service Associations. My Government appointment and my election to the Chair of the SCSA as one person concerned with both sides of the equation, public service and public servant, was however fortuitous and I was much encouraged by congratulations from all races and levels.

The advertisement for the position had used the term 'Localization and Training' and its broad purpose was defined as 'The development of a genuinely local public service'. Within six weeks our small team produced a slender, foolscap size volume in pink card covers entitled 'First Interim Report on Localization, November 1960'.* In it I made bold to assert:

> "The inescapable conclusion is that localization must have as a definite aim the introduction of a minimum proportion of Africans at all levels in which they are not adequately represented ... a decision on this matter, which is fraught with political and economic hazards, cannot be long delayed."

No one afterwards seriously questioned the need and the word Africanisation came into common parlance, if not into immediate bureaucratic usage.

The report pin-pointed a number of linked questions which had to be faced. A provisional target date for Independence was a prerequisite for planning. Lacking any official guidance, we adopted our own time scale for working purposes as between 1963 and 1965. The date would determine pace and pace would affect the morale both of those displaced and of their eager, untrained successors. The much extolled 'maintenance of standards' would demand proper training, as well as emotional acceptance by some grudging expatriates that there already existed what I described as 'overlapping brackets of ability' linking the races. Provision for training, both in new institutions and doubling up on the job, would require large funding. Phased compensation arrangements for loss of career would need to be negotiated and guaranteed, both in fairness and to avoid an outrush of qualified staff too fast for controlled replacement, as threatened Julius Nyerere and Chief Secretary Fletcher-Cooke in Tanganyika.

We suggested three crude policy options for the speed of Africanisation: a crash programme under extreme pressure: accelerated replacement with selective displacement: replacement of normal wastage of up to ten per cent annually. It was throughout assumed that each option referred primarily to Kenya Africans rather than to locally employed non Africans.

The Chief Secretary, no less, issued a general policy circular, which I was called upon to draft, based upon the second option, accelerated Africanisation to reflect the relative proportions of the population. The field of action was defined as the top 17,000, out of a total of 60,000 public service posts, in which there was any presence of all three races, more or less coinciding with the constituency of the Senior Civil Servants' Association. The priority stratum was that of the upper 10,000 posts almost

*Copy deposited in Rhodes House Library; Oxford.

exclusively filled by 6,000 Europeans and 4,000 Asians. There were only a few hundred Africans at the lower margin and into the next stratum of 7,000 intermediate posts, which included Police, nursing and secretarial staff.

We set a provisional target of one third, or 3,000 Africans, in the top 10,000 posts by Independence, that is from the end of 1963 by our guestimate. This required a detailed analysis and ready reckoner of every single post held by non Africans, displaying precise points for intervention. The task challenged the talent and energy of Nisar Mir, who on his own initiative inspanned his supervisory peer group across the service. His printed summary and detailed tables made it easy, by following a single vertical column down 100 flipped pages to pick out any multi-digit entry at a glance, checking adjoining columns for function, contract status and expiry date to reveal the African recruitment and training need.

With this as guide we were able to prepare with Treasury backing a Five Year Plan from 1961 to 1965, costed at five million pounds (at 1961 parity with sterling). Accounting expertise was provided free by Fred Altorfer and Joe England from Local Government. Inspired improvisation came through the scribblings of the Under Secretary for Finance, blonde, tousle haired Tasmanian, Philip Haddon-Cave. Given a range of projects, white linen jacket doffed and eyes agleam through pebble glasses, he would toss off figured scraps of paper, often to the floor, for ordering by his secretarial genius into an acceptable format of estimates. Philip had a gift of informal brilliance and a persistent dynamism which he later transferred to the service of Hong Kong. Africanisation in Kenya was brought about in good part by Philip, Fred, Joe, Nisar Mir and Elizabeth Saldanha.

During this breakneck activity Peter Ricketts was laying the political tracks by setting up an Advisory Committee, which included the vociferous participation of Tom Mboya who quite reasonably queried executive positions in localization being held by expatriates, in particular by the President of SCSA, (me), who might have conflicting interests. Conversely there were initial advantages in co-operation, research and speed of movement when there were common interests. Without any pressure, I resigned from SCSA, as soon as both the Five Year Plan and satisfactory terminal arrangements for displaced expatriates were in hand. Eric Prince succeeded as Chairman, followed later by Alan Simmance. In their letters of appreciation Eric and Betty Annesley little knew how much they had all given back to me. About this time I was upgraded in my post to Under Secretary. It was the second promotion in two years since the 'circumstances' of my transfer from Kiambu.

Peter Ricketts and I went off to Nigeria and Ghana to see how they were handling the Africanisation of their expatriates in senior posts, neither colony having anything like the racial imbalances as Kenya, since they had no local white pool on which to draw and a much larger supply of African graduates going back for at least a generation. Northern Nigeria had a great training institution cum embryonic university at Zaria under an outstanding liberal Principal, Maurice Bennion, succeeded by a supercharged Crown Counsel cum Administrative Officer who sprang from the Secretariat at Lord Lugard's custom built Regional Capital at Kaduna. He was Sam Richardson, whose later meteoric academic career took off from the sale to Unilever for a rumoured £60,000 of his patent dog food canned, he said, in his bath! (Vice Chancellorships in Mauritius and Australia beckoned).

Ghana had much to offer us, not least in the quality of its African Heads of Department, some with Danish surnames dating from the old slave trading post guarded by seventeenth century Christiansborg Castle. Philipps was Secretary for Finance, Engmann Head of Posts and Telegraphs and E. V. Mamphey was in Establishments with a tenacious expatriate *eminence ecossais* called David Anderson, who discreetly dispensed the art of management from Accra across to Nairobi and Lusaka, borne on the silken carpet of the Ford Foundation. I admired Mamphey's straightforward approach to Foreign Aid. "Give them a shopping list; tell them who will offer what and when. If they don't come up with the goods, pick another one. They are preparing for the post Independence game and want to be first on the field." He showed me a framed photograph of his bewhiskered grandfather in cap and gown from Fourah Bay College in Sierra Leone, cradle of West African graduates.

Above and beyond the process of Africanisation was the vast Volta River(s) Hydro-electric Project, whose social and economic ramifications dwarfed even the £144,000,000 expenditure estimate of 1953. Nothing like it had been seen before and it absorbed numbers of expatriate civil servants, who in a sense helped provide a back-stop for the country. By some serendipitous choice a husband and wife partnership of genius came to the helm; Robert Jackson, former Australian Naval Commander and UN Assistant Secretary General, together with Barbara Ward, Economist Dame extraordinary. Between them they designed a model of creative development. They were, each quite distinctly, the most modest and approachable people I ever met, while mounting the summits of their professions.

Ghana, famed 'Golden coast of Guinney' was profusely endowed by any African standards and sat on solid currency reserves. It sustained a top hamper of powerful Ministers, above our ken but well served by the quality of senior civil servant we met. The charismatic President, 'Showboy' Kwame Nkrumah, was mentor to Kenya's political prodigy, Tom Mboya, who had been elected in 1958 first Chairman of the Pan African Peoples Congress in Accra. Nkrumah urged him "first to seek the political kingdom", a parlous piece of advice for Mboya.

Funeral Ceremony of Senior Chief Waruhiu, *
killed by a Mau Mau assassin, 1952.
Eulogy by Edward Windley PC.
Attending Eric Davies (centre) CNC,
Frank Loyd (right) DC.

* *'Evelyn Baring: The Last Proconsul'*: Charles Douglas Home: Collins; St James's Place, London: 1978; p.231. "It was at Waruhiu's funeral that Evelyn saw Kenyatta for the first and only time before he was detained. They faced each other across the grave and Evelyn was conscious of some of what he felt was the demonic force of Kenyatta's personality."

Enoch Powell PC, MP.
Questions in Parliament, 1959.

Hola Detention Camp: Irrigation Scheme
Tana River.

Mrs Jemima Gecaga presents prizes
at Kiambu Show, 1959. (TG at hand.)

Traditional Oath Administrator
swears in Kiambu tribunal elders
with sacred twigs and stone.

Nicole Gavaghan presents
prizes at Limuru Show, 1959.
TG with Divisional DO Keith Shaw.
(Son David expected!)

Tom Mboya,
Elected member of Leg. Co.
For Nairobi and Trade Union
leader.
(On visit to India with
Wilfred Maciel,* P.R.O.)

* Footnote.
Brother of Mervyn Maciel,
author of Memoir of Goan
Service: "Bwana Karani",
Merlin Books, 1984.

Eliud Mathu,
first African
Member of
Legislative
Council.

James Gichuru,
Acting Chairman
of Kenya African
Union; for Jomo
Kenyatta.

Oginga Odinga,
Member of Leg. Co.,
for Kisumu.

Charles Njonjo,
Senior Crown Counsel:
Solicitor General.

Julius Gikonyo Kiano,
elected member of
Leg. Co., for Kiambu
1957/58.

DAILY NATION   October 1960

AFRICANIZATION OF THE CIVIL SERVICE

Few will envy Mr Gavaghan his task. But it is no exaggeration to say that the peace and progress of Kenya during the next decade will very largely depend on the success of his efforts over the coming 12 months.

DAILY NATION   April 1961

All 25 of the Kenya general arts and economics students who sat their degree examinations at Makerere College in April have been offered senior posts by the Kenya Government.

Ahamed Abdalla (far right rear), became Director in the International Monetary Fund.

Jomo
'Burning Spear'!

'Stepping out'

with Wilfred Maciel,   —   *and Alastair Matheson,*
Public Relations Officer.   *Chief Press Officer at right.*

*Home at Gatundu with his former 'Custodian',
John Ch. Cardovillis of Maralal.*

*(After 'Uhuru') 'Mzee' waving Harambée with
Heir Apparent Daniel Torotich Arap Moi.*

*Governor Sir Patrick Renison
and Lady Renison
outside Government House
1961
with senior administrators and wives.*

(Back row, left to right) Geoff Ellis, Police ADC; Denis Hall, PC Coast; Tom Neil, PS/Dep. Chief Secretary; Dick Wilson, PC Central; Ken Cowley, PC Southern; Peter Derrick, Sen. DC; Sir Eric Griffith-Jones, Dep. Governor; Jack Wolfe, PC Rift; Robin Wainwright, CNC/Minister for African Affairs; Henry Huth, Comptroller Govt. House; Frank Loyd, PS Cabinet Office; Bob Wilson, Sen. DC; Peter Walters, PC Northern; Peter Johnson, Pr. Sec. to H. E.; John Dowson, Officer-in-Charge, Nairobi.

Accra, for all its ramshackle back street squalor, had a full blooded Roman vigour, the high templed men decked out in Senatorial robes of costly 'Kinte' weave, colourfully displaying a sense of power and rude enjoyment. We marvelled at Legon University grown out through many years gestation from nearby Achimota, the celebrated College of the Gold Coast. Legon's dramatic entrance block soared above descending terraces paraded by the preening peacocks of academe. The site only lacked a supply of water which was made up in its boundless spirit. Indeed it was known locally as 'the home of spirits'. The next Vice-Chancellor was the mercurial politico-literary *enfant terrible* from Ireland, Conor Cruise O'Brien, Private Secretary in the Congo operations to United Nations Secretary General, Dag Hammerskold, before his fatal air crash in September 1961. Another fascinating figure from the turmoil of the Congo was George Ivan Smith, Australian United Nations Chief Emissary who would drop off in my office to change to towel and shorts for squash. Later when we spent a night grounded from a Boeing 707 at Kennedy Airport, he told me over Black Label complimentary drams that his span of names was not entirely genuine. An Irish aunt Sullivan had left him money in her will conditional upon his adopting her name, which he naughtily shortened to Ivan. Her gift was the making of his international repute and he was always known by all three. Edda, his adopted African child was with us.

Israel was showing a marked interest in Kenya within a broad policy of extending influence and good relations in sub-Saharan Africa. There was emphasis on training, irrigation and the labour movement 'Histadrut'. The trade union affiliated road and building construction body, 'Solel Boneh', had helped Tom Mboya, Secretary General of the Kenya Federation of Labour, in building Solidarity House, at the back of the bazaar in Nairobi and he had been invited to visit Israel. Quite by chance, through an introduction in Nairobi by a bewitching 'Madame Arcati' like personage called Joan Higgins, we had met the Hon. Edwin Samuel, son and heir of the 1st Viscount Samuel of Carmel. The honorific location Carmel derived from his service as first British High Commissioner for Palestine and the title was awarded for extraordinary social and philosophical achievements, including being leader of the Liberal Party, the first Jewish Cabinet Minister (Disraeli's father had become an Anglican) and the founder of Borstals for boys. Edwin followed him with zest in his own roles as Director of the Public Administration Institute at the Hebrew University and Chairman of the Anglo-Jewish Society. He invited us both to visit him in Israel and it was arranged with my office that we could deviate from our flight schedule to study opportunities for training there while heading on leave.

At Lod Airport near Tel Aviv we were taken over by a strapping blonde official called Ben Ari, who initiated us into the frenetic dawn to

W

290

night schedules expected of serious pilgrims. At first light we saw small
scraps of humanity from the ghettos of the Diaspora devotedly attempting
callisthenics on the sand, before taking Hebrew lessons and undergoing six
months directed employment, however qualified, from venereal diseases to
postman! It was difficult to connect them with the fair and russet giants they
bore, the new generation well called the 'sabra', prickly pears outside but
sweet within, the product of sunlight and nourishment. We met them in the
unique 'Kibbutz(im)' and 'Moshav(im)' styles of rural communal living, in
the uniformed national service of 'Gadna' and in the gun toting fighting
youth called 'Nahal', assigned to guard new settlements.

Ben Ari laid out a detailed programme for touring the country, from
Tel Aviv to Eilat on the Gulf of Akaba, and ending beneath the Golan
heights. He was to transfer us at dawn to an apparently known colleague
coming from the Foreign Office in Jerusalem, whom he spoke of as Sinai
Rom. In the chill of false dawn black Chevrolet official cars converged and
halted. The meeting parties advanced silently on foot, as if to exchange
defectors at 'check-point Charlie', until Ben Ari stopped dead in sudden
recognition. "Jesus Christ" he shouted unfittingly at Sinai Rom. "It's Yanni
Ackerman! Don't you remember me, Japi Maritz?"* Thereupon two
reconstructed class mates from Johannesburg fell upon each others necks.

Sinai Rom, dark and slender with his lovely wife Malka (princess),
made us welcome and sped us about the countryside; to Kibbutz Naan for
Irrigation Technology; to desert market town Beersheba for Agricultural
Research; and down to Eilat for Port Management, now in the hands of our
friend whom we had met in Genoa, Captain Enrico Levi. I discussed with
him sailing 'captive' seaborne training classes in Zim Line cargo boats
plying between Eilat and Mombasa ports, which might wish to 'twin',
although Levi and Captain Hamley would make odd bedfellows. Back in
Jerusalem it snowed and we descended to the torrid congestion of
Bethlehem, where religious tourism defiled the Holy Places with jostling
hucksters and unseemly prelates shouting their wares, sacred and profane.

We spent time with Edwin Samuel and the charming Hadassah at their
apartment. With a view to training exchanges with Kenya I visited his
Institute where he taught the principles of public administration in several
languages, using as his basic functional model the common bicycle, while
at the same time observing the different psychological responses of trainees
from Anglophone and Francophone colonies. In regard to Congolese
administrative trainees his colleague, Aryeh Semo, noted a 'split
personality' in their copying the familiar Belgian colonial style, while
seeking to serve their new nation. Edwin asked about our Kenya Police
Commissioner, Richard Catling, who had served in the Palestine Police and

*Misremembered!

whose name cropped up at a working lunch with the Chiefs of Staff of the Israeli forces. One with a severe limp had his leg pulled by the others demanding that he admit how he had jumped from the first floor window where we sat, just ahead of arrest by a Superintendent Catling of the CID. A gentler occasion was a visit to the 'Orde Wingate' Academy of Ballet near Haifa where the enchanting pupils hardly conjured up the unpredictable war hero, who had won puzzling acclaim as an Intelligence Officer during the Arab revolt. It was a time when the population of Israel was noticeably assimilating more new immigrants from North Africa and the Yemen with proportionately less from Europe, Russia and America. There was no such systematic fusion between Israel and the Arabs, within or without the borders, and Palestinian refugee camps were sequestered albeit very visibly throughout the region. We spent three perfect days at the small hotel Galei Kineret where I drafted my report on the wooden jetty beside the sea of Galilee, overlooked by the menacing Golan Heights.

Back in Nairobi, while the Five Year Plan was being negotiated, an extensive university scholarship programme was initiated from within the Education Ministry to which an abrasive, no-nonsense Colonial official, 'Wac' Matheson was seconded as Minister. The driving force was a formidable Senior Education Officer, Mrs Brotherton, one could call her no other, and her Kikuyu assistant in the Scholarship Section, the sturdy and durable young Kenneth Matiba.* A competitive initiative was already launched by Tom Mboya with US Aid, African America Students Foundation and Kennedy Foundation sponsorship. It was known as the Mboya Airlift and counterbalanced the Russian and Bulgarian plans for securing influence through university places.

A key part of the Five Year Plan for Africanisation was the establishment of a Kenya Institute of Administration. Following a meeting in 1958 with the International Federation of Employees in the Public and Civil Service, the germ of the idea came from an Easter weekend draft memo by former Colonel Tom Neil, himself a Staff College graduate and meticulous planner, who was Permanent Secretary in the Office of the Chief Secretary and thus top dog among the several Permanent Secretaries serving the emerging political Ministers. Tom Neil's paper envisaged the training of an élite cadre of Kenya African administrators on lines tried and tested in Her Majesty's Oversea Civil service, handing over what we knew worked well for an independent government to adapt to its purposes. Tom Mboya expressed strong views on freeing the Institute, the trainers, the service and the Civil Service Commission of 'colonial mentalities', while acknowledging that some old stagers might be useful to continuity of experience. Although some incoming academics, such as Professor Colin

*Presidential candidate in the 1990s!

Leys, belatedly took up paper cudgels on the side of the 'guardian angels', something of a coming together took place in the style adopted on the ground by the new Provincial Administration, who were not overseen by political 'commissars' as in Tanganyika/Tanzania. Beyond the lofty academic and political level of the debate we deliberately widened the catchment area of the Institute by dropping from its title the usual P for Public, making the Kenya Institute of Administration, KIA, unique in Africa in its declared openness to management in the private sector. The KIA then evolved in stages to house Administrative, Executive, Local Government, Co-operative and Community Development training in separate branches. For such an ambitious project we had to find a worthy home.

A gently sloping site of 68 acres along the Kabete road lay temptingly under-developed past the trim grass frontages of the residential, formerly coffee, estates of European commuters. The site had long been partly used by various well established but underfunded social welfare activities, including the rambling pre-war and wartime housing and Nissen huts of Jeanes School, *Maendeleo ya Wanawake* (women's progress) and Boy Scouts. Intending to absorb or stimulate such functions within the KIA, we more rather than less moved in on the whole campus. An interim Principal was at once made available from the Provincial Administration, who proved ideal for the initial stage having some rapport with both Kenyatta and Mboya and training experience in Nyanza. Eric Gordon was a dauntless, agriculturally qualified, field District Officer, prepared to lead with his considerable chin and blitz the site of all but sound structures to make way for a ground plan. Mounted proudly on his gleaming Sunbeam tourer, bonnet finned and strapped, he set about the task with a will while belated protests raged in Leg. Co., some asking for my head.

US Aid was eager to be in on the act even before Independence. In close co-operation with 'quiet American' Bob Power, his VW Kombi always full of children, and small, modest Gavin Lawson with his sweet Elli, we set about framing a single 'mid Atlantic' project plan, which would meet the presentational needs of both Washington and the Kenya Treasury. We wanted money and quickly. They wanted influence by way of visible American plant and buildings with an American academic presence through a 'contractor' university. At our personal level some friendly barter took place. Put crudely it was one American academic place for each quarter of a million dollars contributed, against which we would show pound for pound contributions in kind by way of land, buildings, personnel etc. We got the money and more at astonishing speed — they said it would take two and a half years from application — and the negotiations for American presence through Syracuse University continued separately, in parallel with the selection of a permanent Principal.

To keep up the pace we had to cut more corners in the provision of buildings of which we had none on the splendid site. Pat Garland of PWD Headquarters and Divisional Engineer Jim Graham ransacked their blueprint shelves and miraculously turned up unused plans, specifications, quantities and costings for a European girls' boarding school at Nakuru, for which political time had run out. A little art work and redating, with adjustments to site, enabled Jim, a twinkling roseate 'prelate' in a halo of white hair and safari boots, to conjure up in weeks the work of months, ready for construction of the four main wings and the common halls of KIA. Within a year Tom Neil's weekend outline concept was open for business.

The position of Principal was pivotal and was established at 'superscale' within the competence of Tom Skinner. The selection of candidates was not mine to make, but I put forward the name of John Howard whom I had admired since taking over Mandera District from him in 1946. Devoted to mankind, water supplies and mountain places he had heroic qualities of leadership. As a Senior DC he was in line to be a PC and wished to stay in the mainstream. Another candidate, John Pinney, doughty field DC in several stations with the common touch, was similarly launched on the Provincial track. Meanwhile, Robin Wainwright, as Minister of African Affairs, had released Peter McEntee to be detailed for discussions in the USA with Syracuse as the designated 'Contractor University' for supporting the KIA, with the Maxwell School of Citizenship and Public Affairs as the lead Agency. At first Syracuse offered a full team of up to twelve American academic counterparts to the Kenya national training staff including the Principal — and with hopes of channelling students to Syracuse thereafter. This was clearly an overload, coming from a different government culture and ethos without African experience, a view shared in part by Mboya. We need not have worried unduly on this score. A Syracuse Report "explicitly stated that it did not feel that American professors should or could teach Kenyans ... peculiarly American administrative practices and theories". The balance was well and truly kept on the Kenya side by a very fine team of trainers and managers, including District Officers Colin Fuller and Robert Chambers, Alastair Anderson, former Kiambu Revenue Officer and Local Government 'Master Class', Jack Followes.

Apart from short term auxiliary roles such as Librarian, Channing Richardson, and Audio-Visual Aids, Winston Cone, the agreed total settled at around three. The forerunner was a ginger haired visionary, Professor Julian Friedman, who rather 'frightened the horses' and moved on. The second was Professor Fred Burke, already Director of East African Studies at Dar es Salaam University alongside British Principal, Professor David Kimble, something of a cult figure as I found. Fred was of solid help in visiting, commenting and reporting in a positive and pragmatic way. Presiding over the relationship was the Dean of the Maxwell School

294

himself, Stephen K. Bailey, who came, saw and blessed the work in a letter
to me with praise and helpful comment. Apart from his personal distinction
and charm he carried great clout through his direct access to President
Kennedy. The stimulus of the Maxwell School was good value, not only for
the three by quarter of a million dollars private deal!

Peter McEntee returned from Syracuse and took over from the stalwart
Eric Gordon, who remained as Vice Principal, later handing over to Alan
Simmance in what seemed to me an ideal succession. Peter's District and
African Courts experience, leading on to his close involvement with the
'Contractor University', made him a natural appointment as Principal. His
personal style of punctilious service orthodoxy, inculcated with a driving
urbanity, set the tone between Eric's solid foundation of orderliness and
Mboya's leaning towards a new approach to training for the future.

Parallel with the KIA project in the Five Year Plan, the downtown,
thriving Nairobi Polytechnic initially prepared to take in clerical and
secretarial classes. I arranged by a personal visit to Peter Pitman in London
that a special fee-paying residential course be provided at Pitman's College
for six high level local secretaries, two of them Goan, whom I was
convinced would be as vital to support, even sustain, Secretariat Officials
and Ministers as they had been to their predecessors, certainly to me! The
Royal College, Nairobi, growing into University status, enthusiastically put
together a special graduate course for 12 potential Assistant Secretaries,
Foreign Service officials and Diplomats. Among the first few were Ahamed
Abdalla* a coast Arab, and others who advanced to the highest levels. The
quicksilver, irrepressible, uproarious lecturer, Aidan St John Hannigan,
with Elizabeth his towering consort, was an inspiration for the planning of
the course, but it was soon overtaken by the speed of events.

An encouraging joint mission came from the Royal Institute of Public
Administration and the Colonial Office. The long established RIPA was not
as grand as its title and was only now spreading its wings beyond Civil
Service and Police training at home. The Director was Raymond Nottage,
who sent his Deputy, John Sergeant, a most encouraging professional, in
company with Civil Service Principal Hobden, to establish links and
prospects. It gave the KIA a prestigious affiliation and a London address in
a Regent's Park Terrace where the Librarian, Ivor Shelley, provided an
invaluable resource over the years.

Despite the momentum, which was cumulative, we could not yet be
sure the target of 30% Africans in the top 10,000 or so posts would be
achieved by Independence in 1963, but near the end of 1961 and my 39th
birthday it was decided that I should be appointed as Under Secretary in the
Governor's Office. I handed over our small group with confidence and

*Ahamed Abdalla was Executive Director of the International Monetary Fund from 1984-8.

pleasure to Senior Education Officer Dick Lake, full of fire and imagination, with his wife, Doctor Beryl. He was followed in turn by warm, pragmatic, dogged Pat Crichton from the Provincial Administration. Peter Ricketts as head of the Service and Training branch of the Treasury sent me a generous personal appreciation.

"There is no doubt that your efforts ... have produced results far beyond what could have been foreseen when you took up the appointment and for this the credit lies entirely with you."

XXI

NAIROBI
THE GOVERNOR'S OFFICE
NOVEMBER 1961–OCTOBER 1962

As the champions of the rival parties squared up in the cockpit of political jousting for the prizes of future rule in the city below (KANU's emblem was a cock), the Colonial Regime retained within the Governor's hand the powers he needed to hold the ring through the inevitable ups and downs of progress to Independence, now generally spoken of as *Uhuru* (freedom). They included constitutional change, security and border affairs, as well as civil service morale and discipline on a shared basis with a transitional leader of Government Business/Chief Minister.

Even at the Under-Secretary level it was hard to see how my own appointment was consistent with these careful dispositions. The allegations occasioning my public expulsion from Kiambu by Monkey Johnston in 1959, if the 'circumstances' later referred to by Charles Atkins were indeed on record, would as surely have disqualified me from my new duties in the precise areas of the stated default. Mine not to reason why, and I gladly accepted another fascinating job, believing it was a further mark of trust by the Governor, Sir Patrick Renison, and not a grudging parole by others, or even some kind of pacifier.

The Governor's Office, or rather that of his Deputy, was a modest brick bungalow set behind the Kenya Police guard post at the main gate of the short driveway to the Governor's Neo-Palladian mansion, known as GH. The building was barely large enough to serve as a 'think-tank' and diffusion point for HE (His Excellency) up the road and a liaison centre with the functional Ministries and Permanent Secretaries. The layout was in a simple V form with the Permanent Secretary, the Deputy Governor, his boardroom and staff up one leg, the Secretariat and Secret Registry across the centre, and my secretary and myself up the other side, with two empty offices near the entrance, which mysteriously filled. The Deputy Governor was Eric Griffith-Jones, the former Attorney General who had devised and introduced the formula of 'compelling' as opposed to 'punitive' force during my responsibility for rehabilitation prior to my promotion to Kiambu in 1958 and who had interrogated me about culpability for events. We entered a new and less fraught relationship.

The Permanent Secretary to whom I first reported was Dick Luyt (-ate). He was what my French friend Haroun Tazieff, when visiting Teleki's volcano, had called the *type parfait* of the Colonial Administrator. His family name hailed from Southern Africa and he had risen through the Ministry of Labour. Neither short nor tall, handsome nor dull, his square jaw and direct look, his fame with bat and ball — he was also a 'Barbarian' — his seemly modesty and rugged charm, combined to lend him gravitas and a reputation for judiciousness. I had to admire and like him, despite flashes of impatience with his capacity for cogitation. On behalf of the service we sent to him on his promotion to Chief Secretary in Northern Rhodesia, by hand of the Kenya Rugby team, a painting of a favourite coastal scene of gently waving palms commissioned from Arthur Firmin, RPS, framed with inscribed silver plaque.

The queen of the office was Mary Postlethwaite, a maturely handsome lady of knowing eye and pithy comment, delivered between husky draws at her cigarette holder. Her mordant humour concealed a kindly heart and a complete command of her job. Maid of all work was 'Maisie', her comfortably Scottish Registry Assistant, who could manage prodigies of overnight production of the corrected secret records of constitutional meetings held at GH, for which her teams of helpers appeared from nowhere. Mary stood for no nonsense when two MI5 officers came, with porters staggering under a huge steel safe and roll-up wall map shutter, to occupy our first two offices, after leaving their accommodation under our former neighbour Colonel Hugo Dent in the Ministry of Defence. One, improbably called Michel de St Jorre, was of great charm and beauty. They urged secrecy upon us all while erecting a lofty wireless mast outside for direct communication with London. Mary called us together, told the obvious truth, which we forgot.

Apart from putting up policy drafts on subjects passed to me by Dick Luyt, I prepared several on my own initiative. One was a proposal that Kenya, which was in part an accidental jig-saw, should divest itself of the perennial and costly problem of administering and containing the vast Somali occupied area of the Northern Frontier District in which I had twice served since 1946. I drew a diagram of a suggested excision from Kenya of the whole north eastern triangle, from the Gaddaduma complex of wells near the Ethiopian border east of Moyale, down past Habbaswein towards the north bank of the great Tana river above Garissa, and cutting directly from Kasabubu to Ras Chiamboni at the toe of former Italian Somalia on the Indian Ocean. This rough boundary would impede most of the south westerly pressure of the then loosely termed 'pure' Somalis, relinquishing to the two newly independent Somali Republics another of the five points of the white star of a 'United Somalia' (Italian Somalia, British Somaliland, French Somaliland, Ethiopian Ogaden) represented on their new flag of United Nations (Trusteeship) blue. A strategic border road could line the boundary on the Kenya side, linking clan watering points and providing protection for the Boran, Sakuye, Pokomo, Bajun and non Somali people within Kenya. Savings in Administration would be considerable. The concept was sidelined because of Ethiopian and Foreign Office traditional objections and because whichever of KANU or KADU concurred in the giving up Kenya territory would suffer at the polls. (A year later I became part of the Somali scene as Chairman of a United Nations Commission, and found the Somali elected member of Kenya Parliament an honoured 'prisoner' enjoying coffee with Somali Prime Minister Shermake).

In another memorandum I suggested that, in view of the continuing uncertainties about future Kenya leadership and with the recent emergence of Lumumba, Tshombe and Mobutu in nearby Congo, it would be useful for the new Kenya Police payroll computer to be turned to an analysis of the tribal composition of all ranks in all the armed services, with another detailed programme designed to throw up charismatic individuals from the rank of Corporal. As the leadership issue resolved into general acceptance of Kenyatta, such an analysis lost relevance until more turbulent times or a military coup threatened.

Before Dick Luyt was replaced by his designated successor, Frank Loyd, and while the Governor Patrick Renison was away in London, I was gazetted Permanent Secretary in the Governor's Office. This came as a surprise to me, pleasant though it was to be perched on the foot-stool of the throne and to have a third promotion published in the Official Gazette.

On the world and African stage the furniture was being pushed around in response to shifts of the balance of power between America, Communist Russia, resurgent Germany and Japan, retentionist France and the shrinking British Empire. From the firmament above our heads the names of Dulles, the curmudgeonly anti-British Secretary of State, the conciliatory Assistant Under-Secretary for Africa, Satterthwaite, the giant Adenauer and economic miracle-worker Erhard, the burgeoning French Community and the Iron Curtain destabilizers stirred the dust above our own cautious path to Independence. The German Foundation for Developing Countries, even while West Germany was still outside the General Assembly of the United Nations, had formulated a politically schematic theory, in regard to their own and other nations' lost African dependencies, of when and how to jump onto the 'roundabout of power' of a new government. South Africa, with its 'Broderbond' had just (been) withdrawn from the Commonwealth, reducing the drag which it had exerted on the evolution of our political and racial norms.

In the back-stage 'green room' of Kenya I became uneasily aware of evening discussions in Griffith-Jones's room involving Bruce Mckenzie, Tom Mboya and a West German Consular Official. There was some hint of substance given to the meetings by a political furore over a 'turnover' piece on 9 August 1961 by *Times* Correspondent John White, drawing attention to the uncertainty of Jomo Kenyatta's future after Renison's Cassandra like speech and in the light of foreign interference. It was unthinkable to me, even as a hypothesis, that a former South African Air Force Colonel, settled as a farm manager in Kenya, veering from right wing politics to succeed multi-racial Michael Blundell as Minister for Agriculture, and pinning his colours to Jomo Kenyatta as 'Father of the Nation', should be suspected of hedging his bets on an Mboya alternative, backed by foreign financial support from such a dubious source. I could dare to do no more than cautiously record my misgivings in a memo as a contingency to be reckoned with or a fantasy to be dismissed. I found it difficult thereafter to relate amicably to Mckenzie, even at the table of my and his trusted friends. (He met his end long afterwards leaving Uganda by air from a meeting with General [etc.] Idi Amin, bearing the gift of a lion's head trophy which concealed a time bomb. Mboya's brilliant promise was prematurely snuffed out after Independence while he was Minister for Labour by an assassin's bullet fired from opposite Chiani's Chemist in Government Road where he had a rendezvous.)

Griffith-Jones was continuously absorbed in constitution drafting, an esoteric craft of which the high priest he called in was a Rolls-Royce borne Conservative MP, Sir Frederick Bennett, whom I saw but never met. Griffith-Jones would crouch over his desk in fierce concentration focused by tugging with his teeth on a white kerchief. One option was a simple unitary one with a two, or even one, party democratic base. Another was a regional one of immense physical and financial complexity and tribal ramifications. Both were worked on before the series of Constitutional Conferences. It was said that the regional or *Majimbo* one bade fair to be the longest in history, being designed chiefly as a means of pre-empting civil strife. The short one formed the basis of agreements finally entered into. Fortunately this was not my *métier* or responsibility at any level, and Griffith-Jones proved throughout my 'acting' period to be a most tolerant and helpful boss without condescension. There was never any mention of his crucial role in diffusing the Hola affair, after which no full Governorship nor Grand Cross of an Order came his way as might have been expected; only the well cushioned chair of Guthrie Rubber Corporation, ironically recalling his Malayan wartime experience.

After my stint as interim Permanent Secretary, Frank Loyd slipped smoothly from leave into the substantive position, having once been Private Secretary at GH, Provincial Commissioner, Central and Nyanza Provinces and acting Chief Commissioner. To repeat his own phrase, I knew his 'form', as he did mine. The recent recovery in my fortunes made discussion of the Kiambu episode superfluous as well as problematical. Frank was much involved in the preparation of the Constitutional Conferences, both in London and at GH. Those of us 'outside locked doors' read the newspaper reports and shared irreverent jokes about Secretaries of State, Reginald Maudling and Duncan Sandys. The former was said to be too

300

naturally gifted to expend any energy on the obvious, while the latter, somewhat deaf, well nourished and well connected, was said to answer with deliberation the question before last, to the puzzlement of the rapporteurs. It was a serious time for Kenya and I reflected on where I would stand if and when Jomo Kenyatta finally came to take over the Cabinet and Council of Ministers. I had said, and did not regret or resile from, many hard things about him during rehabilitation. This might not be exactly conducive to a future relationship unforeseeable at the time, although I had through everything regarded him, in Kianu's greeting to me, as a 'favourite enemy'.

On the fringe of the hard graft of politics several well intentioned groups sought to smooth the sharp edges of friction between the races. The Capricorn Africa Society, founded by inspirational SAS Colonel David Sterling, had an early seminal influence, but belonged more to the southern ideology of Rhodes' 'all civilized men', than to Blundell's optimistic multi-racialism. As Fraser and Gorrell-Barnes had let slip to me at Maralal, Blundell was their "instrument to hand", but I could never see how power could be shared when the mace or the gun was handed over. Two leading actors in bringing people closer at a certain level were Derek Quicke Erskine and Abdul Ghafur Sheikh, 'Gaby' to everyone.

Derek Erskine was a well bred maverick. Born an Edwardian, of a blood strain he claimed as mingling that of Queen Pocahontas and the twelve tribes of Israel, he listed Eton and prize cadet at Sandhurst on his career path before founding in 1928 Nairobi's most distinguished grocery house, Erskine and Duncan. He and his wife, Elizabeth, had once served me on my way to Mandera in 1946 with their unrivalled peppermint creams. Elected to Leg. Co in 1948, he achieved instant notoriety in a heated debate about finger printing and identity cards for all, to replace the useful but despised *Kipande** or native work certificate. From then on he was in the forefront of provocative liberal thought, commanding attention with his rangy cavalry physique, devilish looks and strident voice, often on the platform of the United Kenya Club with Gaby Sheikh. A happy warrior and a Knight to be.

Gaby came from a family of wealthy Muslim entrepreneurs of charitable reputation. After Indian High School in Kenya he sailed serenely through New York, Dartmouth and Harvard Universities, graduating in Business Studies, with scarcely an American lilt touching his melodious voice. By natural grace, upbringing and good will he involved himself in every cause of benefit to the community and environment, from public affairs, to youth, to wildlife. He was congenial across the boundaries of colour and sex and was almost laughably without blemish on his exotic

*'Kipande House' in Kenyatta Avenue became a 'listed building'.

social butterfly reputation, which incurred a certain mockery on that account. If he knew it, he did not show it.

The Editor of the *Daily Nation* tabloid newspaper, owned by the Aga Khan, was John Bierman, who had edited the London *Daily Express* and knew his way around. He and his tall, auburn wife Alice were our neighbours on Park Estate, cross visiting and entertaining by the pool. John was a mixture of passionately incisive caustic pressman and worldly wise observer of human nature. He asked me once what to do about disreputable allegations against Government brought to him by a certain young District Administrative officer known to me, which could leave them both exposed, even if published in good faith. The circumstances described were no more weighty than was the penny-whistle-blower himself, but the irony of my advice being sought about disloyalty to the Government from that quarter had its comic side. I suggested that John Bierman tell him to go public and be damned on his own, which may have influenced the style and animus of future academic publications.

During the last full year before approaching Independence fears and prejudices left from past turmoil were being chewed finer in the jaws of endless debates and conferences. A sense of the possibility of a bright future was dawning, if only there was a new broom to sweep away the final clutter of human obstacles. In this the nature of Sir Patrick Renison was regarded as pivotal. After his 'leader to darkness and death' speech, whatever the elements which informed his decision, he was said not to be in tune with the incoming leaders. He was seen to hit the muffled buffers at the Colonial Office and after less than three years he ceased to be Governor in December 1962. He was shunted at the age of fifty two into a siding as Vice Chairman of British Red Cross and an Adviser on sport and physical education to Conservative Party power broker Lord Hailsham. I was told that on leaving Kenya he recited a Bentleyan clerihew.

> I stand on my head on the table bare
> I wave my lily-white legs in the air
> I wash my hands of the whole affair
> I don't care.

I was sure he did care, as he confided bitterly to Dame Margery Perham in his brief retirement at 'Freeman's Farmhouse', ended by premature death in 1965. He was decent to me and did his duty by his honourable lights.

There was premature talk of the possible choice of the next and final Governor. The mighty Baring stud had been the progenitor of splendid racehorses, not bred for the coarser events. Now a completely different human species of power was canvassed, no less than the son of the first Labour Prime Minister, Ramsay MacDonald. Malcolm MacDonald had risen from the top through the ranks of community, the Fabian Society, the Labour Party, Parliament, political office and plenipotentiary posts in Asia. He had been Colonial Secretary in his thirties, three decades before. He was a results man not a service one. In his socially unorthodox and utterly self confident style he had no one to fear at any level and nothing to lose by boldness. Kenyatta's 'common touch' could find common cause with such a man. Who would wish to have been the second last Governor?

A parallel comedy was played out with our former Chief Secretary Dick Turnbull, now known as the 'Tiger of Tanganyika'. At dinner in Muthaiga with Nicole's former Public Relations Director, gallant Alan Hall and the exquisitely feline Pam, they introduced us to their visitor, one Charles Longbottom, MP who was Parliamentary Private Secretary to Iain Macleod and married to Anita Trapani, of the famed Thames Valley, Bell Inn Restaurant, and Mavroleon shipping lineage. Charles greatly impressed us with his importance, which had qualified him to 'propose' himself as guest at Government House, Dar es Salaam. A no doubt apocryphal tale was told of Turnbull's ire at the 'hotel booking' and of his list of dinner guests, which was intoned deadpan by the ADC. He had mustered every available prefixed, suffixed, hyphenated, misspelt or mispronounced Bottom in the Territory.

My unexpected levitation from Africanisation to Cabinet Office, whether under Dick Luyt, acting on my own between times, or under Frank Loyd, had not made me feel 'cabin'd, cribbed, confined' for lack of a field command or staff function. It afforded personal freedom of contact across a gamut of experiences and friendships and ready access to new ones with fresh perspectives and opportunities. Outside of family matters, service and political partying, our social forays extended into art and architecture, theatre, the media, the diplomatic circuit, commerce, wildlife, safari, sport and good eating. Like Groucho Marx, membership clubs were never in my line, not even those of religion, which left social life very mobile, if not upward.

A typically secretive and rather touching Kikuyu phenomenon was the sound of my name, always with full initials, obliquely whispered in places like petrol stations or restaurants or even on the pavement. It was a strangely emotional link with detention camps, which each whisperer expected I would individually remember as to name and place. I did often and in general, but sometimes pretended, which evidently gave equal satisfaction. I could not yet fulfil my pledge to return after Independence to allow any scores to be settled. In the nature of my service just before and since Samburu days, most of my close relationships were with Kikuyu.

One far from restrained encounter was in Bazaar Road, where the buses still had Groganville on their destination rollers. I was seized with a roar of *Karuga Ndua* by a wall-eyed old reprobate from the Kiambu-Maasai border called Kungu Karumba, whose village in the Ndeiya I had once picketed at dawn. He seemed to regard his years of incarceration, as one of Jomo Kenyatta's closest prison mates, as establishing a nostalgic bond between us as we polka-danced through the blaring traffic. Of another kidney, I met again in Jomo Kenyatta's entourage the dramatic figure of Waira Kamau, last met with skins and spear as cheerleader and fund-raiser of the Age Grades, at the inflammatory meeting I had attended at Githunguri Teachers' College before the mass detention. His distinguished white hair and sideburns above formal suiting made him a striking leader in another guise.

Visits to Kiambu District kept me in touch with the Waruhiu family, with the Mau Mau detainee Rehabilitation Officers, who were on the way up the ladders of Civil Service, education, politics or commerce, and with many others already making their mark. The sons of the murdered Senior Chief Waruhiu were increasingly influential; in the District Council, David; in Administration, Simon; in Academia, Sam. My rehabilitation colleagues took the Government path; Wilfred Thimba as Chief, Isaiah Mwai as PC, farmer and politician, and Jeremiah Kiereni to the very summit of the Civil Service, with all its appurtenances. Mareka Gecaga, Crown Counsel, and our first citizen of Riruta New Town, was sought after to head international companies and the University. Jemima Gecaga was also the sister of rising political star, the glamorous Doctor Mungai Njeroge, with his Peace Corps backed dispensary at Dagoretti Corner. Their father, Headman Njeroge, had been a friend of many years. Former Kiambu District Councillor, gentle Peter Thande had a prosperous dairy farm, to which he invited me, and was soon to be Vice Consul for Spain.

Pre-eminently, there was Charles Njonjo, son of Senior Chief Josiah. Charles had a style of his own, debonair, rose button-holed, chalk striped suit, with snub good looks, a quizzical manner and sophisticated charm to engage anyone. Attorney General was on his career path, with the threat of personal and tribal jealousy lurking always in the thickets of power. He was a family friend and later attended my 40th birthday cum farewell party.

Although I had not met him since his election to Legislative Council for the Rift Valley seat, covering Samburu, I took some satisfaction in the continued advancement of Daniel Torotich arap Moi as Vice President of KADU and its significance for the status of the congeries of so-called 'fighting tribes', whose power had waned during the rise of the agriculturalists. Another former headmaster among them was Samburu champion javelin thrower, Paulo Rurumban, who now stalked the corridors of Nairobi power like a KADU Nimrod.

The great parliamentary performer from Nyanza was Jaramogi (a traditional Luo warrior) Oginga Odinga, whose stature was in no way diminished by his half admiring European nickname of 'dingle dangle'. He was the only personality on the national stage of the calibre to stand up to Kenyatta. He bewildered the other races by his impregnable Africanness of dress and behaviour. A wealthy businessman owning a printing works, he espoused Communism, but when accused of being left wing, he had blandly retorted that when the pendulum was stuck at top right there was nowhere else for it to go. His parliamentary performances were priceless and often effective. He would assemble himself ostentatiously and start off in honeyed tones so gentle as to command attention. "Mr Speakah, Sah", melodiously and repeated for emphasis. This was followed by a crescendo of descriptive oratory in which hyperbole hurled the subject of debate into the members' imagination. Fat kine, deep grass, oppressed peasantry hovered in the air until, like a hypnotist, he would quietly snap the fingers of his voice to allow them to come to. I knew him only slightly, but always enjoyed his turbulent interventions, right or wrong. It was also a special pleasure now to find on the African Land Development Board, Zakayo Opondo, in whose Central Nyanza home at Gem Ahono in 1945 I had taken tea with the water boiled on methane gas generated by his own cows' manure in tanks outside the banana thatched house from which he had set out to be a thrifty local Native Council driver. Organic man indeed.

Homosexuality was a feature of Kenya society at several levels which I had frequented. In a paradoxical way it seemed more widely tolerated across the Kenya European community, since the war at least, than heterosexual relations were condoned across the colour line. As elsewhere, relations between males were more usual in cultural circles of every kind than in bucolic ones, though there were exceptions as suggested by the Laikipia farming area affectionately known as 'buggers' ridge'. One or two respected DCs and one Police Inspector I knew who fantasized about leading a Jihad, were spoken of as if to the manner born, and intimate relations, with their young 'protégés', sometimes also quite educational, were not unknown. The nature of any intimacy between celibate young warriors in the bush was a mystery to most of us, who wondered at their grace, vanity and beauty, which rejected any such aspersion with disgust.

Among my, and our, closest friends, whose personal lives were not ever exposed to question, were a banker and a restaurateur, both of whom would tolerantly mock my own reputed fixation with the opposite sex. Such friendships over decades were beyond price. Alan Bobbé I had first met as Assistant Manager of the new Stanley Hotel in 1946 when he had given me a 3" mortar bomb box full of classical 78 records to play on solitary Mandera nights. After a circuit of the good hotels he set up in business as 'Alan Bobbé's Bistro' in a Nairobi arcade, where the fame of his French cuisine and the loyal civility of his Comoro staff never faltered. He set a standard for all races and the smiling flick of his waspish wit was the sharpest of welcomes. Godfrey Herbert, ideally named to match his mellifluously cross-gartered splendour of voice and presence, did not attempt to separate the Thespian from the banking platforms, where his performances were as much enjoyed as his outrageous party banter, not least by himself. As Manager of both the Standard Bank and the Diners' Club he was a seriously loving man.

In the Asian community we had happy relations with Bahadur Singh, the Commissioner for India in East Africa, who had enjoyed convivial times with my former mother-in-law, Hilda Tofte, and treated me as an honorary Indian, having been born in Allahabad, for Indian National Days. At the last occasion we had attended in 1961 his predecessor, Commissioner B. K. Tandon, had shown little tact in abruptly announcing the invasion and annexation of Goa to his largely foreign guests, whose historical sympathies were as ambivalent as those of the highly regarded Kenya Goan community. In the business and professional world were Ibrahim Nathoo, a wealthy political heavyweight in support of Africanisation, and his brother Hassan, a fashionable Nairobi dentist married to a society beauty. Hassan had done a discreet service to the future nation in adjusting a snaggle tooth which had puckered Jomo Kenyatta's full lower lip. The two brothers had lifted my spirits by sending me notes of encouragement at difficult times. Taj Nanji, young owner of Nairobi's favourite new Supermarket behind the Kenya cinema and Chinese restaurant set a new standard of commercial elegance with a fine white mansion set across a corner plot in the diplomatic suburb of Muthaiga graced by the Begum, as we called her for her tantalizingly aloof beauty, from whom a hint of smile was reward enough.

In the cultural circles of private architects and artists exotic immigrant names from continental Europe abounded, like Imre Rosza, Heinie Lustman, Zbigniew Trzebinski, George Vamos, Per Abend with Phil Braun of the New Stanley Art Gallery. There was a Celtic fringe of Amyas Connell, Kevin Craig-McFeely, a fey Police Commissioner, Michael Sylvester O'Rourke, surprising watercolourist of Maasai cattle floating in a mirage, and a competing pair of Hughes, Dorothy and Richard, stylistically ancient and modern. Dashing Thornley Dyer was Government Chief Town Planner and thus 'Boss' (?) of our indomitable friend Erica Mann, Township planner of everywhere, environmentalist, creator of semi-precious ethnic jewellery, compulsive collector of Africana and succulents, and with Igo the twin dynamo of 'Freedom from Hunger'.

Thornley collaborated with Architect Amyas Connell in the first purpose-built House of Parliament, the traditional harmonious line of which was spoilt by decorative rosettes, like icing on a wedding cake. An extension by Amyas was of a bolder, more African, idiom shaped like the hull of a barque, its square prow breasting upwards and embellished by his wife, Margaret, with symbolic figureheads. Behind the junction was an open lawned area for chat between debates. I minuted a warning that an

X

assassin, firing from a bedroom window in the new Intercontinental Hotel two hundred metres away, could pick off his target with certainty. Having dumped his weapon he could descend to the dual carriageway past the hotel slip road, step into a getaway vehicle and take off routinely from Wilson Airport to anywhere, almost before the direction of death had been calculated. Hotel interests or apathy won: the risk remained: no new structure intervened. Across the road from Parliament toward the old sandstone Colonial Law Courts and Secretariat they built new Attorney General's Chambers, epitomizing separation of the powers. The design was a box structure contained within a sandy coral honeycomb with a whirligig external staircase in ceramic blue tiles and what resembled matching bathing tents in a walled yard. It was a daring concept for Colonial times and was dubbed the 'Moorish harem'.

Amyas, who had emigrated to Kenya in his fifties, was bearded as a hermit but was a sensually virile and astute Liverpool Gold Medallist. His British Partnership was in the 'Classical Modernist' movement and his own 'High and Over' concept must have inspired the spacious log cabin in which he dwelt, jutting over a deep set Kikuyu rivulet flowing past Cockburn's poultry farm. It was designed around the perfect acoustic amplification of classical music apparently only received when seated upon an interior swing suspended in space on cords from the apogee of a vaulted tongue and groove ceiling framed on telegraph poles as rafters. My dizzy rapture used to feel a trifle queasy.

Abruptly and quite unexpectedly the time came to us to step aside from the Government, the Colonial Administration and Kenya and enter United Nations Service in Somalia. I felt complimented to be handing over as substantive Under Secretary in the Governor's Office to John Cumber. John was exactly two years older, ranked a Senior District Commissioner and had been Private Secretary at GH. He had a broader range of talents and earlier experience, including jungle warfare, the Nuremberg Trials, art school and the London School of Economics. He was a large man in all senses, matched by his splendid wife, Margaret. His strict adherence to good order and discipline gained him a formidable reputation for their enforcement during Mau Mau. He had a keen sense of the ridiculous, given full vent as a cartoonist of line and phrase, albeit with some affection for the victims of his derision. A tilt of the head and a whisper in an ear seen across a crowded reception was a warning to duck from view. For all the court jesting façade, he was personally vulnerable, invariably charming and modestly faithful to causes and people he believed in. (He was destined to find Knightly reward as Director General at the side of the Royal Patron of Save the Children, Princess Anne.)

A man who then came to be a continuing influence in our lives was Bernard Chidzero, a Zimbabwean (after 1980) of Shona blood, who had joined the United Nations Economic Commission for Africa in Addis Ababa during 1960, while I was drafting the Africanisation programme for Kenya. With Africa, Oxford and a Ph.D from McGill University in Canada it was fitting that at 35 he be appointed United Nations Resident Representative for Technical Assistance in Nairobi. (It was he who, when our task in Somalia was done, cabled the Kenya Police sandbag fort blocking the bush track from Kismayu to admit me alone in my Fiat 1800 B station wagon through the prevailing Kenya-Somali 'war zone' to rejoin my family at Westwood Park beyond Nairobi — an epic 17 hour drive. Bernard had the genial gift of understanding the essential link between philosophy and Guinness. His wife was Micheline, an enchanting French Canadian and a chorister in Geneva. Our family paths criss-crossed until I was engaged from Ireland through the Rowntree Trust as an undercover change agent during the Rhodesia/Zimbabwe conflict between 1973 and 1980, when Bernard left UNCTAD to become the economic tiller of the Republic of Zimbabwe, at the request of President Mugabe.)

In our last days in Kenya I walked again across the rolling Ngong Hills, while the family rode and swam at Westwood Park in Karen. Happily it was not a 'Country Club', as self styled, but a free and friendly place with a welcome from the beautiful, jodhpur clad, Muriel Gross and mine host Freddie, formerly of the Equator Inn, where Nicole had spent her first days in Kenya. The dapper, gnomish Seychellois Manager, Jacques, was mischievous master of all ceremonies, controlling access to the *sauna* cabin beside the pool, which could have told many a compromising tale of politics and intimacy in warm embrace.

Far beyond the radio mast on the first crest of the Ngongs and past the sturdier hikers, the game track still dwindled between thick bush, where dark wrinkled pats warned of the buffalo ahead, who might have circled back with intent. Once again I saw a maned lion sunning himself on the grass slope near Denys Finch Hatton's memorial, high over Karen's home, quite oblivious of his fabled vigil. He turned toward me slumbrously and without interest.

I sat for hours on the warm tufty lip of the steep descent to the vast expanse of the Uaso Kedong valley. I watched again the echoing Maasai herds grazing between widely spaced, living manyattas with their fresh brown dung encrusted roofs and the deserted ones, cracked and scorched white without their soaking of pungent, life restoring urine. The contemplation evoked the golden years in Samburu and some of the desolate ones between, bringing gratitude for the life and lives Kenya had given me, tranquillity of mind and hope for a new beginning.

308

EPILOGUE
1962–4
KWAHERI YA KUONANA

While we were preparing the Five Year Plan for Africanisation and establishing the Kenya Institute of Administration, two outsiders with totally different backgrounds and purposes had offered a fresh direction in our lives. One was Dr Eric James of the United Nations, the other Richard C. Fenton, President of Pfizer International, the Brooklyn based pharmaceutical combine.

Dr James, a naturalized Jamaican American, was Director of the Sudanese Institute of Public Administration, (SIPA), then the showcase of the United Nations Public Administration Division's programmes in Africa. He and his schoolteacher wife whom we had entertained in Nairobi had apparently reported Nicole and myself to be "dedicated persons" in the parlance! As a result the Director of the United Nations Technical Assistance Recruitment Service, (TARS), put me on their New York computer roster and made me an immediate offer of the Chairmanship of an *ad hoc* United Nations Establishment Commission to unify the public services of the former British and Italian Somali territories which had just come together as a single independent Republic. It was an offer I could not refuse!

Richard C. Fenton was a naturalized American, plus a middle initial. He had been extremely successful in managing Pfizer's huge diversified business at Sandwich in Kent and was now bent on devolving Pfizer's European based area management for Africa away from Paris.* While I was still thrown by the Kiambu episode before appointment to Africanisation, I had answered a banner advertisement in the London *Sunday Times* for 'Director of Personnel for Africa'. Fenton, fiftyish, graceful and tough, came to Nairobi and interviewed Nicole and myself separately for several hours in the new Stanley Hotel. He offered me the job on the spot and agreed to hold it for a year until I had completed my first contract with UN in Somalia. He also favoured my admittedly biased recommendation that Pfizer African Area Headquarters should be established in Nairobi. In a manuscript note on my personal file, which later came to me, he had recorded "Anglo-Indian wife", a tribute to Nicole's Kenya tan!

In November 1962, with Kenya Government and Colonial Office permission, I was released on eleven months' accumulated leave, enabling me to fill both positions in turn, while my Kenya Government record of

*Pfizer had enjoyed a serendipitous growth explosion during the Pacific War from the conversion of its salicylic acid fermentation tankage to mass production of a perfected tetracyclin called Terramycin; the perfect *Terra* being found near its Indiana installations. They gave me a bronze replica 'culture'.

Ex-Minister leads Assembly walk-out

CRISIS IN SOMALIA POWER STRUGGLE

From a Special Correspondent

THE Somali Republic is faced with a new political constitutional crisis —perhaps the most serious since it gained independence two years ago.

DR. SHERMARKE
Premier under attack

MR. MOHAMED EGAL
Man with ambitions*

Thirty Deputies in the National Assembly, led by the former Minister of Education, Mr. Egal, walked out during a debate on Monday on a Government motion calling for a vote of confidence. The motion was approved by the other 70 Deputies, belonging to the Somali Youth League and the United Somali Party, but it is conceded that the challenge to the Prime Minister, Dr. Shermarke, and his supporters is the most significant that has occurred in weeks of political jockeying.

Observers in Mogadishu interpret current moves as a struggle for power—primarily between Dr. Shermarke and Mr. Egal. The latter was Prime Minister—for five days—of the former British Somaliland before it merged with Somalia in 1960.

At that time the Somali National League—the third party forming what was originally a Coalition Government—saw the prospect of one of its supporters gaining the premiership because of an ominous split in the ranks of the major party, the Somali Youth League.

Some uneasiness

It was known that Mr. Egal entertained ambitions, but the prospect did not materialise and a certain uneasiness has persisted.

The significance of this week's line-up in the National Assembly is that 18 Somali National League Opposition Deputies were supported by 12 Somali Youth League members who have resigned from the party.

The Opposition maintains that the Government, established by agreement after independence and without resort to elections, is illegal now that the National League has withdrawn its support.

It is demanding that the Government should go to the country to test popular opinion, and the feeling in Mogadishu last night was that President Osman might dissolve the Assembly to allow elections.

The issue has been complicated by the fact that Dr. Shermarke is due to leave Mogadishu today on his way to Washington for a five-day State visit. He will be in Nairobi tonight.

Dr. Shermarke, who is also due to visit Bonn and to pay a courtesy call on the British Prime Minister, Mr. Macmillan, is not expected back in Mogadishu until December 10.

MR. T. J. GAVAGHAN
Sent from Kenya

Main task

Meanwhile, an officer of the Kenya Government, Mr. T. J. Gavaghan, who has served in the Governor's office since last year, has been seconded to the United Nations to serve for a year as chairman of the Establishment Commission of the Somali Republic. He was formerly officer in charge of Kenya localisation and training.

He is due to leave Nairobi for Mogadishu in a few days' time.

Mr. Gavaghan's main task will be to help in the co-ordination and integration of the republic's civil service, which is now completely "Somalised".

However, difficulties which were not unforeseen have arisen because of different administrative systems to which Government employees became accustomed under former British and Italian authorities.

The view is also held that the Civil Service is over-staffed, and it is possible that a considerable number, perhaps as many as 400, will lose their jobs.

** Realised in 1993.
(Overleaf)*

Y

Haji Mohamed Ibrahim Egal is inaugurated as
President of Somaliland at Borama in 1993,
(Author present for Save the Children).

service also ran on to Independence in 1963. This serial good fortune enabled me to honour my promise to the Mau Mau detainees to return to Kenya after Independence, establish a home in Nairobi with my 'lumpers' and my Pfizer salary and put up my name board at the gate.

My appointment to the UN in Somalia was given a very good press in Nairobi to an embarrassing degree. The widely read Friday *East African Standard* of November 1962 had merged two topical stories. One concerned a power struggle inside the Somali Government between the southern, Italian speaking, Prime Minister, Doctor Abdirashid Ali Shermake,* and the northern, English speaking, Education Minister, Mohamed Ibrahim Egal.** The other story was about my UN Commission task of co-ordinating the systems personnel and languages of the totally different British and Italian inheritances, which resembled my Africanisation and training job in Kenya. The Friday newspaper, which I had not read before take-off, pictured on the front page top left, "Premier Shermake under attack" above "Mohamed Egal ... with ambitions", with me centred opposite over the caption, "Gavaghan sent from Kenya". It was not the most diplomatic introduction, but nobody meeting me on arrival at the clapboard Mogadishu Airport seemed to have noticed and the Commission's Report earned good words from both the Head of the Public Administration Division in New York, Hamzah Merghani, of a mighty Sudanese family, and the new Prime Minister of Somalia, Abdi Razak Hussein.

At the Wabi Shebelli Hotel, a prefabricated box structure rushed up to house diplomats attending the 1960 Independence Day celebrations, all was empty and silent except for an excited susurration from three Somali elders in bush attire seated on a plastic sofa. Fifteen years slipped away as I saw they were old friends from Mandera District, Chiefs Hussein Salad of the Degodia, Abdi Nur Gursi of the Murille and Mohamed Alio of the Gurreh. We clasped and unclasped hands and they drew me among them on the couch, treating me to thorough finger-tip kneading in the intimate physical expression of Somali greeting.

My new life and the old were intertwined. It was to be *Kwaheri ya Kuonana* to Kenya.

---

*Dr Shermake handed over as PM to Abdi Razak Hussein, was elected President and assassinated.
**The same Dr Egal was installed as President of the Independent 'Somaliland Republic' at an inauguration ceremony in Borama on 23 May 1993, at which I was the only European guest, on behalf of Save the Children, with photographer Hamish Wilson.

312

INDEX

The select index lists some 1,000 names. They are as then known to the author, personally or by repute, without correction by hindsight, except in footnotes from later sources. The first or main mention of names is indicated by the chapter in which they occur.

318

321

Short, Robin, XVII
Siambu; Chief, XVI
Simba; Sergeant, XVI
Simmance, 'Phina', XVIII
Simmance, Alan, XVIII
Sim, Jack, VIII
Sinatra, Frank, XVI
Sinden, Donald, XVI
Skinner, Jill (m. Brauer), XVI
Skinner Tom, XX
Skov, Gitta, XVIII
Skov, Kai, XVIII
Slade, Humphrey; QC, XVIII
Slade-Hawkins (DC), XII
Smallwood (Inspector), X
Smith, Ian, X
Smith, George, Ivan, XX
Smuts; General, XIV
Solly, Noel, XV
Solly, Gillian, XV
Sondhi, Krishna, XIX
Sorrenson, M. P. K., XVIII *Footnote
Southall (Manager Uplands), VI
Southon; Colonel, VI
Spencer, Paul, XVI
Spencer, Sam, XIII
Stallone, Fr., Michael, XVI
Steel, Anthony, XIV
Stephens, John, XVI
Sterling, David; Colonel, XXI
Stevens, Alan, XI
Stewart, James, XV
Steyn, Bert, XI
Stirton, Sheila, VII
Stirton, Jock, VII
Stones, Don, XI
Storey, Sylvia, XVI
Storrar, 'Sandy', VIII
Sudi; Sen. Chief, XI
Sumner Wells, III
Surridge, E. R., II
Swann, Bt., Anthony, XII
Swynnerton, Roger, XVIII
Sylvester, Victor, XVIII

Taberer, W. F. M., XIV
Tameno, J. Ole, XVI
Tapsell, Peter, XV
Tapsell, Eustace, XV
Tarleton, Alan, XVI
Tasker, Jack, XIX
Tatton-Brown, 'Bobby', XIX
Taussig, Emil, XVI

Taylor, Harold, XV
Taylor, Douglas, XVII
Taylor, Freda, VI
Tazieff, Haroun (France), XVI
Teleki, Count, XVI
Templer, Sir Gerald, XVII
Tennant, John, XVII
Terry; Colonel, XVII
Thacker, Ransley; Justice, XVIII
Thande, Peter, XXI
Theodoropoulos, Ritsa, XIV
Theodoropoulos, 'Theo', XIV
Thimba, Wilfred; Chief, XVII
Thiongo, Stephen, XV
Thomas, Dylan, XVIII
Thompson, 'Tommy', W., XVIII
Thompson, Mary, VIII
Thompson, 'Tommy', VIII
Thompson, Joseph, XV
Thoms, Peter, XI
Thornley-Dyer, XXI
Thuku, Harry, VI
Tilney, Sir John, XX
Timms, Peggy, XVIII
Tippu Tip, XIV
Tofte, Cecily (m. Author), XI
Tofte, Jack, XI
Tofte, Cedric, XI
Tofte, Doreen, XI
Tofte, Hilda, XI
Tomlinson, 'Tommy', XVI
Towers, Camilla, XIV
Towett, Teita arap, VI
Tracey; (Surveyor), XV
Trafford, H., XIV
Trafford, Tim, XIV
Travadi, R. K., XVIII
Travis; Alderman, XV
Trennery, Cecil, XI
Trevelyan, José, XV
Trim; Dr., XVI
Tryon; Captain, VI
Trzebinski, Errol, XVIII
Trzebinski, 'Zbish', XVIII
Tshombe, Moise, XXI
Turnbull, Sir Richard, XXI
Turner, Hilda, VIII
Turner; Dr. Hugh, VIII

Usher, Elizabeth, XVII

Valle Family, XVIII
Vamos, George, XXI

Putney.
September 1999

To Seán + Clodagh

an dear friends from
everywhere to everywhere.

GRÁ AGUS SOLAS !

Thunce